SOUND UNBOUND

SOUND UNBOUND

Sampling Digital Music and Culture

edited by Paul D. Miller aka DJ Spooky that Subliminal Kid

The MIT Press
Cambridge, Massachusetts
London, England

For information about special quantity discounts, please email special_sales@mitpress.mit.edu.

This book was set in Minion and Syntax on 3B2 by Asco Typesetters, Hong Kong, and was printed and bound in the United States of America.

Library of Congress Cataloging-in-Publication Data

Sound unbound : sampling digital music and culture / edited by Paul D. Miller.
  p. cm.
Includes bibliographical references and index.
ISBN 978-0-262-63363-5 (pbk. : alk. paper) — 978-0-262-25428-1 (e-book)
1. Music—21st century—History and criticism. 2. Music and technology. 3. Popular culture—21st century. I. DJ Spooky That Subliminal Kid.
ML197.S694 2008
780.9′05—dc22
                                                                2007032443

For a free download of the audio files for this book, contact digitalproducts-cs@mit.edu.

Contents

Contents

Foreword

Cory Doctorow

I was stuck in a hotel room in Geneva, attending a standards body meeting where a group of broadcasters and big entertainment companies were trying to break the Internet so that it's worse at copying.

I fired up Skype and stuck on a headset and rang my girlfriend in London, who slipped on her headset. It was lonely in Geneva. Geneva's the kind of place where nearly everyone who isn't a native has to be there for work, and the natives know it. Geneva's a great place to get robbed, or screwed at a crappy hotel you wouldn't kennel a dog in, or fed a meal whose price/performance ratio is worse than a Hummer's. Sitting in my hotel room, skyped into my girlfriend's bedroom in London, I was in two places at once. The familiar ambient sounds of London, the screech of black cabs' brakes, and the roar of the chavs watching footie at the pub all leaked through my little earbuds. Cyberspace is the place where a phone conversation takes place—that's what William Gibson said. For that witching hour, I was in Geneva and I was in London and I was in neither.

We didn't say much, my girlfriend and I. I was typing and she was typing and we heard each others' keystrokes. She took a call. I took a call. It was like being back at home, so long as I didn't look up from my screen at the grimy paint of the Hotel Terminus.

I can't work without music. I've got about 10,000 tracks in iTunes—itself, incidentally, a piece of software created by a company that is deploying lots of technology in an attempt to break the Internet by making it worse at copying—and I've rated every track from 1 to 5. I start every day with my playlist of 4- to 5-star music that I haven't heard in thirty days, like making sure that I visit all my friends at least once a month (I wish my phone and email were smart enough to remind me which of my best pals I've forgotten to ping this month). After that, I listen to songs I haven't rated, and rate them. Then it's on to 4- to 5-star songs I've heard fewer than five times, total. I don't want random shuffle: I want directed, optimized shuffle.

I put on the shuffle. I mixed the iTunes volume into my cans so that it ran about half my girlfriend's speaking volume. She did the same. We have wildly divergent musical tastes, so usually when we're at home, we both wear headphones with only one earpiece in so that we can still converse without inflicting our music on one another. She's promised to kill me if I play one more Bob Wills yodel for her.

Now here we both were, separated by thousands of klicks, in different countries, but on the same Internet and in the same conversational space.

Our music, however, was in a third place. My music was in my virtual environment, but not mixed into the mic. When I hummed, it was to the tune in my ears, not the one in hers. Likewise, she was grooving to something of her own. Our bodies were separate, our music was separate, our minds were converged.

I was at a party thrown by Linden Labs, who make the multiplayer game Second Life. They'd rented a chic, grimy gallery in San Francisco's SOMA. They'd also modeled the gallery virtually in Second Life. Many of us were present in real body in SOMA; many of the players were present virtually in the virtual gallery, which was up on a big jumbotron being fed by a beamer. A DJ spun for us, but we're geeky conference-attendees; accordingly, we talk instead of dancing when we gather.

The gamers, though, were there to dance. They had painstakingly programmed or purchased dance routines for their avatars, and the virtual hotties on the screen over our heads were really burning the house down.

But for all that, every avatar was dancing to a different beat. Presumably, every player was listening to a different song. And none was dancing in time with our DJ.

They tell us the Internet drives us apart. Music brings us together. It's not clear to me whether the Internet was driving those gamers apart, nor is it clear that the DJ who was drowning out our chatter was bringing us together.

Somewhere in the network and the music, there's a mix that brings us together because we're apart.

In the 1930s, the vaudeville artists hated Marconi's radio. They argued that even if the radio could deliver its crazy dotcom promises of big advertising business, it wasn't a radio exec's place to tell a musician how to make a living. Being charismatic on a stage was what being a musician was about—it was *holy*, like the first story told before the first fire in the first cave. Who was Marconi to doom musicians to being mere clerks, and what would become of those live performers whose magic was in the stagecraft, who couldn't be boiled down and captured on an infernal talking machine?

Seventy-some years later, their spiritual descendants are damning the Internet. We tell them, be the Grateful Dead: use your fluid, highly mobile recordings to advertise your gigs, make your money at the door and not the record store. They ask us where we get off telling them how to make a living. They're not trained monkeys, to caper and gibber on a stage for our amusement! They're *white-collar workers*—they work indoors, communing with the muse until it is time to release the finished product to their audience. Besides, what about all those studio wizards who have the charisma of a catfish? Will we doom them to the scrapheap of history?

Technology giveth and technology taketh away. No business model, art form, or practice has the inherent right to exist: it has to fit in with the social, technological, and market realities of its day. The world is poorer because short stories and poems have fallen out of favor, but legislating poetry back into the market would be insane. Successful poets today write songs, just as successful metalworkers today hack hardware, not horseshoes.

Technology enables creativity, community, art, and love. Crippling it to save someone's outmoded business-model is a crime against humanity.

An Introduction, or My (Ambiguous) Life with Technology

Steve Reich

In the mid-1960s I became extremely interested in tape loops, particularly of people speaking. At the same time I was looking at musical notation of Ghanaian drumming in A. M. Jones's great book, *Studies in African Music*. In late 1964 I recorded a black Pentecostal preacher in Union Square in San Francisco. He was preaching about Noah and the Flood. At home I made various tape loops of his incredibly musical voice. One was of him saying "It's gonna rain!"

I had two cheap mono recorders and made two identical copies of the loop. I put one on each machine and put on my headphones. By chance, the two loops were exactly lined up in unison. The sound appeared to be in the middle of my head, but as I listened, it started to move to the left—first to my left ear, then down my left arm, out across the floor to the left, then finally a kind of reverb between the channels. I kept listening until the loops were 180 degrees out of phase and I could hear "It's gonna, its gonna, rain, rain." I kept on listening and slowly, very slowly, the two loops came back into unison. This was clearly something to pursue.

In late January 1965 I finished "It's Gonna Rain." Later that year I moved back to New York and in 1966 I did a second speech-loop piece called "Come Out." The voice was that of Daniel Hamm, arrested for murder and later acquitted, describing how he had been beaten by police and had to show he was bleeding in order to get to the hospital. He said, "I had to like open the bruise up and let some of the bruise blood come out to show them." His speech melody was very clearly E-flat, C, C, D, C on the words "come out to show them."

I remained totally involved with this idea of gradually shifting phase between two identical loops, but I also kept feeling that unless the process could be performed by live musicians then it was just a gimmick. This ate away at me for several months since I assumed that while gradual phase change happened with railroad warning bells and windshield wipers on old buses, it just wasn't possible for people to perform. Finally I decided "OK, I'm the second tape recorder." I recorded a short melodic pattern I played on the piano, made a tape loop of it, sat down at the piano, and to my amazement found I could actually move slowly ahead of the stationary tape. A little later I discovered that a friend and I could play it on two pianos.

This quickly led to "Piano Phase" (1967), "Violin Phase" (1967), and finally "Drumming" (1971). By that point I felt enough was enough and I never used the phasing process again. I also used no technology in performance except microphones for the next eighteen years.

In 1988 I discovered first that I could use a music notation program on a Macintosh computer to make scores and second that there were sampling keyboards. This led to "Different Trains" later that year for string quartet (Kronos) and tape. The idea was to finally combine speech melody with live instruments. As the documentary voices on the tape (my nanny, then in her seventies, a black former Pullman Porter then in his eighties, and three Holocaust survivors) spoke, I wrote. Their speech melodies were doubled by viola for the women, and cello for the men. The violins often doubled the train whistles, also on the tape in the background. "Different Trains" won a Grammy and became a line in the sand for me. Now there was a technology I really was interested in sampling.

What about synthesizers? Well, I really didn't like them. If I need a violin, then I use a violin, and so on for all other instruments. I did use a synth in "Sextet" in 1986 because it was too expensive to tour with two extra English horns and two clarinets. Beyond such a marriage of convenience, I had no use for synths.—But samplers are another story. They made it possible to bring in noninstrumental, documentary sounds, like speech, on the third beat of the fifth measure.

"Different Trains" and samplers also opened the door to opera and music theater. Years earlier I had been asked by the Frankfurt Opera, and separately, by the Holland Festival, "Would you write us an opera?" I told them I was happy to be asked, etc., but, "No." I didn't have any sympathy for operatic bel canto voices, and I had stopped writing for the orchestra. (I don't need eighteen first violins—I need one, amplified.) I always felt there must be *something* that I could do instead of conventional opera, but I just didn't know what. Then, in 1988 it came to me: what if you could not only hear the prerecorded voices, but also see them on videotape, while you would simultaneously see musicians and singers doubling their speech melody? *This* was my way to make music theater. Video artist Beryl Korot proved to be the perfect collaborator. The result was "The Cave" in 1993. Here the voices were Israelis, Palestinians, and Americans answering the questions, "Who for you is Abraham?" "Sarah?" "Hagar?" "Ishmael?" "Isaac?" Their edited answers became the libretto.

After that I wrote "City Life," where samplers are played live as part of the ensemble. Sounds I had recorded in New York City became part of the instrumental fabric. After that I really felt I needed a break—from technology.

"Proverb" (1996), for singers, organs, and vibes, was the answer. The text was from Wittgenstein: "How small a thought it takes to fill a whole life." It was a pleasure and a relief to just write music.—Then back to the lab.

In late 1997 Beryl Korot and I began the second video opera, "Three Tales," which is actually about technology in the twentieth century: "Hindenburg," "Bikini" (the A-bomb tests in 1946–54), and "Dolly" (the cloned sheep). In the first two acts we used archive film and sound mixed in with the live ensemble of musicians and singers. In "Dolly" the tale was pretty short and we decided to use it as a springboard to let prominent scientists talk about cloning, artificial intelligence, robotics, and where we're headed. We videotaped interviews with James Watson (genetics), Rodney Brooks (robotics), Richard Dawkins (Darwin), Stephen Jay Gould (cloning), and many others. Their edited interviews became the libretto for "Dolly." Some of their remarks were instructively amusing:

We've always thought of our brains in terms of our latest technology. At one point our brains were steam engines. When I was a kid, they were telephone-switching networks. Then they became digital computers. Then, massively parallel digital computers. Probably, out there now, there are kids' books which say that our brain is the World Wide Web. We probably haven't got it right yet. (Rodney Brooks)

Other remarks were amusing in other ways:

You go and buy this module in the Mind Store and have it connected to your brain and then you do four- or five-part counterpoint. (Marvin Minsky)

Actually, as soon as we finished "Hindenburg," I felt I needed a break from technology again and spent most of 1999 composing "Triple Quartet" for Kronos. The bonus here was that the harmonic structure of that piece became a model for the harmony in "Bikini." By the time we finished "Three Tales" in 2002, I felt I needed a few years of just instrumental vocal music before I was ready for another trip back to the lab.—And that's where I am right now.

It seems to me that composers can learn a great deal from sampling both in concert music and music theater of all sorts. At the very least it's a new area of instrumentation to be developed where you can literally use any sound at any precise (or not so precise) point in time.

I know there are folks making music with their PowerBook only, and I really understand how that came to be. I can imagine young composer-DJs bringing these strands together in unforeseen ways. But I don't see live music showing the slightest sign of fatigue. Whether it's post-garage rock, postminimal, DJs, neo-Romantic, or what have you, the music goes on.

2

In Through the Out Door: Sampling and the Creative Act

Paul D. Miller aka DJ Spooky that Subliminal Kid

... free content fuels innovation ...

—Lawrence Lessig, *The Future of Ideas: The Fate of the Commons in a Connected World*

Silence is one of contemporary info culture's rarest commodities. In a world where there are several thousand satellites in the sky constantly beaming down at us information, cell phone relays, GPS signals, and weather patterns, even the idea of light pollution takes on a more than metaphorical value. We see the lights in the sky, but we don't hear the frequencies beaming through every nook and cranny of a world put in parentheses by human-made objects in the sky. It's a different sentence, to say the least, when nature and nurture blur to the extent that they have over the last century, and we've created a new syntax of human culture, as our inability to find another "intelligent species" in the universe attests—we speak only to ourselves, so far—we're alone in the universe. That's the current info-culture scenario. We speak to ourselves because that's what lonely people do sometimes. If the metaphor of architecture and frozen music evokes structure, then I need to update the phrase, give it a spin, and see what pops out of the centrifuge—after all, if there's one thing *Sound Unbound* is about, it's the remix—it's a sampling machine where any sound can be you, and all text is only a tenuous claim to the idea of individual creativity. It's a plagiarist's club for the famished souls of a geography of now-here. Get my drift?

Buildings in architecture are nothing more than correspondences between relationships—presence and absence, form and formlessness—and these ideas are extracted from diagrams drawn and configured within an information environment—people working, living, and breathing together to create a structure. I bet the twenty-first-century remix of the idea of architecture will be an FTP server. Archive fever becomes the Napster impulse for the attention-deficit generation. FTP—File Transfer Protocol. It's a simple triad of words, but a good one to start a book about sound and multimedia. Think of the idea of the archive (same root word as *architecture*), and think of structure as exchange. Is there any way to think outside of the networks of exchange that pervade our lives from every angle—from the sky, from the fiber optic cables embedded in the earth beneath our feet, from the texts that ask us at every turn—"Who are you? Where are you going?" Search the FTP server for files ending in .mp3, .wma, .ogg, .wav, .mov, .mpg, etc., and you will find nothing that would precipitate this question. After all, it's all just data. Map one metaphor onto the other, remix, and press play. The sampling machine can handle any sound, and any expression. You just have to find the right edit points in the sound envelope—it's that structure thing come back as downloadable shareware for the informationally perplexed.

The metaphor proceeds: There's a famous story about the artist Marcel Duchamp. No one knows if it's really true, but that's how stories work. Sometime over a period of years in the mid-twentieth century, he decided to stop painting, saying he stopped simply because he had started to just "fill things in...." This is what's going on now. When I talk about the crowded spaces of info-modernity—I'm talking about a world filled with noise, and if there's one thing we learned from the twentieth century, it's this: noise is just another form of information. Duchamp's unwillingness to just "fill things in" has other parallels—it reminds us of Rauschenberg's collaboration with de Kooning, *Erased de Kooning Drawing*, back in the mid-twentieth century, and it recalls a scene from David Boyle's "The Storming of the Accountants":[1] "it's like the 18th-century mathematical prodigy Jedediah Buxton, who, asked if he had enjoyed a performance of *Richard III*, could say only that the actors had spoken 12,445 words."

Stop. Think about it. Every sensation you have comes from one source: civilization. When you finish this paragraph, put down the book for a little while and look around you—check out your surroundings. What can you see, hear, smell, taste, that does not originate in or is not mediated by civilized people? Crickets chirping on a *Sounds of the Environment* CD doesn't count.

This is all very, very, very strange. Stranger still—and extraordinarily revealing of the degree to which we've not only accepted this artificially imposed situation, but have actually turned the process into a "perceived" good—is the way we've made a fetish and religion (and science, for that matter, and business) of attempting to define ourselves as separate from—even in opposition to—the rest of nature. The "nature versus nurture" argument has been thrown out of the metaphorical window, and on a planet put in parentheses by human-made objects in the sky, the songs we hear are stories we tell ourselves. Civilization isolates all of us, ideologically and physically, from the source of all life—nature. We don't believe that trees have anything to say to us: not stars, not wolves, not cats, not even our dreams. We've been convinced that the world is silent save for civilized human beings and the information we generate. Once again, that echo of form and function, fact and fiction: It was the often eccentric nineteenth-century architect Louis Sullivan who admonished that "form should follow function." But what happens when you have a situation that, like the Goethe and Schelling adage that "architecture is nothing but frozen music," becomes reverse engineered, remixed into a different scenario—and we thaw the process. Music becomes liquid architecture. Sound becomes unbound. Shortly after September 11, 2001, NPR's *Lost and Found Sound*, a program run by independent radio producers, new media producers, artists, historians, and listeners across the country, began to collect and preserve "sound memories" of the World Trade Center, its neighborhood, and the events of that day. The Sonic Memorial Phone Line was set up for people to leave their stories, recordings, and audio artifacts, both personal and historic as a kind of invisible monument to their lost loved ones. Hundreds of people called with their testimonies and remembrances, music, and small shards of sounds that they felt represented the Towers' presence in their daily reality. Those stories were woven together into radio broadcasts on NPR, and this memorial is now an online archive that can be found at http://www.sonicmemorial.org/. Again—that echo of the FTP mindset—search the FTP server for files ending in .mp3, .wma, .ogg, .wav, .mov, .mpg, etc., and you'll find nothing that would precipitate this mourning, but that's the point. People had found new ways to express the grief of a mediated loss; the Towers were phantom limbs of a psychological landscape unprecedented in human history. Form and function, fact and fiction, art and architecture—all woven into a testimony of human reconstruction in media. Think about this for a moment, and pause.

Another scenario: consider the mysterious case of Netochka Nezvanova, a Web-based software agent for the art/multimedia collective NATO. Basically, Netochka is a video-remixing software that posts to mailing lists and sends really bitter email to anybody who crosses "her." Think of her as an update to Walter Benjamin's "The Work of Art in the Age of Mechanical Reproduction"[2]—the remix is "persona in the age of mechanical reproduction" or even better—just plain "no one no where"—which is how the name "Nezvanova" translates. For someone who doesn't exist except as a series of angry emails that are posted on Nettime and on a couple of other listservs, Netochka Nezvanova has a really hardcore reputation. She's a computer programmer. She's a polemicist. She doesn't like it when someone "talks" back to her. She's a performance artist. She's an attack journalist, like David Brock on steroids—a hyperpolemical critic of capitalism and fascism, as well as a capitalist and a marketeer. She markets software. She doesn't exist. But a lot of people know about her and use her products. Her software Nato.0+55 (made obsolete by a lot of developments in the video "VJ" software scene) was once one of the mainstays of the digital video scene: anyone who was cool used Nato to process and create a lot of the weird images you'd see when you went to some wild party downtown—it was used to manipulate video for live performance and installations. But Netochka herself is a work of art—a "person" made of text—an online fiction many years running that's one of the Net's great word-of-mouth stories.

Netochka is the humanized "version" of a software toolkit. She's basically an extension of an editing environment that's used to sample and morph digital video in real time. Netochka knows the media scene—she does interviews and even haunts the lecture circuit. She even appears at digital art and technology conferences to promote the software—except, like Warhol did so many years ago, when she shows up in person, she's frequently represented by different women. No one really knows if there's a "real" Netochka.

She explains—sort of—via email sent to Salon.com a while ago (http://www.salon.com/tech/feature/2002/03/01/netochka/index.html): "NN's reputation is based on mouth 2 mouth adverti.cement. When something is very well konstruckted and designed with a degree of integrity it stands on its own.... All the cool girls wear NN."

Flip that same idea of "all the cool girls" into the remix scene and you get a mirror image of Nezvanova: Luther Blissett. Like Nezvanova, Blissett is a pusher of dematerialized merchandise—instead of software, "he" tells stories, and makes remixes of other people's music tracks online. In his own words, taken from http://www.altx.com/manifestos/blisset.html:

Luther Blissett is both the story-teller and the Mac Guffin of a board-game played on the stage of the world. It is essentially a grim theory of conspiracy which mostly makes use of techniques tested in the Mail Art (Ethe)real Network (MULTIPLE NAMES, "Add, Pass & Return" creations etc.) in order to manipulate and overturn the language of myths, the archetypes of the popular culture as well as the neo-pagan religious experience. It is a sort of lucid shamanism which does not belong to a pre-democratic and pre-individual view of the world (i.e. a claim to a totalitarian social unity); on the contrary it puts itself BEYOND democracy and the individuality, in the name of a free chaotic empathy between the creatures, as if we were charming Betazoids. Sometimes the links between the elements of the project happen to recall the most entangled detective stories (e.g. "The Long Goodbye" by Raymond Chandler or "White Jazz" by James Ellroy), or maybe "Paco Ignacio Taibo meets Paracelsus at an Illegal Rave."

This is the remix. Where Nezvanova is part and parcel of the mythology of the online software scene, Blissett is a process of osmosis—he takes what he can, flips it inside out, and then writes a manifesto about it. Think of him as the equivalent of DJ Kay Slay's mix tapes where Ja Rule, Eminem, Busta Rhymes, and 50 Cent battle it out over rhymes dispersed on mix tapes—that underground Samizdat scenario, and you get the idea. Triangulate between ghetto street stories, myths of people on the Web, the files that we use to process culture, and again—that echo—form and function, fact and fiction. The remix becomes "faction." Check the vibe at www.hotmixx.com.

Every software has a story. Every sound has an origin. I get asked what I think about sampling a lot, and I've always wanted to have a short term to describe the process. Stuff like "collective ownership," "systems of memory," and "database logics" never really seem to cut it on the lecture circuit, so I guess you can think of this introductory essay as a sound bite for the sonically perplexed. *Sound Unbound* is about volume—of content as sound bite, of attention with no definite deficit, of memory as a vast playhouse where any sound can be you. Press "play" and this anthology says "here goes":

Think. Search a moment in the everyday density of what's going on around you and look for blankness in the flow. Pull back from that thought and think of the exercise as a kind of mini-meditation on mediated life. Pause. Repeat. A word passes by to define the scenario. Your mind picks up on it, and places it in context. Next thought, next scenario—the same process happens over and over again, it's an internal process that doesn't even need to leave the comfortable confines of your mind. A poem of yourself written in synaptic reverie, a chemical soup filled with electric pulses, it loops around and brings a lot of baggage with it. At heart, the process is an abstract machine that searches for the right place for the right codes. The information in your mind looks for structures that give it context. The word you have thought about is only a placeholder for a larger system. It's a neural map unfolding in syntaxes linked right into electrochemical processes—it's the perceptual architecture that makes up not only what you can think, but how you can think. Inside, we use our minds for so many different things that we can only guess at how complex the process of thinking is. Outside, it's a different scenario. Each human act, each human expression, has to be translated into some kind of information for other people to understand it—some call it the "mind–brain" interface, and others, like Descartes, call it a kind of perceptual (and perpetual) illusion. In our day and age, the basic idea of how we create content in our minds is so conditioned by media that we are in a position that no other culture has ever been in human history. Today, that interior world expresses itself in a way that in the "real" world can be changed. When it's recorded, adapted, remixed, and uploaded, expression becomes a stream unit of value in a fixed and remixed currency of the ever-shifting currents of the streams of information running through the networks we use to talk with one another. It wasn't for nothing that Marx said so long ago that "all that is solid melts into air"—perhaps he was anticipating the economy of ideas that drives the network systems we live and breathe in. In different eras, an invocation of a deity, a prayer, a mantra—these were common forms, shared through cultural affinities and affirmed by people who spoke the code, the language of the people sharing the story.

Today, it's that gap between the interior and exterior perceptual world that entire media philosophies have been written about, filmed, shot, uploaded, resequenced, spliced, and diced—and within the context of that interstitial place where thoughts can be media, whether they are familiar to you or not, the "kinds" of thoughts don't necessarily matter. In this world, there is no taxonomy of the imagination. It's the structure of the perceptions, and the texts and memories that are conditioned by the thought process that will echo and configure the way texts you're familiar with rise into prominence when you think. We live in an era where quotation and sampling operate on such a deep level that the archaeology of what can be called "knowledge" floats in a murky realm between the real and unreal. Look at *The Matrix* as an updated version of Plato's cave, a parable piece in his *Republic* written more than two thousand years ago, but still resonant with the idea of living in a world of illusion. For that matter, look at the collaboration between standardization and the notion of rhythm. "Ratio," of course, being the root of "rationality," is the core angle on this scenario, and the longitudinal system— the global grid organizing experience in the world map—is a good metaphor for the way we systematize human experience. This excursion is meant to be a dialogue about different forms of sculpture—how physical objects "map" sound objects onto the kinds of metaphors we use to hold contemporary information culture together—think of it as hearing the sound of the world unfold in rhythm. The sound aspect of longitude was based on the Harrison clocks from the eighteenth century that King George III and British Parliament used to create the grid system that still guides navigation routes and configures our perception of "time zones" to this day. We have inherited the sounds of the H4 clock used by the British Admiralty in the eighteenth century to use as a global sculpture—a mix governing how we perceive the entire planet.

Longitude is an exercise in what I like to call "planetary dynamics"—it explores how we hold an artificial sense of time and space together with the socially constructed frames of reference we like to call the "nation-state." Imperial time aspires to be universal, and the grid system, and even rationality itself, is no exception. Back in the eighteenth century, when global travel by sea was coming into its own, hundreds of ships and thousands of mariners were being lost at sea or wrecked on shore because, once out of sight of land, they had no reliable way of telling where they were on the world's seemingly infinite oceans. In 1714, Parliament offered a £20,000 prize to anyone who could solve one of the greatest scientific problems of the day: how to measure longitude accurately at sea. While others looked for the answers in the stars in the sky, John Harrison, an eighteenth-century, self-educated Yorkshire carpenter, who had already built one of the most accurate clocks in the world, thought he could make a clock that would still be able to keep time on board a ship—something that many people pretty much thought "impossible"—like flying to the moon, or splicing the DNA of a jellyfish with a rabbit. The timepiece he imagined would allow sailors to chart their exact position and avoid further maritime tragedies—and create a new form of navigation based on precise Mercator-style coordinates. The emergence of the "longitude" system is literally Harrison's story of how he struggled to perfect his idea in defiance of the physical challenges of the ocean and the more intellectual hurdles and challenges of the Board of Longitude, set up by Parliament to adjudicate the prize. Guess which was harder to deal with? People versus people. Ideas versus ideas. It didn't matter what the best idea was—but how many people believed it.

Harrison, convinced his idea would work, moved to London and set about building his first sea-clock. In 1727 he made a clock with a "gridiron" pendulum that was made of nine alternating steel and brass rods that eliminated effects of temperature changes on the clock's mechanisms. In the decades that followed, this internal mechanism was used to make four clocks each to rise to the challenge of the longitude problem. By 1762, at the end of a 147-day sea voyage, H4 had lost only 1 minute and 55 seconds—it was probably one of the most complex devices of its era—if not one of the most subtly influential.[3] It set the "tone" of time for the next several centuries. Mix the sound of its clock mechanisms with the sound of the U.S. cesium-particle-based "atomic" clocks that are used to standardize Internet time and all aspects of modernity onto one basic time system, and you have a massive social sculpture. Rhythm, after all, can be both visible and invisible, and this is the sound track to a different kind of "world order."[4]

Let's look at it this way: as the World Wide Web continues to expand, it's becoming increasingly difficult for users to obtain information efficiently. This has nothing to do with the volume of information out there in the world, or even who has access to it—it's a kind of search engine function that's in a crisis of meaning. The metaphor holds, the poem invokes the next line, word leads to thought and back again. Repeat. The scenario: internal becomes external becomes involution. The loop of perception is a relentless hall of mirrors in the mind. You can think of sampling as a story you are telling yourself—one made of the world as you hear it, and the theater of sounds that you invoke with those fragments is all one story made of many. Think of it as the act of memory moving from word to word as a remix: complex becomes multiplex becomes omniplex. In physicist David Bohm's book on this topic, *Thought as a System,*[5] the idea of progress is shown to be a convergence of these "visual cues" that hold the eye and hand together when we think. Multivalent and multicultural approaches to language, and all of the sundry variations it's going through right now, are what make this kind of stuff so interesting. Or think of Antonin Artaud, who in 1938 invented the term "virtual reality" in his *The Theater and Its Double*[6] at the beginning of the section entitled "The Theater and Its Shadow"—where one era looked for theater, another looks for code in the era of information culture. Artaud asks—how has life become total theater? It all depends on how you hear the sound of science: like I always enjoy saying, "mimesis is the method of the mode." Artaud's question still hangs over us in the twenty-first century like some shroud made of invisible frequencies—a memorial for a dead era.

Another permutation, another sound file–flip mode excursion: In his 1938 essay "On the Fetish-Character in Music and the Regression of Listening," the theoretician Theodor Adorno bemoaned the fact that, like so many other performance-based arts, European classical music was becoming more and more of a recorded experience. He had already written an essay entitled "The Opera and the Long Playing Record" a couple of years before, and the "Fetish" essay was a continuation of the same theme. People were being exposed to music that they barely had time to remember because the huge volume of recordings and the small amount of time to absorb them presented to the protomodernist listener a kind of sound-bite mentality—one we in the era of the Web continue to be growing all too familiar with. He wrote: "the new listeners resemble the mechanics who are simultaneously specialized and capable of applying their special skills to unexpected places outside their skilled trades. But this despecialization only seems to help them out of the system."[7] When Tim Berners Lee wrote some of the original source code for the World Wide Web, it was little more than a professors' club—a place that entailed such exciting activities as giving briefs on atomic particle research at CERN in Switzerland condensed formats, or trading the latest developments on signal packet switching with DARPA project coordinators, or fielding queries on the latest developments in signal–noise reduction at Bell Labs—but it echoed that same sense of abbreviation that Adorno mentioned.

I tend to think of sampling and uploading files as the same thing, just different formats—to paraphrase John Cage, sound is just information in a different form. Think of DJ culture as a kind of archival impulse applied to a kind of hunter-gatherer milieu—textual poaching, becomes zero-paid, becomes no-logo, becomes brand X. It's that interface thing rising again, but this time around the mind–brain interface becomes an emergent system of large-scale economies of expression. As more and more people joined the Web, it took on a much more expanded role, and I look to this expansion as a parallel with the coevolution of recorded media. Lexical space became cultural space. Search engines took on a greater and greater role as the Web expanded because people needed to be able to quickly access the vast amount of varying results that would be yielded—search engines look for what they've been told to look for, and then end up bringing back a lot of conflicting results. Metadata breaks down websites' contents in very easy-to-search-for "metatags" that flag the attention of the distant glances of the search engines—the process is essentially like a huge Rolodex whose tabs are blue and the paper they describe is hidden behind them. So too with sound.

I'm beginning this anthology on multimedia, sampling, and memory with a metaphor for search engines and the World Wide Web because I see the Web as a kind of legacy of the way that DJs look for information—it's a shareware world on the Web, and the migration of cultural values from one street to another is what this essay is about. Think of streets as routes of movement in a landscape made of routes and manifolds. The roads convey people and goods through a densely inhabited landscape held together by consensus. Like James Howard Kunstler said in his *The City in Mind*,[8] of the cities he loves to write about, it's "as broad as civilization itself." Look at the role of the search engine in Web culture as a new kind of thoroughfare, and that role is expanded a millionfold—the information and goods are out there, but you stay in one place. The architecture of where your information resides, in this geography of nowhere—in the relationships holding the structure together: Empty, as in the Buddhist sense of the mantra, repetition, and reinforcement of motif—code the text—in this scenario, empty can be really full.

An artist named Warren Sack created a "conversation map" a little while ago to track the way we map language onto spatial relationships[9] as a "system for summarizing and visualizing large volumes of e-mail." Two other artists, Ben Rubin and Mark Hansen, did a similar project entitled "Listening Post."[10] Their press release reads like a psychoanalytic update on contemporary culture, and could easily be condensed to be a sound-bite sample for this essay because, after all, I am writing about the art of appropriation:

Listening Post is a biorhythmic visual and sonic response to the content, magnitude, and immediacy of virtual communication. This collaborative multimedia installation is composed of a suspended grid of more than two hundred small electronic screens that display fragments of texts culled in real time from thousands of unrestricted Internet chat rooms, bulletin boards and other public forums. Dissociating the communication from its conventional on-screen presence, the project presents the texts according to the frequency of randomly selected words, topics emerging and changing from hour to hour and day to day. A coordinated audio component alternates between musical passages and sections that vocalize certain messages, underscoring the text on the screens.

But it's not fun citing press releases, so we skip from metaphor to trope, from content to code and back again—and come to the conclusion that this is an associative context—we bring meaning to the search, and the sounds that we want to hear reflect back some of our encoded relationships. The information defining what you're looking for and the end result is a file somewhere, and the Web's search engines are the link between you and that end result. Because most search engines read format languages like HTML or SHTML, search results reflect formatting tags more than actual page content, which is expressed in natural language. Back in 1939 John Cage wrote one of the first compositions for phonographs. It was called "Imaginary Landscape No. 1" and essentially it was meant, in his own words, "to be subsequently broadcast or heard as a recording. It is in effect a piece of proto-musique concrete, though naturally, since at that date there was no tape, the instruments were records of constant and variable frequencies (then available chiefly for audio research)."[11] From the rotation of records made of frequencies, we get a metaphor for a wireless imagination, a Semantic Web describing a new type of hierarchy and standardization that will replace what had been in his era a web of compositions (reminiscent of Vannevar Bush's quest for the "memex" audio archive during World War II—the "Imaginary Landscape" was meant to be a kind of chance operation of memory and material). Cage wanted to replace his current "web of links" with a "web of meaning." Today, when we browse and search, we too invoke a series of chance operations, we use interfaces, icons, and text, as a flexible set of languages and tools. Our Semantic Web is a remix of all available information—display elements, metadata, services, images, and especially content—made accessible. The result, like Cage's piece intimated so long ago, is an immense repository of information accessible to a wide range of new applications—it's an archive of almost anything that has been recorded. The word "phonograph" has so many connotations—I always like to think of it as a collision of two words—phonetics and graphology. *Phono* plus *graph*—the sheer variety of styles and underground phenomenon are pretty much universes unto themselves. Edison, Sarnoff, Marconi, Garrett A. Morgan ... Constellations of sound, memory, and expression are pretty much the core structures of this multiverse.

A good read is the equivalent of a good mix. Think of 'em as a kind of "amicus curiae brief" for the sonically perplexed—render judgment not on the singular track but on the mix as a whole. It's philosophy for the audio-splice generation—on a mix tape made by Burroughs VS Grand Master Flash etc.—anything goes. That's kind of the point.

The Ring Cycle. *La Mer.* Imaginary Landscapes. The art of noise. *Musique d'ameublement. Pli Selon Pli. Kraanerg. Gebrauchsmusik.* Names that are common in the contemporary classical music reconfigure into templates for a different kind of classic: Afrika Bambaata's "Death Mix," Grand Master Flash's "Adventures on the Wheels of Steel," Steinski and Double D's "The Lesson," DJ Q*bert's "Wave Twisters," and so on ... This handbook for the Semantic Web covers, among other topics, software agents that can negotiate and collect information, markup languages that can tag many more types of information in a document, and knowledge systems that enable machines to read Web pages and determine their reliability. But it also fosters a sense of participation in what Heidegger called the "Age of the World Picture." The truly interdisciplinary Semantic Web combines aspects of artificial intelligence, markup languages, natural language processing, information retrieval, knowledge representation, intelligent agents, and databases. A good DJ has a lot of records and files and knows exactly where to filter the mix. They don't call the process online "collaborative filtering" for nothing—it's those loops again, coming back, like E. T. A. Hoffman and Sigmund Freud's Frankenstein and the Uncanny flipped with the original Mary Shelley scenario and updated, weblog style—trace it back to the origin, and you're left with an imaginary landscape. As George Clinton would put it, "you are one with the clones of Dr. Funkenstein." Check the remix. *Sound Unbound* is an anthology that gleefully says— "To hell with your divisions and name descriptions! This is what's going on!"

Think of the semantic webs that hold together contemporary info culture and the disconnect between how we speak, and the machines that process "culture speak" to one another in our efforts to have anything and everything represented and available to anyone everywhere. It's that archive fever that makes the info world go round, and as an artist you're only as good as your archive. It's that minimalist, and that simple. That's what makes it deeply complex. At the site of inside out, in through the portal into the here and now, out through the exit sign, there's always a discrepant engagement. Totally alive, wave patterns, cloud formations, vortices and eddies, and flows in the life patterns of the earth as seen from way above. It's all rhythms, all patterns: the meteorology of the world we inhabit, syncopated fragments of geology, space and time, rendered into ripples of perception—like a place where everything—the sky, the sand, the clouds, the waves on the ocean's surface, the breath emanating from my body—everything—is alive and moving gracefully with everything else.

There's always a rhythm to the space between things. Pause, hold the thought, check the moment. Repeat. Wait. There it goes again. Another thought, another pause in the stream of conscious in another abstraction—the reader, the listener. Speak these words out loud, and the same logic applies—there's always a rhythm to the space between things. It's been a truism for a while, ever since Schelling and Goethe pronounced that "architecture is nothing but frozen music," that sound and the forms we inhabit are intimately intertwined. What happens when you reverse engineer the process, and think of sound as nothing but thawed architecture? The moment between sounds, the moment between thoughts and perceptions—it's one of those intangible structures that gives meaning to the things it separates, and that's what this collection is about. Blurring the lines between forms of thought echoes in the aftereffects of their actions and things generated by those thoughts, and well, in this day and age, that's something to give one—pause. Private discourse made public, public discourse becomes a new kind of sustenance in an ecosystem of hunter-gathers of moments suspended in a culture founded on a world where information moves only because someone invented and shared it. It's a milieu where a network is defined as a quote ending a quote: "and a system is defined as another quote of a quote." Music of floating signifiers—software as editing environment, dematerialization of the studio at a bit rate that can only accelerate. This is the end result: An incidental drift across definitions takes the place of any sense of fixed meaning—like slang, we look at sounds as a vernacular process. They're a syntax of the "what-if"—how will these sounds appear in this mix when we place them over another sound, in another file, in another program? Again and again, one of the main things I see people asking when I travel is—"what software do you use?"

Today's computer networks are built on software protocols that are fundamentally textual. Paradoxically, this linguistic medium of software isn't only nearly undecipherable to the layperson, but it has created radical, material transformations through these linguistic means—computers and networks as forces of globalization. "Translation Map," like "Listening Post," develops an approach to inhabit and visualize computer-based or computer-mediated language as a space or material form. As Henri Lefebvre said so long ago in his 1974 classic *The Production of Space*: "the body's inventiveness needs no demonstration, for the body itself reveals it, and deploys it in space. Rhythms in all their multiplicity interpenetrate one another. In the body and around it, as on the surface of a body of water, rhythms are forever crossing and recrossing, superimposing themselves upon each other, always bound to space."[12]

An intangible sculpture that exists only in the virtual space between you and the information you perceive—it's all in continuous transformation, and to look for anything to stay the same really is to be caught in a time warp of another era, another place when things stood still and didn't change so much. But if there is one thing I hope this essay has pointed out it's been to move us to think as the objects move, to make us remember that we are warm-blooded mammals and that the cold information we generate is a product of our desires, and that it manifests some deep elements of our being. The point of all this? To remind us that, like Ellington and so many musicians said so long ago, "it don't mean a thing if it ain't got that swing." As the information age shifts into high gear, it would be wise to remember the cautionary tales of shades and shadows. To recall and remix the tale of a bored billionaire living in a dream world of Don DeLillo's, who said in his *Cosmopolis*: "It was shallow thinking to maintain that numbers and charts were the cold compression of unruly human energies, every sort of yearning and midnight sweat reduced to lucid units in the financial markets. In fact data itself was soulful and glowing, a dynamic aspect of the life process. This was the eloquence of alphabets and numeric systems, now fully realized in electronic form, in the zerooneness of the world, the digital imperative that defined every breath of the planet's living billions. Here was the heave of the biosphere. Our bodies and oceans were here, knowable and whole."[13]

Sometimes, it's all that simple. Welcome to *Sound Unbound*.

Notes

1. *New Statesman*, January 21, 2002.

2. Walter Benjamin, "The Work of Art in the Age of Mechanical Reproduction," in *Illuminations*, trans. Harry Zohn (London: Fontana, 1992).

3. Notes and further information on the development of Harrison's clocks can be found on the CD *Standard Time*, a collaboration between Miklos Pinther, Chief

Cartographer of the United Nations, Julian Laverdiere, and Paul D. Miller—for more info and to hear the sound of the H4 clock go to: www.djspooky.com/art.html/.

4. A good discussion of the impact of Harrison's clocks can be found in Dava Sobel's *Longitude: The Story of a Lone Genius Who Solved the Greatest Scientific Problem of His Time*, Penguin Press, 1995.

5. David Bohm, *Thought as a System*, Routledge, 1994.

6. Antonin Artaud, *The Theater and Its Double*, Grove Press, 1958 (orig. published 1938).

7. In Theodor Adorno, *Essays on Music*, with notes and commentary by Richard Leppert, trans. Susan H. Gillespie, University of California Press, 311.

8. James Howard Kunstler, *The City in Mind*, The Free Press, 2001.

9. See www.translationmap.walkerart.org/ or www.sims.berkeley.edu/~sack/cm/.

10. See http://www.earstudio.com/projects/listeningPost.html/.

11. John Cage, "The 25 Year Retrospective Concert of the Music of John Cage" (liner notes to the album, 14 and 29, Wergo, LP, 6247-2).

12. Henri Lefebvre, *The Production of Space*, trans. Donald Nicholson Smith, Blackwell Publishing, 1974, 205.

13. Don DeLillo, *Cosmopolis*, Scribner, 2003, 25.

The Future of Language

3

Saul Williams

in the beginning was the word. word. and the word was with God. and the word was God. word up. and God said, let there be ... and (then) there was. Word is bond. and the word was made flesh. word life.

  a latin transcription of the word "person" is "being of sound." as human beings we communicate with each other and with the greater universe through sound vibration. it is, thus, the essence of our collective being. all sounds reverberate with meaning. every sound vibration has an effect, and every sound connected with every word we speak, in every syllable, is connected to its eternal meaning, its eternal reverberation. the original inhabitants of egypt (KMT) actually documented the esoteric meaning of each sound vibration. they believed that all consonant sounds communed with energies of a temporal reality, whereas vowel sounds connected us with energies of the eternal reality. in their written text they wrote only consonants, for the eternal reality was too sacred to be transcribed. the ancient egyptian language like all other languages of antiquity was, needless to say, rooted in passion. yet, over time, many cultures have become disconnected from the passionate roots of their language and thus, perhaps, we have become disconnected from the roots of our existence.

nada brahma: the world is sound

in the east, it is widely believed that the word/sound "om" is the seed of the universe and the seed of all creation that can be heard reverberating within all life forms. practically all religions over time have focused on the power of sound vibration. whether through the chanting of "om," buddhist and hindu chants, islamic prayers and calls to worship, or reciting hail mary and the lord's prayer, the common thread has been an investment in the belief that change will come about through voicing these sacred words, aloud. yet, like that of the ancient egyptians, many of these belief systems have also contained the idea that there is a realm of eternal reality that cannot be put into words. in the words of the eastern mystic lao-tsu:

the tao that can be told is not the eternal tao.
the name that can be named is not the eternal name.
the unnamable is the eternally real.
naming is the origin of all particular things.

thus, the future of language would involve our getting closer and closer to being able to articulate the unspoken. consciousness, like technology, evolves over time. in the same way that there are advances in technology that may take a decade or more before they reach the public, there are also shifts in consciousness that gradually become understandable to the masses over time—so that an idea that perhaps the twelfth dalai lama achieved through meditation however many years ago may just today be reaching the level of common understanding by the average young american. ideas and concepts that perhaps our parents could not grasp until reaching a midlife crisis may now be grasped by adolescent teens. and things that once could be put into words only by the most learned philosophers can now be expressed by the average emcee (and in my estimation most emcees that i hear are average).

i had the privilege of cowriting a film called *slam*, the story of a young kid who learns the power of words and uses it to transcend his given reality. in writing this film i decided to give the main character the last name joshua, based on the biblical story of joshua who fought the battle of jericho by simply marching around the city's walls seven times while playing his trumpet to make the walls come tumbling down. i figured that if the film was played on seven hundred screens the walls of babylon would come tumbling down, mainly because of the spells laced into the poetry of the film. i have often thought of my poetry in terms of incantations: spells (note: magic is done through casting spells which is the same way words are made) or prayers to be recited in the darkest caves and highest mountain tops. in writing, i often feel as if i am deciphering age-old equations and am often as baffled an audience member as any other listener or reader. i have also found numerous occasions where i have felt that i wrote or recited a situation into existence.

i write in red ink
that turns blue
when the book closes

language usage is a reflection of consciousness. thus, the future of language is connected to the ever-evolving state of human awareness. as we become more aware of our existing reality it becomes clearer that we live with the power to dictate our given situations and thus the power to determine our future. our present reality is *pre-sent,* dictated by what we asked for previously. no, i am not saying that everything that happens to us is within our control, but through our perception we have the ability to determine much more of our reality than we realize (all puns intended). and what we say (which is clearly a reflection of what and how we think) is of the ut-most (utter-most) importance. what we say matters (becomes a solid: flesh). word life.

so then the question becomes, what role does hip-hop play in the future of language, or rather, what role does the future of language play in hip-hop? there does seem to have been a lyrical evolution in hip-hop. vivid, descriptive narratives of ghetto life seem to have come at the cost of imaginative or psycho-spiritual exploration. in other words, niggas have come up with amazing ways to talk about the same ol' shit. the problem is, when we recite the same ol' shit into microphones which increase sound vibration the same ol' shit continues to manifest in our daily lives, and only gets more deeply embedded. but of course employing one's imagination is problematic when the aim is to keep it real.

in a book called *illusions* by richard bach, the main character finds that when jesus reportedly said that all one needs is faith the size of a mustard seed to move mountains he actually only used the word faith because at the time there wasn't a word for imagination. it is imagination applied to our daily lives and use of language that brings about interesting futures. hip-hop, as is, is mainly concerned with depicting a rough street life devoid of hope or an upscale designer life devoid of reflection and in doing so dictates its own outcome. if biggie's album had not been entitled *ready to die* would he still be alive today? did his vocalized profession dictate his destination? the fact that we were so ready to hear about how he was ready to die increased the sound vibration of his recitation through playing it on a million radios and televisions at once, to the point where it affected our reality and his.

word is bond.

"these are the words that i manifest"

—guru

we are the manifestation of our thinking patterns. and we think in terms of terms. words. sooner or later we must realize that we are liable for what and how we think and say and thus must alter (altar) our use of language. sentence structures predate pyramids and are as complex. realize, even in asking me to describe the future of language, i am simply playing my part in determining it by helping those who read this to become more aware of the importance of what they say. and that (this) is how the future comes about.

word.

The Ecstasy of Influence: A Plagiarism Mosaic　　　4

Jonathan Lethem

All mankind is of one author, and is one volume; when one man dies, one chapter is not torn out of the book, but translated into a better language; and every chapter must be so translated....
—John Donne

Love and Theft

Consider this tale: a cultivated man of middle age looks back on the story of an *amour fou*, one beginning when, traveling abroad, he takes a room as a lodger. The moment he sees the daughter of the house, he is lost. She is a pre-teen, whose charms instantly enslave him. Heedless of her age, he becomes intimate with her. In the end she dies, and the narrator—marked by her forever—remains alone. The name of the girl supplies the title of the story: *Lolita*.

The author of the story I've described, Heinz von Lichberg, published his tale of Lolita in 1916, forty years before Vladimir Nabokov's novel. Lichberg later became a prominent journalist in the Nazi era, and his youthful works faded from view. Did Nabokov, who remained in Berlin until 1937, adopt Lichberg's tale consciously? Or did the earlier tale exist for Nabokov as a

First published in *Harper's* Magazine, vol. 314, no. 1881. Copyright © 2007 by Jonathan Lethem. Reprinted by permission of The Richard Parks Agency.

hidden, unacknowledged memory? The history of literature is not without examples of this phenomenon, called cryptomnesia. Another hypothesis is that Nabokov, knowing Lichberg's tale perfectly well, had set himself to that art of quotation that Thomas Mann, himself a master of it, called "higher cribbing." Literature has always been a crucible in which familiar themes are continually recast. Little of what we admire in Nabokov's *Lolita* is to be found in its predecessor; the former is in no way deducible from the latter. Still: did Nabokov consciously borrow and quote?

"When you live outside the law, you have to eliminate dishonesty." The line comes from Don Siegel's 1958 film noir, *The Lineup*, written by Stirling Silliphant. The film still haunts revival houses, likely thanks to Eli Wallach's blazing portrayal of a sociopathic hit man and to Siegel's long, sturdy auteurist career. Yet what were those words worth—to Siegel, or Silliphant, or their audience—in 1958? And again: what was the line worth when Bob Dylan heard it (presumably in some Greenwich Village repertory cinema), cleaned it up a little, and inserted it into "Absolutely Sweet Marie"? What are they worth now, to the culture at large?

Appropriation has always played a key role in Dylan's music. The songwriter has grabbed not only from a panoply of vintage Hollywood films but from Shakespeare and F. Scott Fitzgerald and Junichi Saga's *Confessions of a Yakuza*. He also nabbed the title of Eric Lott's study of minstrelsy for his 2001 album *Love and Theft*. One imagines Dylan liked the general resonance of the title, in which emotional misdemeanors stalk the sweetness of love, as they do so often in Dylan's songs. Lott's title is, of course, itself a riff on Leslie Fiedler's *Love and Death in the American Novel*, which famously identifies the literary motif of the interdependence of a white man and a dark man, like Huck and Jim or Ishmael and Queequeg—a series of nested references to Dylan's own appropriating, minstrelboy self. Dylan's art offers a paradox: while it famously urges us not to look back, it also encodes a knowledge of past sources that might otherwise have little home in contemporary culture, like the Civil War poetry of the Confederate bard Henry Timrod, resuscitated in lyrics on Dylan's newest record, *Modern Times*.

The same might be said of *all* art. I realized this forcefully when one day I went looking for the John Donne passage quoted above. I know the lines, I confess, not from a college course but from the movie version of *84, Charing Cross Road* with Anthony Hopkins and Anne Bancroft. I checked out *84, Charing Cross Road* from the library in the hope of finding the Donne passage, but it wasn't in the book. It's alluded to in the play that was adapted from the book, but it isn't reprinted. So I rented the movie again, and there was the passage, read in voiceover by Anthony Hopkins but without attribution. Unfortunately, the line was also abridged so that, when I finally turned to the Web, I found myself searching for the line "all mankind is of one volume" instead of "all mankind is of one author, and is one volume."

My Internet search was initially no more successful than my library search. I had thought that summoning books from the vasty deep was a matter of a few keystrokes, but when I visited the website of the Yale library, I found that most of its books don't yet exist as computer text. As a last-ditch effort I searched the seemingly more obscure phrase "every chapter must be so translated." The passage I wanted finally came to me, as it turns out, not as part of a scholarly library collection but simply because someone who loves Donne had posted it on his homepage. The lines I sought were from Meditation 17 in *Devotions upon Emergent Occasions*, which happens to be the most famous thing Donne ever wrote, containing as it does the line "never send to know for whom the bell tolls; it tolls for thee." My search had led me from a movie to a book to a play to a website and back to a book. Then again, those words may be as famous as they are only because Hemingway lifted them for his book title.

Literature has been in a plundered, fragmentary state for a long time. When I was thirteen I purchased an anthology of Beat writing. Immediately, and to my very great excitement, I discovered one William S. Burroughs, author of something called *Naked Lunch*, excerpted there in all its coruscating brilliance. Burroughs was then as radical a literary man as the world had to offer. Nothing, in all my experience of literature since, has ever had as strong an effect on my sense of the sheer possibilities of writing. Later, attempting to understand this impact, I discovered that Burroughs had incorporated snippets of other writers' texts into his work, an action I knew my teachers would have called plagiarism. Some of these borrowings had been lifted from American science fiction of the 1940s and '50s, adding a secondary shock of recognition for me. By then I knew that this "cut-up method," as Burroughs called it, was central to whatever he thought he was doing, and that he quite literally believed it to be akin to magic. When he wrote about his process, the hairs on my neck stood up, so palpable was the excitement. Burroughs was interrogating the universe with scissors and a paste pot, and the least imitative of authors was no plagiarist at all.

Contamination Anxiety

In 1941, on his front porch, Muddy Waters recorded a song for the folklorist Alan Lomax. After singing the song, which he told Lomax was entitled "Country Blues," Waters described how he came to write it. "I made it on about the eighth of October '38," Waters said. "I was fixin' a puncture on a car. I had been mistreated by a girl. I just felt blue, and the song fell into my mind and it come to me just like that and I started singing." Then Lomax, who knew of the Robert Johnson recording called "Walkin' Blues," asked Waters if there were any other songs that used the same tune. "There's been some blues played like that," Waters replied. "This song comes from the cotton field and a boy once put a record out—Robert Johnson. He put it out as named 'Walkin' Blues.' I heard the tune before I heard it on the record. I learned it from Son House." In nearly one breath, Waters offers five accounts: his own active authorship: he "made it" on a specific date. Then the "passive" explanation: "it come to me just like that." After Lomax raises the question of influence, Waters, without shame, misgivings, or trepidation, says that he heard a version by Johnson, but that his mentor, Son House, taught it to him. In the middle of that complex genealogy, Waters declares that "this song comes from the cotton field."

Blues and jazz musicians have long been enabled by a kind of "open source" culture, where preexisting melodic fragments and larger musical frameworks are freely reworked. Technology has only multiplied the possibilities; musicians have gained the power to *duplicate* sounds literally rather than simply approximate them through allusion. In 1970s Jamaica, King Tubby and Lee "Scratch" Perry deconstructed recorded music, using astonishingly primitive predigital hardware, creating what they called "versions." The recombinant nature of their means of production quickly spread to DJs in New York and London. Today an endless, gloriously impure, and fundamentally social process generates countless hours of music.

Visual, sound, and text collage—which for many centuries were relatively fugitive traditions (a cento here, a folk pastiche there)—became explosively central to a series of movements in the twentieth century: futurism, cubism, Dada, *musique concrète*, situationism, pop art, and appropriationism. In fact, collage, the common denominator in that list, might be called *the* art form of the twentieth century, never mind the twenty-first. But forget, for the moment, chronologies, schools, or even centuries. As examples accumulate—

Igor Stravinsky's music and Daniel Johnston's, Francis Bacon's paintings and Henry Darger's, the novels of the Oulipo group and of Hannah Crafts (the author who pillaged Dickens's *Bleak House* to write *The Bondwoman's Narrative*), as well as cherished texts that become troubling to their admirers after the discovery of their "plagiarized" elements, like Richard Condon's novels or Martin Luther King Jr.'s sermons—it becomes apparent that appropriation, mimicry, quotation, allusion, and sublimated collaboration consist of a kind of sine qua non of the creative act, cutting across all forms and genres in the realm of cultural production.

In a courtroom scene from *The Simpsons* that has since entered into the television canon, an argument over the ownership of the animated characters Itchy and Scratchy rapidly escalates into an existential debate on the very nature of cartoons. "Animation is built on plagiarism!" declares the show's hot-tempered cartoon-producer-within-a-cartoon, Roger Meyers Jr. "You take away our right to steal ideas, where are they going to come from?" If nostalgic cartoonists had never borrowed from *Fritz the Cat*, there would be no *Ren & Stimpy Show*; without the Rankin/Bass and Charlie Brown Christmas specials, there would be no *South Park*; and without *The Flintstones*—more or less *The Honeymooners* in cartoon loincloths—*The Simpsons* would cease to exist. If those don't strike you as essential losses, then consider the remarkable series of "plagiarisms" that links Ovid's "Pyramus and Thisbe" with Shakespeare's *Romeo and Juliet* and Leonard Bernstein's *West Side Story*, or Shakespeare's description of Cleopatra, copied nearly verbatim from Plutarch's life of Mark Antony and also later nicked by T. S. Eliot for *The Waste Land*. If these are examples of plagiarism, then we want more plagiarism.

Most artists are brought to their vocation when their own nascent gifts are awakened by the work of a master. That is to say, most artists are converted to art by art itself. Finding one's voice isn't just an emptying and purifying oneself of the words of others but an adopting and embracing of filiations, communities, and discourses. Inspiration could be called inhaling the memory of an act never experienced. Invention, it must be humbly admitted, does not consist in creating out of void, but out of chaos. Any artist knows these truths, no matter how deeply he or she submerges that knowing.

What happens when an allusion goes unrecognized? A closer look at *The Waste Land* may help make this point. The body of Eliot's poem is a vertiginous mélange of quotation, allusion, and "original" writing. When Eliot alludes to Edmund Spenser's "Prothalamion" with the line "Sweet Thames, run softly, till I end my song," what of readers to whom the poem, never one of Spenser's most popular, is unfamiliar? (Indeed, the Spenser is now known largely because of Eliot's use of it.) Two responses are possible: grant the line to Eliot, or later discover the source and understand the line as plagiarism. Eliot evidenced no small anxiety about these matters; the notes he so carefully added to *The Waste Land* can be read as a symptom of modernism's contamination anxiety. Taken from this angle, what exactly is postmodernism, except modernism without the anxiety?

Surrounded by Signs

The surrealists believed that objects in the world possess a certain but unspecifiable intensity that had been dulled by everyday use and utility. They meant to reanimate this dormant intensity, to bring their minds once again into close contact with the matter that made up their world. André Breton's maxim, "Beautiful as the chance encounter of a sewing machine and an umbrella on an operating table," is an expression of the belief that simply placing objects in an unexpected context reinvigorates their mysterious qualities.

This "crisis" the surrealists identified was being simultaneously diagnosed by others. Martin Heidegger held that the essence of modernity was found in a certain technological orientation he called "enframing." This tendency encourages us to see the objects in our world only in terms of how they can serve us or be used by us. The task he identified was to find ways to resituate ourselves vis-à-vis these "objects," so that we may see them as "things" pulled into relief against the ground of their functionality. Heidegger believed that art had the great potential to reveal the "thingness" of objects.

The surrealists understood that photography and cinema could carry out this reanimating process automatically; the process of framing objects in a lens was often enough to create the charge they sought. Describing the effect, Walter Benjamin drew a comparison between the photographic apparatus and Freud's psychoanalytic methods. Just as Freud's theories "isolated and made analyzable things which had heretofore floated along unnoticed in the broad stream of perception," the photographic apparatus focuses on "hidden details of familiar objects," revealing "entirely new structural formations of the subject."

It's worth noting, then, that early in the history of photography a series of judicial decisions could well have changed the course of that art: courts were asked whether the photographer, amateur or professional, required permission before he could capture and print an image because the photographer was *stealing* from the person or building whose photograph he shot, pirating something of private and certifiable value. Those early decisions went in favor of the pirates. Just as Walt Disney could take inspiration from Buster Keaton's *Steamboat Bill, Jr.*, the Brothers Grimm, or the existence of real mice, the photographer should be free to capture an image without compensating the source. The world that meets our eye through the lens of a camera was judged to be, with minor exceptions, a sort of public commons, where a cat may look at a king.

Novelists may glance at the stuff of the world too, but we sometimes get called to task for it. For those whose ganglia were formed pre-TV, the mimetic deployment of pop-culture icons seems at best an annoying tic and at worst a dangerous vapidity that compromises fiction's seriousness by dating it out of the Platonic Always where it ought to reside. In a graduate workshop I briefly passed through, a certain gray eminence tried to convince us that a literary story should always eschew "any feature which serves to date it" because "serious fiction must be Timeless." When we protested that, in his own well-known work, characters moved about electrically lit rooms, drove cars, and spoke not Anglo-Saxon but postwar English—and further, that fiction he'd himself ratified as great, such as Dickens, was liberally strewn with innately topical, commercial, and time-bound references—he impatiently emended his proscription to those explicit references that would date a story in the "frivolous Now." When pressed, he said of course he meant the "trendy mass-popular-media" reference. Here, transgenerational discourse broke down.

I was born in 1964; I grew up watching Captain Kangaroo, moon landings, zillions of TV ads, the Banana Splits, *M*A*S*H*, and *The Mary Tyler Moore Show*. I was born with words in my mouth—"Band-Aid," "Q-tip," "Xerox"—object-names as fixed and eternal in my logosphere as "taxicab" and "toothbrush." The world is a home littered with pop-culture products and their emblems. I also came of age swamped by parodies that stood for originals yet mysterious to me—I knew Monkees before Beatles, Belmondo before Bogart, and "remember" the movie *Summer of '42* from a *Mad* magazine satire, though I've still never seen the film itself. I'm not alone in having been born backwards into an incoherent realm of texts, products, and images, the commercial and cultural environment with which we've both supplemented and blotted out our natural world. I can no more claim it as "mine" than the sidewalks and forests of the world, yet I do dwell in it, and for me to stand a chance as either artist or citizen, I'd probably better be permitted to name it.

Consider Walker Percy's *The Moviegoer*:

Other people, so I have read, treasure memorable moments in their lives: the time one climbed the Parthenon at sunrise, the summer night one met a lonely girl in Central Park and achieved with her a sweet and natural relationship, as they say in books. I too once met a girl in Central Park, but it is not much to remember. What I remember is the time John Wayne killed three men with a carbine as he was falling to the dusty street in *Stagecoach*, and the time the kitten found Orson Welles in the doorway in *The Third Man*.

Today, when we can eat Tex-Mex with chopsticks while listening to reggae and watching a YouTube rebroadcast of the Berlin Wall's fall—i.e., when damn near *everything* presents itself as familiar—it's not a surprise that some of today's most ambitious art is going about trying to *make the familiar strange*. In so doing, in reimagining what human life might truly be like over there across the chasms of illusion, mediation, demographics, marketing, imago, and appearance, artists are paradoxically trying to restore what's taken for "real" to three whole dimensions, to reconstruct a univocally round world out of disparate streams of flat sights.

Whatever charge of tastelessness or trademark violation may be attached to the artistic appropriation of the media environment in which we swim, the alternative—to flinch, or tiptoe away into some ivory tower of irrelevance—is far worse. We're surrounded by signs; our imperative is to ignore none of them.

Usemonopoly

The idea that culture can be property—*intellectual* property—is used to justify everything from attempts to force the Girl Scouts to pay royalties for singing songs around campfires to the infringement suit brought by the estate of Margaret Mitchell against the publishers of Alice Randall's *The Wind Done Gone*. Corporations like Celera Genomics have filed for patents for human genes, while the Recording Industry Association of America has sued music downloaders for copyright infringement, reaching out-of-court settlements for thousands of dollars with defendants as young as twelve. ASCAP bleeds fees from shop owners who play background music in their stores; students and scholars are shamed from placing texts facedown on photocopy machines. At the same time, copyright is revered by most established writers and artists as a birthright and bulwark, the source of nurture for their infinitely fragile practices in a rapacious world. Plagiarism and piracy, after all, are the monsters we working artists are taught to dread, as they roam the woods surrounding our tiny preserves of regard and remuneration.

A time is marked not so much by ideas that are argued about as by ideas that are taken for granted. The character of an era hangs upon what needs no defense. In this regard, few of us question the contemporary construction of copyright. It is taken as a law, both in the sense of a universally recognizable moral absolute, like the law against murder, and as naturally inherent in our world, like the law of gravity. In fact, it is neither. Rather, copyright is an ongoing social negotiation, tenuously forged, endlessly revised, and imperfect in its every incarnation.

Thomas Jefferson, for one, considered copyright a necessary evil: he favored providing just enough incentive to create, nothing more, and thereafter allowing ideas to flow freely as nature intended. His conception of copyright was enshrined in the Constitution, which gives Congress the authority to "promote the progress of science and useful arts, by securing for limited times to authors and inventors the exclusive right to their respective writings and discoveries." This was a balancing act between creators and society as a whole; second comers might do a much better job than the originator with the original idea.

But Jefferson's vision has not fared well, has in fact been steadily eroded by those who view the culture as a market in which everything of value should be owned by someone or other. The distinctive feature of modern American copyright law is its almost limitless bloating—its expansion in both scope and duration. With no registration requirement, every creative act in a tangible medium is now subject to copyright protection: your email to your child or your child's finger painting, both are automatically protected. The first Congress to grant copyright gave authors an initial term of fourteen years, which could be renewed for another fourteen if the author still lived. The current term is the life of the author plus seventy years. It's only a slight exaggeration to say that each time Mickey Mouse is about to fall into the public domain, the mouse's copyright term is extended.

Even as the law becomes more restrictive, technology is exposing those restrictions as bizarre and arbitrary. When old laws fixed on reproduction as the compensable (or actionable) unit, it wasn't because there was anything fundamentally invasive of an author's rights in the making of a copy. Rather it was because copies were once easy to find and count, so they made a useful benchmark for deciding when an owner's rights had been invaded. In the contemporary world, though, the act of "copying" is in no meaningful sense equivalent to an infringement—we make a copy every time we accept an emailed text, or send or forward one—and is impossible anymore to regulate or even describe.

At the movies, my entertainment is sometimes lately preceded by a dire trailer, produced by the lobbying group called the Motion Picture Association of America, in which the purchasing of a bootleg copy of a Hollywood film is compared to the theft of a car or a handbag—and, as the bullying supertitles remind us, "You wouldn't steal a handbag!" This conflation forms an incitement to quit thinking. If I were to tell you that pirating DVDs or downloading music is in no way different from loaning a friend a book, my own arguments would be as ethically bankrupt as the MPAA's. The truth lies somewhere in the vast gray area between these two overstated positions. For a car or a handbag, once stolen, no longer is available to its owner, while the appropriation of an article of "intellectual property" leaves the original untouched. As Jefferson wrote, "He who receives an idea from me, receives instruction himself without lessening mine; as he who lights his taper at mine, receives light without darkening me."

Yet industries of cultural capital, who profit not from creating but from distributing, see the sale of culture as a zero sum game. The pianoroll publishers fear the record companies, who fear the cassette-tape manufacturers, who fear the online vendors, who fear whoever else is next in line to profit most quickly from the intangible and infinitely reproducible fruits of an artist's labor. It has been the same in every industry and with every technological innovation. Jack Valenti, speaking for the MPAA: "I say to you that the VCR is to the American film producer and the American public as the Boston Strangler is to the woman home alone."

Thinking clearly sometimes requires unbraiding our language. The word "copyright" may eventually seem as dubious in its embedded purposes as "family values," "globalization," and, sure, "intellectual property." Copyright is a "right" in no absolute sense; it is a government-granted monopoly on the use of creative results. So let's try calling it that—not a right but a *monopoly on use*, a "usemonopoly"—and then consider how the rapacious expansion of monopoly rights has always been counter to the public interest, no matter if it is Andrew Carnegie controlling the price of steel or Walt Disney managing the fate of his mouse. Whether the monopolizing beneficiary is a living artist or some artist's heirs or some corporation's shareholders, the loser is the community, including living artists who might make splendid use of a healthy public domain.

The Beauty of Second Use

A few years ago someone brought me a strange gift, purchased at MoMA's downtown design store: a copy of my own first novel, *Gun, With Occasional Music*, expertly cut into the contours of a pistol. The object was the work of Robert The, an artist whose specialty is the reincarnation of everyday materials. I regard my first book as an old friend, one who never fails to remind me of the spirit with which I entered into this game of art and commerce—that to be allowed to insert the materials of my imagination onto the shelves of bookstores and into the minds of readers (if only a handful) was a wild privilege. I was paid $6,000 for three years of writing, but at the time I'd have happily published the results for nothing. Now my old friend had come home in a new form, one I was unlikely to have imagined for it myself. The gun-book wasn't readable, exactly, but I couldn't take offense at that. The fertile spirit of stray connection this appropriated object conveyed back to me—the strange beauty of its second use—was a reward for being a published writer I could never have fathomed in advance. And the world makes room for both my novel and Robert The's gun-book. There's no need to choose between the two.

   In the first life of creative property, if the creator is lucky, the content is sold. After the commercial life has ended, our tradition supports a second life as well. A newspaper is delivered to a doorstep, and the next day wraps fish or builds an archive. Most books fall out of print after only one year, yet even within that period they can be sold in used bookstores and stored in libraries, quoted in reviews, parodied in magazines, described in conversations, and plundered for costumes for kids to wear on Halloween. The demarcation between various possible uses is beautifully graded and hard to define, the more so as artifacts distill into and repercuss through the realm of culture into which they've been entered, the more so as they engage the receptive minds for whom they were presumably intended.

Active reading is an impertinent raid on the literary preserve. Readers are like nomads, poaching their way across fields they do not own—artists are no more able to control the imaginations of their audiences than the culture industry is able to control second uses of its artifacts. In the children's classic *The Velveteen Rabbit*, the old Skin Horse offers the Rabbit a lecture on the practice of textual poaching. The value of a new toy lies not in its material qualities (not "having things that buzz inside you and a stick-out handle"), the Skin Horse explains, but rather in how the toy is used. "Real isn't how you are made.... It's a thing that happens to you. When a child loves you for a long, long time, not just to play with, but REALLY loves you, then you become Real." The Rabbit is fearful, recognizing that consumer goods don't become "real" without being actively reworked: "Does it hurt?" Reassuring him, the Skin Horse says: "It doesn't happen all at once.... You become. It takes a long time.... Generally, by the time you are Real, most of your hair has been loved off, and your eyes drop out and you get loose in the joints and very shabby." Seen from the perspective of the toymaker, the Velveteen Rabbit's loose joints and missing eyes represent vandalism, signs of misuse and rough treatment; for others, these are marks of its loving use.

Artists and their surrogates who fall into the trap of seeking recompense for every possible second use end up attacking their own best audience members for the crime of exalting and enshrining their work. The Recording Industry Association of America prosecuting their own record-buying public makes as little sense as the novelists who bristle at autographing used copies of their books for collectors. And artists, or their heirs, who fall into the trap of attacking the collagists and satirists and digital samplers of their work are attacking the next generation of creators for the crime of being influenced, for the crime of responding with the same mixture of intoxication, resentment, lust, and glee that characterizes all artistic successors. By doing so they make the world smaller, betraying what seems to me the primary motivation for participating in the world of culture in the first place: to make the world larger.

Source Hypocrisy, or Disnial

The Walt Disney Company has drawn an astonishing catalogue from the work of others: *Snow White and the Seven Dwarfs, Fantasia, Pinocchio, Dumbo, Bambi, Song of the South, Cinderella, Alice in Wonderland, Robin Hood, Peter Pan, Lady and the Tramp, Mulan, Sleeping Beauty, The Sword in the Stone, The Jungle Book*, and, alas, *Treasure Planet*, a legacy of cultural sampling that

Shakespeare, or De La Soul, could get behind. Yet Disney's protectorate of lobbyists has policed the resulting cache of cultural materials as vigilantly as if it were Fort Knox—threatening legal action, for instance, against the artist Dennis Oppenheim for the use of Disney characters in a sculpture, and prohibiting the scholar Holly Crawford from using *any* Disney-related images—including artwork by Lichtenstein, Warhol, Oldenburg, and others—in her monograph *Attached to the Mouse: Disney and Contemporary Art.*

This peculiar and specific act—the enclosure of commonwealth culture for the benefit of a sole or corporate owner—is close kin to what could be called *imperial plagiarism*, the free use of third-world or "primitive" artworks and styles by more privileged (and better-paid) artists. Think of Picasso's *Les Demoiselles d'Avignon*, or some of the albums of Paul Simon or David Byrne: even without violating copyright, those creators have sometimes come in for a certain skepticism when the extent of their outsourcing became evident. And, as when Led Zeppelin found themselves sued for back royalties by the bluesman Willie Dixon, the act can occasionally be an expensive one. *To live outside the law, you must be honest*: perhaps it was this, in part, that spurred David Byrne and Brian Eno to recently launch a "remix" website, where anyone can download easily disassembled versions of two songs from *My Life in the Bush of Ghosts*, an album reliant on vernacular speech sampled from a host of sources. Perhaps it also explains why Bob Dylan has never refused a request for a sample.

Kenneth Koch once said, "I'm a writer who likes to be influenced." It was a charming confession, and a rare one. For so many artists, the act of creativity is intended as a Napoleonic imposition of one's uniqueness upon the universe—*après moi le déluge* of copycats! And for every James Joyce or Woody Guthrie or Martin Luther King Jr. or Walt Disney who gathered a constellation of voices in his work there may seem to be some corporation or literary estate eager to stopper the bottle: cultural debts flow in, but they don't flow out. We might call this tendency "source hypocrisy." Or we could name it after the most pernicious source hypocrites of all time: Disnial.

You Can't Steal a Gift

My reader may, understandably, be on the verge of crying "Communist!" A large, diverse society cannot survive without property; a large, diverse, and modern society cannot flourish without some form of intellectual property. But it takes little reflection to grasp that there is ample value that the term "property" doesn't capture. And works of art exist simultaneously in two economies, a market economy and a *gift economy*.

The cardinal difference between gift and commodity exchange is that a gift establishes a feeling-bond between two people, whereas the sale of a commodity leaves no necessary connection. I go into a hardware store, pay the man for a hacksaw blade, and walk out. I may never see him again. The disconnectedness is, in fact, a virtue of the commodity mode. We don't want to be bothered, and if the clerk always wants to chat about the family, I'll shop elsewhere. I just want a hacksaw blade. But a gift makes a connection. There are many examples, the candy or cigarette offered to a stranger who shares a seat on the plane, the few words that indicate goodwill between passengers on the late-night bus. These tokens establish the simplest bonds of social life, but the model they offer may be extended to the most complicated of unions—marriage, parenthood, tutorship. If a value is placed on these (often essentially inequal) exchanges, they degenerate into something else.

Yet one of the more difficult things to comprehend is that the gift economies—like those that sustain open source software—coexist so naturally with the market. It is precisely this doubleness in art practices that we must identify, ratify, and enshrine in our lives as participants in culture, either as "producers" or "consumers." Art that matters to us—which moves the heart, or revives the soul, or delights the senses, or offers courage for living, however we choose to describe the experience—is received as a gift is received. Even if we've paid a fee at the door of the museum or concert hall, when we are touched by a work of art something comes to us that has nothing to do with the price. The daily commerce of our lives proceeds at its own constant level, but a gift conveys an uncommodifiable surplus of inspiration.

The way we treat a thing can change its nature, though. Religions often prohibit the sale of sacred objects, the implication being that their sanctity is lost if they are bought and sold. We consider it unacceptable to sell sex, babies, body organs, legal rights, and votes. The idea that something should never be commodified is generally known as *inalienability* or *unalienability*—a concept most famously expressed by Thomas Jefferson in the phrase "endowed by their Creator with certain unalienable Rights...." A work of art seems to be a hardier breed; it can be sold in the market and still emerge a work of art. But if it is true that in the essential commerce of art a gift is carried by the work from the artist to his audience, if I am right to say that where there is no gift there is no art, then it may be possible to destroy a work of art by converting it into a pure commodity. I don't maintain that art can't be bought and sold, but that the gift portion of the work places a constraint upon our merchandising. This is the reason why even a really beautiful, ingenious, powerful ad (of which there are a lot) can never be any kind of real art: an ad has no status as gift; i.e., it's never really *for* the person it's directed at.

The power of a gift economy remains difficult for the empiricists of our market culture to understand. In our times, the rhetoric of the market presumes that everything should be and can be appropriately bought, sold, and owned—a tide of alienation lapping daily at the dwindling redoubt of the unalienable. In freemarket theory, an intervention to halt propertization is considered "paternalistic," because it inhibits the free action of the citizen, now reposited as a "potential entrepreneur." Of course, in the real world, we know that child-rearing, family life, education, socialization, sexuality, political life, and many other basic human activities require insulation from market forces. In fact, paying for many of these things can ruin them. We may be willing to peek at *Who Wants to Marry a Millionaire* or an eBay auction of the ova of fashion models, but only to reassure ourselves that some things are still beneath our standards of dignity.

What's remarkable about gift economies is that they can flourish in the most unlikely places—in rundown neighborhoods, on the Internet, in scientific communities, and among members of Alcoholics Anonymous. A classic example is commercial blood systems, which generally produce blood supplies of lower safety, purity, and potency than volunteer systems. A gift economy may be superior when it comes to maintaining a group's commitment to certain extra-market values.

The Commons

Another way of understanding the presence of gift economies—which dwell like ghosts in the commercial machine—is in the sense of a *public commons*. A commons, of course, is anything like the streets over which we drive, the skies through which we pilot airplanes, or the public parks or beaches on which we dally. A commons belongs to everyone and no one, and its use is controlled only by common consent. A commons describes resources like the body of ancient music drawn on by composers and folk musicians alike, rather than the commodities, like "Happy Birthday," for which ASCAP, 114 years after it was written, continues to collect a fee. Einstein's theory of relativity is a commons. Writings in the public domain are a commons. Gossip about celebrities is a commons. The silence in a movie theater is a transitory commons, impossibly fragile, treasured by those who crave it, and constructed as a mutual gift by those who comprise it.

The world of art and culture is a vast commons, one salted through with zones of utter commerce yet which remains gloriously immune to any over-all commodification. The closest resemblance is to the commons of a *language*: altered by every contributor, expanded by even the most passive user. That a language is a commons doesn't mean that the community owns it; rather it belongs *between* people, possessed by no one, not even by society as a whole.

Nearly any commons, though, can be encroached upon, partitioned, enclosed. The American commons include tangible assets such as public forests and minerals, intangible wealth such as copyrights and patents, critical infrastructures such as the Internet and government research, and cultural resources such as the broadcast airwaves and public spaces. They include resources we've paid for as taxpayers and inherited from previous generations. They're not just an inventory of marketable assets; they're social institutions and cultural traditions that define us as Americans and enliven us as human beings. Some invasions of the commons are sanctioned because we can no longer muster a spirited commitment to the public sector. The abuse goes unnoticed because the theft of the commons is seen in glimpses, not in panorama. We may occasionally see a former wetland paved; we may hear about the breakthrough cancer drug that tax dollars helped develop, the rights to which pharmaceutical companies acquired for a song. The larger movement goes too much unremarked. The notion of a *commons of cultural materials* goes more or less unnamed.

Honoring the commons is not a matter of moral exhortation. It is a practical necessity. We in Western society are going through a period of intensifying belief in private ownership, to the detriment of the public good. We have to remain constantly vigilant to prevent raids by those who would selfishly exploit our common heritage for their private gain. Such raids on our natural resources are not examples of enterprise and initiative. They are attempts to take from all the people just for the benefit of a few.

Undiscovered Public Knowledge

Artists and intellectuals disheartened by the prospects for originality can take heart from a phenomenon identified about twenty years ago by Don Swanson, a library scientist at the University of Chicago. He called it "undiscovered public knowledge." Swanson showed that standing problems in medical research may be significantly addressed, perhaps even solved, simply by systematically surveying the scientific literature. Left to its own devices, research tends to become more specialized and abstracted from the real-world problems that motivated it and to which it remains relevant. This suggests that such a problem may be tackled effectively not by commissioning more research but by assuming that most or all of the solution can already be found in various scientific journals, waiting to be assembled by someone willing to read across specialties. Swanson himself did this in the case of Raynaud's syndrome, a disease that causes the fingers of young women to become numb. His finding is especially striking—perhaps even scandalous—because it happened in the ever-expanding biomedical sciences.

Undiscovered public knowledge emboldens us to question the extreme claims to originality made in press releases and publishers' notices: is an intellectual or creative offering truly novel, or have we just forgotten a worthy precursor? Does solving certain scientific problems really require massive additional funding, or could a computerized search engine, creatively deployed, do the same job more quickly and cheaply? Lastly, does our appetite for creative vitality require the violence and exasperation of another avant-garde, with its wearisome killing-the-father imperatives, or might we be better off ratifying *the ecstasy of influence*—and deepening our willingness to understand the commonality and timelessness of the methods and motifs available to artists?

Give All

A few years ago, the Film Society of Lincoln Center announced a retrospective of the works of Dariush Mehrjui, then a fresh enthusiasm of mine. Mehrjui is one of Iran's finest filmmakers, and the only one whose subject was personal relationships among the upper-middle-class intelligentsia. Needless to say, opportunities to view his films were—and remain—rare indeed. I headed uptown for one, an adaptation of J. D. Salinger's *Franny and Zooey*, titled *Pari*, only to discover at the door of the Walter Reade Theater that the screening had been canceled: its announcement had brought threat of a lawsuit down on the Film Society. True, these were Salinger's rights under the law. Yet why would he care that some obscure Iranian filmmaker had paid him homage with a meditation on his heroine? Would it have damaged his book or robbed him of some crucial remuneration had the screening been permitted? The fertile spirit of stray connection—one stretching across what is presently seen as the direst of international breaches—had in this case been snuffed out. The cold, undead hand of one of my childhood literary heroes had reached out from its New Hampshire redoubt to arrest my present-day curiosity.

A few assertions, then: Any text that has infiltrated the common mind to the extent of *Gone With the Wind* or *Lolita* or *Ulysses* inexorably joins the language of culture. A map-turned-to-landscape, it has moved to a place beyond enclosure or control. The authors and their heirs should consider the subsequent parodies, refractions, quotations, and revisions an honor, or at least the price of a rare success.

A corporation that has imposed an inescapable notion—Mickey Mouse, Band-Aid—on the cultural language should pay a similar price.

The primary objective of copyright is not to reward the labor of authors but "to promote the Progress of Science and useful Arts." To this end, copyright assures authors the right to their original expression, but encourages others to build freely upon the ideas and information conveyed by a work. This result is neither unfair nor unfortunate.

Contemporary copyright, trademark, and patent law is corrupted. The case for perpetual copyright is a denial of the essential gift-aspect of the creative act. Arguments in its favor are as un-American as those for the repeal of the estate tax.

Art is sourced. Apprentices graze in the field of culture.

Digital sampling is an art method like any other, neutral in itself.

Allusion is a step toward making the modern world possible for art.

Despite hand-wringing at each technological turn—radio, the Internet—the future will be much like the past. Artists will sell some things, but also give some things away. Change may be troubling for those who crave less ambiguity, but the life of an artist has never been filled with certainty.

The dream of a perfect systematic remuneration is nonsense. I pay rent with the price my words bring when published in glossy magazines and at the same moment offer them for almost nothing to impoverished literary quarterlies, or speak them for free into the air in a radio interview. So what are they worth? What would they be worth if some future Dylan worked them into a song? Should I care to make such a thing impossible?

Any text is woven entirely with citations, references, echoes, cultural languages, which cut across it through and through in a vast stereophony. The citations that go to make up a text are anonymous, untraceable, and yet *already read*; they are quotations without inverted commas. The kernel, the soul—let's go further and say the substance, the bulk, the actual and valuable material of all human utterances—is plagiarism. For substantially all ideas are second-hand, consciously or unconsciously drawn from a million outside sources, and daily used by the garnerer with a pride and satisfaction born of the superstition that he originated them; there is not a rag of originality about them anywhere except the little discoloration they get from his mental and moral caliber and temperament, and which is revealed in characteristics of phrasing. Old and new make the warp and woof of every moment. There is no thread that is not a twist of these two strands. By necessity, by proclivity, and by delight, we all quote. Neurological study has lately shown that memory, imagination, and consciousness itself is stitched, quilted, pastiched. If we cut-and-paste our selves, might we not forgive it of our artworks?

Artists and writers—and our advocates, our guilds and agents—too often subscribe to implicit claims of originality that do injury to these truths. And we too often, as hucksters and bean-counters in the tiny enterprises of our selves, act to spite the gift portion of our privileged roles. People live differently who treat a portion of their wealth as a gift. If we devalue and obscure the gift-economy function of our art practices, we turn our works into nothing more than advertisements for themselves. We may console ourselves that our lust for subsidiary rights in virtual perpetuity comprises some heroic counter to rapacious corporate interests. But the truth is that with artists pulling on one side and corporations pulling on the other, the loser is the collective public imagination from which we were nourished in the first place, and whose existence as the ultimate repository of our offerings makes the work worth doing in the first place.

As a novelist, I'm a cork on the ocean of story, a leaf on a windy day. Pretty soon I'll be blown away. For the moment I'm grateful to be making a living, and so must ask that for a limited time (in the Thomas Jefferson sense) you please respect my small, treasured usemonopolies. Don't pirate my editions; do plunder my visions. The name of the game is Give All. You, reader, are welcome to my stories. They were never mine in the first place, but I gave them to you. If you have the inclination to pick them up, take them with my blessings.

KEY: I IS ANOTHER

This skeleton key to the preceding essay names the source of every line I stole, warped, and cobbled together as I "wrote" (except, alas, those sources I forgot along the way). First uses of a given author or speaker are highlighted in bold-face. Nearly every sentence I culled I also revised, at least slightly—for necessities of space, in order to produce a more consistent tone, or simply because I felt like it.

Title

The phrase "the ecstasy of influence," which embeds a rebuking play on **Harold Bloom**'s "anxiety of influence," is lifted from spoken remarks by Professor **Richard Dienst** of Rutgers.

Love and Theft

"... a cultivated man of middle age ..." to "... hidden, unacknowledged memory?" These lines, with some adjustments for tone, belong to the **anonymous editor or assistant** who wrote the dust-flap copy of **Michael Maar**'s *The Two Lolitas*. Of course, in my own experience, dust-flap copy is often a collaboration between author and editor. Perhaps this was also true for Maar.

"The history of literature ..." to "... borrow and quote?" comes from Maar's book itself.

"Appropriation has always ..." to "... Ishmael and Queequeg...." This paragraph makes a hash of remarks from an interview with **Eric Lott**, conducted by **David McNair** and **Jayson Whitehead**, and incorporates both interviewers' and interviewee's observations. (The text-interview form can be seen as a commonly accepted form of multivocal writing. Most interviewers prime their subjects with remarks of their own—leading the witness, so to speak—and gently refine their subjects' statements in the final printed transcript.)

"I realized this ..." to "... for a long time." The anecdote is cribbed, with an elision to avoid appropriating a dead grandmother, from **Jonathan Rosen**'s *The Talmud and the Internet*. I've never seen *84, Charing Cross Road*, nor searched the Web for a Donne quote. For me it was through Rosen to Donne, Hemingway, website, et al. I avoid spiritual matters in my own writing, and so I experienced a peculiar discomfort hijacking Rosen's gently searching tone.

"When I was thirteen ..." to "... no plagiarist at all." This is from **William Gibson**'s "God's Little Toys," in *Wired* magazine. My own first encounter with William Burroughs, also at age thirteen, was less epiphanic. Having grown up with a painter father who, during family visits to galleries or museums, approvingly noted collage and appropriation techniques in the visual arts (Picasso, Claes Oldenburg, Stuart Davis), I was gratified, but not surprised, to learn that literature could encompass the same methods.

Contamination Anxiety

"In 1941, on his front porch ..." to "... 'this song comes from the cotton field.'" **Siva Vaidhyanathan**, *Copyrights and Copywrongs*.

"... enabled by a kind ... freely reworked." **Kembrew McLeod**, *Freedom of Expression*. In *Owning Culture*, McLeod notes that, as he was writing, he happened to be listening to a lot of old country music, and in my casual listening I noticed that *six* country songs shared *exactly* the same vocal melody, including Hank Thompson's "Wild Side of Life," the Carter Family's "I'm Thinking Tonight of My Blue Eyes," Roy Acuff's "Great Speckled Bird," Kitty Wells's "It Wasn't God Who Made Honky Tonk Angels," Reno & Smiley's "I'm Using My Bible for a Roadmap," and Townes Van Zandt's "Heavenly Houseboat Blues." ... In his extensively researched book, *Country: The Twisted Roots of Rock 'n' Roll*, Nick Tosches documents that the melody these songs share is "ancient and British." There were no recorded lawsuits stemming from these appropriations....

"... musicians have gained ... through allusion." **Joanna Demers**, *Steal This Music*.

"In 1970s Jamaica ..." to "... hours of music." Gibson.

"Visual, sound, and text collage ..." to "... realm of cultural production." This plunders, rewrites, and amplifies paragraphs from McLeod's *Owning Culture*, except for the line about collage being the art form of the twentieth and twenty-first centuries, which I heard filmmaker **Craig Baldwin** say, in defense of sampling, in the trailer for a forthcoming documentary, *Copyright Criminals*.

"In a courtroom scene ..." to "... would cease to exist." **Dave Itzkoff**, *New York Times*.

"... the remarkable series of 'plagiarisms' ..." to "... we want more plagiarism." **Richard Posner**, combined from The Becker-Posner Blog and *The Atlantic Monthly*.

"Most artists are brought ..." to "... by art itself." These words, and many more to follow, come from **Lewis Hyde**'s *The Gift*. Above any other book I've here plagiarized, I commend *The Gift* to your attention.

"Finding one's voice ... filiations, communities, and discourses." Semanticist **George L. Dillon**, quoted in **Rebecca Moore Howard**'s "The New Abolitionism Comes to Plagiarism."

"Inspiration could be ... act never experienced." **Ned Rorem**, found on several "great quotations" sites on the Internet.

"Invention, it must be humbly admitted ... out of chaos." **Mary Shelley**, from her introduction to *Frankenstein*.

"What happens ..." to "... contamination anxiety." **Kevin J. H. Dettmar**, from "The Illusion of Modernist Allusion and the Politics of Postmodern Plagiarism."

Surrounded by Signs

"The surrealists believed ..." to the Walter Benjamin quote. From **Christian Keathley**'s *Cinephilia and History, or the Wind in the Trees*, a book that treats fannish fetishism as the secret at the heart of film scholarship. Keathley notes, for instance, Joseph Cornell's surrealist-influenced 1936 film *Rose Hobart*, which simply records "the way in which Cornell himself watched the 1931 Hollywood potboiler *East of Borneo*, fascinated and distracted as he was by its B-grade star"—the star, of course, being Rose Hobart herself. This, I suppose, makes Cornell a sort of father to computer-enabled fan-creator reworkings of Hollywood product, like the version of George Lucas's *The Phantom Menace* from which the noxious Jar Jar Binks character was purged; both incorporate a viewer's subjective preferences into a revision of a filmmaker's work.

"... early in the history of photography" to "... without compensating the source." From *Free Culture*, by **Lawrence Lessig**, the greatest of public advocates for copyright reform, and the best source if you want to get radicalized in a hurry.

"For those whose ganglia ..." to "... discourse broke down." From **David Foster Wallace**'s essay "E Unibus Pluram," reprinted in *A Supposedly Fun Thing I'll Never Do Again*. I have no idea who Wallace's "gray eminence" is or was. I inserted the example of Dickens into the paragraph; he strikes me as overlooked in the lineage of authors of "brand-name" fiction.

"I was born ... *Mary Tyler Moore Show*." These are the reminiscences of **Mark Hosler** from Negativland, a collaging musical collective that was sued by U2's record label for their appropriation of "I Still Haven't Found What I'm Looking For." Although I had to adjust the birth date, Hosler's cultural menu fits me like a glove.

"The world is a home ... popculture products ..." McLeod.

"Today, when we can eat ..." to "... flat sights." Wallace.

"You're surrounded by signs. Ignore none of them." This phrase, which I unfortunately rendered somewhat leaden with the word "imperative," comes from **Steve Erickson**'s novel *Our Ecstatic Days*.

Usemonopoly

"... everything from attempts ..." to "defendants as young as twelve." **Robert Boynton**, *The New York Times Magazine*, "The Tyranny of Copyright?"

"A time is marked ..." to "... what needs no defense." Lessig, this time from *The Future of Ideas*.

"Thomas Jefferson, for one," to "... respective writings and discoveries." Boynton.

"... second comers might do a much better job than the originator...." I found this phrase in Lessig, who is quoting Vaidhyanathan, who himself is characterizing a judgment written by **Learned Hand**.

"But Jefferson's vision ... owned by someone or other." Boynton.

"The distinctive feature ..." to "... term is extended." Lessig, again from *The Future of Ideas*.

"When old laws ..." to "... had been invaded." **Jessica Litman**, *Digital Copyright*.

"I say to you ... woman home alone." I found the Valenti quote in McLeod. Now fill in the blank: Jack Valenti is to the public domain as _____ is to _____.

The Beauty of Second Use

"In the first ..." to "... builds an archive." Lessig.

"Most books ... only one year...." Lessig.

"Active reading is ..." to "... do not own...." This is a mashup of **Henry Jenkins**, from his *Textual Poachers: Television Fans and Participatory Culture*, and **Michel de Certeau**, whom Jenkins quotes.

"In the children's classic …" to "… its loving use." Jenkins. (Incidentally, have the holders of the copyright to *The Velveteen Rabbit* had a close look at *Toy Story*? There could be a lawsuit there.)

Source Hypocrisy, or Disnial

"The Walt Disney Company … alas, *Treasure Planet*.…" Lessig.

"Imperial Plagiarism" is the title of an essay by **Marilyn Randall**.

"… spurred David Byrne … *My Life in the Bush of Ghosts*.…" **Chris Dahlen**, *Pitchfork*—though in truth by the time I'd finished, his words were so utterly dissolved within my own that had I been an ordinary cutting-and-pasting journalist it never would have occurred to me to give Dahlen a citation. The effort of preserving another's distinctive phrases as I worked on this essay was sometimes beyond my capacities; this form of plagiarism was oddly hard work.

"Kenneth Koch …" to "… *déluge* of copycats!" **Emily Nussbaum**, *The New York Times Book Review*.

You Can't Steal a Gift

"You can't steal a gift." **Dizzy Gillespie**, defending another player who'd been accused of poaching Charlie Parker's style: "You can't steal a gift. Bird gave the world his music, and if you can hear it you can have it."

"A large, diverse society … intellectual property." Lessig.

"And works of art …" to "… marriage, parenthood, mentorship." Hyde.

"Yet one … so naturally with the market." **David Bollier**, *Silent Theft*.

"Art that matters …" to "… bought and sold." Hyde.

"We consider it unacceptable …" to "… certain unalienable rights.…" Bollier, paraphrasing **Margaret Jane Radin**'s *Contested Commodities*.

"A work of art …" to "… constraint upon our merchandising." Hyde.

"This is the reason … person it's directed at." Wallace.

"The power of a gift …" to "… certain extra-market values." Bollier, and also the sociologist **Warren O. Hagstrom**, whom Bollier is paraphrasing.

The Commons

"Einstein's theory …" to "… public domain are a commons." Lessig.

"That a language is a commons … society as a whole." **Michael Newton**, in the *London Review of Books*, reviewing a book called *Echolalias: On the Forget-*

ting of Language by **Daniel Heller-Roazen**. The paraphrases of book reviewers are another covert form of collaborative culture; as an avid reader of reviews, I know much about books I've never read. To quote **Yann Martel** on how he came to be accused of imperial plagiarism in his Booker-winning novel *Life of Pi*:

Ten or so years ago, I read a review by John Updike in the *New York Times Review of Books* [*sic*]. It was of a novel by a Brazilian writer I'd never heard of, Moacyr Scliar. I forget the title, and John Updike did worse: he clearly thought the book as a whole was forgettable. His review—one of those that makes you suspicious by being mostly descriptive ... oozed indifference. But one thing about it struck me: the premise.... Oh, the wondrous things I could do with this premise.

Unfortunately, no one was ever able to locate the Updike review in question.

"The American commons ..." to "... for a song." Bollier.

"Honoring the commons ..." to "... practical necessity." Bollier.

"We in Western ... public good." **John Sulston**, Nobel Prize–winner and co-mapper of the human genome.

"We have to remain ..." to "... benefit of a few." **Harry S Truman**, at the opening of the Everglades National Park. Although it may seem the height of presumption to rip off a president—I found claiming Truman's stolid advocacy as my own embarrassing in the extreme—I didn't rewrite him at all. As the poet **Marianne Moore** said, "if a thing had been said in the *best* way, how can you say it better?" Moore confessed her penchant for incorporating lines from others' work, explaining, "I have not yet been able to outgrow this hybrid method of composition...."

Undiscovered Public Knowledge

"... intellectuals disheartened" to "... quickly and cheaply?" **Steve Fuller**, *The Intellectual.* There's something of Borges in Fuller's insight here; the notion of a storehouse of knowledge waiting passively to be assembled by future users is suggestive of both "The Library of Babel" and "Kafka and His Precursors."

Give All

"... one of Iran's finest ..." to "... meditation on his heroine." **Amy Taubin**, *Village Voice,* although it was me who had made the discovery at the Walter Reade Theater and who had the fresh enthusiasm for Iranian cinema.

"The primary objective ..." to "... unfair nor unfortunate." **Sandra Day O'Connor**, 1991.

"Allusion is a step ... possible for art." **T. S. Eliot**, in his review of Joyce's *Ulysses*.

"... the future will be much like the past" to "... give some things away." Open-source film archivist **Rick Prelinger**, quoted in McLeod.

"Change may be troubling ... with certainty." McLeod.

"... woven entirely ..." to "... without inverted commas." **Roland Barthes**.

"The kernel, the soul ..." to "... characteristics of phrasing." **Mark Twain**, from a consoling letter to Helen Keller, who had suffered distressing accusations of plagiarism(!). In fact, her work was a composite of received phrases; under her particular circumstances, Keller's writing could be understood as a kind of allegory of the "constructed" nature of artistic perception. I found the Twain quote in the aforementioned *Copyrights and Copywrongs*, by Siva Vaidhyanathan.

"Old and new ..." to "... we all quote." **Ralph Waldo Emerson**. These guys all sound alike!

"People live differently ... wealth as a gift." Hyde.

"... I'm a cork ... blown away." This is adapted from the Beach Boys' song, "'Til I Die," written by **Brian Wilson**. My own first adventure with song-lyric permissions came when I tried to have a character in my second novel quote the lyrics, "There's a world where I can go and tell my secrets to/In my room/In my room." After learning the likely expense, at my editor's suggestion I replaced those with "You take the high road/I'll take the low road/I'll be in Scotland before you," a lyric in the public domain. This capitulation always bugged me, and in the subsequent British publication of the same book I restored the Brian Wilson lyric, without permission. *Ocean of Story* is the title of a collection of **Christina Stead**'s short fiction.

Saul Bellow, writing to a friend who'd taken offense at Bellow's fictional use of certain personal facts, said: "The name of the game is Give All. You are welcome to my facts. I gave them to you. If you have the strength to pick them up, take them with my blessings." I couldn't bring myself to retain Bellow's "strength," which seemed presumptuous in my new context, though it is surely the more elegant phrase. On the other hand, I was pleased to invite the suggestion that the gifts in question may actually be light and easily lifted.

KEY TO THE KEY

The notion of a collage text is, of course, not original to me. **Walter Benjamin**'s incomplete *Arcades Project* seemingly would have featured extensive interlaced quotations. Other precedents include **Graham Rawle**'s novel, *Diary of an Amateur Photographer*, its text harvested from photography magazines, and **Eduardo Paolozzi**'s collage-novel *Kex*, cobbled from crime novels and newspaper clippings. Closer to home, my efforts owe a great deal to the recent essays of **David Shields**, in which diverse quotes are made to closely intertwine and reverberate, and to conversations with **Sean Howe** and **Pamela Jackson**. Last year **David Edelstein**, in *New York* magazine, satirized the Kaavya Viswanathan plagiarism case by creating an almost completely plagiarized column denouncing her actions. Edelstein intended to demonstrate, through ironic example, how bricolage such as his own was ipso facto facile and unworthy. While Viswanathan's version of "creative copying" was a pitiable one, I differ with Edelstein's conclusions.

The phrase *Je est un autre*, with its deliberately awkward syntax, belongs to **Arthur Rimbaud**. It has been translated both as "I is another" and "I is someone else," as in this excerpt from Rimbaud's letters:

For I is someone else. If brass wakes up a bugle, it is not his fault. That is obvious to me: I witness the unfolding of my thought: I watch it, I listen to it: I make a stoke of the bow: the symphony makes movement into the depths, or comes in one leap upon the stage.

If the old fools had not found only the false significance of the Ego, we should not now be having to sweep away these millions of skeletons which, since an infinite time, have been piling up the fruits of their one-eyed intellects, proclaiming themselves to be the authors!

"Roots and Wires" Remix: Polyrhythmic Tricks and the Black Electronic

5

Erik Davis

How does one orient oneself within electronic culture? Our first impulse, metaphorically at least, is probably to try and see it more clearly. We seek to read the signs of the times, to look forward, to focus on the fluctuating horizon. But I fear that the clarity we expect from sight, the bird's-eye view of the mappable field, can no longer be relied on to illuminate the network of relations that surround us. Instead, I suspect we might do better to prick up our ears, to sound the sensorium that engulfs us. In other words, electronic culture is a space to plumb, an immersive sea we discover through the dive. But to sound also means to listen, and to listen to the now means to listen, at least in part, to the sounds and music emerging from electronic machines.

I am not just talking about listening as an act of sensation, but as a fundamentally different mode of engaging the world, one that tugs against long-standing habits of perception, knowledge, and experience. According to Marshall McLuhan, whose tendencies toward technological determinism by no means undermine his continuing relevance to electronic culture, "visual space" became the dominant mode of Western consciousness following the Italian Renaissance. McLuhan argued that Renaissance perspective not only provided a powerful new representational mode of organizing the visual field, but also engendered a very specific form of subjectivity. He associated this subjectivity with the point of view produced by the techniques of perspective painting, but he also related it to print technologies and to some formal properties of the printed book. In essence, he argued that the self we inherit from the Renaissance is a visual self.

Renaissance perspective thus serves as an analogy for a much more general phenomenon: the power to create a distinct, single point of view that organizes thought and perception along linear lines. We know this space from Descartes and from William Gibson's cyberspace: a homogeneous field organized by an objective coordinate grid that simultaneously produces an apparently coherent individual subject who maintains control over his or her unique point of view. Not only do we conventionally overlay this panoptic grid onto the far more ambiguous visual field that our nervous system constructs on the fly, but we have embraced it as the dominant conceptual image of space itself. McLuhan related visual space to print technologies—and print culture—because, he argued, these technologies inculcate within us a habit of organizing the world as a field of objects distributed in a largely linear, atomized, and sequential fashion. Central to the concept of visual space is the axiom or assumption that "different" objects, vectors, or points are not and cannot be superimposed; instead, the world is perceived as a linear grid organized along strictly causal lines.

McLuhan contrasts this construction of visual space, and the kind of subjectivity associated with it, with what he calls "acoustic space." Simply put, acoustic space is the space we hear rather than the space we see; and he argued that, in contrast to print technologies, electronic media submerge us in this acoustic environment. Acoustic space is multidimensional, resonant, invisibly tactile, "a total and simultaneous field of relations." Where visual space emphasizes linearity, acoustic space emphasizes simultaneity—the possibility that many events can occur in the same holistic zone of space-time. Unlike visual space, where points either fuse or remain distinct, blocks of sound can overlap and interpenetrate without necessarily collapsing into a harmonic unity or consonance, thereby maintaining the paradox of "simultaneous difference."

Acoustic space isn't limited to a world of music or sound; the environment of electronic media, visual as well as aural, itself engenders an acoustic mode of organizing and perceiving information and experience. Still, our increasingly aural orientation helps explain why music, and especially electronic music, plays such a crucial role in sounding the acoustic space of technoculture. On both academic and popular levels, electronic music has articulated and generated an impressive number of soundscapes, atmospheres, and immersive environments that evoke metaphors of space far more readily than metaphors of time.

This secret sympathy between electronics and space also marks the imaginal realm, a dimension easily as important as more technical or purely musical domains. As a particularly convenient example, you can trace the changing fortunes of Leon Theremin's eponymous electronic instrument, which the Russian inventor first developed in the early 1920s. Theremin felt that the eerie glissandi of his instrument belonged in the concert hall, and the theremin's first great practitioner, Clara Rockmore, played a conventional repertoire. But the instrument would not find its cultural home until its use in the soundtracks of UFO movies from the 1950s forevermore linked its synthetic vocal tones with outer space, cosmic communication, and the uncanny.[1]

In the 1960s, the connection between electronic music and space became more explicit, with the popular success of composer Morton Subotnick's "Silver Apples of the Moon" and the early use of the Moog on the hippie-exploitation album *Cosmic Sounds* ("Must be played in the dark"). In the heady days of the counterculture, the outer space of Forbidden Planet and the inner space of human subjectivity, expanded through drugs or mysticism or other good vibrations, became fused within the nebulous category of the cosmic, with its extraterrestrial emphasis on virtuality, disorientation, and transport. The progressive rock tradition, always friendly to electronics, later helped spawn "space music," an often cheesy genre that looped together analog synthesizers, astronomical images, and the ancient dream of booting up altered states of consciousness through vibrating and resonating sounds. Later, many new age musicians and psychedelic trance producers would consider the synthesizer to be a transdimensional biofeedback device; by generating invisible landscapes through mostly invisible circuits, these machines seemed to lead listeners within themselves, into disembodied states of consciousness that mirrored the emptiness of deep space.

Electronic space also emerged within the more Afrofuturistic dimensions of black American music. The wailing guitar on the first track of Jimi Hendrix's *Axis: Bold as Love* not only mimicked a flying saucer, but carved out space by panning between stereo channels (thereby zooming between "the rooms behind your minds"). On albums such as *Cosmic Tones for Mental Therapy* and *We Travel the Spaceways*, Sun Ra led his iridescently costumed Intergalactic Jet-Set Arkestra from big band to free jazz and back; with bizarre albums like

1964's *Other Planes of There*, Ra also pioneered the use of synthesizers in jazz. With less eminence and more flash, George "Starchild" Clinton psychedelicized and technologized funk music with Parliament-Funkadelic. Besides fusing high-production values with fat and greasy riffs, Clinton brought flying saucers onstage, and created an elaborate comic-book mythos of Clone Funk Afro-nauts, Maggot Brains, and Mothership Connections.

I'll call this Afrofuturistic dimensions of electronic space—which I'll explore for the remainder of this paper—the Black Electronic, a term I've dubbed from the British cultural theorist Paul Gilroy. Gilroy uses the phrase the "Black Atlantic" to denote the "webbed network" of the African diasporic culture that penetrates the United States, the Caribbean, and, by the end of the twentieth century, the U.K. Gilroy considers the Black Atlantic a modernist countercultural space, a space that, for all the claims of black cultural nationalists, is not organized by African roots but by a "rhizomorphic, routed" set of vectors and exchanges: ships, migrations, creoles, phonographs, European miscegenations, expatriate flights, dreams of repatriation. The image of the criss-crossed Atlantic ocean is essential for Gilroy's purpose, which is to erode the monolithic notion of roots and tradition by emphasizing the "restless, recombinant" qualities of Afrodiasporic culture as it simultaneously explores, exploits, and resists the spaces of modernity.[2]

The Black Electronic characterizes those electroacoustic spaces that emerge from the historical-cultural context of the Black Atlantic. Though the roots of these spaces do indeed lie in West Africa, I am more concerned here with their decidedly rhizomorphic behavior as they wire up that acoustic dimension that David Toop has called, in a somewhat different context, the twentieth century's "ocean of sound."[3] In particular, I want to explore one specific zone within the Black Electronic: the remarkable acoustic spaces that emerge when the polyrhythmic sensibility found in traditional West African drumming encounter those electronic instruments, at once musical and technological, that record, reproduce, and manipulate sound. Though the linkage of rhythm with musical space may seem somewhat counterintuitive, I'd like to suggest that West African polyrhythm carves out a unique and powerful dimension of acoustic space by generating a "nomadic" space of multiplicity that unfolds on the fly. In other words, polyrhythm does not so much generate acoustic space as show us how one might move through it. Polyrhythm impels the listener to explore a complex space of beats, to follow any of a number of fluid, warping, and shifting lines of flight, to submit to what the old school hip-hop act A Tribe Called Quest calls "The rhythmic instinction to yield to travel beyond existing forces of life."

Drumming Up Polyrhythmic Space

The Fon tell that one day the supreme being Mawu-Lisa decided to appoint a chief for her children, the divine brood who rule the world. She proposed a contest: whoever could come before her and simultaneously play a gong, a bell, a drum, and a flute, while dancing to the music at the same time, would win the position. The most aggressive deities all tried their hands and failed. But the agile boy Legba, her youngest and most spoiled child, performed the task with ease.

Legba is a messenger god, an opener and closer of gateways, the West African equivalent of Hermes-Mercury or the great Hindu lord Ganesh. But he is first and foremost a linguist. In the beginning, Mawu-Lisa gave her seven children different realms of the world to rule—earth, sea, animals, and so on. She also gave them each a language separate from her own. But she allowed Legba to remain with her and to act as her linguist, a translator and relayer of information between her and her children. It is this ability to shift and translate between different codes and points of view—what Robert Pelton describes as Legba's "metaphysically fancy footwork"—that enabled the god to balance the competing claims of the various instruments and beats. Communication of any sort takes place within a dynamic and unstable network of forces, disruptions, and contrary points of view. As the first myth above suggests, the "manyness" of polyrhythmic ensembles can capture this zone of shifting boundaries, where the greatest dancers not only follow the beat of a different drummer, but the beats of many different instruments at once. And it's with this "at once" in mind that I would like to look at the rhythms that underlie West African music, a "system of beats" whose deep aesthetic, philosophical, and even spiritual dimensions now subtly undergird electronic space.

It must be said that the West has a rather repellent history of reducing African and Afrodiasporic culture to its rhythms. At the same time, we should not let Hollywood images of savage and frenetic drumming (or the more subtle distortions that emerge with overgeneralized discussions such as my own) obscure the profound and pivotal role that rhythm plays in West African aesthetics, social organization, and metaphysics. Nor should the evident psychophysiological power of drums and their intimacy with dancing bodies obstruct their more abstract, conceptual, or virtual powers. As I hope to make clear, West African drumming can serve as an excellent analogue for a variety of pressing technocultural discussions about distributed networks, the philosophy and perception of multiplicities, and the emergent properties of complex systems.[4]

Though I prefer the looser and more playful term "polyrhythm," traditional West African drumming is perhaps more accurately described as polymetric. The meter is the standard unit of time that divides European music. In most symphonies or ensembles, all instruments basically follow the same meter; the shared rhythm is counted evenly and stressed on every main beat. Musicologists thus call Western rhythm divisive because it is divided into standard units of time. But the traditional rhythms of West African music are considered additive, a term which already gives us an indication of their fundamental multiplicity. The music's complex percussive patterns bubble up from the shifting and open-ended interaction between many different individual drum patterns and pitches. As Chernoff puts it, "in African music there are always at least two rhythms going on."[5]

In order to notate this music, which is traditionally passed on mnemonically and orally, Western musicologists are forced to assign different meters to different instruments—hence, polymetric. Written down, the measures that organize the repetitive beat sequences associated with each instrument can be of variable lengths and time signatures. Neither the bar lines nor the main beats associated with each instrument coincide, but instead are staggered throughout a music whose rhythmic motifs are constantly appearing and disappearing. Individual musicians thus practice what is called apart-playing, maintaining a definite distance between their beats and those of the other drummers, a differential "space" which refuses to collapse or fuse into a unified rhythmic point. In turn this produces permanent conversations or cross-patterns between each drum, a dialogue which is also a complex dimension of difference introduced between elements that are themselves often simple and repetitive.

Though this description is overly schematic, we can nonetheless understand that polyrhythm has little to do with pure repetition. As Deleuze and Guattari point out in "On the Refrain," their crucial chapter on aesthetics from *A Thousand Plateaus*, "It is the difference that is rhythmic, not the repetition, which nevertheless produces it: productive repetition has nothing to do with reproductive meter" (my emphasis).[6] Even to call West African drumming "polymetric" is already to define it from a perspective it eludes. As Deleuze and Guattari write, "Meter, whether regular or not, assumes a coded form whose unit of measure may vary ... whereas rhythm is the Unequal or the Incommensurable that is always undergoing transcoding. Meter is dogmatic, but rhythm is critical: it ties together critical moments, or ties itself together in passing from one milieu to another. It does not operate in a homogeneous space-time, but by heterogeneous blocks. It changes direction."[7]

But what exactly constitutes these "milieus" within an actual polyrhythmic ensemble? "Every milieu is vibratory," according to Deleuze and Guattari: "In other words, a block of space-time constituted by the periodic repetition of the component. Every milieu is coded, a code being defined by periodic repetition."[8] This much seems clear: each specific milieu is a block of space-time produced by the exacting repetitions of each individual drum. Polyrhythmic communication thus unfolds as an interdimensional play of milieus—a mutating array of slices, splits, folds, and fusions; an acoustic hyperspace. "One milieu serves as the basis for another, or conversely is established atop another milieu, dissipates in it or is constituted in it. The notion of the milieu is not unitary: not only does the living thing [the dancer or listener] continually pass from one milieu to another, but the milieus pass into one another; they are essentially communicating. The milieus are open to chaos, which threatens them with exhaustion or confusion. Rhythm is the milieu's answer to chaos."[9]

With the ancient mediation of the drum, this potent play between chaos and rhythm carries us outside of theory and into the dance of multiplicity that characterizes our experience of unfolding through an unfolding world. Polyrhythmic music provides a primary and unusually intuitive avenue, not just to conceptualize, but to train ourselves to cross and combine heterogeneous spaces, chaotic ruptures, and zones of communication directly into our body–minds. As we weave ourselves into polyrhythm's fibrillating tapestry of molecular beats and percussive patterns, we taste a kind of wisdom, not the reflection in repose we conventionally imagine, but the wisdom of networked differences, whether social, ecological, or spiritual. In humanistic terms, we are shown how the action of standing apart from others can actually support the entire group, and how novelty is not so much an imposition of creative individual will as a kind of active remix of other beings and energies.

To demonstrate just how polyrhythm mobilizes philosophical and ethical considerations, I want to turn to John Chernoff's indispensable *African*

Rhythm and African Sensibility. In the following extensive sample, which I have cut and spliced from various points of his book, the author, self-consciously writing from a Western perspective, unfolds a sort of pragmatics of polyrhythmic listening. Though the philosophical aspects of his discussion are only implied, I ask you to listen as well for these overtones:

The effect of polymetric music is as if the different rhythms were competing for our attention. No sooner do we grasp one rhythm than we lose track of it and hear another. In something like Adzogba or Zhem it is not easy to find any constant beat at all. The Western conception of a main beat or pulse seems to disappear, and a Westerner who cannot appreciate the rhythmic complications and who maintains his habitual listening orientation quite simply gets lost.... The situation is uncomfortable because if the basic meter is not evident, we cannot understand how two or more people can play together or, even more uncomfortably, how anyone can play at all.... We begin to "understand" African music by being able to maintain, in our minds or our bodies, an additional rhythm to the ones we hear. Hearing another rhythm to fit alongside the rhythms of an ensemble is basically the same kind of orientation for a listener that apart-playing is for a musician—a way of being steady within a context of multiple rhythms.... Only through the combined rhythms does the music emerge, and the only way to hear the music properly, to find the beat ... is to listen to at least two rhythms at once. You should attempt to hear as many rhythms as possible working together yet remaining distinct.[10]

Because listeners are forced to adopt any of a number of possible rhythmic perspectives—cognitive patterns which reorganize the acoustic space that surrounds them—Chernoff rightly insists that they are "actively engaged in making sense of the music."[11] We must enter into polyrhythm; by selecting particular rhythmic clusters, and cutting and combining them with other beats, our body–minds generate a sense of coherent flux within a space of multiplicity, a kind of balanced line of flight that constantly criss-crosses a shifting and unstable terrain. Listening and dancing to polyrhythm, we sample the phenomenon of emergence, as fluid lines arise from the complex and chaotic interaction (or communication) of numerous smaller and simpler repetitions and individual beats.

In addition to the layering of repetitive beats, West African drumming also introduces the crucial improvisational figures unfurled by the lead drummer. Playing over and against the stacked repetitions of the other musicians, the lead drummer improvises not so much by spontaneously generating new patterns as by precisely cutting and splicing the rhythms of the other drums. As Chernoff writes, "The drummer keeps the music moving forward fluidly, and by continually changing his accents and his beating, he thus relies on the multiplicity of possible ways to cut and combine the rhythms."[12] The lead drummer's lines thus emerge from a space of multiplicity that could be said to constitute the ensemble's virtual dimension.

And what the lead drummer deploys most forcefully is the cut or break. These intense, almost violently syncopated "off-beat" lines criss-cross and interfere with the other rhythms, pushing and pulling at the dancer-listener's precarious internal sense of the beat. Though these assaults can be quite intense, they should not go too far: "A musician should deliver not too many and not too few off-beat accents because people can get thrown off the beat, and at a certain point either their orientation to the rhythms will shift or they will begin hearing the separate rhythms as a single rhythm."[13] Making an analogy with nonlinear dynamics, we could say that the lead drummer must maintain an open field of competing rhythmic attractors. The game is to push the beats to the edge of bifurcation without allowing them to settle into a singular basin of attraction. For listeners that means remaining constantly open to productive chaos: to the disorienting surprise of beats struck earlier than expected, or to the little voids that open up when beats are unpredictably dropped out—an experience Chernoff brilliantly likens to missing a step on a staircase.

While it's fruitful to speak of polyrhythmic experience in the language of the dance, we should also remember that the body so mobilized may be entirely virtual. As Richard Waterman points out, "African music, with few exceptions, is to be regarded as music for the dance, although the 'dance' involved may be entirely a mental one."[14] And I'd like this figure of the "mental dance" to lead us into electronic space, into the simultaneously premodern and postmodern spaces opened up by the tactile yet disembodied machine beats of the Black Electronic.

Dubbing the Drum

Among the pantheon of the Black Electronic's mental dancers, alongside Sun Ra, George Clinton, Jimi Hendrix, Grandmaster Flash, and Derrick May, stands one Lee "Scratch" Perry, perhaps Jamaica's most inventive reggae producer and one of the leading architects of dub music—the mutant spawn of reggae produced entirely in the studio from prerecorded rhythm tracks. Explaining the esoteric correspondences between rhythm and the body, Perry once wielded out the roots cliché that "The drum is the beat of the heart." But the bass, he said, "is the brain."[15] More than just subverting the common cultural association between bass frequencies and the base moves of the hips, Perry was suggesting that drums and bass make head music, with all the resonance that term conjures up—abstraction, drugs, interiority, virtual worlds. As Perry put it when discussing his preference for mixing tracks without vocals: "the instrumental is formed in the mental."[16]

Of course, Perry's instrumentals were also formed in the machine, and it's this imaginal network between the machinic and mental realms that opens up both the disembodied architectures of cyberspace and the more abstract dimensions of the drum. West Africa's polyrhythmic ensembles can already be seen as deploying a kind of abstract machine, their enormous intensities engineered with a notable coolness, precision, and craft. As Chernoff writes, "A drummer avoids 'rough' beating because the precision of play is necessary for maximum definition of form.... the truly original style consists in the subtle perfection of strictly respected form."[17] This crisp and cool sensibility informs the Black Electronic's unique reconfiguring of the physically alienated or "mental" labor necessary to engineer electronic musical spaces, and goes a long way to explaining why, as Andrew Goodwin perceptively notes, "we have grown used to connecting machines and funkiness."[18]

The image of the funky machine undermines the usual associations of black music, which has long carried the burden of representing the folk-cultural body within Euro-American society. This body is either demonized as primitive or lionized as an authentic and natural corrective to an abstract West identified with mind and machines. Besides eliding the fact that, as Gilroy argues, the African Diaspora is actually integral to the West, this opposition tends to erase the extraordinary technological sensibility of modern black music's musical, aesthetic, and even mythic imagination. This sensibility, rooted in the abstract dynamics of the drum, seemed fully capable of creatively engaging the conditions of industrial and informational economies as they emerged. Chernoff reports the legend that once some African stevedores, who had their own songs for loading and unloading boats, "first understood the machine to be the white man's music."[19] The author also tells of visiting a customs office in Ghana where a bureaucrat hammered out rhythms on his typewriter, even continuing to "play" the shift key as he searched for the next phrase to type.[20]

Here I'd like to trace the connection between machines and funkiness to 1970s Jamaica, when record producers and engineers created dub reggae by manipulating and remixing prerecorded analog tracks of music coded on magnetic tape. Though Lee Perry became one of dub's most surreal experimenters, he did not invent the form. That honor goes to Osbourne Ruddock, aka King Tubby, an electrical engineer who fixed radios and other appliances in Kingston in the 1950s and who built his own sound system amplifiers to get the big bass sound. A musical genius, Tubby was also a gearhead, a tinkerer, an experimental geek. After discovering that he could remix (or "version") the backing track of a popular tune into a new piece of music, Tubby played these "dub plate specials" to enthusiastic crowds at his Home Town Hi-Fi dances, where Tubby would stand behind his customized mixing console, tweaking the beats on the fly while the DJ U Roy "toasted" over the rhythms.

In the studio, dubmasters like Tubby would saturate and mutate individual instruments with reverb, phase, echo, and delay; abruptly drop voices, beats, and guitars in and out of the mix; strip the music down to the bare bones of drums and bass and then build it up again through layers of distortion, percussive noise, and electronic ectoplasm. As the trend spread, Tubby stayed ahead of the game by working with top producers like Bunny Lee and Lee Perry while endlessly tinkering with what Prince Buster called the "implements of sound." Tubby constantly toyed with his four-track console, jury-rigging echo delay units and created sliding faders that allowed him to bring tracks smoothly in and out of the mix. He also just played tricks with the machine, generating his famous "Thunderclap" sound by physically hitting the spring reverb unit, or using frequency test tones to send an ominous sonar through the depths of dub's watery domain, calling into being a deeply spatial sensibility.

At a time when roots reggae was proclaiming a literally religious mythos of folk-cultural authenticity, dub subtly called it into question by dematerializing and eroding the integrity of singers and song. There is no original, no motherland outside the virtual, no roots that are not at the same time rhizomes remixed on the fly. Yet by improvising and mutating repetitions of prerecorded material, dub added something distinctly uncanny to the mix. Dub's analog doppelgängers, spectral distortions, and vocal ghosts produced an imaginal space no less compelling in its own way than the virtual African Zion that organized so much of reggae's Rastafarian longings. And for all its unmistakable Caribbeanisms, dub's concerns with warped analog spaces, electromagnetic noise, and technologically mediated disorientation also recall the galactic explorations of German progressive rockers in the early 1970s. Dub too is a kind of *Kosmiche Musik.* As Luke Ehrlich wrote, "If reggae is Africa in the New World, dub is Africa on the moon."[21]

But while the space of dub is certainly "out" in both the extraterrestrial and Sun Ra sense of the term, its heavy use of echo also produces a sense of enclosure, an interiority that, along with a variety of moist and squooshy effects, conjures up distinctly aquatic surroundings. With dub we do not find ourselves in the incorporeal deep space of sci-fi soundtracks and acid rock, but in a kind of "out" inner space, a liminal womb. This unresolved spatial tension not only explains the druggy or even mystical qualities of the music (qualities rooted in psycho-physiological effects that erode the experiential division between interior and exterior), but also explains why '70s dub so powerfully anticipates the virtual spaces of today's electronic media—spaces which seem at once extensive and implicate (or implied), intensive and unfolded, inside and out.[22] As Jeff Salamon wrote in *Artforum,* "one might hypothesize that entering dub's vertiginous expanses is good training for exploring [virtual realities], where depth perception and a mastery of the intricate layers of nested windows will be invaluable."[23]

Whereas the almost psychedelic qualities of dub can be attributed to its "spacey" effects, and perhaps to the role of ganja in both its production and consumption, the heady pleasures of the music arise at least as much from its trippy polyrhythmic play—a play that unfolds possibilities latent within the reggae beat. Strictly speaking, modern Jamaican dance music adheres to the same 4/4 beat that drives the vast majority of Western popular music. But when dub hit the scene, reggae's "dread ridims" were already unusual in accenting the second and fourth beats of the measure and in "dropping" the initial beat, all of which produced the music's unmistakable snaky pulse. An even more crucial element of reggae rhythms is the pivotal role played by the bass guitar. Back when Jamaica's sound systems—basically mobile discos— were playing American R&B in the 1950s, the techies gave their American grooves an unmistakable Jamaican twist by severely amplifying the bass, transforming R&B's low end into a veritable force of nature. This is the kind of bass that does not just propel or anchor dancers, but saturates their bones with near cosmic vibrations. The rock steady music that morphed into reggae anchored the beat with the bass guitar rather than the drum kit. This deterritorialized the drums, allowing musicians to explore more polyrhythmic percussive play outside and around the main beat. As Dick Hebdige points out, by the end of the '70s, drummers like Sly Dunbar were playing their kits like jazz musicians, improvising on cymbals, snares, and tom-toms to "produce a multi-layered effect, rather like West African religious drumming."[24]

Dub translated this rhythmic complexity into an abstract electro-acoustic space, using technology to further destabilize the beats and to stretch and fold the passage of time. While stripping the music down to pure drums and bass, dubmasters also thickened the mix with extra percussion and what the producer Bunny Lee called "a whole heap a noise." More importantly, dubmasters introduced extended counter-rhythms by multiplying chunks of sound (voices, guitars, drums) through echo and reverb, producing stuttered pulses which split off from the main beat and generate cross-rhythms as they stray and fade into the virtual void. Dub is not strictly polymetric, as it rarely sustains such staggered-apart playing for very long. At the same time, by abruptly dropping guitars, percussion, horns, and keyboards in and out of the mix, dubmasters teased the rug out from under the listener's habitual rhythmic orientation toward the 4/4, creating a subtle virtual analog of the tripping, constantly shifting conversations of West African drums.

Quite like master drummers, many dubmasters would improvise their studio mixes on the fly. This should not surprise us, for West Africa's polyrhythmic ensembles already anticipate the breakdown of the distinction between the mechanical labor of the recording engineer and the creative labor of the musician—a distinction that organizes much popular music production and that dub and later electronic dance music dissolves. One can see polyrhythmic ensembles as an assemblage of various distinct rhythmic tracks whose molecular beats are remixed, cut, and spliced through the cool mediation of the master drummer, his apparently spontaneous and chaotic cuts introducing noise that becomes signal, feeding back into and enlivening the ensemble's "total and simultaneous field of relations."

By giving flight to the producer's cybernetic imagination, dub created room within Afrodiasporic culture for a cyborg mythology grounded in technical practice. Here's Lee Perry again, explaining his almost animistic relationship to the machine:

The studio must be like a living thing. The machine must be live and intelligent. Then I put my mind into the machine by sending it through the controls and the knobs or into the jack panel. The jack panel is the brain itself, so you've got to patch up the brain and make the brain a living man, but the brain can take what you're sending into it and live.[25]

Here we are on the imaginary border between the premodern and the postmodern, between roots and wires, an imaginary mobilized by Perry's whole persona and astounding career. Claiming at various times to be "Inspector Gadget," the "Super-Ape," or "The Firmament Computer," Perry also pioneered the use of phasers, drum machines, and the borrowing of existing records to "scratch" in a patch of sound. Aesthetically exploiting the electromagnetic play between information and noise, Perry integrated signal degradation directly into his thick and spongy polyrhythmic textures—as the producer Brian Foxworthy points out in *Grand Royal*, "Tape saturation, distortion and feedback were all used to become part of the music, not just added to it."[26] Perry would also plant records and tape reels in his garden, whirl like a dervish behind his SoundCraft mixing board, and blow ganja smoke directly onto the tapes rolling through the battered four-tracks at his Black Ark studio. As Perry told Toop about the Ark, "It was like a space craft. You could hear space in the tracks."[27]

This kind of surreal Afrodiasporic science fiction also appears on the cover art of much dub. Mad Professor's *Science and the Witchdoctor* sets circuit boards and robot figures next to mushrooms and fetish dolls, while *The African Connection* shows the Professor—significantly wrapped in European safari garb—reclining at a West African tribal dance, the jungle trees housing bass woofers and tape machines while the sacred drums nestle EQs. *Scientist Encounters Pac-Man at Channel One* shows the Scientist manhandling the mixing console as if it were some madcap machine out of Marvel comics.

It's perhaps no accident that in Jamaican patois, "science" refers to *obeah*, the island's African grab-bag of herbal medicine, sorcery, and occult lore. In his book on the trickster in West Africa, a study in "mythic irony and sacred delight," Robert Pelton also points out the similarities between modern scientists and traditional trickster figures like Legba, Eshu, and Anansi: "Both seek to befriend the strange, not so much striving to 'reduce' anomaly as to use it as a passage into a larger order."[28] We could ask for no better description of the electronic polyrhythmic tricks pulled by the great dubmasters.

It's a Jungle in There

Although the torch of golden-age roots reggae has passed mostly into the hands of Waspafarian bands, dub's deeply technological imagination has enabled it to make a rich and multilayered transition into the cultural science of the digital regime. As the excellent 1995 British music compilation *Macro Dub Infection* argues in both its title and selections, dub came to be seen as a technological virus, its silly-putty beats, active silences, and bubbling, booming bass as nomadic codes that have wormed their way into a host of musical genres: ambient, industrial, trip-hop, two-step, dancehall, techno, pop, jungle, and experimental rock. Indeed, dub helped erode the artificial differences often erected between these types of music, rendering such generic categories increasingly subservient to an open conversation between forms.

In the early and mid-1990s, when digital culture reached perhaps the most vital and open-ended phase we have yet to see, one particular electronic contagion stood out in its digital transcoding of the technologically mediated polyrhythmic space that characterizes '70s dub: jungle music, aka drum'n'bass. With its dizzying tempos and nonlinear beats, jungle certainly counts as one of the most aggressively syncopated, even polyrhythmic, dance music forms ever spawned in the modern West. And yet much of it was generated entirely on personal computers loaded with Cubase and a fat folder of sound files. Distorted soul samples and rude boy taunts got layered over smooth R&B chords; giddy high-hats, and hyperfast snares teetered on the edge of collapse; machine-gun martial beats and ominous bass lines liquefied your gut like an apocalyptic undertow.

Though a multicultural scene, jungle was essentially the first homegrown dance music to spring directly from Britain's black population, making it perhaps the most significant mutation of the Black Electronic since techno originator Derrick May read Toffler's *The Third Wave* or hip-hop producers began to build tracks with samplers as well as turntables. While dub is one definite influence, jungle's roots are, appropriately enough, tangled, and the following sketch drastically oversimplifies this backstory. In the early 1990s, when electronic dance music producers started whipping up the repetitive beats of techno to ungodly velocities, some folks took to speeding up breakbeats as well (breakbeats are the stimulating chunks of rhythmic surprise drawn from other records and that form the bedrock of American hip-hop). The resulting music—known as hardcore, or the more descriptive drum'n'bass—became something like breakbeat's mutant British twin, unfurling a tactile, hacked-up mix of drums and bass that foregrounded its own recombinant production like few other genres of dance music. Over time, the bass got thicker and dubbier, so that soon a slow ganja pace chugged along beneath the amphetamine snares; various cross-overs with the ragamuffin toasts of Jamaican dancehall MCs helped fix the name "jungle" in the public's mind just as the music started seeping out of the underground.[29]

The fact that jungle's maniacal tempos now sound old hat to most listeners of electronic dance music should not allow us to forget how revolutionary they sounded in their heyday. Upon first encountering jungle, most listeners probably suspected that in the Deleuzian contest between chaos and rhythm, rhythm had conceded defeat. Here's Simon Reynolds, describing hardcore for *Artforum* in 1994: "Sped-up break-beats are reverbed, treated, 'time-stretched,' and overlaid with itchy'n'scratchy blips of sounds that evoke the mandible-rustling telecommunication of the insect world. Polyrhythms are piled on, oblivious of the 'correct' way to organize rhythm: a spastic sound-clash of incompatible meters (funky hip-hop breaks, dub reggae sway, Latin rolls)."[30] At the same time, jungle does resemble "correct" polymetric drumming in allowing dancers to satisfactorily hook into and pass between different rhythmic milieus nested within the same cut: one can skank to the slow bass pulse or attempt to articulate the frenetic, unpredictable multiplicities exploding up top.

In other words, while jungle's programmed percussive samples are thickly layered, sped-up, and hypersyncopated, in most jungle tracks they stumble across downtempo dub lines that ultimately anchor the madness. But in the hands of the music's more aggressive and experimental creators, jungle can induce a remarkably delicious sense of disorientation, as reverbed cymbals and chopped-up snares savagely tug against the bass beat, upsetting the listener's habitual desire to "fill in" the music with a comprehensible rhythm. The stronger jungle tracks also intensify their breaks (the passages dominated by cuts and cross-rhythms) to a degree that shatters the usefulness of the term "syncopation." For these reasons, intense drum'n'bass can produce the same kind of disturbing confusion that West African drumming does; only instead of being threatened by the frenetic chaos of the primitive, the drums are threatened by the digital chaos of sampled code reiterating itself out of control.

In a sense, then, one must learn to listen and dance to jungle's complex and extremely recombinant rhythmic language. Many of the rhythmic units in jungle—such as the Wilsons' "Amen, Brother" sample—are generic and constantly recycled, cut and pasted across the thousands and thousands of tracks that junglists crank out on their PCs and Amigas. Novelty lies at least as much in the recombinant rearrangement and pacing of these generic elements as in the generation of novel motifs and sounds. I am reminded here of Chernoff's emphasis on the abstract precision of the many patterns that underlie West African drumming, and his point that "new forms are built from simple modifications of existing patterns, perhaps through the replacement of a single note."[31] Moreover, new forms are perhaps less important than the fresh rearrangement or pacing of received elements that everyone recognizes. As Chernoff writes, "It is the duration of time that a drummer plays a particular rhythm, the amount of repetition and the way the rhythms change, to which the drummers pay attention, and not so much any particular rhythmic invention."[32]

On the one hand, the junglists' attention to the crafty assemblage of beats make their rhythms more supple and compelling than those found in most other electronic dance music. In their apparently spontaneous articulation and madcap organization, they can seem almost organic. But for a period of time, drum'n'bass also seemed to be on the verge of unfolding some strange new non-Euclidian dimension, as cyborgs like Photek or 4 Hero painstakingly engineered an abstract space-time architecture from nano-beats that seemed to have been spliced and diced in a digital cuisinart.[33]

Jungle shares with dub the visceral root of the bass, as well as the deft deployment of gaps and silences that stretch and rend space-time, opening little voids that cannot help but empty us out of ourselves. But in contrast to the aquatic, resonant, almost meditative zones opened up by dub, the spaces generated by the more intense junglists emerge as a perpetually morphing array of compressed, malformed, and fractured "intermilieus." In part this distinctive mutation in the spaces of the Black Electronic arises from the qualitative distinction between digital and analog modes of production—a difference whose effects are particularly notable in electronic music. But the jarring hyperspace of jungle arises at least as much from the music's almost eschatological polyrhythm, its deployment of "heterogeneous blocks of space-time" that cut across the conventional dimensions of acoustic space. These blocks pull against dance music's tendency to conform to a central rhythm; they also compress that space through intensity and speed, creating little black holes of multiple beats. Perhaps this is what Marshall McLuhan heard when he pricked up his ears and decided that, as electronic subjects, "we live in a single constricted space resonant with tribal drums."[34]

Coda, 2002

Though I have made changes throughout, the bulk of "Roots and Wires" was written in 1994–95 and its conclusion should be read as much as possible in that context. Like many listeners, I found that jungle did not explore the most interesting territories it opened up. The polyrhythmic play hinted at in its earlier iterations gave way to, on the one hand, pleasant cocktails of carbonated fusion, and on the other, a nihilistic tedium that reduced the music's syncopated aggressivity into a jack-hammer monotony better deployed by death metal. Though edgier dancehall carries on the torch of drum'n'bass, the polyrhythmic potential of electronic dance music still remains in many ways untapped. The club remains dominated by the easy sell of four-to-the-floor, while most self-consciously avant-garde electronic music continues to keep the dance—mental or not—at arm's length.

The adherence to a central organizing beat is partly the fault of music software: genuine apart-playing is difficult to arrange, since most programs insist on a single meter and even automate beat-matching. There are promising signs, including the digital beat science of progressive hip-hop and the explosion of electronic dance music in developing countries like Brazil and South Africa, where even the most superficial desire to sample local color will thicken the rhythmic stew. IDM's fragmentation of rhythm into the skittering, textural para-beats made famous by Autechre can also only go so far, as producers—some armed with modular software giving them greater control over loops—realize that adhering to or undermining the beat is not nearly as interesting as allowing it to diversify and reorganize on another level. At that point multiplicity—about which I have spoken too much in this essay—will no longer simply serve as an engine of deconstruction or disorientation, but as a springboard for new, emergent forms of interconnection, communication, and holistic play. And since, as I hope I've shown, rhythm can be a training ground for the soul, such forms may move more than our feet.

Notes

1. Significantly, the action of the theremin brought up spatial issues of proximity and distance: to control pitch, the player moves her hands toward or away from a vertical antenna that is generating a weak electromagnetic field.

2. See Paul Gilroy, "The Black Atlantic as a Counterculture of Modernity," in *The Black Atlantic* (Harvard University Press, 1993), 1–40.

3. I share with Gilroy—who takes a position he calls "anti-anti-essentialism"—the sense that the lived realities of culture and history act as a powerful restraint on the loopier postmodern arguments for radical constructionism. Rhizomes are not roots, but they still conform themselves organically to the actual shapes of the land they encounter.

4. Along these lines see Ron Eglash, "African Influences in Cybernetics," in *The Cyborg Handbook*, ed. Chris Hables Gray (Routledge, 1995), 17–28.

5. John Miller Chernoff, *African Rhythm and African Sensibility* (University of Chicago Press, 1979), 42.

6. Gilles Deleuze and Felix Guattari, *A Thousand Plateaus*, trans. Brian Massumi (University of Minnesota Press, 1987), 313.

7. Ibid.

8. Ibid.

9. Ibid.

10. Chernoff, *African Rhythm and African Sensibility*.

11. Ibid., 50.

12. Ibid., 112.

13. Ibid., 100.

14. Ibid., 50.

15. Video documentary, *The History of Rock: Punk*, PBS.

16. Interview, *Grand Royal*, vol. 2, 69.

17. Chernoff, *African Rhythm and African Sensibility*, 112.

18. Cited in John Corbett, *Extended Play: Sounding Off from John Cage to Dr. Funkenstein* (Duke University Press, 1994), 19.

19. Chernoff, *African Rhythm and African Sensibility*, 35.

20. Cited in Michael Ventura, "Hear That Long Snake Moan," in *Shadow Dancing in the USA* (Tharcher, 1985), 123.

21. Cited in Corbett, *Extended Play*, 23.

22. This ambiguity can be captured in one simple query: Is the Internet exploding or imploding?

23. Jeff Salamon, "Dub and Dubber," *Artforum* (summer 1997), 35.

24. Dick Hebdige, *Cut'n'Mix* (Comedia, 1987), 82.

25. Interview in David Toop, *Ocean of Sound* (Serpent's Tail, 1995), 113.

26. Bob Mack, "Return of the Super Ape," *Grand Royal*, vol. 2, 64.

27. Toop, *Ocean of Sound*, 114.

28. Robert Pelton, *The Trickster in West Africa* (University of California Press, 1980), 268.

29. For these reasons and others, "jungle" is not a universally accepted terms, and many still prefer the more descriptive "drum'n'bass."

30. Earlier draft from author.

31. Chernoff, *African Rhythm and African Sensibility*, 112.

32. Ibid., 100.

33. As Simon Reynolds points out, the jungle scene hosts such copious and rapid mutations that singling out its stars denies the collective intelligence that drives its recombinant creativity; citing Brian Eno, he says that we should speak not of "genius" but of "scenius."

34. Marshall McLuhan, *The Gutenberg Galaxy* (University of Toronto Press, 1962), 31.

Bruce Sterling

As a science fiction writer, I have a deep and abiding interest in electronic arts, multimedia, computer networks, CD-ROMs, virtual reality, the Internet, the Information Superhighway, cyberspace—basically, the less likely it sounds, the better I like it.

These are topics I dare not ignore. It would mean ignoring the nervous system of the information society, the laboratory of information science, the battlefield of information warfare, the marketplace of the information economy—as well as one of the strangest areas of the art world.

Jules Verne invented science fiction when he was a stockbroker. Almost by accident, he discovered that nineteenth-century France had a large market for techno-thrillers. Jules Verne discovered and fed the tremendous nineteenth-century cultural appetite for romantic, futuristic technologies like the hot-air balloon, the electric submarine, the airborne battleship, the moon cannon.

I feel a great sense of solidarity with Verne as my spiritual ancestor when it comes to topics such as virtual reality, telepresence, and direct links between brain and computer. I can scarcely restrain my natural urge to inflate some of these big shiny high-tech balloons with the hot air of the imagination.

But I have seen this done for so long now, and for so many times, and to so many different technologies, that I can no longer do it myself with any sense of existential authenticity. I must confess to you quite openly and frankly that I am having a crisis of conscience.

Do information technologies need any hot-breathing promotion from science fiction writers? I would suggest otherwise. The good old techno-booster role of science fiction writers has been taken over by a professional class of public relations hucksters and intellectual property attorneys. Science fiction writers are no longer needed to serve as handmaidens for these blundering colossi.

Contemporary science fiction writers should fulfill another role. Science fiction writers should be examining aspects of media that cannot be promoted and sold—aspects of media that corporate public relations people are afraid to look at and deeply afraid to tell us about. We should be attempting to achieve a coherent understanding of media.

Media is a commodity. Media is something that is sold to us. Media can be something that we are sold to, even. Media is an everyday thing. You can buy bandwidth in job lots. You can watch television, buy books, videos, records, CDs—but that's not all. That's not what's interesting.

Media is an extension of the senses.

Media is a mode of consciousness.

Media is extrasomatic memory. It's a crystallization of human thought that survives the death of the individual.

Media generates simulacra. The mechanical reproduction of images is media.

Media is a means of social interaction.

Media is a means of command and control.

Media is statistics, knowledge that is gathered and generated by the state.

Media is economics, transactions, records, contracts, money, and the records of money.

Media is the means of civil society and public opinion. Media is a means of debate and decision and agitpropaganda.

None of these is a full working definition of the term "media," but taken together they compose a list of those qualities of this phenomenon that I find relevant and compelling.

To treat this matter seriously, I need a far better understanding than I have. We're getting in really deep now, ladies and gentlemen; we can't trifle with this thing anymore. As a society, we have bet the farm on the digital imperative. I need to speculate from new principles and new assumptions. I want a new synthesis; I want to really know and understand how media live and die.

Maybe I'll get my heartfelt little wish, and maybe I won't. But now I want to tell you how I plan to go about attempting this.

First, I want to destroy the Whig version of technological history. In the Whig version of history, all events in the past have benevolently conspired to produce the crown of creation, ourselves. In the Whig version of media history, all technological developments have marched in progressive lockstep, from height to height, to produce the current exalted media landscape. This is a very simple story. It's convenient and it flatters our self-esteem. Its very cheering to supporters of the media status quo (if there are any supporters left, or even any status quo left), but it can be proven untrue.

It can be proven untrue by disinterring and dissecting dead media. One understands evolution by studying the fossil record: the arcane, the offbeat, the forgotten; the failures, the lost and the buried, the media *maudit*—the dead precursors of later successes. Some forms of media are rendered obsolescent, but others are murdered. Some innovations are pushed very hard by clever and powerful people with lots of money, and yet they still fail. I find that aspect particularly interesting.

I'm not alone in my interest in this topic. My friend and colleague Richard Kadrey is also a science fiction writer, and together we have launched an effort called the Dead Media Project. We're using the Internet to bring people together to catalog and study extinct forms of human communication. We're in the media autopsy business. We're into media forensics.

If this scheme works, it will work in the way the Internet works: through prestige, netiquette, and acts of intellectual generosity. I think that books can and even should be constructed in the same way that the Internet is constructed. I'm going to give it a try.

Let's consider cinema. Cinema is not a dead medium—cinema is a hundred years old, and obviously alive, and more or less well. At least, it's still generating plenty of revenue in those squinchy little multiplex theaters. But cinema killed quite a few other media: the magic lantern, the phenakistiscope, the phantasmagoria, the praxinoscope, the zoetrope, the mutoscope, the fantascope. If you look closely at the evolution of cinema you can see that cinema is not a monolith, it's a radiation of species—E. J. Marey's *chambre chronophotographique*; Edison's kinetoscope; Anschutz's tachyscope; the vitagraph, the cinematographe, the theatrograph, the animatograph, the Urbanora.

Cinema as a medium did not make a sudden triumphant leap from silent movies to sound. People were attempting to jam sound into cinema from almost the beginning. We remember the much-publicized triumphs like *The Jazz Singer*, but we have been taught to disregard the numerous experiments that died on the barbed wire of technological advance: Edison's kinetophone, Gaumont's chronophone, the synchronoscope, the movietone, phonofilm, the graphophonoscope, the vitaphone.

These mutant forms of talking and singing cinema weren't ignored because they failed to work. In a lot of cases they worked just fine. Nobody who invented these devices ever set out to build a failure. The truly failed experiments never even made it out of the lab. These dead species of cinema were always imagined and proclaimed to be the cutting edge, the state of the art, and they were generally unveiled in a state of wild enthusiasm and a furious drumbeat from the press. They died because of contingency, not destiny.

Take Gaumont's chronophone, for instance. The name sounds rather arcane and silly, but that is not a technical judgment. Cinevision, Cinerama, Odorama—do these names really sound any less silly? How about Apple QuickTime, or CU-SeeMe, or Yahoo? But hey, those can't be silly—those are modern! "I hope you're not trying to suggest that some day people will laugh at us. Hey man, we're cyberculture—we'll never be obsolete."

Some media shed a few dead species, but the genus goes on living. Other media are murdered.

Have you ever heard of the quipu of pre-Colombian Peru? If you have, it's a minor miracle. The archives of the Incan quipus were burned by the Spanish conquerors, after the Council of Lima in the year 1583. There are about 400 authentic quipus left in the entire world. Every last one of the quipus we possess nowadays was dug out of a human grave.

Well, not quite every last one. I happen to have a brand-new quipu here in my pocket. I was doing quite a bit of reading about the quipu, so I decided I'd make one.

The word quipu means "account" in the Quechua language, so the quipu was basically a kind of accounting device and calculator. This is a fabric network to carry data. This was the only recording medium that the Incas had. It served all the recording functions of their society.

No one today seems to have any real idea how these quipus worked. They all looked more or less like mine; they had a thick fabric backbone, with a series of dependent fringes. But the fringes could also have fringes. Sometimes there were as many as six subdirectories coming off the backbone of the network. They had a variety of different knots. They had quite a wide variety of colors. People have only the vaguest ideas what the colors may have signified.

Mine is a very small quipu. The largest remaining quipu weighs about forty pounds and has well over two thousand dependent cords. No one has any idea what this device signifies or what message it carries. It was buried with a Peruvian gentleman who was modestly well-to-do, but he doesn't appear to have been particularly prominent.

The Incas had no idea that the planet harbored any civilization other than their own. As far as they were concerned, these quipus were the absolute apex of human intellectual accomplishment. And one must admit they have a lot to offer. They're very light—wool and cotton—they're portable and durable. Crush-proof. No problem with power surges or headcrashes. A good thing they were portable too, because one of their primary functions was the census.

It appears that everyone without exception in the Inca realm existed as a knot in a quipu somewhere. The Incas were great masters of ethnic cleansing. They thought nothing of ordering thousands of people out of their homes to distant realms as pioneers and settlers. Everyone simply loaded all their possessions onto their backs and left immediately. Thanks to the quipu, there was simply no way they would ever manage to slip by the authorities.

The Inca economic system was a centralized command economy. A third of the nation's economic output was stored in vast ranks of stone cells. Everything down to the last sandal was recorded on quipu.

I don't think there was ever an alphabet recorded on quipu. I don't think that the Inca were literate in that fashion, because their empire was only a hundred years old. There was nothing to pronounce that you could find on a piece of string. But there may have been genealogies in string: hierarchies, maybe family trees; maps, even—three days' journey, they forded a blue river, they fought a red battle—you can imagine how usefully suggestive this might have been. Maybe you could attack language even more directly with a quipu: meter, stress, quantity, pitch, length of the poem—why should this be hard to believe? In English we sometimes call telling a story "spinning a yarn."

These Incas were fine textile makers. They had a lot of wool and cotton. The government made them grow it, and their women spun yarn every day of their lives. When a quipucamayoc read one of these recording devices, I don't think his lips moved. There was nothing crude or halting or primitive or painful about the experience—a quipu is certainly a more tactile and sensual and three-dimensional experience than a book.

The quipu was a medium. It was a way to cast the world into an entire new form of order. It was a medium invented by and for very careful and methodical people, people who liked to fit huge boulders together so snugly that you couldn't slip a knife-blade between them. For the Incas, this was the Net—a net that caught their population in a sieve that dominated the whole material world, a sieve that no one could escape.

You know, in today's ultramediated world, I think it's quite a good idea to go into a quiet room with a quipu. Go to a room and shut off the electricity. Don't look at the quipu with scorn or condescension. Just hold it in your hands and try to pretend that this is the only possible abstract relationship, besides speech, that you have with the world. Really try to imagine what you are *missing* by not comprehending all economics, all governmental business, all nonverbal communication, as a network of colored yarn. Think of this as a discipline, as an act of imaginative concentration, as a human engagement with a profoundly alien media alternative.

It's truly pitiful how little is known or remembered about the quipu, a dead medium that was once the nervous system of a major civilization. And yet that is by no means the only form of knot record. There's also the Tlascaltec nepohualtzitzin, the Okinawan warazan, the Bolivian chimpu; and Samoan, Egyptian, Hawaiian, Tibetan, Bengali, Formosan knot records. So far, I know almost nothing about these beyond their names. I'd like to learn more.

Before I began the Dead Media Project I had no idea that native North American wampum might be historical records. I always thought that wampum was a kind of currency. Maybe, like the quipu, wampum was both currency and record at the same time. Imagine if our currency were a medium. Maybe our currency should be a medium. If you're an experimental media artist, why don't you start writing poetry on twenty-dollar bills and see what happens? Maybe you should just write the address of your favorite website on money, and see what happens then as the bill travels from hand to hand. Peculiar notion, isn't it—communicating with money? Maybe we've just been trained to find that notion peculiar.

As a writer, I use electronic text these days, because the typewriter is dying. In the early days of typewriters, what wonderful names they had: Xavier Progin's "Machine Kryptographique" (1833), Giuseppe Ravizza's "Cembalo-Scrivano" (1837), Charles Thurber's "Chirographer" (1843), J. B. Fairbanks'

"Phonetic Writer and Calico Printer," and so forth. A minor horde of typing machines, many of them scarcely recognizable as such to the modern eye. Soon they'll all be gone—swept away by the computer.

The computer. Its tide is so inexorable. Its power is so immense. Its triumph is so complete. What do we mean exactly when we say: "I've modernized. I own a computer"? Are we really in possession of a machine less mortal than Giuseppe Ravizza's Cembalo-Scrivano?

Take the Macintosh Powerbook. An impressive machine, isn't it? I admire that name—PowerBook. It says a lot about the kind of rhetoric our culture cherishes. The name "PowerBook" somehow suggests that this device can last as long as a book, though even the cheapest paperback will outlive that machine quite easily.

PowerBook is a good name, but not a really pretty name. Personal computers have had much prettier names. Like the Intertek Superbrain II. It must have been extremely difficult not to buy an Intertek Superbrain II, even though that machine is absolutely as dead as mutton.

Forgive me while I indulge in a brief sentimental roll-call of vanished glories, the vast and ever-growing legion of dead personal computers: The Altair 8800. The Amstrad. The Apple Lisa. The Apricot. The Canon Cat. The CompuPro "Big 16." The Exidy Sorcerer. (How can a sorcerer end up dead on the junk heap? That's not supposed to happen, we're not even supposed to think about that. A computer is a sorcerer with a superbrain—it's not supposed to be lying in a landfill with great-grandma's victrola.) The Hyperion, the Mattel Aquarius. The NorthStar Horizon and the Osborne Executive. The Xerox Alto and the Yamaha CX5M.

But wait! There's more! Dead mainframes! Dozens and dozens of fantastically complex and expensive dead mainframes. Dead supercomputers. Dead operating systems. Windows 95 is an operating system which is refreshingly honest, because it has an expiration date written right on it. We know that operating systems are of absolutely critical importance in computing, but how often do we honestly recognize that?

Suppose you compose an electronic artwork for an operating system that subsequently dies. It doesn't matter how much creative effort you invested in that program. It does not matter how cleverly you wrote the code. The number of hours of labor invested is of no relevance. Your artistic theories and your sense of conviction are profoundly beside the point. If you chose to include a political message, that message will never again reach a human ear.

Your chance to influence the artists who come after you is reduced drastically, almost to nil. You are inside a dead operating system. Unless someone deliberately translates you into a new one—with heaven only knows what liberties of translation—you are nailed and sealed inside a glamorous sarcophagus. You have become dead media. Almost as dead as the quipu.

This is, of course, the dirty little secret of the electronics industry, and therefore it is the mark of Cain for electronic art. When we are surfing the Web, we are surfing on a vast dark sea of dead computers. We have to surf, you see—because we are just a white scrim of foam up on the surface. The waves of machines rolling in beneath us are moving in with the hideous relentlessness of Moore's Law, doubling in power every eighteen months, one order of magnitude a decade. If you are working on a cutting-edge computer today you are working on one percent of the cutting-edge computer you will have twenty years from now.

And beyond that—the awe-inspiring prospect of teraflops, gigaflops, petaflops; Quantum Dot computers, ten thousand times faster than today's fastest microchips; optical computers, one hundred thousand times faster; holographic data storage, one hundred thousand times faster.

Sometimes you think that computation has to slow down, that it has to bureaucratize, become more like a normal industry. But then you're confronted with yet another awesome vista of absolute possibility!

You see, ladies and gentlemen, we live in the Golden Age of Dead Media. What we brightly call "multimedia" provides a whole galaxy of mutant recombinant media, most of them with the working lifespan of a pack of Twinkies. Mastering a typical CD-ROM is like mastering an entire new medium by using a frozen watch-cursor. And then the machine dies. And then the operating system dies. And then the computer language supporting that operating system becomes as dead as the Hittite language. And in the meantime, our entire culture has been sucked into the black hole of computation, an utterly frenetic process of virtual planned obsolescence.

But you know—that process needn't be unexamined or frenetic. We can examine that process whenever we like, and the frantic pace is entirely our own fault. What's our big hurry anyway? When you look at it from another angle, there's an unexpected delicious thrill in the thought that individual human beings can now survive whole generations of media. It's like outliving the Soviet Union once every week! That was never possible before, but for us, that is media reality.

It puts machines into a category where machines probably properly belong—colorful, buzzing, cuddly things with the lifespan of hamsters. My PowerBook has the lifespan of a hamster. Exactly how attached can I become to this machine? Just how much of an emotional investment can I make in my beloved three-thousand-dollar hamster?

I suspect that the proper attitude—one that more and more people will share in the coming millennium—is a kind of Olympian pity. We are as gods to our mere mortal media—we kill them for our sport.

Ladies and gentlemen, let me implore your pity and understanding for dead media. If you're really electronic frontier people, then in all justice, you ought to eat what you are killing. Let's try to see the greater sense of tragedy and majesty in this whirlwind we're creating. Perhaps this realization will free us from the hypnotism of our own PR. I dare not suggest that it will make us better artists—but at least it may help establish where we are and what is coming. Somehow, it might help us survive. It might even help us prevail.

Dick Hebdige

For five consecutive days in 1972, John Lennon and Yoko Ono cohosted the Mike Douglas TV show on Channel 11 in a talk-fest that took up no less than seven and a half hours of network TV time. On day one, Valentine's Day as it happened, Lennon, then 31, and Yoko Ono, just a couple of days short of her 39th birthday, explained to a national audience clearly understood by both them and the show's producers to represent "Middle America"—understood more as a spiritual or psychological condition than as an actual social or geographical location—that in the coming week they were going to be talking about, to use their own words, "love, peace, communication, Women's Lib ... war, racism, prison conditions and life in general"[1] with a string of invited guests including George Carlin, Ralph Nader, Rena Uviller, Chuck Berry, Bobby Seale, Marsha Martin, and Jerry Rubin, because, as John explained: "they represent a certain part of the youth and they are movement heroes to their own people and I think it's time they spoke for themselves and showed their humanity."

What seems unimaginable more than thirty years down the line is the extent to which both the boomers and Brokaw's "Greatest Generation" that begat them tended in 1972 to regard youth not just as the most advanced point of social change but as the new revolutionary vanguard: as agents and harbingers of an imminent global transformation.

The digital revolution and the antiglobalization movement notwithstanding, I think that particular Love–Peace–Teen–Dream thing is over. Today the kids as a collective are more likely to be linked, at least in the United States, to Columbine than to Woodstock. Rather than being deferred to as the transcendental seers of the future, the vast suburban majority of American adolescents are now subject to the constant pressure of homework and SAT scores, to the summary suspension of their civil liberties (via statutory curfews, etc.), and to the prospect of being tried as adults for the serious crimes in which, the statistics indicate, a significant and growing minority of them periodically engage.

But back in 1972, Love still held sway. In one of the performance pieces John and Yoko presented, along with an improvisation with electronic composer, David Rosenboom (incidentally, now Dean of Music at CalArts), that was based on rhythms supplied by the couple's amplified alpha brainwaves, and a processual piece involving the on-air gluing back together over the course of the week of a broken cup and saucer,[2] Yoko had the guests on the first day dial random numbers and tell whoever picked up that they loved them. At one point, Mike Douglas modified the rule and phoned David Frost's office to deliver the good news:

Voice on phone: Mr. Frost is out of the country. He won't be back until Monday afternoon.
Mike Douglas: Listen. Who am I talking to? Is this Mr. Frost?
Voice: This is his assistant.
Mike Douglas: This is Mike (Douglas) . . . I'm just calling because I want to tell David Frost that I love him very much. And tell him to pass it along so that everyone gets the message, could you, please? Tell him to tell Merv Griffin, and Dick Cavett and Johnny Carson . . .
Audience laughter
John Lennon: Right on!

What was unprecedented about the Yoko Ono–John Lennon partnership and the collaborations, artworks, and interventions that grew out of it was not just or not so much the way it brought together, on the one hand, experimental art—here the international New York–centered Fluxus avant-garde—the zendered-more-than-gendered avant-garde—and, on the other, youth-identified U.S.- and U.K.-centered international rock and pop music—here the first Brit rock invasion at the dying postpsychedelic end of its arc of development. Because in itself that conjunction was not new. Some years before Andy Warhol had engineered a similar match—although with more incestuously related and somewhat blanker components in his sponsorship and promotion of Nico and the Velvet Underground. As for the broader symbiosis between contemporary art practices, rock, and other recorded musics, think, for instance, *inter alia*, early Who, David Bowie, Captain Beefheart, Genesis P-Orridge, more or less all of U.K. and New York punk, and the interpenetration to the point of virtual merger of today's metropolitan art, fashion, and DJ scenes.

What was new was the degree to which John and Yoko turned the medium of celebrity itself into a platform for the dissemination of an uncompromisingly utopian vision and an ecstatic revolutionary message: namely, the re-enchantment of the world through the affirmation of love, the transformation of everyday life through the glorification of the ordinary, and the annihilation of boredom (that's where the Zen comes in), and finally, to borrow the language of the yippies and the Situationists through the conversion of the Spectacle into the Event, and through the war on war, specifically the war against the war in Vietnam, in other words, the war against the draft.

What Lawrence Grossberg calls the "rock formation"[3]—that assemblage of affective alliances, progressive political commitments, and an essentialized image of youth on which the baby boomers built a short-lived counterculture and a rather more enduring ideology of the transformative power of unregulated pleasures has been eroding now for decades. Rock, we know now, is like any other cultural form in that it has no intrinsic, fixed, or guaranteed meaning. It has no intrinsic social or political belonging. It can be shifted left or right or scrolled right off the page. It can be articulated to literally anything —placed in service to quite disparate and contradictory projects: Live Aid, Pepsi, Budweiser, Coors, Clinton, Bush, Rock Against Racism, racist skinhead Oi! music, or heartland Christian rock.

Nonetheless, I'd isolate two moments when something like the late-1960s rock formation was reassembled and brought back, albeit in mutated form, with enough force to produce a critical moment of contestation in the wider culture: the U.K. punk movement in the '70s, and rave and dance culture in the '90s. First punk:

Punk took the "ideological apparatuses"—the family, work, school, religious and political allegiance—stripped them down and held them up to see if there was anything viable left. And it did the same with sex and sexual relations. In the 60's the utopian idea was that power and power relations polluted the human potential for love whereas the punks began to explore the possibility that power and power relations actually produce sexual desire. So if sexual desire operated like a machine, you could fiddle with the knobs and change the positions and that's maybe how punk moved into a dialogue with S&M, the language of tops and bottoms, cross-dressing, bondage, fetishism and so on.[4]

Contrary to the sexual liberation theology of the '60s and early '70s, love is not a unitary or a necessarily unifying force. Love itself, like sex "itself" is myriad and legion. The forms it takes and the desires, censures, and permissions that direct, define, regulate, and shape its diverse articulations vary over time and space, as Foucault's work on sexuality and the genealogy of ethics makes especially clear. Hence, for instance:

rave wasn't about being rooted and organic, squatting in the mud at Woodstock. In the 60's the metaphors of alliance and bonding were all based around kinship and the family—brotherhoods and sisterhoods and so on—whereas rave seems to be more about networking, being mobile and on the move. It's more about casual, temporary alliances with strangers and maybe that can include love like in the 60's but this is love in the age of AIDS....[5]

Rave and dance culture were the West's weak echo of what was called in Eastern Europe in the late '80s "people power" as the crowds gathered in the public squares of Leipzig, Dresden, and Prague, not just to witness the dying days of Soviet Communism but to accelerate that process through the action of their collective witness. Rave and dance culture was a collective movement which reaffirmed the right to congregate in public. It was a movement against the domestic archipelago, against the conservative assertion of "family values" and the associated logic of containment. It was a movement against the homogenized interior, architectural colonics: the gating of communities. It was a movement against the subtraction of risk from pleasure, against the privatization and malling of public space. It was about finding comfort in strangers. It was about finding safety in numbers.

But rave also marked a shift with regard to the star system based in part on the recognition in a hyperwired world of the potentially lethal implications of celebrity (literally so in Lennon's case) and the dangers of the promiscuity of contact that celebrity entails: a recognition of the inferno constituted by incessant visibility, the unbearable killing weight of mass projection. Celebrity is now seen to be, in part at least, quite toxic. In this regard, the most prophetic innovation of the antiglobalization movement evident in its public debut at the demonstrations against the WTO in Seattle in terms of youth identity politics may reside less in the carnival of difference and difference-transcended—eco-pagans and bare-chested lesbians marching alongside workers in hard hats!—but in the widespread erasure of the dissident face as more and more protesters opted not for "coming out" but for staying out (of range), choosing masking and concealment over self-disclosure.[6]

This brings me back finally, to 1972, the overexposed, televised revolution, and to now: early 1972 and late 2001, the twin peaks of stand-off and lockdown in a long historical trajectory of corporate interests and corporate-sponsored norms and behaviors prevailing over older patterns that were based on a utopian-democratic model of vigorous debate within a truly heterogeneous and open civil society. In this last clip, John Lennon on day two of the five-day TV talk show marathon, introduces a clearly unenthusiastic Mike Douglas to his good friend Jerry Rubin, whom he'd met for the first time the year before with Abbie Hoffman in New York City. When Douglas asks Rubin what he's thinking about these days, Rubin replies:

I'm glad you asked me that because we're gonna support Nixon for President because by going to China he's furthering communist revolutions throughout the world and also encouraging communism at home. Anything to get elected. Even though he's not supported by the right wing, it's appreciated by the left. I'm just kidding. What he's really done is automate the war in Vietnam so that it's machines killing people. Create a situation where 43 people can be murdered at Attica. Create a situation where four kids can be killed at Kent State and the people are afraid.... It's the atmosphere in the country ... is one of just death.[7]

Rubin spins the Marxist–Lennonist line: Groucho Marx, John Lennon. Now you might think that intervention outrageous or courageous or crass or just plain charmless, but, whatever else it was or wasn't, it's certainly unimaginable today. As Howard Hampton wrote more than a decade ago about Dylan (and we could substitute the names of Lennon and Ono at this point): "Society has structured itself round the suppression of the kinds of demands Dylan's music once made ... (to such a degree) ... that it might make such speech unimaginable again."

Again, the key word here is "unimaginable": as unimaginable as it had been back in Senator McCarthy's day, before people like Dylan and Ono and Lennon came onto the scene. Just imagine for a moment.

Imagine there's no dissent.
No way to speak your mind.
No confidential consultation.
All constitutional rights declined.

When the organizers of this symposium settled on their theme I don't imagine they imagined that we, all of us—citizens and noncitizens alike—would be pushed up against a fault line which is potentially as polarizing and forbidding as the one that divided the U.S. body politic back in 1972. Yet that's precisely where we're all positioned at the beginning of the twenty-first century and for the foreseeable mid- to long-term future. As President Bush put it a few weeks back: "You're either for us or against us."

And to declare war on terrorism in the year 2001 is, as many people have pointed out, to declare a war that, whatever the sincerity of the original intention, however atrocious the precipitating cause, is both dangerously vague in terms of its targets and terrifyingly infinite in its potential range and duration. It is an instrument designed to place the entire planet on permanent alert, and its effect is to reinforce rather than reduce the ambient sense of terror— ("Fear proves itself" as William Whyte once said)—by producing multiple reverberating silencings: the suspension in the name of national security of our obligation, our human right to question, to reason and debate. Its effect is to produce a different kind of silence, a silence of a completely other and more sinister order than the sapient and contemplative silence induced by so much of Yoko Ono's work in the 1972 show.

What's clear after September 11, 2001, is the insistent authoritarian monologue on a particular version of national belonging and the proclaimed inviolability and self-evident virtue of American national interest: the patriotic closure and the heavy price you or I or anybody else not in the room is likely to pay for detaching from that rigid nexus—these are anything but academic issues. It may well be that we are moving into a more violently polarized political environment than anything we've seen since the era of the protests against the Vietnam War, so the subject of this panel is, I think (and this is where I'll stop), to say the least, timely.[8]

Notes

1. *The Mike Douglas TV Show*, recorded January 1, 1972, broadcast February 14, 1972.

2. *The Mike Douglas TV Show*, recorded January 1, 1972, broadcast February 14, 1972.

3. Lawrence Grossberg, *We Gotta Get Out of This Place: Popular Conservatism and Popular Culture* (Routledge, 1992).

4. The author in a video interview for "Land of 1000 Dances" (dir. Rotraut Pape, 1999).

5. The author in a video interview for "Land of 1000 Dances."

6. Deck Hebdige, "Even Unto Death: Improvisation, Edging, and Enframement," *Critical Inquiry* 27, no. 2 (winter 2001).

7. *The Mike Douglas TV Show*, recorded February 1, 1972.

8. This paper was originally presented in November 2001 at the Annual Wax Wasserman Forum on Contemporary Art for a panel entitled "Losing the Revolution: A Discussion on the Loss of Seditious Potential When Avant-Garde Art and Rock Music Stopped Sleeping in the Same Bed." In addition to the author, the panelists were Paul Miller, Laura Cottingham, and Dan Graham. The panel was designed to complement the exhibition "Yes Yoko Ono," then showing at the MIT List Visual Arts Center, Cambridge, Massachusetts.

Freaking the Machine: A Discussion about Keith Obadike's *Sexmachines*

8

Keith + Mendi Obadike

It has to do with stimulation: from the images I do the music, from the music I do the sound. But sound is not something foreign to adorn the film. It is intrinsic to the film.... Oral tradition is a tradition of images.

—Djibril Diop Mambety, filmmaker

[Sounds] penetrate not only through the ears, but over the skin, not only into the hearing, but also into certain cavities of the body, continue in bone courses and other channels, in order to enter the whole body acoustically.

—Bernhard Leitner, architect and sound artist

A picture held us captive, and we could not get outside it for it lay in our language and the language seemed to repeat it to us inexorably.

—Ludwig Wittgenstein, philosopher

To be naked is to be speechless.

—Ogotemmeli, sage

Are some desires and histories beyond speech? What role does desire play in the making of avant-garde art and the telling of its history? Why are some narratives more appealing than others? In my recent work I've become increasingly concerned with constructing a metalanguage that can function as a personal art history–sonic praxis. This device should be useful not only for expressing momentary concerns but also in creating a conceptual lineage for my work.

Sexmachines is a chapter in this series of investigations. In 1967, Nam June Paik created Opera Sextronique, a performance/music piece with Charlotte Moorman. In 1969–70, James Brown recorded "Sex Machine." These events were an aural anticipation of a future filled with Internet porn sites, erotic CD-ROMs, and satellites dedicated to beaming sex flicks around the globe. *Sexmachines* is a sonic portrait of Nam June Paik (the Godfather of Video Art) and James Brown (the Godfather of Soul) in the moment at which they emphasized the intersection of pleasure, art, and technology. There are three modules in *Sexmachines*. Each module in this triptych is abstracted from textures created by one sex toy.

Keith Townsend Obadike
Hear *Sexmachines* at Audiophfile 6.0: http://www.nomadnet.org/audiophfile6/index.htm/.

As Keith Obadike's collaborative partner and wife, I often have the privilege of talking to him in our studio about his individual work. We often discuss goals for our work and our concerns about creative lineage. This interview is a more formal version of our private conversation and comes from our desire to communicate with the world beyond our apartment.

Keith remembers seeing Paik's work before he really even knew what art was. What struck him was the way Paik made television and other machines feel organic. As the Godfather of Soul, James Brown is usually thought of as the opposite of mechanical. Keith points out, however, that the way Brown has been sampled by hip-hop artists is not only a result of how fertile funk is for this newer genre or how funky James Brown is. It is also a result of the fact that, unlike many musicians' work, Brown's rhythms and riffs are tight enough, repeatable enough, mechanical enough to be sampled and placed against other rhythms and riffs.

Keith has always reached for what is organic in electronic instruments. Growing up as a hip-hop artist, he sampled other musicians and himself in order to create new sounds, textures, and rhythms. Listening to the popular music on the radio, he criticized artists who used the factory sounds programmed into synthesizers or used samplers only to replay another song, uncomplicated by the artist's personal style. When he discovered audio art, he found more freedom to experiment with sounds, but he has always wanted to push the limits of electronic media. He has always tried to freak the machine.

For Keith Obadike, Nam June Paik and James Brown represent successful unions between what is moving and what is mechanical. A funk artist and a video artist are not the most obvious parents of an audio artist, but Keith's homage to his two unlikely fathers is a testament to the pleasure and productivity of engagement with their work.

Mendi Lewis Obadike

MLO: In your statement above you say *Sexmachines* is a sonic portrait. Are you mainly referencing the visual with the idea of portraiture or are you trying to get at something beneath that visual practice?

KTO: I think we recognize people as much by sound as by sight. While the idea of portraiture is usually associated with visual art, I think sonic portraits are also fairly common. Perhaps sonic self-portraits are even more common. Everything from early hip-hop rhymes to our voicemail messages can be understood as sonic self-portraits.

But with this particular project I was concerned with creating and placing myself within a lineage or sonically linking myself to Paik and Brown. This for me is related to the ways that families make photo albums filled with snapshots in order to remember and also to say where they come from. And at least since the late '60s or early '70s when recording technology became more affordable many families have been making audio recordings of their children's voices as a way to preserve an aural memory. This is a prime example of sonic portraiture. However, what I discovered with this project is that the challenge of creating a sonic portrait becomes exponentially more difficult when you create a sonic portrait of a composer. How do you render a sonic image of someone who makes sonic images?

MLO: What is your process like? How did you go about making these sounds? I mean, because I was at home as you were composing, I know you sat in our studio playing with sex toys in front of a microphone. But I still don't know what you thought about the sonic potential of each toy as you approached it or whether you think of each piece in the triptych as having some kind of narrative arc.

KTO: I decided that I would not quote from their work directly (by using samples). In order to highlight their conceptual connection I thought that I should work with what might be most commonly understood as a "sexmachine." This is a triptych and each image is created with one sexmachine. Image one is derived from a vibrator, two is from a dildo, and three is from a butt plug. Each image is created from multiple close recordings of the sex-machine with a stereo pair of condenser microphones. These sounds were then cut up and repositioned using a couple of different audio software applications and then treated with outboard effects. In terms of sonic potential—I think most things have sonic potential. But I also believe that if something has been designed (like a dildo) with an emphasis on its tactile qualities, I think it is probably full of rich sonic possibilities. Each piece was created with a definite narrative arc as well as some musical allusions but I hope listeners will bring their personal aural memories into the piece as well.

MLO: I read your choice to reference Paik and Brown (among all the influences you could have chosen) as reflecting something specific about your choice to make art with sex toys. Am I on track or is there something you want to say about your interest in Paik and Brown that goes beyond your interest in their takes on pleasure, art, and technology?

KTO: Well generally what I admire and want to learn from the work of Paik and Brown is a kind of playful seriousness. That's what I see as the real beauty in their work. But in terms of these particular pieces—*Opera Sextronique* and *Sexmachines*—I think they both succeed in creating a holistic vision of what an art-pleasure-technology piece can be. And I think these pieces can serve as useful models in the moment because there is very little pleasure or art in much contemporary media art.

Paik and Brown are also interesting in that they blur the lines between "popular" and "avant-garde" artists. I don't think many people could imagine a more "avant-garde" recording artist than James Brown or a more popular and accessible "fine artist" than Nam June Paik.

MLO: Is it significant for you that they are both men and of color?

KTO: It is very significant. I think up until that point there were very few images of men of color dealing with sexuality on their own terms or making overtly sexual work in the American public sphere.

MLO: On a more general note, how did you reach the point of making sound art? When we were growing up, you identified heavily as a musician and it seems to me that what you actually do when making sound art or sound design isn't that different now. You have said as much, as a matter of fact. But you identify now as all three: sound designer, sound artist, and musician. What do you want from sound art that you can't get from music or sound design? And could you (would you) have possibly made a conceptual project about these ideas without sound?

KTO: As a child I studied European classical music. In my early teens I was introduced to American avant-garde composers like Sun Ra, Ornette Coleman, Cecil Taylor, and later composers like John Cage and Olly Wilson. After working in hip-hop professionally and studying visual art as an undergraduate, I naturally started making work that combined all of these influences.

At this point I don't believe there is a clear line between my "sound art," "music," and "sound design" projects. I could have made a project about this idea without sound but sound art seems like the most direct way to talk about a sonic history or lineage.

MLO: How do you see your work here against your other (past or future) projects that are not sound based, like *Blackness for Sale*?

KTO: For me all of these works are closely related. Maybe I expect people to have a more visceral response to my sound-based projects. But there is always sonic information in my projects. Even net.art works like *Blackness for Sale* are intended to be read aloud.

9

Freeze Frame: Audio, Aesthetics, Sampling, and Contemporary Multimedia

Ken Jordan and Paul D. Miller aka DJ Spooky that Subliminal Kid

Paul D. Miller's Preamble

In an era of intensely networked systems, when you create, it's not just how you create, but the context of the activity that makes the product. Let's think of this as a hypothetical situation become real, and then turn the idea inside out and apply it to music—operating systems, editing environments, graphical user interfaces—these are the keywords in this kind of compositional strategy. During most of the spring of 2002 I was working on an album called *Optometry*. I thought of it as a record that focused on "the science of sound—as applied to vision." Think of it as a kind of "synesthesia" project navigating the bandwidth operating between analog and digital realms. *Optometry* was constructed out of a series of audio metaphors about how people could think of jazz as text, of jazz as a precedent for sampling—of jazz as a kind of template for improvisation with memory in the age of the infinite archive. In sum, the album was a play on context versus content in a digital milieu using sampling as a "virtual band" of the hand. Flip the situation into the here and now of a world where file swapping and P2P bootlegs are the norms of how music flows on the Web, and *Optometry* becomes a conceptual art project about how the "hypertextual imagination" holds us all together. Seamless, invisible, hyperutilitarian ... those are some of the words that describe the composition process of *Optometry*.

What's new here? In 1939 John Cage made a simple statement about a composition made of invisible networks that was called *Imaginary Landscape.* The piece was written for phonographs with fixed and variable frequencies (there was no magnetic tape at that time), and radios tuned to random stations. The idea for Cage was that the music was an invisible network based on "chance operations." As Cage would later say in his famous 1957 essay "Experimental Music," "Any sounds may occur in any combination and in any continuity." The sounds of one fixed environment for him were meant to be taken out of context and made to float—think of it as audio free-association, and you get the first formalist ideas of the origins of DJ culture.

But what does this have to do with jazz? In 1964 Ralph Ellison gave a discussion before the Library of Congress about writing jazz criticism. In it he discussed Henry James's fascination with Americanness—think of it as an echo of the Cage notion, and flip the code into a different cipher—you arrive at Henry James' critique of Americanness as "a complex fate." The Ellison lecture was called "Hidden Name/Complex Fate" and Ellison takes us on a journey through elements "absent from American life." In this text Ellison would flip the mix and build a template for a new kind of literature—that's the echo of *Imaginary Landscape* that intrigues me. He said: "So long before I thought of writing, I was playing by weather, by speech rhythms, by Negro voices and their different timbres and idioms, by husky male voices and by the high shrill singing voices of certain Negro women, by music by tight places and wide spaces in which the eyes could wander...."—again, the invocation of an imaginary landscape made of the hyperreal experiences of living in a world made of fragments. That's what *Optometry* inherits. Think of it as a dialectical triangulation between the idea of being made from files of expression put through places that are not spaces, but code. Gesture is the generative syntax, but once the sounds leave the body, they're files. And that's the beginning.

Introduction

When computers communicate over a network, they do so through sound. Before information can be sent over wires run between computers, it must first be translated into tones. The composer Luke Dubois, of Columbia University's electronic music department, has described the static you hear when a modem connects as a hyperaccelerated Morse code, a billion dots and dashes sung each second, too fast for the human ear to discern. This has been true since the dawn of networked computing. When the first two nodes of the Internet, at UCLA and Stanford, were brought online in 1969, Charlie Kline at UCLA famously initiated the connection by typing "login." After keying the letter "l" he received the appropriate echo back along the phone line from Stanford. The same with the letter "o." But when he hit "g" the system crashed; the audible reply from Stanford never reached its destination.

In 1972, Ray Tomlinson modified a program meant for ARPANET, the precursor to the Internet, that would let people send each other data as small "letters." He chose the "@" sign for addresses for a simple reason: the punctuation keys on his Model 33 Teletype made it easy to type; it was a convenient way to lend a geographic metaphor to an otherwise abstract place made up of data and people's interaction with the nodes that hold the data together. In one fell swoop, Tomlinson signaled that data could be both a place and a linguistic placeholder for digital information as a complete environment. By using the @ symbol, he restated what modernist artists and composers had been pointing out for over a century: when information becomes total media in the Wagnerian and the Nietzschean sense, we arrive at the *Gesamtkunstwerk*, "the total artwork." The Situationists referred to this as a "psycho-geography." Antonin Artaud wrote an essay about it called "Theater and Its Shadow"; for him it was based on the interaction of different forms of alchemy. When Artaud coined the term "virtual reality" in his 1938 essay "The Alchemical Theater," he anticipated a realm where signs, symbols, letters, and ciphers were all placeholders in the rapidly changing landscape of a society that faced the surging tides of industrial culture's mad race to become an information culture. It was a phrase to describe a mind trying to make sense of the data roadkill on the side of the information highway being built in the minds of artists whose dreams punctuated an immense run-on sentence typed across the face of the planet as technology carried the codes out of their minds and into the world. In the twentieth century, one symbol— "@"—ushered in a new world linked by the intentions of people to communicate. This is a world of infinitely reflecting fragments, vibrating, manifesting a hum, making music.

The connection between sound and networked computing is more than the product of technical convenience. It can be traced to the first visionary articulation of the digital age. In his seminal essay from 1945, "As We May Think," Roosevelt's science advisor, Vannevar Bush, proposed the creation

of a device he called the memex, which provided the inspiration for what later
became the networked personal computer. Bush's memex system had the
ability to synthesize speech from text, and, conversely, to create text records
automatically from spoken commands. He wrote enthusiastically of the
Voder, which was introduced at the 1939 World's Fair as "the machine that
talks." "A girl stroked its keys and it emitted recognizable speech," Bush
wrote. "No human vocal cords entered in the procedure at any point; the
keys simply combined some electrically produced vibrations and passed these
on to a loud-speaker." Bush also discussed another Bell Labs invention, the
Vocoder, an early attempt at a voice recognition system. Central to his vision
of the memex was the notion that sound would circulate through the system,
available for easy retrieval and manipulation.

Today that ease of access and malleability is transforming the way musicians conceive of and make music. It is now simple to convert sound into
digital streams, so it can flow anywhere across the computer network, to be
manipulated by a continually growing array of software. Real-time collaborations between musicians across the Net are becoming common. Online
collaborations that are not real time are commonplace. The combination of
databases (for storage), software (for manipulation), and networks (for interactivity between databases, software, and musicians) is challenging many long-
held notions of what music-making can or should be. Established boundaries
are blurring.

This blurring comes from a basic premise behind computing: all information can be translated from its original form into binary code and then re-
articulated in a new form in a different medium. Texts can be stored in a
database as ones and zeros, and later output as images or sounds. Ted Nelson,
who coined the terms "hypertext" and "hypermedia" in the mid-1960s, was
among the first to appreciate the full range of opportunities that networked
computers make possible. In 1974, he proposed the playful idea of "tele-
dildonics," a computer system that would convert audio information into tactile sensations. Why should music only enter the body through the ear? Why
not through the skin, or through the eye? Artists have been using computer
networks for collaboration at least since 1979, when I.P. Sharp Associates
made their timesharing system available to an artist's project called *Interplay*.
Organizer Bill Bartlett contacted artists in cities around the world where IPSA
offices were located, and invited them to participate in an online conference—
essentially a "live chat"—on the subject of networking. At the time this tech-

nology was rare and expensive; artists had no access to it. *Interplay* is often referred to as the first live, network-based, collaborative art project.

Around the same time, the innovative use of satellites by artists such as Nam June Paik, Joseph Beuys, Douglas Davis, Kit Galloway, and Sherrie Rabinowitz were connecting performers across great distances in collaborative, interactive pieces. A dancer in New York would improvise to music played in Paris, while a video of the two would be edited into a single performance for broadcast in, say, Berlin.

Although these pioneering telematic works did not make use of networked computing—bandwidth and processor speeds were not yet great enough to allow for it—they set precedents for the real-time network-based interaction between artists that became possible in the 1990s, as the technology improved and costs came down.

Online collaboration today takes many forms. Using Web-based music technologies, artists are working together to create new music. There are online studios that connect artists across great distances, and Web-based jams between musicians who have never laid eyes on one another. At the same time, even more popular are "collaborations" between artists who are not even aware that a "collaboration" is taking place. Referred to as "remixes," "mashups," or "bootlegs," digital files of a wide range of recorded material are being cut up and manipulated into entirely new works of art—blending distinct and unlikely source materials into singular creations. Of course, this kind of unsolicited collaboration challenges some long-held notions of intellectual property, and of an artist's unique affiliation with his or her own output. But at the same time, it brings back the idea of a shared folk culture, where creative expression is the property of the community at large and can be shared for everyone's benefit. Digital technology may be a route that reconnects us to aspects of our tribal roots.

As new as these techniques are, however, they retain a continuity with pre-digital compositional approaches. The network simply allows musicians to perform together online, replicating the experience they have always had when jamming in the same room. At the same time, the mixing of distinct aural elements certainly does not require digital technology; analog sound mixing dates at least to John Cage's 1939 performance of *Imaginary Landscape No. 1*, which featured a mix of turntables and radios. From this perspective, computer networks simply contribute to long-standing tendencies in composition that preceded the digital era. However, some composers are exploring a wholly original, uncharted musical terrain, one that is unthinkable without networked computers. In these works, the sound experience is created through the real-time participation of the listener in the making of the performance itself. These online sound art pieces rely on the interactive engagement of the listener, who helps to shape the specifics of the performance through her choices and actions, which are communicated to the music-making software over the wired network. In this way, the traditional distinction between "artist" and "audience" begins to melt away, as the "listener" also becomes a "performer."

Composing with Software

When the software conditions the experience, it conditions the music. One thing that many people notice when they start making music online is that the Web is a powerful vortex; it doesn't let you go. There is no single way to end a session; rather, there are many ways. There are bootlegs of everything that has ever made it onto the Net. Multiplicity is an unwavering factor in the online experience. Look at sites like Afternapster.com. You will find hundreds of peer-to-peer networks, each of which is the private preserve of a file-sharing community. These can be seen as the operational mode of a culture of distributed networks, held together by a common thread: each represents a particular taste as distributed through the system. As Artaud said (in an incredible precognition of the digital era's constant stream of information guiding any creative act): "All true alchemists know that the alchemical symbol is a mirage as the theater is a mirage.... [It's] the expression of an identity existing between the world in which the characters, objects, images, and in a general way all that constitutes the virtual reality of the theater develops."[1] In a way, collaborative music-making on the Net requires an interaction of people and software that turns almost all normal contact between musicians into a mediated experiment with the hypothetical. Is there a human on the other side of the screen? The sounds can only give you a hint. The software is a window onto a realm governed only by the uncertainty of that fact. The connections displace physicality in a way that leaves you a victim of context. This is the experience of telecomposing. It makes the creative act become a cog in the abstract machines of the software that mediate it. Using online studio software, such as Rocket, Pro Tools, or Reason, allows you to mix equally with either musicians or found sounds. Through the software interface, there is a certain equivalency. Collaboration can take place in real time between people, or between the remnants of creativity that people leave behind—the Net is full of such suggestive debris. In this context, the only limitation comes from the bottleneck that bandwidth places on file exchanges. The quicker the speed, the richer the environment.

Another effect of software is to dematerialize the musical instrument. It does this by distributing the qualities of an instrument across the various peripherals that control the sounds that the software generates. Algorithm displaces rhythm and becomes the environment in which to create. MAX/MSP is an open-ended software environment that lets you create templates for virtual instruments—it allows you to make an aggregate of whatever sounds you run through its parameters. Almost all process-oriented software behaves like this. Editing environments such as Pro Tools or Digital Performer function as dissecting tables of sound; they allow the musician to compose material from multiple layers of tracks and files, and then to condition the total output. It's like building music out of LEGO blocks.

That is, either LEGO blocks or samples. Online, everything is a sample. Every audio element becomes a potential fragment for manipulation and recontextualization. Sampling follows the logic of the abstract machinery of a culture where there are no bodies—just simulations of bodies. The fragment speaks for the whole; the whole is only a single track drifting through a vast database. The basic structure of "assemblage," the method of collage, holds sway here. Think of this terrain as object-oriented programming with beats. Take the file, edit it: import/export/MIDI/SMTP.

Time code synchronizes the fragments, and makes it work wherever you are ... FTP controls the data exchange as a basic source of file exchange ... Lee Perry popularized the term "versioning" by using a series of vocal tracks that were taken out of context and defamiliarized through sound effects programming. This can be done either as a live process or improvised on a virtual "mixing board."

Software that allows real-time online jamming is appearing from every corner of the globe. But is your online collaborator a person or a bot? Or a combination of the two? On the Web, collaborators can come in all guises. The White Stripes have no bass player. Steve McDonald, the bass player for Red Kross, felt that the White Stripes tunes could use more bottom end. So each week he adds a bass guitar part to one or two White Stripes songs, and makes them available as bootleg MP3s. Jack White, the White Stripes' front man, has apparently given these remixes his blessing.

Interacting with Intelligent Networks

Once, every sound had a distinct source. A door slammed shut, a horn was blown, a guitar string was strummed. Audio came from a discrete event; it was tied to a discernible action. Networked music challenges this notion by displacing sound from its origin, moving audio freely from one location to another, giving it a presence in and of itself. John Cage brought this quality into modern music with his 1939 piece, *Imaginary Landscape No. 1*. A performance that combined turntables and radio broadcasts, this work introduced networked interactivity into music making. Cage mixed into his performance various transmissions that came over the airwaves, and with them created an entirely new composition. Sound separated from its source in this manner becomes a "free-floating signifier," to borrow a phrase from Roland Barthes. The musical elements are liberated from a specific time and place, allowing them to be recontextualized in the final composition.

Robert Rauschenberg pursued something similar in the mid-1960s with his interactive, sound-emitting sculpture, *Oracle*. Rauschenberg's collaborator on the project, Bell Labs engineer Billy Kluver, described *Oracle* as "a sound environment made up of five AM radios, where the sounds from each radio emanates from one of the five sculptures. The viewer can play the sculpture as an orchestra from the controls on one of the pieces, by varying the volume and the rate of scanning through the frequency band. But they cannot stop the scanning at any given station. The impression was that of walking down the Lower East Side on a summer evening and hearing the radios from open windows of the apartment buildings."[2]

By the early 1970s, as the technology became more accessible, more artists began to explore the potential of networked media—both audio and video—to create unique forms of interactive expression. These artworks grew from the notion that meaning would emerge from media as it circulates freely within a network—and that meaning can be enhanced through strategic interventions by the artist or audience. Douglas Davis's 1971 performance, *Electronic Hokkadim*, produced at the Corcoran Gallery, was based on the interactions between telephone callers and broadcast television. Nam June Paik pursued what he referred to as a "cybernated art," based on the transmission of information through video and audio networks. Paik's 1973 television broadcast, *Global Groove*, stands as a landmark event in this trajectory. Fragments of performances by artists of various traditions—Western and Eastern, popular and elitist, traditional and modern—were strung together in a frenetic, continuous flow across the screen. Paik himself "performed" the broadcast as a live mix, choosing his streams as a DJ does today, manipulating images through a video synthesizer, using rhythm as the underlying principle of composition.

Enabling and manipulating the continuous flow of information was a principal concern behind the design of the networked personal computer. But before the mid-1980s, bandwidth constraints and limited processing power made the use of these tools prohibitively expensive for artists. However, it was long apparent to the pioneers of networked media—such as Davis, Paik, and Roy Ascott—that their artistic explorations with satellites and local wired networks would lead to computer-based work, once the technology had caught up to their vision.

Among the earliest musicians to dedicate themselves to the potential of networked computing were the members of The League of Automatic Music Composers, perhaps the world's first "computer network band," founded at Mills College in 1985, some of whom went on to found The Hub in the mid-1980s.[3]

One member of The Hub describes their method as follows:

Six individual composer/performers connect separate computer-controlled music synthesizers into a network. Individual composers design pieces for the network, in most cases just specifying the nature of the data which is to be exchanged between players in the piece, but leaving implementation details to the individual players, and leaving the actual sequence of music to the emergent behavior of the network.

Each player writes a computer program which makes musical decisions in keeping with the character of the piece, in response to messages from the other computers in the network and control actions of the player himself. The result is a kind of enhanced improvisation, wherein players and computers share the responsibility for the music's evolution, with no one able to determine the exact outcome, but everyone having influence in setting the direction. The Javanese think of their gamelan orchestras as being one musical instrument with many parts; this is probably also a good way to think of The Hub ensemble, with all its many computers and synthesizers interconnected to form one complex musical instrument. In essence, each piece is a reconfiguration of this network into a new instrument.[4]

Implicit in this approach is the idea that, within the network, a kind of intelligence is in circulation. David Wessel, at the University of California at Berkeley, has been working with his colleagues along these lines since the late 1980s, bringing together the fields of computer music and neural networks. Could an instrument become intelligent, and adapt in an automated manner to a musician's playing style? Could it learn the preferences of a particular musician, and modify itself in response to what it learns? Using the MAX programming environment, Wessel began to experiment with musicians in a network context. "We have obtained reliable recognition of complex guitar strumming gestures and limited numbers of spatial gestures," he wrote. "With such procedures and much more research, we might conceivably move towards adaptive, personalizable instruments.... one will have to decide when to standardize or fix the instrument and let the musician learn the appropriate gesture and when to let the instrument adapt to the specialized approach of a player. How to rig the training harnesses on ourselves as players and on our instruments as expressively responsive musical tools will be a question of scientific, aesthetic, and social concern."[5] Once meaningful information is circulating within a computer network, the opportunity emerges for a relevant interaction. As Wessel suggests, networked computer tools will lead musicians to make choices about aspects of their performance that previously never even had to be questioned, such as: how "smart" do I want my instrument to be?

The notion that music can emerge from an intelligent, interactive environment has drawn some composers to compositional forms that would be inconceivable without telecommunications technology. One example is Atau Tanaka's 1998 installation, *Global String*. The work consists of a physical string, fifteen meters long, that stretches from a floor diagonally to the ceiling of a room. At the ceiling, the string is connected to the Internet. "It is a musical instrument wherein the network is the resonating body of the instrument through the use of a real-time sound-synthesis server," writes Tanaka. "The concept is to create a musical string (like the string of a guitar or violin) that spans the world. Its resonance circles the globe, allowing musical communication and collaboration among the people at each connected site."[6] *Ping*, a site-specific sound installation by Chris Chafe and Greg Niemeyer, takes a similar approach. *Ping* has been described as "a sonic adaptation of a network tool commonly used for timing data transmission over the Internet. As installed in the outdoor atrium of SFMOMA," for the millennial exhibition 010101,

"*Ping* functions as a sonar-like detector whose echoes sound out the paths traversed by data flowing on the Internet. At any given moment, several sites are concurrently active, and the tones that are heard in *Ping* make audible the time lag that occurs while moving information from one site to another between networked computers."[7] In effect, *Ping* makes music out of the data flow of the Net—the constant motion of digitized fragments in real time is given an aesthetic form.

The composer and theorist Randall Packer has explored this line of telematic composition in a number of pioneering collaborative installations. For *Mori*, an "Internet-based earthwork" first mounted in 1999 by Packer with Ken Goldberg, Wojciech Matusik, and Gregory Kuhn, the trembling movements of California's Hayward Fault are picked up by a seismograph, converted into digital signals, and sent over the Internet to the installation. This data stream triggers a series of low-frequency sounds that vibrate through the installation, viscerally connecting the visitor to the moment-by-moment fluctuations of the Earth's actual movement.

In what he has referred to as "artistic research projects," Packer has further explored the possibilities of interactive, telematic musical works. One such installation, *Telemusic*, was staged by Packer and his collaborators Steve Bradley and John P. Young at the Sonic Circuits VIII International Festival of Electronic Music and Arts in St. Paul, Minnesota, in November 2000. *Telemusic* brought together live performers, audio processing of their performances, and real-time participation by the public through a website, www.telemusic .org. As the performers read from a script, their delivery was affected by audio processing triggered by the mouse clicks of visitors to the website. The final mix in the room was then streamed to the website, so a visitor could hear the final musical composition that she had contributed to by clicking a mouse.

In order to create this direct form of interactivity, Packer's team had to develop an interface between impulses captured over the Internet and a server hosting MAX software. This circular experience, in which listener is also a participant in the making of a musical work, is indicative of the direction in which the Internet is suggesting that music should go—as the distinction between "artist" and "audience" begins to slip away, and we find ourselves dipping into the data flow, listening to the music that it makes, and that we make with it.

None are more hopelessly enslaved than those who falsely believe they are free....
—Goethe

Notes

1. Antonin Artaud, *The Theater and Its Double* (New York: Grove Press, 1958), 49.

2. Billy Kluver Interview with Randall Packer, November 2001.

3. Http://crossfade.walkerart.org/brownbischoff/. Accessed October 3, 2007.

4. Http://www.artifact.com/release.php?id=1008/. Accessed October 3, 2007.

5. *Computer Music Journal* 15, no. 4 (winter 1991). Available at http://www.cnmat .berkeley.edu/News/Wessel/InstrumentsThatLearn.html/. Accessed October 3, 2007.

6. Http://www.fondation-langlois.org/html/e/page.php?NumPage=284/. Accessed October 3, 2007.

7. Http://www-ccrma.stanford.edu/~cc/sfmoma/topLevel.html/. Accessed October 3, 2007.

10

A Theater of Ideas: An Interview with Steve Reich and Beryl Korot on *Three Tales*

David Allenby

DA: How did the idea for *Three Tales* first come about?

SR: When *The Cave* premiered in 1993 its first commissioner, Dr. Klaus Peter Kehr of the Vienna Festival, asked if we'd ever thought about doing a piece about the twentieth century. One of the things that came to mind very quickly was that the twentieth century had been driven more by technology than almost any other human endeavor. This wouldn't create a music theater piece in itself—we needed some events, some signposts from the early, middle, and late parts of the century that would be emblematic of the period and its technology.

Hindenburg came to mind rather rapidly. It signaled the end of a failed technology when the airship exploded and crashed in New Jersey in 1937. It was also the first major disaster captured on film. The image of an enormous hydrogen-filled zeppelin, with huge swastikas on its tail fins, flying over Manhattan and bursting into flames in New Jersey just before World War II, was unforgettable.

The atom bomb was in many ways the emblematic technology of the century. For the first time we'd created a technology with which we could destroy the planet. Hiroshima and Nagasaki seemed overly well documented. We settled instead on the tests at Bikini, which were between '46 and '52, signaling the end of World War II and the start of the Cold War. It brought together the most ultrasophisticated hi-tech known to man at that time and some of the least technological human life on the face of the Earth—the Bikini people of the Marshall Islands in the Pacific.

For the third tale we were originally going to use the explosion of the *Challenger* spacecraft, but we soon felt this was one disaster too many for the piece. Then in 1997 Dolly the sheep was cloned and we both took one look at each other and said "That's it!" It's a totally different technology, growing out of medicine and biology, and pointing to what life might be like for the rest of the twenty-first century.

BK: Also, in contrast to the first two acts, "Dolly" is looking within, to ourselves, to the impact of technology on our own physical bodies. And it symbolized the whole range of issues now brought about by technology to impact on our bodies, not only by manipulating the basic blueprint of that body, but by actually bringing technology into our bodies.

DA: How did your personal experiences with technology feed back into your creative work?

BK: Even in the early 1970s, when I first started working in the genre of multiple channels, I looked to the ancient technology of the hand loom for ideas on how to program multiple channels of video. The loom was after all the most ancient of programming tools and held out very useful ideas to me of how to think about programming multiple images. I have always liked the tension between working with a modern technology and thinking about the older tools which preceded it and learning from those tools. The impact of media on the social and cultural environment in which we live was the focus of a magazine I coedited in 1970 called *Radical Software*. That double-edged sword of the gains and losses of each new technology that we incorporate into our lives is one of the subtexts to *Three Tales*.

SR: When I first began working with tape in the '60s nothing seemed more interesting than gradually changing the phase relations between two identical tape loops. This produced *It's Gonna Rain* and *Come Out*. Rather quickly I felt that if this were something only for machines, it wasn't worthwhile pursuing. I then discovered, to my amazement, that I could produce that gradual change of phase with myself and another musician playing two pianos, which led to *Piano Phase*. Phasing itself is really just a variation of canonic technique where the rhythmic distance between two or more voices is flexible. While the electronics suggested something, it was the connection to living musical tradition that made that suggestion fruitful and worthwhile. Right now I am obviously attracted to making music with digital samplers to playback speech and sound recordings as part of a video opera, and at the same time I have no interest in using synthesizers to substitute for traditional instruments. I also find that after working with technology, as in *Three Tales*, I then need to compose a piece or two, or more, just for acoustic instruments and voices.

DA: Do you see any contradiction in using sophisticated audio and video technology to question the role of technology? Is *Three Tales* advising us to turn away from technology?

SR: No, to both questions. If you want to know, for example, about a certain kind of car or a certain kind of medical procedure, you go to someone who can tell you what's good about them and what's not so good. You don't take advice from someone who knows nothing about them or has no experience with them. This piece needed artists who had feelings about technology based on years of experience.

In terms of being antitechnology, Beryl and I use and enjoy the technology necessary to make this work and have used it before in *The Cave*. Computers, video tape, samplers, and so on are all part of our culture. They are what is used to make our folk music—rock and roll. It would be strange if artists didn't use this technology for music theater.

What we *are* exploring, are differing human attitudes to technology. In *Hindenburg* and *Bikini* one senses the unqualified faith in "the march of progress" that typified those periods. Then in *Dolly*, the audience sees and hears scientists themselves, and all with very different attitudes toward what they are doing. People then draw their own conclusions about the character and intent of these scientists and one religious figure.

BK: It used to take hundreds of years for a technology to develop and have an impact. Now it takes decades, or less (think about the Internet). When tools develop and become upgraded so quickly, offer so much accessibility, their physical and social impact on our lives is transformative, and we have very little say over this impact. Is this part of our evolution? Are we in control? Can we be? Have we ever been? Bill Joy suggests we have no brakes. Adin Steinsaltz says, "The sin of Adam, in eating . . . He was too hasty."

DA: "He was too hasty." What does that mean?

SR: The idea that Adam was too hasty comes from the Zohar, the central book of Jewish mysticism. The Torah makes no mention of which fruit Adam and Eve ate. The apple is never mentioned anywhere in the tradition.

The Talmud suggests three possibilities; a fig, a grape, or wheat. The fig has clear sexual implications, the grape leads to wine which can alter consciousness, and wheat is the cornerstone of agriculture which made possible cities and eventually all our other technologies. Adam and Eve were created on the sixth day and the Zohar says they ate the fruit just two hours before sundown when the Sabbath begins. If they had waited they would have been able to bless the Sabbath with wine, then bread, and then enjoy making love, which is particularly encouraged on the Sabbath. The forbidden fruit would have been permitted when the context was right.

DA: What are the differences between the technologies employed in *The Cave* and *Three Tales*?

BK: The differences are enormous. Within two or three years of completing *The Cave* it became possible to get a computer and work with programs that could combine photography, film, video, and drawing, all within a single frame. *Three Tales* exists on a single screen, unlike *The Cave* where the complexities came from the relationships between the images and the timings of the images on five different screens. It's still mind-boggling to me that an artist can work at a computer, import the raw materials for the work, and then transfer the finished work to a tape deck sitting next to the computer, and hand it to a projectionist as a finished product for performance. You can make a work with considerably powerful tools at your disposal, sitting at home working alone.

There are also techniques I developed in the course of the work to create distance from the documentary source material. For instance, in *Bikini* I turned the live film footage of the islanders into photographic stills, made these stills painterly and then animated them at a different frame rate from the usual thirty frames per second. It creates a very different feeling from usual slow motion and places the documentary material in a new context, which is the intent throughout the work.

SR: In *The Cave*, as in *Different Trains*, I followed the speech exactly—as they spoke, so I wrote. The result, because there are a lot of short speech samples, was a constant changing of key and of tempo which makes it, particularly in *The Cave*, difficult to play and often lacking in rhythmic momentum. In *Three Tales* I thought OK—*prima la musica*. Musical concerns (as opposed to samples) would predominate and the sound samples would be altered to fit the music. This allows the musicians to work up some momentum in one tempo over a longer period of time as in most of my other pieces. It also allows me to control the overall harmonic movement of the music and make the samples fit that. This is particularly appropriate in this piece which, particularly in *Dolly*, deals with how we are beginning to alter our bodies using technology.

I also use two new techniques that I originally thought about in the 1960s, but have only recently become technically possible. The first is what I call slow-motion sound, which is slowing down a speaker or other sound without changing pitch or timbre. The second is the equivalent of freeze frame in film. While one of the interviewees is speaking on videotape I make an extension of a single vowel in time so that it becomes a kind of audible vapor trail and, in fact, becomes part of the harmony. This also means that what the interviewee was speaking about, the thought itself, becomes extended, along with the vowel, into what follows, which is of course an intensification of something that happens with speech and ideas in our lives.

DA: Following performances of *Hindenburg* as an individual work in 1998, you've made some changes.

SR: Yes, *Hindenburg* was originally five scenes, now it's four. The second scene was about General Hindenburg himself, leading up to Hitler and the burning of the books. It was just too laborious and heavy-handed, so we chucked it. The following short scene, called "Nibelung Zeppelin," is a musical reworking of the hammering Wagner leitmotif from *The Ring* while you're watching the German workers in 1935 building the zeppelin in Frederikshaven. The music takes the Nibelung leitmotif from Wagner's *Das Rheingold* and uses it as a repeating pattern played against itself in canonic variations. Wagner's dominant pedal harmony (transposed from B-flat minor to F minor) is also maintained and extended in length. At the end you see the enormous finished Zeppelin, huge swastikas on its tail fins, a show piece for Nazi Germany which, in many ways, realized Wagner's ideals. So this scene indirectly covers the Nazi era without ever going into it directly at all. There's also a tightening up in the first scene, so all in all *Hindenburg* went down from 24 to 16 minutes.

BK: Just to diverge slightly, when Steve was thinking of the reworking of Wagner's leitmotif, I was thinking of the Judson Dance Troupe of the 1960s. I'd been watching the archival material of the workers building the *Hindenburg* that I'd gathered at the National Archive in College Park, Maryland.

What struck me was the incredible gracefulness and dancelike quality of the workers in their everyday activities, especially several of the workmen climbing and walking on the scaffolding. So I masked these out of the original footage, frame by frame, and set them to the music. You have a conjoining here of two of the most unlikely influences, and I think it's one of the high points of the work.

DA: Moving on to *Bikini*, how do you make connections between the atom bomb tests and the biblical stories of the creation of humans and the Garden of Eden?

SR: The chief reporter for the *New York Times* who was stationed at Bikini during the tests writes about seeing a huge tree—a Tree of Knowledge—with alpha-particle and beta-particle fruits. The atom bomb was the device whereby mankind could destroy the planet and that conjured up religious imagery. The physicist Robert Oppenheimer quoted the Bhagavad Gita about how we had become like Shiva, able to destroy worlds. We decided to present parts of our own biblical tradition which deal with the creation of humans as a way of gaining a bit more perspective on the situation. There are, in fact, two stories. The first is the one that many people know, describing how G-d created man and woman at the same time and gave them dominion over the birds and beasts and everything on the face of the Earth. If you read some social critics nowadays you'll find them using that to beat us Westerners over the head—of course we're going to rape the earth, because Genesis tells us we were given dominion over everything. Unfortunately, those critics ignore the fact that the text goes on and there is a second retelling of the story.

BK: These two creation stories in Genesis describe two types of human beings, which are aspects of all of us to different degrees. In the first story man and woman are created together and achieve dominion over the Earth and its creatures. In the second, man is made from the dust of the Earth, woman from his rib. They are placed in the Garden of Eden "to serve it and to keep it"—a more humble type of human being. In the events that combined to create the situation at Bikini in 1946, the man of dominion came upon a humble man and asked (or rather told) him to make a sacrifice of their homeland for the sake of all mankind. The Bikinians are a paradigm for the plight of displaced people, past and present, to return to their homeland. These two aspects of humankind represent an ongoing struggle, both internally within a single human being, and also between nations.

SR: We do have dominion, and therefore responsibility, whether we like it or not, yet at the same time we get sick, we die, we doubt ourselves, we don't really understand our significance in the universe—and that's not because of a lack of scientific knowledge.

DA: Turning to Dolly, the cloned sheep, we're brought up to the end of the century.

SR: Cloning is emblematic of the many biological procedures and digital devices by which we are now beginning to manipulate the human body. The possibilities are endless and the question arises whether we are the right beings for the job. *Dolly* meditates on this and the religious background from which we came.

DA: In *Dolly*, one of the interviewees says, "It's a religious war, it's a war between religions." What is he referring to?

SR: Well, unfortunately, some people thought he was referring to the conflict between the creationists versus Darwin starting almost one hundred years ago. In fact he was referring to "Darwinism" itself becoming a kind of scientific religion that purports to explain absolutely everything, versus any kind of spiritual outlook on the world, be it Judaic, Christian, Islamic, Hindu, Buddhist, Taoist, or any other.

For me, and for many others, there is no conceivable contradiction between religion and science. Science investigates the nature of the physical world. Religion investigates how we should act as human beings. If I say something scientifically, like "This book weighs one pound," we can put the book on the scale and find out if that is true or false. If I say, "Natural laws are the expression of G-d's will," there is nothing conceivable that will ever prove or disprove this. I'm not looking for evidence. I'm expressing an attitude that implies life is sacred.

DA: With *Dolly*'s dominance of "talking heads" we seem closer to a theatrical world of human characters. But what sort of theater are we talking about here?

BK: Our private subtitle to this work is "Two Tales and a Talk." It's a theater of ideas. As with *The Cave*, we used a very tiny percent of the overall recorded material. Some truly terrific interview material did not make it into the final cut. Sometimes the presentation of the ideas wasn't what we wanted, or didn't fit with the other answers we were editing. Sometimes someone might have given us fantastic answers but if that person didn't deliver the words in a certain way, or look convincing when delivering those words, then they didn't make it into our final cut. So in a way the interviewees are being cast like actors. The video provides both the visual action and the theatrical set, which in performance is underscored or subtly elaborated on by Nick Mangano, stage director, Matt Frey, lighting designer, and Anita Yavitch, costume designer. The performers are fairly static and iconographic, but add a live presence that both extends into live space and supports what is on the screen. This is not theater with a capital "T" trying to be a classic form of opera or drama. The theater is really there to serve the video and music.

SR: The main theatrical action is on the screen. The singers act as a kind of chorus, reflecting on the action on screen. Each of the three acts not only looks and sounds like its historical period, each is formally organized quite differently to comment on that period. *Hindenburg* is in four scenes with short pauses between them in a more or less conventional way you might have found at that time. *Bikini*, as Beryl originally conceived it, is in three image–music "blocks" which are each repeated three times as a kind of meditation with a coda at the end. There are no pauses. *Dolly* is much harder to diagram formally. It is nonstop with certain kinds of material recurring in no clearly discernible pattern. Musically one might say *Dolly* was a kind of free rondo. The forms of each act reflect the historical period they describe.

In regards to the "talking heads" in *Dolly*, we picked interviewees who are important scientists at places like MIT and Oxford. They are very accomplished in their field and they are "doers" talking about their activities and theories. It is clear from the onset that they are very different personalities, and their characters reveal themselves more and more as the piece progresses. The speech melodies of these eminent scientists provide dramatic revelation through utterance. One can observe different attitudes within this scientific community through the way they present things and perhaps most significantly by their capacity for humility.

DA: Having completed *Three Tales*, will the work influence your future plans?

BK: In the 1980s I left video behind to paint. As I've mentioned, after *The Cave*, by 1996, I was able for the first time to combine many different elements, film–photography–video–text within a single frame instead of working in the multiple channel form which I'd been doing since the early 1970s. In working on *Three Tales*, with a single image comprised of many different sources, there were many ideas that occurred to me, or briefly appeared, that

I was not able to develop because of the needs of this particular work. I look forward to developing these visual ideas, creating much shorter, more visually intense works, which I think of as video paintings.

SR: First off, I need to compose some purely musical pieces, which is what I did after *The Cave* and after composing *Hindenburg.* This is a kind of working rhythm that I've developed recently that feels right and that keeps my energy up. Music theater, then pure music, then back to music theater. We'll see. I think the use of sampling and video in opera and music theater is clearly growing. It's simply an honest expression of the life we are living now. "Timeless" music theater has in fact always reflected its time and its place.

Quantum Improvisation: The Cybernetic Presence

11

Pauline Oliveros

Dedicated to the memory of Robert Erickson, who encouraged us all to improvise

According to Ray Kurzweil in his book, *The Age of Spiritual Machines: When Computers Exceed Human Intelligence*:

In a hundred years there may be no clear distinction between humans and computers. There will be enormous augmentation of human perceptual and cognitive abilities through neural implant technology.

Humans who do not use such implants are unable to participate in meaningful dialogue with those who do—knowledge is understood instantaneously through assimilated knowledge protocols. The goal of education and intelligent beings is discovering new knowledge to learn.

The speculations for the future in the Kurzweil book and others concerning self-aware machines with the ability to reproduce into future generations with patterns of matter and energy that can perpetuate themselves and survive set me wondering. It's already evident that computers and human intelligence are merging. What would I want on a musician chip if I were to receive the benefit of neural implant technology? What kind of a twenty-first-century musician could I be? Humans, with the aid of technology, already see and hear

Keynote address presented at the Improvisation Across Borders conference at the University of California, San Diego, April 11, 1999. © Copyright 1999 Deep Listening Publications.

far beyond the capability of the unaided senses. It's not long according to Kurzweil when such aids will be available at the personal level as implants like personal computers or digital assistants. All of us improvisers could have new input from this and new challenges. I'll return to the question of my musician chip after looking back a hundred years for some reminders and highlights:

The first magnetic recording came in 1899. One hundred years ago—sound is recorded magnetically on wire and a thin metal strip. By 1900 the Gramophone Company advertised a choice of 5,000 recordings.

The human desire to record—to replicate and preserve—resulted in 52,000 CD titles produced in 1998!

Early Jazz improvisation emerged after the civil war and emancipation. Improvisation developed in parallel with radio broadcast and recording technology. It is not surprising that all styles and forms of improvisation from historical to free have been empowered by recording. Recording is the memory and documentation of improvisation and testifies to an enormous creative effort by innumerable musicians. Musicianship for written forms of music has been empowered by recording as well.

The African aesthetic imposed on American and European dance music leads to the decade of the birth of the blues and blues-influenced jazz—1920–30. Ma Rainey and Bessie Smith mothered this music and rose to short-lived stardom as blues queens during the migrations from the South to Northern metropolitan centers. Horn players of innumerable bands followed the lead of Ma Rainey, Bessie Smith, and other singers in a tremendous era of creativity and enterprise by people of African descent.

By 1930, 60 percent of all American households have radios. Improvised music spreads out from recordings and radio broadcasts. Music by Americans of African descent is heard throughout the land and influences all of American music. This enormous creativity is recognized and appropriated by the white entertainment establishment. The black–white exchange and interaction continues throughout the century and grows into the billion-dollar music industry which exists today.

In 1953 the first consumer-model tape recorders are available. This means that musicians can record themselves at home or in their studios—a sound mirror is available to use anytime. Musicianship escalates with the aid of technology. Today's musicians are phenomenal in their performance skills in all styles of music improvised and written.

Currently another wave of creativity originating from 1970s hip-hop sweeps youth culture—influencing the whole world. All recordings are sources for improvisation. Rather than frozen historical objects, recordings become live material through DJ scratching and remixing.

Classical music as taught in American establishment institutions and conservatories regards improvisation as a kind of craft, subordinate to the more prestigious art of composition. It's well known that Mozart as well as Beethoven improvised on their tours. Improvisation as a lost art was excluded from the curriculum and all but disappeared in America except for church organists and occasional cadenzas in concertos. The denial of the validity of improvisation has a racist tinge and origin. In America in the first half of this century improvisation grew mostly from jazz and blues—heart music of Americans of African descent—the disenfranchised. After 1950 improvisation appears in white avant-garde music through the influence of marginalized indeterminate or aleatoric procedures, exposure to jazz and blues and to recordings and live imports of non-Western music—also disenfranchised music.

What's the purpose of creating music in performance without reference to memory or written form—improvisation? The purpose varies according to the function of the music. One purpose is to enter into direct dialogue through sound with oneself and others. If the improvisation is creative then new mental and physical patterns could be born such as happened with Ornette Coleman and Cecil Taylor breaking away from jazz traditions in the '50s, and later Musica Electronica Viva, San Francisco Tape Music Center, and AMN breaking away from classical music restrictions with improvisation. If the improvisation is historical, such as replicating Charlie Parker, John Coltrane, or the legacies of other great improvisers without introducing new elements, then the purpose is to affirm a tradition.

The improvising musician has to let go of each moment and also simultaneously understand the implications of any moment of the music in progress as it emerges into being. In historical improvisation the course is charted or set by the conventions and codifications of the style—the classicism of the music; in so-called free improvisation nothing is known about the music before it happens—this edge is the challenge for human and for machine intelligence. Unless the styles of the musicians improvising were already absorbed by the machine then what information would there be to calculate a response? If the outcome is known in advance it is not free improvisation, it is historical improvisation.

What in fact does happen when a creative musician makes new music? How can it be new or free? What is it free of? What could be new about it? What is happening with a solo improvising musician? a group? The soloist gives herself feedback and enters a dialogue with herself and musical space —the group stretches the possibilities for dialogue and new relationships come about creating a myriad of new possibilities even though the course of the music—new as it may be—will flow with ineluctable inevitability. The recorded legacies of innumerable musicians are waiting to answer these questions.

What happens when a new musician chip is implanted in a human or a machine? All ranges are increased. Processing is possible beyond known present human capabilities. What could be heard? Could a new musical paradigm include a new spatial domain? Moments of local sound—moments of moving sound with the ability to detect locations from light years away—defining new interdimensional spatiality? What would a spatial melody sound like—a pitch beginning on Saturn moving to Aldeberon to Sirius to Earth? Space-related frequency and amplitude—multidimensional melody—color/space/sound melody. Who would be playing this tune? Who would be listening and where? Melody across space stretched out and also happening everywhere simultaneously. Space is the place—I hear you Sun Ra!

According to the article "Is Space Finite?" by Luminet, Starkman, and Weeks:

The universe may look infinitely large, but that could be an illusion. If space folds back on itself like the braids of a pretzel, it might be boundless, and light could spool around the cosmos endlessly. The usual assumption is that the universe is, like a plane, simply connected, which means there is only one direct path for light to travel from a source to an observer. A simply connected Euclidean or hyperbolic universe would indeed be infinite. But the universe might instead be multiply connected, like a torus, in which case there are many different such paths. An observer would see multiple images of each galaxy and could easily misinterpret them as distinct galaxies in an endless space, much as a visitor to a mirrored room has the illusion of seeing a huge crowd.

What if we could sound out, hear, and perceive the shape of the universe by bouncing sound around the torus? We don't have to be limited to the physical definitions of our perceptual ranges. What about imagination? Here is the challenge of the machine—the promise of hybrid human–machine forms through implants. The challenge of new beings with formidable powers of perception, memory, reasoning, and interpretation. Non-carbon-based beings created by humans to eventually replace humans. Are we creating new beings to replace humans, or are we expanding our minds—making a quantum leap into the neocortex to develop our own potential power?

Back to the highlights:

In 1948, Norbert Wiener coins the word "cybernetics" meaning the science of control and communication in the animal and machine. The cybernetic presence is definitely with us. Kurzweil says in his time line: "10 years from now (2009) human musicians routinely jam with cybernetic musicians." This is a shallow statement because there is no revelation concerning style, complexity, or form. In fact many musicians are already improvising with machines programmed to respond to improvised input. Will Kurzweil's cybernetic musicians be self-determining in ten years?

In 1977 the first desktop computers from Apple become available. Musicians and hobbyists continue to work out programs to make and play music now in their own studios away from Bell Labs, Princeton, Stanford, and other institutions for computer music research.

At this time, improvisation is also developing and merging with new forms of interaction made possible by machine intelligence. Computers expand the reach of solo as well as group improvisers. Laurie Spiegel, David Behrman, Warren Burt, Joel Chadabe, George Lewis, Elliott Sharp, Jim Tenny, Deep Listening Band, Chris Brown, the Hub, and many others come to mind.

By 1990 computer hard disc recording and editing is available. A powerful and revolutionary combination—the merging of recording and computing. What a wonderful tool for the creative musician.

From Kurzweil, again: "In twenty years virtual musicians with their own reputations are emerging." We need to know what constitutes a musician. How will humans with or without implants compete or collaborate with the cybernetic presence? I don't feel comfortable with the notion of surgical implants. I hope that some noninvasive reversible form may be available.

"Thirty years from now direct neural pathways for high bandwidth connections to the human brain perfected. There will be a range of neural implants to enhance auditory and visual perception and interpretation, memory and reasoning." What would be enhanced? What and how would such powers be measured and valued and by whom? What about imagination? What kind of improvisation could and inevitably will result?

Music and especially improvised music is not a game of chess—improvisation, especially free improvisation, could definitely represent another challenge to machine intelligence. It won't be the silicon linearity of intensive calculation that makes improvisation wonderful. It is the nonlinear carbon chaos, the unpredictable turns of chance permutation, the meatiness, the warmth, the simple, profound humanity of beings that brings presence and wonder to music.

We have looked one hundred years before and one hundred years ahead of the 1999 conference Improvisation Across Borders. Now for what I would want on my musician chip—what skills should the twenty-first-century musician have? What could she know?

In 1937, the Church–Turing thesis stated that "All problems that humans can solve can be reduced to a set of algorithms, supporting the idea that machine intelligence and human intelligence are essentially equivalent."

Returning to the future Star Date 2336, we find a machine intelligence—minus human emotions that evidently don't reduce to a set of algorithms until lately—at work on the *Starship Enterprise*. *Star Trek*'s android Lieutenant Commander Data is an imagining of the future predicted by the Church–Turing theory. Data solves problems and is a sentient life form with the same rights as other life forms. His ultimate storage capacity is 800 quadrillion bits and his total linear computation speed is 60 trillion operations per second. Data can remember every fact he is exposed to and can imitate voices so perfectly that he can even fool the computer of the *Enterprise* into thinking he is someone else. *Star Trek*'s Data has performed as a classical musician on several episodes. His classical musician chip allows him to perform any music superbly, having absorbed all known styles and all available recorded interpretations of written music. The musician who learns to perform classic forms and idioms is a conservative who affirms and preserves tradition. All of known music could be listened to, absorbed, analyzed, and interpreted by machine intelligence and be contained on a chip.

The composer is an organizer who designs and formalizes music prior to performance through notation. Computers already aid a variety of composer's design calculations. Computers can engage in rule-based composition, and can calculate and realize musical forms. *Experiments in Musical Intelligence* by David Cope describes the basic principles of analysis, pattern matching, object orientation, and natural language processing. This system makes it possible to generate new compositions in the styles of various composers, from Bach and Mozart to Prokofiev and Scott Joplin. The program SARA (Simple Analytic Recombinant Algorithm) produces new compositions in the style of the music in its database. Already audiences are hard put to tell what music is composed by a human and what is composed by a machine. All known styles of composition could be contained on the composer chip.

Data could certainly handle all known styles of composition and historical improvisation. Improvisor is a computer program that creates original music, written by Paul Hodgson, a British jazz saxophone player. Improvisor can emulate styles ranging from Bach to jazz greats Louis Armstrong and Charlie Parker—historical improvisation. What about the improvising musician as an evolutionary? What would an improviser chip have to include for Data as a machine intelligence to engage in free improvisation? To boldly go where no musician has gone before, sounding through dimensions of space—of time? Finding new sounds and new sound relationships?

Data could probably analyze all known instruments for instrument makers, all performance abilities for performers, and all known musical forms for composers. The edge, though, is the unknown of imagination for performers, improvisers, composers, and instrument makers, and the unification of all these roles.

On my musician chip I would like the following features:

The ability to recognize and identify instantaneously any frequency or combination of frequencies in any tuning, timbre, in any tempo or rhythm, in any style of music or sound in any space.

The ability to produce any frequency or sound in any tuning, timing, timbre, dynamic, and articulation, within the limits of the selected instruments or voices used. Maybe I would also like to morph from any instrument to any other instrument or voice, at will.

The ability to recognize, identify, and remember any piece of music—its parts as well as the whole, no matter the complexity.

The ability to perceive and comprehend interdimensional spatiality.

The ability to understand the relational wisdom that comprehends the nature of musical energy—its form, parts, and underlying spirituality—as the music develops in performance.

The ability to perceive and comprehend the spiritual connection and interdependence of all beings and all creation as the basis and privilege of music making.

The ability to create community and healing through music making.

The ability to sound and perceive the far reaches of the universe much as whales sound and perceive the vastness of the oceans. This could set the stage for interdimensional galactic improvisations with yet unknown beings.

I suppose it would be great to be able to print it all out as well in 3-D color.

Are improvisers conscious? Do they have self-perception, self-awareness, the ability to feel? What is conscious improvisation? For that matter, what is unconscious improvisation? The body knows what to do even if the small mind does not comprehend. The body "dances" the music—the nerves fire and the mind notices slightly after it happens. Conscious improvisation involves strategy—responding strategically even if the outcome is unknown. A strategy of conscious improvisation might be: play only if you are listening—or, trust the body to respond. This melds of course the notion of conscious–unconscious improvisation.

The capability of the human mind is unplumbed. We have far more capacity than we currently use in the neocortex waiting for evolutionary expansion. Computers may actually instruct us in this process, as we continue to merge with the machine intelligence that we are creating and as we continue to develop improvisation interaction. We must decide, though, what a fifty-year-old structure of silicon is going to tell a five-billion-year-old structure of carbon before making irreversible physical changes.

Quantum computing is a revolutionary method of computing based on quantum physics that uses the abilities of particles such as electrons to exist in more than one state at the same time. Quantum computation can operate simultaneously on a combination of seemingly incompatible inputs.

By analogy or metaphor, quantum improvisation could mean a leap into new and ambiguous consciousness opening a new variety of choices. Ambiguous consciousness would mean the ability to perform in more than one mental state simultaneously in order to reach or bridge past and future as an expanding present. There could be new sound combinations anchored by increasing order, even though choices might seem incompatible. Such a quantum leap could mean the utilization of more of the neocortex, the seat of creativity and problem solving. The newest part of the brain is waiting to evolve in association with the limbic system—the amygdala—the "old brain" and seat of the emotions. Quantum improvisation could find new ways to express and understand the relationships between mind and matter.

Ordinarily we use only a relatively small percentage of the neocortex—this reflects the style of most content-oriented education in institutions, which limits or suppresses rather than encourages creative problem solving. After enormous growth spurts in the brain by age sixteen, many people are no longer interested in creativity. Education—content-oriented education particularly—does not necessarily access the neocortex. Rather there is the classic learning of forms—cortical learning—recognizable forms with no encouragement or support for innovation, which requires creative problem solving. This situation is particularly true of music. Performance of traditional music is rewarded and encouraged rather than acts of creation. Performance and creativity both could be rewarded and encouraged.

What is needed now is a complete program—an Improvatory of Music for pre-K through post-doc in aural music, including all forms of improvisation and aural traditions, to complement conservatories. As soon as possible young children could be encouraged to improvise and create their own music. They could be introduced to sound gathering and listening strategies. This program would not replace traditional music learning but would complement, enhance, and make it possible for all people to participate in creative music making. An Improvatory would necessarily be interdisciplinary and include all the arts and technology.

There exist now 100 years of recordings of the complete range of improvisation from historical to free. This is ample documentation that could yield many fruitful studies for advanced degrees. Improvisational strategies could be introduced early and advance through graduate levels. Here is one example of an improvisational strategy: "Only sound what has not been sounded before."

Once an improvisation has happened, is recorded, and studied, it becomes historical. Too much replication can be destructive of creativity. Replication guarantees survival and perpetuation of form but it would be critical to hold the space for creative problem solving—proposing an advanced problem to solve would be how to do this. Music teachers could encourage playing by ear as well as reading and writing music. The use of recording and computing could accelerate the learning of reading and writing music through intelligent courseware.

What would one learn at an Improvatory of Music? Basic listening skills, including the listening effect. Music only happens with conscious listening. Maybe one would learn quantum listening—listening in more than one state simultaneously. If you are not listening the music is not happening. A conscious observer is necessary. Conscious observation affects sound. One could also learn ways of sounding and listening—strategies; starting from scratch—making music by any means possible (e.g., bottle caps, found objects).

Other areas of study at the Improvatory:

Sound ecology—what happens in the environment?
Sound gathering through recording.
Sound sensitivity.
Sound provision with live feeds from sonically stimulating environments such as ponds, oceans, natural soundscapes, the weather, and many other sources including industrial and urban sites.
Sound as intelligence.
Relational techniques or relationality.
Relational organization.
Informality.
Egalitarian ethics.
Political structures.
Evolving open form processes.
Computing—computers may push us or teach us about the mind and facilitate a quantum leap into unity of consciousness.
Technology—especially tools for expanding the mind through listening.
Instrumental research and development.
Acoustics.
Psychoacoustics.
Organizational strategy.

An Improvatory requires an architecture that is supportive of the process—ideally. Chaos is a key resource in pushing evolution. Meeting places might provide an appropriately chaotic environment with reconfigurable levels, color, textures, sonorous objects, acoustics, recording opportunities, and open spaces. There could be many choices to make.

The Improvising Across Borders conference has brought a new dignity to a creative activity, which has been marginalized by the Western, established musical order. It is time now for an inclusive curriculum where improvised music is no longer ignored or denigrated. Borders should not only be crossed, but should dissolve. Degrees in both aural and written musics should be available equally. Aural music informs written music and vice versa. Improvisation is a key process for creative problem solving and the expansion of mind that is needed to meet the challenge of the machine intelligence that we are creating. Improvisation is creative problem solving and is a portal to quantum thinking—thinking in more than one state simultaneously.

What exactly is free improvisation?—nothing is known in advance of making the music. What's the algorithm for that condition? It may or may not be free of historical patterns, or it may use historical patterns in new ways. Theoretically free improvisation is utterly spontaneous, like the big bang of creation. Maybe the big bang was the first and only genuine free improvisation. Algorithms anyone? How about holding the possibility of the first unknown sound to begin an improvisation at an unknown time in a group of players who are all new to one another? Imagine then a crowd of creative people improvising together.

Acknowledgments

I thank the organizers of the Improvising Across Borders conference for their courage and imagination. Special thanks for reading my paper and offering comments to: Ione, Monique Buzzarté, Stuart Dempster, Norman Lowrey, Richard Povall, William Osbourne, Ka sha Unger.

References

Cope, David (1996). *Experiments in Musical Intelligence.* A-R Editions.

Floyd, Jr., Samuel A. (1995). *The Power of Black Music: Interpreting Its History From Africa to the United States.* Oxford University Press.

Gershenfeld, Neil, and Isaac L. Chuang (1998). "Quantum Computing with Molecules." *Scientific American* (June 1998). Available at http://www.media.mit.edu/physics/publications/papers/98.06.sciam/0698gershenfeld.html/.

Kurzweil, Ray (1999). *The Age of Spiritual Machines: When Computers Exceed Human Intelligence.* Viking.

Luminet, Jean-Pierre, Glenn D. Starkman, and Jeffrey R. Weeks (1999). "Is Space Finite?" *Scientific American* (April).

Prevost, Edwin (1995). *No Sound Is Innocent: AMM and the Practice of Self–Invention.* Copula.

Scanner aka Robin Rimbaud

I believe in ghosts.

Now let me clarify that statement. I am not referring to a menacing spectral presence that hovers several meters above the floor in a long white sheet that is suggested by this image, but rather the ghosts of our memories and the resonance held by specific locations over history.

Every day we use batteries—in our Walkmans, bicycle lights, and watches—but the battery is an intriguing object, for it is a form that can retain an energy and potential far outweighing its size and often modest stature. Rechargeable batteries can develop "memories," recalling how many times they have been recharged, and over time their full potential slowly retreats until all energy has been sapped. One needs to constantly discharge a battery, relieve it of its "memory" so that it can retrace its original source of strength and dynamics. Similarly I believe that buildings and spaces also retain a particular memory, a sense of time or place. What would it be like if we could, like a digital computer tool that can search out the remnants of a lost hard drive that we once thought was long erased, simulate this process within the confines of a gallery space or a CD recording? What if we could find the ghosts, the lost narratives, the stories that once echoed around a building—how would we fill in the stories, how would we experience them today?

Now let's pause for a brief history lesson. Back in the autumn of 1941, Attila von Szalay, of Van Nuys, California, attempted to record spirit voices on 78 R.P.M. records, initiating an effort to capture the voices of spirits on a machine of permanence. Several years later, the Swedish filmmaker Friedrich

Jürgenson apparently succeeded in tape-recording the voices of the dead in 1959. Noticing these voices buried within the mix of recordings of bird song, he discovered he could also capture the voices in tape recordings of normal conversation. Shortly afterward Dr. Constantin Raudive, a Latvian psychologist living in Germany, visited Jürgenson in Sweden. Jürgenson and Raudive spent long laborious hours over tape recorders connected to a radio tuned into the abstract white noise band between commercial stations in an attempt to improve the quality and volume of the spirit voices. Then in 1968, Raudive announced he had replicated Jürgenson's experiments without the application of Jürgenson's psychic abilities: he had finally established communication with the dead solely through electronic means.

Back in my awkward teenage years I had a chance encounter with a neighbor's ham radio, an early form of radio communication favored by truckers on the road long before cellular telephones, which meant that often when I listened to records or the radio at home, their voices would feature as uninvited guests with my amplifier acting as a receiver for their banal communications. These conversations became a common ghostly presence within my field of sound and combined with my eclectic listening habits of the time—Throbbing Gristle, John Cage, Brian Eno, David Byrne, and Robert Fripp—led to the first of several Scanner CD recordings on Ash International in 1992. Intercepting cellular phone conversations of unsuspecting talkers, and editing them into minimalist musical settings as if they were instruments, brought into focus complex issues of privacy and the dichotomy between the public and the private spectrum. Sometimes the high frequency of cellular noise would pervade the atmosphere; at other junctures it would erupt into words and melt down to radio hiss. During interception of the data stream, transmissions would blend, blurring the voices and rupturing the light, creating audio transparencies of dreamy, cool ambience.

With the technology to peel open virtually any zone of information and consume the contents, I used the scanner device itself—a modestly sophisticated radio receiver—to explore the relationship between the public and private spheres. Working with sound in this manner suggested a means of mapping the city, where the scanner device provided an anonymous window into reality, cutting and pasting information to structure an alternative vernacular. It was a rare opportunity to record experience and highlight the threads of desire and interior narrative that we weave into our everyday lives, to explore the invisible, the ghostly presences all around us but impossible to pinpoint.

In scientific research by the likes of Raudive in the last century, recordings would be made of empty locations. On listening back to these apparently vacuous spaces one could identify mysterious voices speaking languages and phrases we barely understood. Analysis and interpretation would be left open—were these really the voices of those long past? Were they trapped outside of sight trying to communicate with us? Or were they simply radio interference or faults on the original tapes? What is real and what is not real? These are questions that are asked constantly within both representational art and modern abstraction. For my work with these cellular interceptions I was zooming in on the spaces in-between—between language and understanding, between the digital fall-out of binaries and zeros, between the redundant and undesired flotsam and jetsam of environmental acoustic space, which finally led to a focus toward the cityscape. If an accent suggested a certain class, age, or attitude, then how suggestive was the raw sound around these conversations, how influential was the location where each conversation was held? Sound is ever present, sometimes as a constantly shifting whir, as a damp grain of footsteps, the dronelike spangle of distant traffic, or as the seemingly motionless air that ripples past our ears, the elegant stuttering trill of a bird overhead. How influential was this common envelope of space, the environment in which we consume sound and music? How does one define the spaces between music and sound? When we listen to a Walkman, how do we distinguish between that which is intended—the sound carrier—and that which is incidental—passing traffic, the roar of a plane, the screech of a train door, our own footsteps? Whether active (creator) or passive (listener), we set up a virtual space in which we are free to each explore the sonorous and acoustic strata of what is an intimate yet global expression of space, a simple translation of the social transformations wrought by new technologies.

My work has always explored the relationship between sound and architectural space and the spaces in between information, places, history, relationships, where one has to fill in the missing parts to complete the picture. Digital technology has allowed us to search beneath the surface of sound and its image within the modern recording studio. Using machines that allow us to replicate and duplicate familiar sounds by "sampling" them we are already experiencing notions of time and memory displaced from their reality. Is this sound sample you are hearing of the present or of the past? How might its future use alter its status? How "real" is it? How much is dependent upon your recollection of its source?

Combining these theories and ideas recently led to my collaboration with American artist Mike Kelley for our work *Esprits de Paris* (2002–2003) shown as part of the Sonic Process show at the Pompidou Centre in Paris. Wishing to explore the ground built through these explorations into these unintelligible signals, we recorded some of the most haunted places in Paris, as well as locations loaded with an electrical presence—everywhere from author Isidore Ducasse's (Lautréamont) apartment in Montmartre where he died in 1870; the grave of Charles Cros, inventor of the phonograph and alien contactee, in Montparnasse cemetery; to recordings inside l'Église de la Sainte-Trinité Church, where composer Olivier Messiaen famously played the organ.

The theory is that somehow certain places may become impregnated by some subtle physical emanation, by the thoughts and emotions of those living and dying within them. An analogy can be found in the display of a physical medium, which seems to become surcharged with a psychic energy, from which phenomena doubtless radiate during the course of a seance. Recording using a thermal camera that allows one to tune into a particular temperature on the film and also a series of acoustic recordings in each of the locations, sometimes with the microphone itself connected but switched off, allowed us to explore a form of "audio mirage" that can emerge from prolonged listening to an identical recording, where you almost begin to hear things not actually recorded on the original tape or disc. Somewhere beneath the surface we were able finally to reveal acoustic data and information, voices formed from the distortions in digital recording. In even the most subtle passages one could hear the most dramatic parts, the hidden shifts in detail and language we were searching out. A space would thus be orchestrated in which the audience could experience the essence of these voices from beyond, a densely orchestrated hiss of information. We listened to the spaces to hear the detail, the silences offering up a narrative unknown.

All of my works have explored the hidden resonances and meanings within the memory and in particular the subtle traces that people and their actions leave behind. The "ghosts" within sound and memory point to where I am currently propelling myself. Capturing these moments, storing them and redirecting them back into the public stream enables one to construct an archaeology of loss, pathos, and missed connections, assembling a momentary forgotten past in our digital future. It is a form of found futurism.

With thanks to Mike Kelley for historical detail

The Musician as Thief: Digital Culture and Copyright Law

13

Daphne Keller

Human culture is always derivative, and music perhaps especially so. New art builds on old art. We hear music, process it, reconfigure it, and create something derivative but new—folk melodies become Liszt's Hungarian Rhapsodies; Roy Acuff's "Great Speckled Bird" becomes Hank Williams's "Wild Side of Life"; and Rodgers and Hammerstein's "My Favorite Things" becomes a John Coltrane classic.

Twentieth-century recording technology brought this pervasive culture of reuse to a new level. Artists can now build upon prior recordings themselves, turning the fixed artifact of an earlier artist's performance into raw material for new work. Early sonic collage, in the analog era, was painstaking and labor-intensive. It took John Cage a year to make his four-minute-long Williams Mix.[1] William Burroughs spent untold hours constructing cut-ups with razor blades and tape. And of course, artists' raw materials for these projects were limited to whatever recorded sound was physically at hand.

Digital recording technology revolutionizes and democratizes this recycling process, making complex manipulation of recorded fragments easy and relatively affordable. And the Internet and other digital communications media bring a treasure trove of recorded sound directly to the sonic cannibal—information formerly fixed in discs or tapes now exists, in one critic's words, "as pure thought or something very much like thought: voltage conditions darting around the Net at the speed of light, in conditions which one might behold in effect, as glowing pixels or transmitted sounds, but never touch or claim to 'own' in the old sense of the word."[2] Contemporary music, from the top forty to the most obscure live DJ set, reflects this technological change, taking the music that came before as raw material for reuse and reconfiguration. As David Sanjek has noted, this cultural practice profoundly blurs the line between creators and consumers of culture, turning listening itself into a platform for creative production and performance.[3]

The cultural practice of sampling meshes very poorly with copyright, the body of law which turns creative expression into private property. The first U.S. sampling case held rapper Biz Markie liable for infringing Gilbert O'Sullivan's copyright in the song "Alone Again (Naturally)." Judge Kevin Duffy began his opinion with scripture—"thou shalt not steal"—and ended it with a referral for criminal prosecution.[4] The law has changed very little in intervening years, despite the burgeoning of sample-based music. As a result, much of today's most innovative cultural production takes place in the shadow of the law: many DJs and other artists produce their work in the knowledge that a copyright holder could sue, that distribution of their work could be enjoined by law, and the sampler held liable for substantial monetary damages.

The law doesn't have to work this way. Judge Duffy's "thou shalt not steal" implies a deeply flawed analogy between physical property and the intellectual property protected by copyright law. Property rights over informational works, such as music, don't work the same way as property rights over land or material goods, for reasons eloquently expressed by Thomas Jefferson:

If nature has made any one thing less susceptible than all others of exclusive property, it is the action of the thinking power called an idea, which an individual may exclusively possess as long as he keeps it to himself; but the moment it is divulged, it forces itself into the possession of everyone, and the receiver cannot dispossess himself of it. Its peculiar character, too, is that no one possesses the less, because every other possesses the whole of it. He who receives an idea from me, receives instruction himself without lessening mine; as he who lights his taper at mine, receives light without darkening me. That ideas should freely spread from one to another over the globe, for the moral and mutual instruction of man, and improvement of his condition, seems to have been peculiarly and benevolently designed by nature, when she made them, like fire, expansible over all space, without lessening their density at any point, and like the air in which we breathe, move, and have our physical being, incapable of confinement or exclusive appropriation. Inventions then cannot, in nature, be a subject of property.[5]

The peculiar properties of intellectual goods—that we can all use them at once without diminishing their value, that we consistently build on elements of older intellectual goods to produce new ones—are reflected in U.S. copyright law. The law limits the rights of intellectual property owners, and grants the public rights to share in the intellectual property's value, in ways that would be unthinkable for tangible property like cars or bushels of wheat. Indeed, many argue—based on the First Amendment and the Constitution's Copyright Clause—that expansive copyright protection of the sort assumed by Judge Duffy in the Biz Markie case exceeds Constitutional parameters. This essay will not detail those arguments. (I refer you to sonic appropriationists Negativland if you are interested in the legal niceties of this issue.[6]) But it will lay out a framework for considering the relationship between copyright, culture, and digital technology.

According to the Constitution, copyright law grants limited rights to authors in order to "Promote the Progress of Science and Useful Arts." The point is to create the economic and legal conditions within which science, learning, and culture can flourish. In pursuit of this goal, a copyright holder is generally granted the right to stop other people from selling copies of her work or derivative works based on it.[7] This ensures that she can get paid, that she will have economic incentives to create and distribute culture. As the Supreme Court has explained, the "Promote the Progress" goal is deeply utilitarian:

[Although] the immediate effect of our copyright law is to secure a fair return for an author's creative labor the ultimate aim is, by this incentive, to stimulate artistic production for the general public good.[8]

"Promot[ing] the Progress" is a goal defined by collective interests, not individual desert. (This utilitarian function of copyright can, in a characteristic Enlightenment-liberal way, be a little harsh. U.S. law has no equivalent to Europe's "moral rights" for a songwriter to control exploitation of her work—she cannot necessarily stop a cruel parody; and if she sells her copyright she retains no power to stop commercial or other uses that she finds distasteful.)

As well as rewarding authors for their work, the law also protects the general public interest in cultural progress by maintaining some public access to old works as raw materials for new ones. All copyrights eventually expire, and the works feed into the public domain where anyone may copy them or prepare derivative works.

In addition, certain reuse rights never belong to the author—they are handed off to the public, and to secondary users, immediately. You are always free to copy the underlying ideas or facts contained in a work; only the author's individual expression is protected by copyright. And you can copy elements of a work that were not original to the author—like 4/4 time, an a-b-a-b rhyme scheme, or a boy-meets-girl plot. Moreover, under the doctrine of "fair use," certain criticism and parodies can copy a work without infringing the work's copyright. When 2 Live Crew mocked Roy Orbison in a goofy cover version of "Pretty Woman," the U.S. Supreme Court held that the fair use doctrine protected the group from copyright liability.

Fair use is not a great legal tool for DJs or appropriationist artists as defendants, though. For one thing, taking a fair use case to court is hugely expensive. For another, it is rarely clear in advance what a court will consider to be fair use, so the defense can be a serious gamble. The 2 Live Crew case illustrates this legal unpredictability: the group's fair use defense was accepted by a federal trial court, then roundly rejected by the appeals court, before being upheld at the Supreme Court level. And the fair use defense has conspicuously failed some artists. Jeff Koons, whose "Banality Exhibition" included a sculpture based on a copyrighted image from a postcard, argued in court that "his sculpture [was] a satire or parody of society at large,"[9] and that he drew on Dadaist and other influences in critiquing "the mass production of commodities and media images [that] has caused a deterioration in the quality of society." He used the postcard's mass-marketed image of a couple holding puppies, he said, in order to "comment critically both on the incorporated object and the political and economic system that created it."[10] The court rejected this defense, holding Koons liable for copyright infringement and suggesting that, "given Koons' willful and egregious behavior, we think [the copyright holder] may be a good candidate for enhanced statutory damages" of $100,000.[11] No fair use case involving music sampling has ever been decided. When U2 sued Negativland for sampling, Negativland wanted to defend on fair use grounds. But the group's record label, aware of the uncertainty and legal pitfalls of the doctrine, settled the case.[12]

Fair use is a conceptually useful doctrine, though, because the statute establishing the doctrine lays out a detailed balancing test. The test asks both how creative or transformative the second work is and whether it displaces the first product in the market.[13] This lets a court get at questions about creativity and questions about money all at once—and these issues tend to blur in the sampling context. Another legal device that effectively merges financial and artistic concerns is the compulsory license for musical compositions (not recordings—just compositions). Anyone who wants to record a new version of a copyrighted composition can do it, as long as he pays the songwriter a fee set by the government. So the owner of the copyright in the composition gets paid whenever someone records a cover—but in most circumstances she can't stop the cover artist or set the terms of payment. Compulsory licensing is one possible legal compromise in allocating rights between artists who sample recordings and artists whose work gets sampled.

The legal limits on copyright holders' power, in particular the fair use doctrine, are legal mechanisms allowing us to engage with, respond to, and reuse information; to turn cultural input into cultural output; to be processors of culture rather than passive consumers. These doctrines protect First Amendment values: if copyright did make it illegal to quote someone in order to criticize what they said, it would run headlong into the First Amendment.[14] And the limiting doctrines serve the Copyright Clause's "Promote the Progress" goal by balancing financial rewards to authors against access rights for the public and for secondary authors who build on elements of the older work.

The balance between the rights of authors and the rights of creative reusers has shifted dramatically over time. Copyright has expanded hugely, particularly in the twentieth century, giving creators ever-greater powers to stop other people from making derivative or secondary uses of their work. The first U.S. Copyright Act, in 1790, only gave authors the right to "print, reprint, publish or vend"—authors had no right to control derivative uses.[15] An 1863 Supreme Court case took a similarly dim view of authorial control over derivative works, holding that Harriet Beecher Stowe could not stop sales of an unauthorized German translation of *Uncle Tom's Cabin*.[16] This holding illustrates a conception, profoundly different from today's, of the reuse rights passed by a copyright holder to her readers. The court explained,

[when an author] has ... given his thoughts, sentiments, knowledge or discoveries to the world ... his conceptions have become the common property of his readers, who cannot be deprived of the use of them.

This nineteenth-century conception of the "the common property of readers" is strikingly robust—according to this holding, a copyright holder grants such significant reuse rights to cultural consumers that they may legally prepare closely derivative works, even translations.

The law has changed greatly since this holding. Stowe's case would come out the other way if litigated today. This expansion of authors' property rights is driven in part by sound economics—authors would have a hard time getting paid if pirates could legally sell derivative works which differed only slightly from the original. But the expansion is also driven by intensive lobbying from major copyright holders, a group which currently prominently includes record companies and movie studios.

Historically, flurries of lobbying and changes in the legal balance between authors' and consumers' rights have tracked changes in popular media and communications technologies. The invention of player piano rolls triggered heated copyright battles, as did the development of photography, the VCR, and digital audio tape. Legislation has consistently favored existing commercial interests over interests newly enabled by technology. In 1905, draft legislation largely ignored the interests of the technologically novel piano roll and phonograph producers. By 1909, these industries had a seat at the bargaining table and helped craft legislation that disfavored the then-nascent motion picture studios. In the 1920s, proposed copyright laws neglected the interests of another emerging group, radio broadcasters.[17] And at no time, of course, have the diffuse interests of the public, or the as-yet-unconceived interests of future creators, been strongly represented in the lobbying process.

But given the Constitutional concerns described above, the interests of the public and of creative reusers of culture should be relevant; the law should be tailored to account for both contemporary technology and contemporary culture. At any given time, legal rules defining what the author can do with a work, and what subsequent creators can do with the work, logically build on two sources (aside from lobbyist pressure): (1) The constitutional mandate to promote progress, and (2) lawmakers' empirical assumptions about how to promote progress—how culture gets made.

The legal question posed by the art discussed in this book is, should digital technologies change lawmakers' empirical predictions about cultural production? Does a change in technology produce a change in how we make culture? And, if we are making culture differently now, how should the law respond?

Marshall McLuhan offers one answer: he says that changes in technology do change culture.[18] For example, he argues, in preliterate societies, a story or song existed only in the moment of being performed—there was no separation of text and performance, and plagiarism was inconceivable, because cultural survival depended on repetition. Writing, the technology of fixing information in physical form, changed our relation to culture. Writing reified information as a thing existing separately from the human being. As a fixed object, the informational work became more easily susceptible to ownership and authorial attribution.[19]

There's clear cause and effect here: a change in technology produces a change in how we use information, and particularly how we think about ownership of information. Another technology, the printing press, is generally credited as the trigger for modern legal copyright protection.

Electronic and eventually digital media introduced another cultural shift. McLuhan identified television as the bringer of post-print culture, disrupting the linearity of previous media. McLuhan's contemporary, Harvard Law Professor Benjamin Kaplan, who dismissed McLuhan as a "professional soothsayer," himself proved almost eerily prescient on this topic.[20] Speaking in 1966, he forecast the rise of networked computers which would allow cheap and instantaneous distribution of text, images, and sound.[21]

This technology, he said, would beget a sea-change in our creative practices and interaction with information, as the "distinction between the author or producer of the stored material and the user of the material [becomes] blurred." In time, he said, such a change will likely "abate feelings of proprietorship and thus modify conceptions of copyright, especially those bearing on plagiarism."[22]

Kaplan's prediction pulls together technology, culture, and copyright law. He suggests, first, that technology will change the way we think about information and produce culture; and, second, that this will bring about a corresponding change in the law.

Looking to the burgeoning production of digitally enabled, sample-based culture, I would say that Kaplan's first prediction has clearly come to pass. Looking to the ever-increasing legal constraints on reuse of prior works, however, I would submit that his second prediction, about the law, has not.

David Toop has written eloquently about the cultural shift brought about by sampling technology. With sampling, he says,

Songs became liquid. They became vehicles for improvisation, or source materials, field recordings almost, that could be reconfigured or remixed to suit the future. In a humiliating way, musicians became technicians, alongside recording engineers, tape ops, editors, and all the other technocratic laboratory assistants cleaning their glasses in the back room. At the front end of the medium was the DJ ... playing music and people as one fluid substance.[23]

Mixmaster Morris put it more succinctly: "We've had sixty, seventy years of making records. That's stage one. Now we sample them."[24]

If this is the way that we make culture now—if, as Chris Cutler suggests, in an age of digital technology "producing is no more than critical consuming"—then perhaps it is time to reconsider how well copyright law's balance of authorial control and public access serves the Constitutional "Promote the Progress" goal.[25] Streamlined compulsory licensing systems and expanded, clarified fair use rights may facilitate contemporary cultural production better than the expansive copyright power currently granted to authors.

Cultural theorists have intelligently theorized the intersection of cultural consumption and cultural production, and provided a framework for thinking about these practices. Dick Hebdige described versioning in Caribbean music as a sort of semiotic democracy: "it implies that no one has the final say. Everybody has a chance to make a contribution. And no one's version is treated as Holy Writ."[26] (Carried by immigrants like Cool DJ Herc, the musical practices which Hebdige describes became part of the early hip-hop culture of the Bronx and an ancestral source of much that is most alive in today's music.) Roland Barthes, too, told us something about the nonpassive consumption of culture when he wrote of "writerly texts," which invite the reader to participate in the production of meaning.[27] Sampling practice may represent more vigorous participation than Barthes envisioned, and suggest that with the right (digital) tools, an intelligent consumer can make any found text "writerly."[28]

Walter Benjamin's works of the 1930s provide especially well-developed theoretical foundations for navigating the relation between technology, semiotic leftovers, and cultural production through consumption. His essay "The Work of Art in the Age of Mechanical Reproduction" suggested that the reproductive technology of film and other media "not only permits . . . but virtually causes mass distribution." As a result, he said, "the distinction between author and public is about to lose its basic character."[29]

Benjamin's writing both about technologies for copying art and about mosaic or collage-format artistic production may provide conceptual tools to explain how, through sampling, an artist can create something new and valuable. His own major uncompleted work, the *Arcades Project*, was to have been entirely sample based. Benjamin explained:

Method of this project: literary montage. I needn't say anything. Merely show. I will purloin no valuables, appropriate no ingenious formulations. But the rags, the refuse—these I will not inventory, but allow, in the only way possible, to come into their own: by making use of them.[30]

In one critic's description, the mosaic model of the *Arcades Project* is a construction of a "history and politics ... which clings tenaciously to the fragment, the miniature, the stray citation, but which impacts these fragments upon each other to politically explosive effect."[31]

Drawing on Benjamin (and oversimplifying, inevitably) we can derive at least two explanations of what is new and creative about sample-based production.[32]

The first point is about collage as a technique: the selection, arrangement, and juxtaposition of the found bits of prior culture is the art. The fragments "impact upon each other to explosive effect"—through the artist's selection and arrangement, she generates novel information. Such collage-based creative production is well established in visual art. In the realm of music, musical sampling artists like Negativland and Canadian plunderphonics creator John Oswald practice analogous techniques with sonic detritus.[33]

The second point derived from Benjamin is that it may be a culturally productive act simply to discover and draw attention to a fragment of text, image, or sound. Part of the mosaic- or collage-creator's art lies in the very process of rescuing the fragment from obscurity and showing it to people. This Benjaminian urge to rescue and re-present culture is conspicuous throughout sample-based genres, and is illustrated in the following description of DJs making organized raids on collective culture—that is, going to record stores. This comes from Jeff Chang, aka DJ Zen, who describes feeling outclassed as a crate-digger by members of the now defunct Solesides collective.

There's nothing worse to them than the kind of guy who won't bid his rent and food money for a Tanzanian Funk 45 or the impossible-to-get Invaders LP. The kind of person who doesn't scour thin phonebooks from foothill counties and find teeny used record stores owned by unwashed proprietors who look like trolls. The kind of person who doesn't know where and when all the record conventions within 1000 miles are going down, and what hour before dawn to show up in a miner's light helmet and a backpack.[34]

This is serious pursuit of cultural fragments—on par with the great-granddaddy of all crate diggers, Grandmaster Flash, who claims to have performed with "something like 45" crates of records behind him.[35] The critical and commercial success of these artists suggests that their compulsion to collect, to reconfigure, to re-present prior recorded sound is finding a receptive audience. To listeners, crate-digging is a highly legitimate foundation for significant and innovative cultural production.

McLuhan gives us a conceptual framework for explaining how technology affects cultural production; Benjamin and others give us analytical tools for describing how production based on copying can be creative and important. A glance at the top forty or visit to a record store gives us evidence of how widespread sampling practice is. All of this evidence strongly supports Benjamin Kaplan's claim that technology will change the way we make culture and disrupt the neat division between cultural producers and consumers.

But the DJs and artists who make culture this way still legally expose themselves to civil and even criminal liability. That brings us to Kaplan's second prediction: that copyright law will adapt to this new mode of production. This prediction has not come to pass. Indeed, so far, copyright law has reacted only to the increased piracy threat posed by digital technology, and not to the technology's creative potential.

Very few music sampling cases have gone to court. Those that have—such as the Biz Markie case—have come out so poorly for the sampler that few musicians would now choose to defend sampling before a judge. So instead of a body of carefully reasoned and Constitutionally constrained case law, we are left with compelling precedent of a different sort: the legendary out-of-court settlements—De La Soul versus the Turtles, Vanilla Ice versus Queen and David Bowie, the Beastie Boys versus everyone.

The law, by creating a background regime of absolute entitlements for copyright holders, creates a very bad bargaining situation for the well-meaning DJ who actually tries to comply with the law and clear her samples. And it creates an impossible situation for acts like John Oswald or Negativland, who (1) sample lots of artists who are very hard to track down, making transaction costs of licensing impossibly high; (2) tend to irritate the artists they sample, making refusal of permission quite likely; and (3) aren't making much money.

It has been my contention that digital technology allows us to interact with information and make culture in a new way. Copyright law should respond to this cultural shift if it is to serve its Constitutional "Promote the Progress" goal and the First Amendment's free expression goal. It's not that we've stopped making music the old way—people still sing and always will, people still play acoustic guitars and Hammond organs, and those people should be able to sell their work and make a living. And it's not that all sampling should be free—very few people would argue that Puffy Combs should not have had to pay for his "Every Breath You Take" sample. But some sampling is so clearly original and expressive, and so harmless to sales of the original work, that it should be free—either on fair use grounds or pure First Amendment grounds. And creative reuse of copyrighted material could be enabled, and legal chilling effects on new musical voices alleviated, through a streamlined compulsory licensing system for sampling. The law should move in this direction in order to adapt to technology and the way culture gets made today, in order to serve the collective cultural progress goal that copyright is designed to facilitate.

But the law is in fact moving in the opposite direction. I will close with a brief overview of recent legal responses to digital technology and digital culture. Major copyright holders have successfully argued to Congress that digital technology and the Internet vastly increase the threat of piracy, making greater protection necessary. They are partly right—a technology which enables free and instantaneous transmission of millions of copies is a very real threat to copyright holders. But the situation is more complicated than that. The same technology also lowers copying and distribution costs for legal sales, which can decrease costs for the copyright holder and help her turn a profit on her work. And on the Internet, the same technology that facilitates piracy also facilitates detection and prosecution of piracy. Moreover, individuals' noncommercial copying and sharing of copyrighted music—which is now labeled piracy by the record industry, particularly if carried out online—has traditionally been far outside the province of copyright law and enforcement. It's not that digital and Internet piracy is not a legitimate threat—but the furor surrounding it is, in the words of copyright professor Jessica Litman, "about 50 percent hype."[36]

The legislative response, however, has been quite real. In the Sonny Bono Copyright Term Extension Act, Congress extended the term of copyright to life plus 70 years, or 95 years for corporate works. (The original copyright term, in 1790, was 14 years extendible to 28 years.) This extension enraged online publishers and others whose business it was to bring public domain works—often works long out of print and unavailable to consumers—into print or online distribution.

And with the Digital Millennium Copyright Act (DMCA), Congress gave copyright holders legal protection that potentially eviscerates consumers' fair use rights. The DMCA established both civil and criminal liability for anyone who breaks through encryption or other "digital fences" surrounding a copyrighted work.[37] The law also criminalizes distribution of programming tools for breaking such encryption. Under the DMCA, it doesn't matter if the defendant actually infringed copyright—if she bypassed the encryption, she broke the law. If the encryption wraps up both a public domain work and a copyrighted one—like a Shakespeare play with a new introduction—and the hacker only copies from Shakespeare, she is still liable under the DMCA. She is also liable if she hacks the encryption in order to make fair use of the material—a film teacher could violate the DMCA by making a montage of clips from movies on encrypted, copy-protected DVDs.

The DMCA has come under heavy attack from computer programmers who work on encryption, because it can prevent them from developing and sharing their work—a restriction which, in addition to being inconvenient, arguably violates both the First Amendment rights of code writers and the "Promote the Progress" goal of copyright. (The DMCA got a lot of bad press when the Recording Industry Association of America threatened to sue Princeton Computer Science Professor Ed Felten for presenting his research on digital music encryption at a scientific conference. Although the RIAA backed off of that case, it reserves the right to sue Felten's graduate student assistants for publishing their encryption research, should they attempt to do so.) But the DMCA is also potentially significant for cultural producers of the sort discussed in this article. By banning decryption tools, it may make reuse of digital format recordings much more difficult as a practical matter. And by banning decryption, it raises the number of laws a DJ may break, and the amount of legal liability she may face, every time she uses an uncleared sample.

The DMCA is just one of several legal shifts that may effectively expand protection so far as to seriously undermine legal reuses (such as fair use) and currently illegal but interesting reuses (such as those carried out by innumerable DJs and artists). Another emerging body of law permits copyright owners to legally bind consumers to the terms of "click-wrap" licenses on digital media.[38] By clicking "yes" and using the copyrighted work, the user legally agrees to comply with small print which may prohibit fair use and even, in some cases, purport to prohibit public criticism of the copyrighted work. Yet another law—as yet unenacted, but working its way through Congress— would compel manufacturers to make computers and other devices comply with technical measures for protecting copyright.

These legal changes respond to one aspect of digital technology, the cheap and easy piracy which it enables. But in so doing, they impede new modes of cultural production enabled by those same technologies. Legal rights to turn cultural consumption into cultural production are eroding at the very moment that such production is becoming possible for large numbers of artists. In legally foreclosing this entire realm of digital culture, copyright law disserves its "Promote the Progress" goal under the Constitution.[39]

Notes

1. Chris Cutler, "Plunderphonics," *Musicworks* 59 (1994), 14.

2. John Perry Barlow, "Selling Wine without Bottles: The Economy of Mind on the Global Net" (1993), available at http://www.eff.org//Publications/John_Perry_Barlow/HTML/idea_economy_article.html.

3. David Sanjek, "'Don't Have to DJ No More': Sampling and the 'Autonomous' Creator," *10 Cardozo Arts & Entertainment Law Journal* 607 (1992).

4. *Grand Upright Music Ltd. v. Warner Brothers Records,* 780 F.Supp. 182 (1992), available at http://detritus.net/rhizome/legal/bizmarkie.txt.

5. Letter from Thomas Jefferson to Isaac McPherson, August 13, 1813, quoted in *The Complete Jefferson,* ed. Saul K. Padover (Duell, Sloan and Pearce 1943), 1011, 1015.

6. See www.negativland.com.

7. Copyright in music is complicated because there are separate copyrights over the underlying composition, on the one hand, and any individual sound recording, on the other. The law is complexly tailored to allow these two sets of rights to coexist. Generally speaking, however, a copyright owner's rights are defined as follows by Section 106 of the Copyright Act (see http://www.copyright.gov/title17/92chap1.html):

Subject to sections 107 through 121 [which create a number of exceptions], the owner of copyright under this title has the exclusive rights to do and to authorize any of the following:

(1) to reproduce the copyrighted work in copies or phonorecords;
(2) to prepare derivative works based upon the copyrighted work;
(3) to distribute copies or phonorecords of the copyrighted work to the public by sale or other transfer of ownership, or by rental, lease, or lending;
(4) in the case of literary, musical, dramatic, and choreographic works, pantomimes, and motion pictures and other audiovisual works, to perform the copyrighted work publicly;
(5) in the case of literary, musical, dramatic, and choreographic works, pantomimes, and pictorial, graphic, or sculptural works, including the individual images of a motion picture or other audiovisual work, to display the copyrighted work publicly; and

(6) in the case of sound recordings, to perform the copyrighted work publicly by means of a digital audio transmission.

8. *Twentieth Century Music Corp. v. Aiken*, 422 U.S. 151, 155 (1975).

9. *Rogers v. Koons*, 960 F.2d 301, 309 (2d Cir. 1992).

10. Ibid.

11. 17 U.S.C. §504 (1992).

12. See Negativland, *Fair Use: The Story of the Letter U and the Numeral 2* (Seeland-Negativland, 1995).

13. 17 U.S.C. §107 provides:

Notwithstanding the provisions of sections 106 and 106A, the fair use of a copyrighted work, including such use by reproduction in copies or phonorecords or by any other means specified by that section, for purposes such as criticism, comment, news reporting, teaching (including multiple copies for classroom use), scholarship, or research, is not an infringement of copyright. In determining whether the use made of a work in any particular case is a fair use the factors to be considered shall include—

(1) the purpose and character of the use, including whether such use is of a commercial nature or is for nonprofit educational purposes;
(2) the nature of the copyrighted work;
(3) the amount and substantiality of the portion used in relation to the copyrighted work as a whole; and
(4) the effect of the use upon the potential market for or value of the copyrighted work.

The fact that a work is unpublished shall not itself bar a finding of fair use if such finding is made upon consideration of all the above factors.

14. The Supreme Court, frustratingly, has never clarified the relationship between the fair use doctrine and the First Amendment. Its clearest statement on this point so far is this: "In view of the First Amendment protections already embodied in the Copyright Act's distinction between copyrightable expression and uncopyrightable facts and ideas, and the latitude for scholarship and comment traditionally afforded by fair use, we see no warrant for expanding the doctrine of fair use [as defendants in the case asked the court to do]." *Harper & Row Publishers, Inc. v. Nation Enterprises*, 471 U.S. 539, 560 (1985).

15. See discussion in Jessica Litman's excellent book, *Digital Copyright*, (Prometheus Books, 2001), at p. 22.

16. *Stowe v. Thomas*, 23 F. Cas. 201 (C.C.E.D. Pa. 1853).

17. Litman, *Digital Copyright*, 46.

18. Marshall McLuhan, *The Gutenberg Galaxy* (University of Toronto Press, 1962); Marshall McLuhan and Quentin Fiore, *The Medium Is the Massage* (Random House, 1967).

19. See Doug Brent, "Oral Knowledge, Typographic Knowledge, Electronic Knowledge: Speculations on the History of Ownership," available at http://www.virtualschool .edu/mon/Economics/BrentHistoryOfOwnership.html, discussing Walter Ong, *Orality and Literacy: The Technologizing of the Word* (Routledge, 1982), in turn drawing heavily on McLuhan's work (but adding considerably more anthropological data).

20. Benjamin Kaplan, *An Unhurried View of Copyright* (Columbia University Press, 1967), 118.

21. Kaplan described "full-scale 'on-line' operations with computers ... linked or integrated systems or networks of computers capable of storing faithful simulacra of the entire treasure of the accumulated knowledge and artistic production of past ages.... The systems will have prodigious capacity for manipulating the store in useful ways, for selecting portions [including sound and graphics files] of it upon call and transmitting them any distance...." Ibid., 119. He suggested that the medium could be the death-knell of copyright as we know it, as "the ingenuity which devises the systems will no doubt be capable of welding-in bookkeeping apparatus" to bill on a per-access basis. Ibid., 121.

22. Ibid., 117.

23. David Toop, *Ocean of Sound* (Serpent's Tail, 1995), 43.

24. Ibid., 52.

25. Cutler, "Plunderphonics," 14.

26. Dick Hebdige, *Cut 'n' Mix: Culture, Identity, and Caribbean Music* (Methuen, 1987), 14.

27. Roland Barthes, *S/Z* (Hill and Wang, 1970).

28. Of course, with the right attitude an artist may not need any tools at all. Consider, e.g., Marcel Duchamp's transformation of a urinal into a "writerly text" in creating his *Fountain* sculpture.

29. Walter Benjamin, "The Work of Art in the Age of Mechanical Reproduction," in *Illuminations* (Schocken, 1969), 217, 244, 232.

30. Walter Benjamin, *The Arcades Project*, trans. Howard Eiland and Kevin McLaughlin (Harvard University Press, 1999), N1a, 8.

31. Terry Eagleton, *Ideology of the Aesthetic* (Blackwell, 1990), 338.

32. For Benjamin, these two points go together: as Terry Eagleton puts it, Benjamin's model "revolutioniz[es] the relation between parts and whole"; the idea's "constituents light each other up in all their contradictoriness" in a way that "safeguards particularity but fissures identity." Ibid.

33. See http://www.negativland.com/changing_copyright.html/.

34. Liner notes from *Solesides Greatest Bumps* (various artists, Quannum Projects, 2001).

35. David Toop, *The Rap Attack: African Jive to New York Hip-Hop* (Pluto Press, 1984), 62, 73.

36. Litman, *Digital Copyright*, 25.

37. 17 U.S.C. §1201.

38. The Uniform Computer Information Transactions Act, enacted in some states, makes click-wrap licenses enforceable. Many courts have held them enforceable under existing contract law.

39. A version of this essay was first delivered at Duke Law School's "Music and Theft" conference in May of 2002.

Beth Coleman and Howard Goldkrand

We would see them show up, these weird distended figures tautly held by their ears. They brought a phalanx of miniature units through which energy was dispersed in sound waves. Overdeveloped ears, they heard with their whole bodies, swaying to the subsonic bass, their slender frames bowed slightly toward the source. Their figures made a gathering of "U"s and "S"s. With multiple sources in attendance, the scene would become some obtuse ballet mechanique, all units moving in an encrypted cross-pattern. As the signals cross and merge new algorithms would form, hanging in the air, then disperse in the birth of a new one. It dawned on us that sound began to creep away from the deserted construction site where we had gathered. Volume instead of growing became inverted in the pink noise cancellation pattern they danced. There was a legend for the pattern, we'd heard, but no one had yet to be able to read it. Secret agents of the crowd, they would show up at the train tracks, in the street, by monuments on holidays and bend the sound of the throng. Their machines ate the urban ambient of metal-in-motion.

Pink noise rests somewhere on the spectrum between white and black. White noise gives you the intensity of a burn. The vanilla factor is a recognized experience among the noise terrorists. The sound is grown in a self-regenerative lattice that mirrors cellular reproduction. One thing fractures and its breaking creates a synthesis. The synthesis makes a mutation, and so on. Like the wailing of an explosion, it crumbles apart in the ear like glass turned back to sand. The sonic build comes from the acceleration of the process, i.e. sound breaks

Figures 14.1, 14.2, 14.3

Mobile Stealth Unit (Pink Noise) Series 002, Beth Coleman and Howard Goldkrand, 1999, mixed-media sculpture (workman tricycle, sound system, Web camera, laptop, software, electronics). Pink noise, the parenthetical in the piece's title, describes sound behaving not as content but as an investigation of context. Pink noise is the name of audio used in tuning sound systems by engineers. It is a signal sent out in frequencies to test the architectural-acoustic dimensions of a space. *Mobile Stealth Unit* is designed as an investigation of the dynamic space created between sound source and listener, between remote audiovisual input and local. In the case of the *MSU,* pink noise describes an investigation of space in the form of a two-way transmission: sound circulates out to the local listener, impacting that immediate environment, while the remote viewer manipulates a virtual visual field from the Net, run concurrent with audio broadcast. Different yet simultaneous spaces are charted and interlinked by the double transmission.

the time associated with witnessing the world as a simple data input by encoding a complex presence of phase relations and harmonies.

open and then open again, continually—that is, continually until entropy catches up with forward motion. The space built from this motion is a clearing ground. Everything gets dead. It builds until the ear reaches stasis and all sound floats. The body tingles in the stillness. The walls of sound press in, filling every bit. The ear and the body discuss the demateral world. Two squirrels chattering over nuts.

Black noise gets you located in time. Immersed in invisible yet physical information. Time code variable, but always set to lead. Witness—*The Mobile Stealth Unit*; antenna, process filter, generator and transmitter. Boom-Biff—Boom-Biff—Bap 8-bit talking drums, fat tree stump speakers sending a signal frequency of which there is only the dynamics of feeling and not words or sounds. Felt again and remembered. Dub tensions and release. An architecture of continuous fragmentation. There they were rockin' hacked hearing aids with remote control processors and dumb, double wide smiles. They look like they're listening to you, but fer real, in their ears, it is you sounding like the teacher from *Peanuts* sucking helium. Good Luck. Black Noise. Hence the smile, intoxicated with witnessing the world as a sample data input. Re-encoding a complex presence of phase relations and harmonics.
—Journal entry 794001, Betty Mann Chronicles

Lucy Walker

Moby: ... everything about the music business is about to change. The way that music is made has changed completely and it will continue to change. It's become so much more egalitarian, democratic, and inexpensive. The way that music is sold, distributed, listened to. The role that music serves in most people's lives. On the one hand music is so much more ubiquitous, but on the other it's so much cheaper. And so it's hard to judge the current state of popular music because every aspect of it is changing. So, making predictions—I have no idea. The only prediction I can make is that music has become so much more egalitarian and ubiquitous and the means of production have become available to almost anybody. Anyone with access to a computer can make music now. You download the software from the Internet and ten minutes later you're making music that sounds just as good as anything you might hear in a nightclub.

Lucy Walker: But if you do think about what is being heard in clubs or the charts—how's that changing, where's that going?

Moby: Well, right now we're in a strange position where if you look at album charts in the States, the records that are being sold are being sold to people who for the most part don't have access or the inclination to download music or burn CDs. So there's this kind of sad irony that good records for the most part tend to get burned and downloaded and the bad records tend to get bought. And eventually the record business is probably finished. It's on its last legs, and within the next five years it'll either change beyond all recognition or it'll just end. I don't see anyway around that.

...

Lucy: Is there a way in which you can feel the mainstream catching up with you?

Moby: I'm a quite utter weird anomaly. I'm a little bald guy from the Lower East Side who makes music in his bedroom. There is no precedent for someone like me going on to become successful—I don't sing particularly well, I don't dance particularly well, I don't have too many pop music skills. My success is anomalous. If you're to make a sort of like naturalistic analogy—I'm the mutation, the plant that starts growing thorns.

Lucy: But to pick your evolution imagery in terms of memes, it seems to me that your art of success that you've innovated is very interesting in [that] you've successfully propagated [it].

Moby: But it's weird. And I feel it's available to just about anyone, but no one is willing to work at it. I mean, for example, the Chemical Brothers. I think they make great records—when they go to a country on tour, they'll do one hour of interviews. You know, most musicians have a rule that they'll only do an hour of interviews per country or maybe two hours of interviews per country if that. And that's one thing I learned from people in the pop world is if you want to reach people you have to make the effort. I can't expect people to beat a path to my door. I have to reach them. What that means is in the last five months doing 1,200 interviews in almost every country in the Western world.

Lucy: But then your marketing is unique . . . ?

Moby: And also overcoming your liabilities. You know like if I looked like Enrique Iglesias—he sells records because he's attractive. The music's nothing to write home about; he sells records because he's a very good-looking man. And the fact that 80 percent of his audience is female—they're buying his records because he's a very attractive man, he's very handsome. I don't have that going for me, I have to figure out, what do I have? Like, adaptation to your environment. If you don't have fur to keep yourself warm in the winter you have to figure out how to build fire; if you can't fly high to see your food you have to figure out how to climb trees. It's overcoming liabilities and making up for shortcomings.

...

Lucy: But when you made, for example, your less popular albums—did you still want to engage people then or was there any kind of a change between that and *Play*?

Moby: Well, in terms of success, I never expected to have—I mean success for me was selling 5,000 records. So I made this record *Animal Rights* in 1996 and by most people's estimates it failed. It sold about 120,000 copies worldwide. But to me 120,000 copies—that's more than my favorite punk rock bands ever sold so I thought it was a success. But it was an aggressive, confrontational record and after that with *Play* and *18* I wanted to make records that were no longer aggressive and confrontational. I wanted to make music that could find its way into people's lives. I'd much rather be invited to a party than complain about not going.

Lucy: And when you made *Play*, did it not occur to you that the work was really good and that the work was something a lot more people might find accessible?

Moby: I thought it was the end of my career. I thought that no one would like it and that my record company would drop me and that I was going to have to figure out something else to do for the rest of my life.

...

Lucy: Changing the subject, how does sampling relate to what you've been able to do?

Moby: Sampling is overcoming my weaknesses and liabilities. Because at an early age I learned that I didn't have a great singing voice...I have an adequate singing voice for certain things but if I wanted to have really wonderful vocal performances on my records, I had to get other people to sing them. Or had to sample other performances. So it's like, you know, necessity being the mother of invention. I had—and the same thing, like I was working out of home studios, so in order to have big amazing drum sounds I had to sample other people's drum sounds, in order to have really great orchestral things sometimes I would have to sample other people's ideas. So without sampling, I probably never would have been particularly successful.

Lucy: And in terms of some of the samples that you used, the most famous example being the blues samples, you're taking obscure work and taking it to an audience, recontextualizing it in a massively more popular way exposing so many more people to it than—thousands of more people than were originally exposed—

Moby: Which is cool, that's not always—when I sample old things it's not because they're old, it's because they're compelling.

Lucy: Not that that's the aim, but it's interesting that you're again being this conduit for lesser-known work.

Moby: But almost accidentally. It's cool if those are the ramifications, like with *Play* selling ten million records: if one of the ramifications of that is more people get exposed to old African-American music that's wonderful, and if one of the ramifications is that suddenly people are more open to more experimental types of electronic music that's wonderful. But neither one of those things was my intention in making the record. My intention was just to make a nice record.

Lucy: Do you ever think now that you have this big and enthused audience you can take them to places that they might not go if they didn't love you so much already? Can you now take your audience—are there less accessible ideas or types of music that you do that you're excited to invite this crowd along now that you have this crowd?

Moby: I never know. It's like, again—I'm never trying to be avant-garde, I'm never trying to be experimental, and I'm just trying to make beautiful music. I like the idea of broadening people's horizons, but I'd rather make a beautiful, conventional song that doesn't broaden someone's horizons than make a mediocre, unconventional song that does broaden someone's horizons, that is challenging and difficult—I don't want to be challenging and difficult. I want to make nice records, which is probably the least cool thing I could probably say in the context of this book.

Lucy: Is there a way in which you feel sort of defensive about, because you are this anomaly—do you feel a need to defend that position?

Moby: Maybe not defend so much as explain, try and explain. I got a lot of criticism for letting my music be used in movies, and TV shows and advertisements; everyone just assumed that the reason I did it was so I could make a lot of money, and you would think if that was the reason I would have spent some of the money, but the whole reason I did it was because I wanted to reach a larger audience. And I wanted people to hear my music.

Lucy: What did you do with the money?

Moby: It's all in the bank.

Lucy: What are you going to do with it?

Moby: I don't know. Buy a house or something. Buy an island full of monkeys and train them all how to work automatic weapons and defend the island.

Lucy: Do you feel there's a difference licensing your music for a car commercial than licensing your music for a PSA?

Moby: It's all subjective. The thing I find fascinating about television ... the way in which people experience media, whether it's movies or TV shows or stereos or whatever, visual images are always experienced on a flat screen whether it's a TV or an in-flight monitor or a movie screen, it's visual information coupled with audio information. And audio information almost always comes out of two speakers. So, there isn't any objective way to establish a hierarchy of audiovisual information; it's purely subjective. Because it's intangible. You can establish an objective hierarchy for food because you can say that an orange has more nutritional value than, say, a Twizzler, and there are objective criteria to back up your claim. With audiovisual information, it's purely subjective.

Lucy: But you do have a lot of opinions about car culture or the environmental politics and so on.

Moby: But what I'm saying is that they're my opinions and they're very subjective. There are certain things I'd never allow my music to be allowed to sell—tobacco and meat products and weapons of mass destruction—but at the same time it's just information and people can tackle it at some hermeneutic level however they so choose.

Joseph Lanza

"Easy listening"—a term that is supposed to describe sweet and relaxing music—continues to elicit cacophonous controversy. This is particularly true in recent times, when the art of playing soft instrumental salutes to old standards and pop hits has incurred prejudicial crosswinds from an otherwise disparate community of musicians and music critics. As dysfunctional as they usually are in forging any kind of consensus, classical, country, jazz, R&B, and rock purists can at least break bread over the assumption that easy listening is "beneath" them, particularly the kind that indulges in the sound of lush, melodic, and unabashedly sentimental strings. In an era when the crowd salivates for jazz improvisation or the ability to sound "raw," such high-gloss orchestral pop has become a guilty pleasure.

Why, amid an urban din of boom boxes, car alarms, and squealing cell phones, would anyone object to the sweet inspiration of shimmering violins playing dulcet melodies? The sizable number of those who enjoyed easy listening during its heyday of the 1950s, '60s, and early '70s would find such a question bewildering. A glance at *Billboard's Top Pop Albums* tells why. Among the instrumental titles, orchestral pop proved to be the most popular, with names like Ferrante & Teicher, Mantovani, and the Jackie Gleason Orchestra boasting a healthy amount of best-selling titles.

The *Billboard* Top 40 singles charts also commanded their salient share of orchestral pop hits, even with the onslaught of rock releases. This suggests that, in the otherwise turbulent '60s, there was once an unofficial musical consensus that is entirely absent from today's tight niche marketing and "multicultural" pretenses. In a climate teeming with conflicting musical forms, orchestral pop supplied a language through which most music lovers could form a common bond. Movie scores used it; so did Broadway original cast albums. Then there were the many hits by vocalists like Perry Como, Johnny Mathis, and Frank Sinatra that featured the mellifluous backings of arrangers like Hugo Winterhalter, Percy Faith, Gordon Jenkins, and Nelson Riddle. And it did not stop there! Even when the British invasion changed many of pop music's rules, artists like Chad & Jeremy, Marianne Faithfull, and Petula Clark released ballads wrapped in pop orchestral blankets.

Velvety violins serenaded much of modern music's history. In many ways, the shimmering strings of Mantovani and Percy Faith were another step in an ongoing light orchestra tradition dating back to late nineteenth-century Romantic composers like Tchaikovsky and Debussy. So-called "serious" musicians (averse to "commercial" music and pop culture anyway) have been especially unkind to music considered too sentimental or "schmaltzy." Even the average record buyer, relatively unschooled in classical music niceties, is now prone to apply knee-jerk snob standards when a full string orchestra plays "The Way We Were" instead of Samuel Barber's "Adagio." But to understand some of orchestral pop's woebegone place in the pantheon of aesthetic correctness, one need only look to the troubled parallel history of the Hollywood score.

Stories abound about film music composers browbeaten by academic peers for the apparent sin of using intricate orchestras to play simple, emotionally accessible tunes. Yet, under the batons of movie music mavens like Max Steiner and Victor Young, huge symphony-style ensembles dedicated to massaging viewer hearts and minds helped forge an entertainment empire. Like most easy-listening instrumentals, many outstanding film themes also command a subtle power through understatement or—to be more precise—underarrangement. This has impelled some musicians to feel a bit ambivalent about this relatively subservient role.

Several film composers have shared profound words about this self-imposed self-effacement. Aaron Copland once claimed that film composers have an "ungrateful" task since their music is more like sonic wallpaper and not the center of attention. In Tony Thomas's book *Film Score: The Art and Craft of Movie Music*, Dimitri Tiomkin claimed that: "The [film] composer, by providing pleasant melodic music, can direct attention from what the make-up artist could not hide." Some could not resist referring to their work in nonmusical terms, alluding to movie music as a form of interior or sartorial design. While Tiomkin invoked the beautician, Jerry Goldsmith has likened his craft to that of a tailor fashioning melodies and rhythms to conform to each film's fabric. Accordingly, some of the most remembered and successful orchestral pop recordings have been movie themes. Obvious examples are Steiner's "Theme from *A Summer Place*," Henry Mancini's "Moon River" from *Breakfast at Tiffany's*, and Michel Legrand's "Theme from *Summer of '42*."

Orchestral pop was also vibrant with the sweet dance bands of the '20s and early '30s. Along with their smooth waltz beats, bandleaders like Guy Lombardo and Isham Jones would often temper their fox trots with violin contoured waltz beats. These celestial serenades played behind crooners like Russ Columbo, Rudy Vallee, and (post–Rhythm Boys) Bing Crosby. But ever since the jazz age, countervailing trends started to reject what Irving Berlin once called that "simple melody." Jazz critics like John Hammond took a fancy to the perceived rebellion of "hot" music and dismissed more sugary strains as "smooth and soporific." Their efforts grew more feverish with the advent of swing.

By the mid-'40s, when swing had already shown signs of waning, big band veteran Paul Weston applied similar symphonic wallpaper principles when he released a 10″ album called *Music for Dreaming*. Weston triumphed with his first excursion into what journalists and marketers soon called "mood music." Into the '50s, his "creamy-on-the-melody" style set the trend for other arrangers and conductors. When assessing the evolution of the form, Weston remains one of the most interesting of mood maestros, precisely because he is arguably the founder of the actual "easy listening" tag. After overhearing a fan declare that his music "makes mighty easy listening," he subsequently released an album forthrightly titled *Music for Easy Listening* and spawned a category that assumed a life of its own. In many respects, it has been a very fitting description. "Easy listening" implies both the crucial role of the listener and the professional manner by which the recordings are sufficiently unobtrusive for the background yet impeccably arranged to invite more focused enjoyment.

Other label moguls saw mood music as an opportunity to optimize new postwar audio gimmicks. Once CBS Labs introduced the 12″ LP in 1948, Columbia Records' Goddard Lieberson started by emphasizing classical music and show tunes, but he soon gave mood music an additional boost with releases from Percy Faith and Andre Kostelanetz, both of whom had already established themselves as light music conductors for radio. For mood music, this long-playing format could spin uninterrupted for at least twenty minutes, giving home listeners more of an opportunity to suspend disbelief and escape into the ambiance of albums like *Percy Faith Plays Continental Music* or Kostelanetz's *Lure of the Tropics*.

Meanwhile, England's Decca label had pioneered "full-frequency range recordings" by placing studio microphones in optimal spots. One of Decca's innovators, the Italian-born conductor Annunzio Paolo Mantovani, employed this equipment for his famous "cascading strings"—a sound that offered a quiet revolution in high-fidelity history. This began by the dawn of the 1950s, when London Records (Decca's American label) asked for an album of waltzes. Mantovani granted that request, so long as he could go one waltz step further. He adopted fellow British composer-arranger Ronald Binge's idea that a forty-piece orchestra could produce an echo-delay if each violin's note overlapped the other. The resulting manipulation of strings re-created the airy acoustics of a cathedral.

Mantovani's foray soon earned him the endearing sobriquet "Niagara Falls of Fiddles." He made a profound impression on American listeners, especially with his 1951 hit recording of the silent movie theme "Charmaine." Like all "mood music," the Mantovani sound gained momentum with hi-fi and stereophonic advances. As his stringsweeps accompanied the countermelodies of accordion, mandolin, and guitar, Mantovani put a refreshing gloss over songs like "Some Enchanted Evening," "September in the Rain," and his own composition "Cara Mia" (which Jay & the Americans later turned into a pop hit). In time, Mantovani would become the first to sell a million stereo records in America and garner over fifty albums in *Billboard*'s Top 50 between 1953 and 1972.

In contrast to Mantovani's cathedralized acoustics, Percy Faith's strings sounded more concentrated. They were set at a higher emotional pitch and often accented with sprightlier tempos. He could also create an effervescent effect with several violinists plucking their violins and violas in unison, a style that David Rose helped articulate back in the '40s with his madcap "Holiday for Strings." In his greatest moments, Faith engineered a mood of weepy romanticism. He once stated back in the '50s that his goal was "satisfying the millions of devotees of that pleasant American institution known as the quiet evening at home, whose idea of perfect relaxation is the easy chair, slippers and good music." Even when he released albums dedicated to Latin rhythms, Faith's orchestra tended to take a lighter-than-air approach, demonstrating how easy-listening artists distinguished themselves from more raucous instrumentalists like Perez Prado.

Faith also got an audio boost from Columbia's "360 Sound," achieving a fuller, more intoxicating effect on albums like *Exotic Strings*. Expanding into what the liner notes boast as "fifty virtuoso strings," his Percy Faith Strings mixed tropical melodies like "Poinciana" with immediately recognizable standards like "Dancing in the Dark." Faith gave his violins, violas, and basses an extra antigravity finesse by adding bells, finger-cymbals, and other dazzling rhythm instruments, guaranteeing a "mood of moonlight, romance and rapture."

At Capitol, meanwhile, Weston had left for Columbia, allowing Jackie Gleason to take time out from his Ralph Kramden persona to become the label's new mood music doyen. His role as an actual conductor is one of dispute, but he did at least provide his orchestra with the right inspiration. (One biographer claimed that Gleason once asked his studio players to approximate "the sound of pissing off a high bridge into a teacup.") Albums like *Music for Lovers Only* and *Music, Martinis, and Memories* combined a bed of fluffy strings with a featured instrument, usually Bobby Hackett's trumpet. But the Gleason series proved more enchanting as the instruments got more varied and more surreal.

Aphrodisia is among the best of the Gleason offerings. It features what the notes call "two complete string orchestras," each one dominating the left and right speakers respectively. The cream in the middle consists of "Wild Bill" Davis's moody organ on songs like "Pastel Flame" and "Pink Chiffon"—titles credited to "The Great One" himself in dedication to "the pursuit, fulfillment and enjoyment of romance." Into the late '60s, Gleason put out *The "Now" Sound for Today's Lovers*—all gossamer interpretations of pop ballads like "Can't Take My Eyes Off You," seasoned with sitar, tabla, an "African finger piano," and, of course, the full orchestra.

In 1955, Nelson Riddle had already proven his affinity for sonic sugardust with the sweeping fiddles, lithe piano, and soothing chorus on his number-one single "Lisbon Antigua." By the early '60s, Capitol proudly released several albums featuring Riddle conducting and arranging instrumental collections with special themes. On albums like *Sea of Dreams* and *Love Tide*, he took a healthy break from the rat-pack swing associated with his arrangements for

Frank Sinatra. He instead opted for a softer, more introspective approach to old favorites as well as a few of his own compositions. His self-penned title song from *Love Tide* demonstrates moody and tender writing at its best. The album *Love Is a Game of Poker* added the brain-tickling juxtaposition of reverberating strings, bells, and chimes to make a song like "Witchcraft" as supernatural as its subject.

At this time, Capitol also had launched its "Staged for Sound" series, showcasing its "full dimensional stereo." Renowned British arranger, composer, and conductor Norrie Paramor applied his trusty "thirty-three strings" on *Strings! Stages for Sound*, an album of richly textured melodies whose moods range from punchy to haunting. The blend of violins, violas, and cellos alternately glide, tremble, cascade, and leap, along with guitar, piano, celeste, harps, flutes, trumpet, and a subtle rhythm section. One track, an original composition called "Janny," sends the strings and the guitar from one part of the stereophonic stage to another in (what the liner notes aptly describe as) a "walkative" manner.

Top 40 radio was also a prime orchestral pop showcase. In the '50s, Mantovani supplied cathedralized treatments to "Around the World" and "The *Moulin Rouge* Theme." Britain's Frank Chacksfield crested fame's wave with "Ebb Tide," Hollywood composer Morris Stoloff combined the sweet with the sensuous on "Moonglow and Theme from *Picnic*," and Roger Williams let his cascading keys sweep along to Glenn Osser's orchestral elegance on "Autumn Leaves." Nelson Riddle's "Lisbon Antigua" adorned a Top 10 travelogue with Hugo Winterhalter's "Canadian Sunset," as well as Les Baxter's "April in Portugal" and "The Poor People of Paris." The trend continued into the '60s with Percy Faith's lushly seductive "Theme from *A Summer Place*," Mr. Acker Bilk's pensive clarinet in "Stranger on the Shore," Horst Jankowski's Orchestra and Chorus on "A Walk in the Black Forest," and Henry Mancini's "Days of Wine and Roses" and "Love Theme from *Romeo and Juliet*."

The 1960s also allowed instrumental stars like Mancini, Billy Vaughn, and television's champagne chevalier Lawrence Welk to venture beyond the Tin Pan Alley songbook and extract melodies from burgeoning pop and rock hits. Percy Faith was among the first to make the transition with his excellent 1963 album *Themes for Young Lovers*, sprinkling droplets of pretty pizzicato on "Rhythm of the Rain" and playing brainy games of melody and countermelody on "Go Away Little Girl." A year later, when the Beatles emerged as the new lords of Capitol Records, arranger-composer Stu Phillips led his studio ensemble the Hollyridge Strings on several successful albums that featured luxuriant, echo-redolent reinterpretations of Fab Four favorites, as well as songs "made famous by" Elvis Presley, Simon and Garfunkel, the Beach Boys, and the Four Seasons. Honorable mention also goes to Arthur Fiedler who, in the early '60s, pleasantly surprised his Boston Symphony Hall audience with a Boston Pops version of "I Want to Hold Your Hand."

Using the symphonic-pop fusion, Andre Kostelanetz came out with some of his best work in the mid-'60s and early '70s. He could add an energized electric guitar on his cover of Little Peggy March's "I Will Follow Him" or make playfully Baroque overtures to "The Sounds of Silence." One very exceptional track is a version of the "Love Theme from *Madame X* (from *The Academy Award–Winning "Shadow of Your Smile" and Other Great Themes*). He combines violins, voices, electric guitar, and an otherworldly electronic keyboard, the overall effects producing some of the most evocative and goose-pimply moments in mood music history.

Many of orchestral pop's most creative arrangers have been of the French persuasion. With his semiclassical flourishes, Roger Roger specialized in the effervescent "let's go shopping" pizzicato found in some of the best library production music. Then there were more flamboyant trendsetters like Francis Lai, Paul Mauriat, Raymond Lefevre, and Franck Pourcel who spiced their orchestras with echo-delays, multitracking, and a profusion of contrapuntal instruments ranging from spacey electronic keyboards to fuzz guitars. Caravelli, who charmed America's "Beautiful Music" FM stations with his instrumental cover of Bob Dylan's "Wigwam," used a curious method of pairing his orchestra with a piano that was initially played back at half the normal speed and then retaped at normal speed for a distinctive double-speed effect on the final recording.

Many pop arrangers and producers plied their vast musical acumen by working orchestral pop into their star-centered releases. Along with George Martin and his string arrangements for some of his Beatles recordings, the redoubtable John Barry used strings to neo-psychedelic effect on his scores to James Bond films, especially the riveting title theme to *You Only Live Twice*. His finesse is also evident in the backgrounds behind his protégés Chad & Jeremy on their early tunes "Yesterday's Gone" and "Like I Love You Today." Frank Hunter, a renowned studio arranger and conductor who also contributed to muzak, offered his lush backings to the duo's subsequent single

"Before and After." Peter Knight conducted the London Festival Orchestra behind the Moody Blues' navel-gazing poeticisms on *Days of Future Passed.*

And thanks to orchestral pop, the much-touted '60s "generation gap" was bridged more often than history remembers. Duane Eddy's "Because They're Young" and Jack Nitzsche's "The Lonely Surfer" could sound wonderful in a beach movie or on a push-button lift to the fourth floor swimwear section of a department store. Even in the turbulent years of 1968 and 1969, when counterculture's living theater of attitudes reached critical mass, Paul Mauriat's ornate "Love Is Blue," Raymond Lefevre's lavishly uptempo "Soul Coaxin'," and Ferrante & Teicher's mind-bending adaptation of John Barry's "Midnight Cowboy" theme commingled on *Billboard*'s Top 40 with the Doors, Steppenwolf, and 1910 Fruitgum Co.

Oddly, the year 1972 became a *Billboard* cutting-off point for many orchestral pop artists. Reasons for this turn of the worm inspire speculations that are a little more engaging than the sundry "Tastes change" cop-out. Possible factors include the generational changing of the guard at record labels, the mounting blitz of stadium concerts, the advent of synthesizers, and even bitter moods triggered by stagflation and the creeping energy crisis.

So, now that its principal players have passed away, disappeared, or been relegated to occasional nostalgia shows, orchestral pop easy listening is in an aesthetic purgatory. It cries for more historians and critical sympathizers to keep it in memory and to win back its just respect. Yet, even during its thriving years, some have expressed angst about its place in the pop stratum. Unlike the categories of classical, country, jazz, or rock, easy listening is usually not embraced by musicians themselves, even those who made a comfortable living creating it. There are no easy-listening schools, scholarships, or lavish PBS documentaries to celebrate its fascinating genesis.

Today, orchestral pop has been almost entirely erased from daily life. The radio stations now avoid it, supermarkets are more likely to pipe in a baby-boomer hit parade of original artists' vocals, and places like Starbucks play "smooth jazz." Imagine an A&P piping out Bobby Vinton's "Take Good Care of My Baby" followed by the Standells' "Dirty Water." It happened! Even muzak has renounced its "elevator music" legacy in favor of a more "foreground" approach.

This leaves the question posed in the beginning of this article: Why are the angelic melodies that soothe so many prone to drive others to unholy thoughts? Several years after dedicating an entire book to the subject, this writer can only conclude that no consistent or rational answer exists. Those growing up in the shadow of rock and roll (the time when antimuzak sentiments came to prominence) saw elevator music as the slow, safe, and sanitized culture of their elders. Many of their elders, arguably less tenacious about their generation's music than baby boomers and subsequent boomer-babies, seem to have just gone with the flow and are content with their direct-marketing "nostalgia" collections.

Even some orchestral pop aficionados have inadvertently contributed to its demise in their misguided attempts to rescue their pet artists from easy-listening limbo at the expense of others. In the process, they fail to adhere to a bigger picture. Sure, some Weston or Gleason fans may hail the semi-improvisational horn interludes; some may take a shine to Faith's intricate "counterlines"; others may have a penchant for Mantovani's more diaphanous arrangements, or be partial to the pseudo-jazzy patter in some of Mancini's work. Having preferences is fine, but erecting a mood music food chain is ultimately counterproductive. Trying to prove to anti-easy-listening skeptics how much Percy Faith is less "elevator music" than Mantovani is akin to trying to convince '50s opponents of rock and roll that Bill Haley shakes, rattles and rolls less than Buddy Holly.

There are, of course, designer politics. Some have come to identify easy listening as too middle-class, whitebread, and blue-note deficient. Despite the fact that Guy Lombardo and His Royal Canadians was Louis Armstrong's favorite band, many current "encyclopedists" impose jazz standards onto music that has essentially nothing to do with jazz. The *Penguin Encyclopedia of Popular Music*, for instance, justifies Lombardo and his "sweetest music this side of heaven" on the basis that, despite his predominantly sweet predilections, he could "swing" once in a while.

One point is more certain: In a world where merchandizing rules urban life, where people joyously sport brand names on their clothing, and when it is increasingly difficult to tell commercials from entertainment, the old canard about elevator music being manipulative seems ludicrous. Back in 1947, the Otis Elevator Company put out a magazine ad boasting how its conveyances play "music by 'Muzak'" so that "the cares of the business day are now wafted away on the notes of a lilting melody." In contrast, today's prevailing soundscape assumes muzak's worst stereotypes. It replaces soothing waltzes with ear-pummeling polyrhythms and is more invasive and manipulative than any music that came before.

Oddly enough, the few reminders that elevator music ever existed are in a spate of recent smart-ass television commercials. Consider the mild cha-cha that plays behind shoppers browsing for "Pork: The Other White Meat," the New Balance footwear spot where office drones languish through an elevator ride with a sweaty gymnast, or, better yet, the elevator airs that two slackers drown out during a Doritos crunching contest. It may be grist for Comedy Central gags today, but who knows? In the din-weary future, the music that once lent mystery to supermarket aisles may end up subverting the status quo.

Jeff E. Winner

> Gentlemen: I have a story that may be of interest to you.
>
> It is not widely known who invented the circuitry concept for the automatic sequential performance of musical pitches—now well known as a "sequencer." I, however, do know who the inventor was, for it was I who first conceived and built the electronic sequencer.
>
> Bob Moog, who visited me occasionally at my lab, was among the first to see and witness the performance of my UJT-Relay sequencer. To digress for a bit, I was so secretive about my development activities—perhaps neurotically so— that I was always reminding Bob that he mustn't copy or reveal my sequencer work to anyone. I understand, now, my personal need for secrecy at that time. Electronic music for commercials and films was my living then, and I thought I had this great advantage, because of my sequencer.
>
> Word naturally got around about the nature of what my device accomplished, but Bob Moog continued to be loyal. I must say Bob Moog is a most honorable person. He steadfastly refrained from embodying my sequencer in his equipment line until the sheer pressure of so many manufacturers using the sequencer forced him to compete. Yet, he used the simplest version, though he knew about my most advanced sequencer. Quite a gentleman, and a super talent besides.
>
> Now, with the passing of years, I guess I regret my secrecy and would like people to know of what I accomplished.
>
> Raymond Scott (from an unaddressed letter, ca. mid-1970s)

Figure 17.1
Raymond Scott, age 29, at work in his lab (March 1938). © The Raymond Scott
Archives: RaymondScott.com

Few of us have the opportunity to choose our name. Raymond Scott was an exception. Obsessed with the sound of everything, he selected the moniker because it had "good rhythm." Then he made it one of the most famous names of his generation.

Raymond Scott sold millions of records during his long career. He wrote his first hit tune at age twenty-five, and only four years later, a 1938 issue of *Time* magazine reported that his popular and eccentric music had "attracted the attention of such musical bigwigs as Igor Stravinsky." Scott was a bandleader on a par with Duke Ellington in the 1940s, and a star of the new medium of television during the '50s. Raymond Scott was a household name.

Then Elvis came along. When Presley made his 1956 TV debut, the show's hosts, Tommy and Jimmy Dorsey—who, like Raymond Scott, were big band stars—couldn't have guessed what was about to happen. Soon, Scott and his peers weren't cool anymore, and this new thing called "rock and roll" was the latest sensation. A figure once well known faded into obscurity.

But thanks to *Bugs Bunny*, his tunes were never forgotten. For each generation since 1943, the music of Raymond Scott has underscored the antics of Bugs, Daffy, Porky, and the rest of the internationally famous Warner Bros. Looney Tunes gang. More recently, *The Ren & Stimpy Show*, *Animaniacs*, and *The Simpsons* have featured Scott's music. To this day, not a thirty-minute time slot can pass without a Raymond Scott composition being played somewhere on cable TV. Ironically, Scott never wrote music for cartoons. He simply sold a chunk of his publishing to Warner Bros. in the early '40s, a coincidence that immortalized his music for the future.

A diverse range of musical artists also kept Raymond Scott's melodies alive throughout the twentieth century; Rush, Gorillaz, Kronos Quartet, Louis Armstrong, J. Dilla, They Might Be Giants, Don Byron, Benny Goodman, Q-Tip, Gwar, Paul Whiteman, John Zorn, Devo, Jim Thirlwell, Christian Marclay, and countless others have covered, sampled, or remixed Scott's music.

In the early 1990s, the discovery of Scott's original '30s recordings led to a revival of interest in the man himself. Kids who grew up listening to Scott's tunes in cartoons finally discovered who created those familiar melodies. Kronos Quartet leader, David Harrington, said that his introduction to Scott's music "was like being given the name of a composer I feel I have heard my whole life, who until now was nameless. Clearly he is a major American composer."[1]

Growing awareness of the other side of Raymond Scott's career, as inventor and electronic music pioneer, began with the 1997 reissue of Scott's "Soothing Sounds for Baby" trilogy. These albums, largely undervalued at the time of their original 1962 release by Epic Records, contained gentle and completely electronic works marketed to calm and delight infants. Scott's pioneering explorations into synthesized minimalism and ambience prefigured subsequent works by Philip Glass, Terry Riley, Kraftwerk, and Brian Eno. And, as Electronic Music Foundation president Joel Chadabe points out, "Scott's music is so perfectly crafted, that it seems all the more wonderful, even mysterious, that it was created with the sophisticated and complex technology he invented."[2]

Yet, Soothing Sounds couldn't prepare the world for the variety of auditory artifacts uncovered in *Manhattan Research Inc.*, the two-CD and book set

Figure 17.2
Raymond Scott in one of his self-built electronic recording studios (late 1950s). © The Raymond Scott Archives: RaymondScott.com

(coproduced by the author) detailing Raymond Scott's groundbreaking electronic work from 1953 to '69. Experiments in abstract musical sculpture are heard alongside decidedly non-kiddie collaborations with a pre-Muppets Jim Henson, Scott's junior by twenty-eight years.

Manhattan Research Inc. also includes vintage commercial interruptions—examples of some of the first TV and radio spots to feature completely electronic music. At the time, electro-music was rarely heard outside academic circles. But as *Spin* magazine senior editor Will Hermes observed, Scott "had Madison Avenue paying him to soundtrack its vision of postwar American Futurism."[3]

The dusty *Manhattan Research Inc.* recordings still "sound like the future" to Peter Buck of R.E.M., while Can's Holger Czukay was moved to disbelief: "This is from the 1950s and '60s? I'm trying to accomplish something like this now! Raymond Scott belongs to the phalanx of unique people like Les Paul, Oscar Sala, and Leon Theremin, to whom we owe so much in developing our own musical identity today."[4]

Eclectic Jazz, Electric Swing

Next door to Gordon's Photography, on the corner of Sutter Avenue and Cleveland, in Brooklyn, New York, Raymond Scott's father Joseph Warnow opened a music shop in 1906. A Russian immigrant and amateur violinist, Joseph sold radios, instruments, Victrolas, records, sheet music, and player piano rolls. The family, including Ray's mother Sarah and older brother Mark, lived above the store. But Raymond, born Harry Warnow in 1908, could usually be found downstairs in the shop.

The most sophisticated music technology in young Ray's environment was the player piano, invented around the turn of the century. By age five, the variable-speed Pianola in his dad's store became his earliest obsession—and his first music teacher. Raymond dedicated himself to countless hours of struggling to match its mechanical perfection. He was in awe, yet focused as he studied the ghostly "invisible man" effect. Most important, the player piano never made a mistake. It hit the correct notes every time. Scott stretched his small hands to keep pace with the precision of the moving parts. For especially complicated pieces, he would slow the playback speed until he could flawlessly mimic the machine. Then he would gradually increase to a super-human tempo.

Popular long before wire and tape recording, paper player piano rolls represented an early desire to preserve musical performances. With their perforation codes, they were not unlike computer punch cards widely used until the 1980s. Piano rolls were software of the day, and Ray loved their automatic accuracy. The precise playback qualities of the player piano would inspire him for the rest of his life.

"For many years, I thought technology could be used to aid both the composition and performance of music. Incidentally, this goes back a long time," the sixty-year-old Scott remembered in 1968. "Even when I was 10 years old I had dreams that it was possible to use technological assistance to perform better. For instance, when I was studying piano as a kid, I didn't play octaves very well. And I had a dream that if I fastened one of these barber shop type massage things to my wrist, and it vibrated the wrist up and down, then all I had to do was hold it on the piano and I could play octaves like mad."[5]

By age twelve, Raymond had assembled his first audio laboratory in the bedroom he shared with his brother. The ability to record sound was exciting and novel. Still long before the development of magnetic tape, Ray committed much mischief with his microphones. Armed with his own acetate cutter and aluminum discs from Fairchild Aviation, Scott swung mics from the third floor window to record the random conversations of passersby, or the neighbors' embarrassing piano lessons. Later he would conduct an in-house broadcast that reached no further than his family's Kolster radio set in the living room.

He also made mayhem with the phone lines. "It would be very confusing," bemoaned Scott's first wife Pearl. "He'd telephone, and while you're talking to him, he's playing back the first part of the conversation. You're talking to a person, and then you hear your voice coming back at you! Very confusing!" Raymond was Pearl's "first real boyfriend," and this was the first time in her life she'd heard a recording of her voice. "But this was an indication of where his interests lay, in the technical things. It had nothing to do with people," Pearl explained. "He did it just to please himself. To show what could be done."[6]

Before Raymond graduated from Brooklyn Technical High School in 1927, he had decided to devote his life to engineering. His brother Mark, a famous CBS radio bandleader (for Frank Sinatra and others), recognized Raymond's talent and insisted he study music instead. Skeptical, Raymond reluctantly enrolled at Juilliard. When he received his degree in 1931, Mark again pushed him into a world of sound: he landed Ray the job as CBS staff pianist. Not wanting to be known as Mark Warnow's little brother, he invented the name "Raymond Scott" for himself in 1934.

Raymond was considered socially awkward and always seemed to prefer the company of his equipment to humans. Pearl recalled that he excused himself from their wedding reception, claiming he "had work to do." Associate Rob Curtis said, "Mechanical things fascinated Raymond. His idea of superman was an automaton, humanoid in shape, with a well developed brain. This he modeled himself after." Even the titles of his compositions revealed his preoccupations: "Powerhouse," "The Principles of Arithmetic," "Kodachrome," and "Love Song to a Microphone."

Throughout his life, Scott explored music technology with remarkable tenacity. His knowledge of radio and recording hardware displayed a technical sophistication rarely seen among composers and bandleaders. In 1935, the twenty-six-year-old had "designed and owned one of New York City's earliest independent recording studios," located in the Radio City/RKO building. (Artie Shaw and a young Judy Garland were among his many clients.) He revolutionized the art of microphone placement, and spent many of his bands' recording sessions monitoring the mixing consoles in the control room.

A 1937 *Down Beat* article, titled "Engineer-Musician Electrifies Swing World with Ideas," described Scott's downtown dwelling as brimming with "all sorts of recording equipment, with microphones all over the place and long wires trailing across the floor." The feature explored Scott's science of "creative acoustics," which involved using a mic to manipulate and capture sounds that differ from those heard by the naked ear. A November 1937 *Popular Mechanics* feature, "Radio Music of the Future," described Scott "placing a 'dead' microphone beside the piano and then turning it on only after the keys have been struck [to] catch the ghostlike effect" of after-tones that are "ethereal, disembodied, [and have] a sense of great space."

At CBS, he formed the hugely successful (if oddly named) six-man Raymond Scott Quintette. Scott insisted they memorize the parts—no sheet music allowed. His difficult compositions could be performed faster by "skipping the eyes," he insisted. While performing for Scott, a job requirement was to become "temporarily superhuman." Scott was a strict perfectionist with little tolerance for improvisation, which often confounded jazz purists. He earned notoriety as a session tyrant and was often criticized for treating his sidemen and vocalists like machines.

Wireless Think Tank

Nothing is impossible in this atomic age. Someday, perhaps within the next hundred years, science will perfect a process of thought transference from composer to listener. Devices already have been perfected to record the impulses of the brain. In the music of the future, the composer will merely think his idealized conception of his music. His brain waves will be picked-up by mechanical equipment and channeled directly into the minds of his hearers. Instead of recordings of actual music sound, recordings will carry the brain waves of the composer directly to the mind of the listener.

Raymond Scott, 1949

Figure 17.3
Raymond Scott with his electronic sequencer invention, Karloff (late 1950s). © The Raymond Scott Archives: RaymondScott.com

Scott expected his bandmates to be like his father's player piano: flawless and utterly predictable. "All he ever had was machines—only we had names,"[7] said Scott's drummer Johnny Williams (father of movie soundtrack composer, John Williams). Singer Anita O'Day worked briefly with Scott's 1940s band and said he "reduced [musicians] to something like wind-up toys."[8] In the mid-'50s, he auditioned an unknown guitarist calling himself Bo Diddley, but Scott rejected his playing as "too sloppy." Percussionist John Blowers remembered Scott eyeing the second hand of a stopwatch while the band played. "He was trying to see if the tempo remained at a certain 'tick' of the watch. Of course, it can't possibly, because you're playing from emotions. You're not like a machine!"[9] But no one dared explain this to Raymond.

A Monster Science Created

In 1946, Raymond Scott established his company, Manhattan Research Inc., to expand the horizons of electronic sound and music. When advertising, Scott claimed to have built "the world's most extensive facility for the creation of Electronic Music." A slogan was "more than a think factory: a dream center where the excitement of tomorrow is made available today."

Scott was spending less time with sidemen, and more time soldering relays. Gradually he dispensed with the human element. Scott felt more comfortable with his machines; they spoke the same language. "Scott's music speaks for itself, and his instruments speak through his music," enthused Joel Chadabe, Bennington College's electronic music director. "Scott developed his instruments to make his music, and he did it so well that what you hear is the music."[10]

Raymond Scott was on a quest to create "new plastic sounds," and his inventions reflect this. In March 1946, he patented an electro-mechanical synthesizer called the Orchestra Machine, which featured a keyboard that could simulate an ensemble of traditional musicians. "This is a device incorporating a number of multiple soundtrack units," Scott wrote in the patent disclosure, "that may be selected as would the musical instruments in an orchestra. The entire mechanical driving system's speed may be varied in order to select any particular musical pitch."

Two years later, in 1948, Scott began a decade of work on a monstrous sound-effects generator. He named it "Karloff" as a tribute to movie actor

Boris Karloff, who made Dr. Frankenstein's monster a sci-fi icon for the ages. Scott demonstrated his beast to columnist Joseph Kaselow of the *New York Herald Tribune*. "Scott's machine has 200 sound sources and is capable of quickly producing infinite and varied musical and electronic effects. The machine uses several electronic tone generators, and others can be added," Kaselow reported. "The control panel directs pitch, timbre, intensity, tempo, accent, and repetition. It can sound like a group of bongo drums. It can give impressions which suggest common noises. It can create the mood of musical tone-poems. And it can also produce limitless emotional variations to suit a variety of musical styles. All, of course, if Scott is at the controls."[11]

In 1952, Scott designed and built two of the world's first multitrack tape machines, capable of recording seven and fourteen parallel tracks on a single reel. Two years later, sonic maverick Les Paul made an eight-track prototype, and inventor Hugh Le Caine devised a way to mix-down six separate tape sources in 1955. But as author Thom Holmes points out, "nobody came close to matching Scott's early achievement."[12] Scott filed two patents for his advancements in magnetic tape technology in 1953, and a third in '59.

From 1950 to '57, Scott funded his technological excursions by conducting the orchestra on NBC's corny but highly rated TV show, *Your Hit Parade*. Every week, millions of Americans watched Raymond and his second wife, singer Dorothy Collins, as they counted down the nation's top tunes. Few, however, suspected the alter ego behind the conductor's stiff stage smile.

Walls of Sound

A Columbia University freshman named Bob Moog was among the privileged few who witnessed Raymond Scott's audio obsessions in action. During the early 1950s, the young Bob Moog was building theremins with his dad as a hobby. Scott wanted to obtain the unique instrument's tone-generating subassembly, so he invited the Moogs to tour his facility in Manhasset, New York.

"First, Raymond showed us his recording studio. Then a very large room with a cutting lathe and all sorts of monitoring and mixing equipment," Moog remembered. "Next, the entire downstairs floor, which was several large rooms. A dream workshop filled with machine tools of the highest quality, a woodworking shop, an electronics assembly room, and a huge thoroughly equipped stock room of electronic parts. It looked like heaven to me!

Figure 17.4
Raymond Scott with his keyboard synthesizer invention, the Clavivox (late 1950s).
© The Raymond Scott Archives: RaymondScott.com

There my father and I were with our mouths hanging open. And I was this electronics nerd who found himself on the track to becoming an engineer."

This encounter commenced a professional and social relationship between Moog and Scott that continued for nearly two decades. "When I first worked for Raymond Scott in the early 1950s, he had a very large laboratory. It was the largest room," Moog explains, "and it was completely filled with rack upon rack of relays, rotating motors, steppers, electronic circuits, all sorts of patch chords, switches, and so on. This was where Raymond experimented with making music—electronic music—mechanically. This was before the time of computers, and before the time of what we call 'electronic sequencers,' that would produce one tone after the other. Raymond's tones were sequenced by mechanical relays. He would go around and adjust various things to change the sound patterns. I'd never seen anything like it—never tried to imagine anything like it. And I'm sure it gave me something to think about over the years. It was a huge 'electro-mechanical sequencer.' "[13]

At the time, bigger was better. And Ray had built the best. His sequencer was more than thirty feet long and stretched from floor to ceiling. He named it "The Wall of Sound."

As an extension of his mid-1940s Orchestra Machine, Scott used a theremin module in the first prototype of his keyboard synthesizer, the Clavivox, which he patented in 1956. The project began five years earlier when Scott fashioned a toy theremin for his first daughter, Carrie. "I must have been 11 or 12, which would be 1950 or '51," remembers Carrie. "We had seen a Broadway play called *Mrs. McThing* which used a theremin, and I loved the way it sounded. But after my dad built it, I discovered I couldn't play it. So he took it back and made it into something else."[14]

The resulting synthesizer allowed a player to glide smoothly from one note to another without a break over a three-octave keyboard. It could be played with an expressive portamento rather than with discrete pitches only. Subsequent improvements allowed staccato attacks, on–off vibrato toggling, and many other effects. It could also simulate the sounds of many traditional instruments.

"This was not a theremin anymore," Bob Moog was careful to point out. "Raymond quickly realized there were more elegant ways of controlling an electronic circuit." In subsequent models, Scott used photocells and a steady light source beamed through photographic film graded from opaque to transparent. This varied the voltage, which changed the pitch of the tone generator.

Automatic Frequency Scans

Scott also holds a patent on an automatic scanning radio which tunes in on stations around the country and changes frequency by itself at any given interval, enabling him to catch most of the nation's disc-jockey shows in a brief span and find out what tunes are being played.

Popular Mechanics magazine, July 1959

The waveform of the sound determined the tone color, and the methods of altering the waveform were similar to analog synths developed many years later. In fact, Moog later explained that "A lot of the sound-producing circuitry of Scott's Clavivox resembled, very closely, the first analog synthesizer my company made in the mid-'60s. The sounds are not exactly the same, but they're close."[15]

When they met in the 1950s, Bob Moog was still a teen—more than a quarter-century younger than Scott. But Moog would eventually become the first inventor to successfully market a voltage-controlled synthesizer. By the late 1960s, everyone from Wendy Carlos to the Beatles had recorded with Moog's instruments.

Beat the Clock

A relentless workaholic, Scott imposed on his musicians the kind of discipline that came naturally to him. In 1957, at age fifty, he endured his first encounter with serious heart trouble. "I had many dead spots around my body," Scott wrote in his journal. "Cardiac specialists gave me one year to live." Instead of slowing, his pace increased. There was lots of work to do, and Raymond feared he was running out of time.

Scott designed and built the Circle Machine, a more compact electronic sequencer, around 1959. Dr. Thomas Rhea, music synthesis professor at the Berklee College of Music, visited Scott's laboratory many times and remembers the Circle Machine as "an analog waveform generator that was this crazy, whirling-dervish thing. It had a ring of incandescent lamps, each with its own rheostat, and a photo-electric cell on a spindle that twirled in a circle above the lights."[16] Each bulb's intensity was individually adjustable, as was the rotation speed of the photocell. As the lights brightened, the pitch ascended.

Arm rotation speed governed the rhythm. The lights could be staggered in brightness, and depending on the pattern, the tone sequence would change accordingly.

Drum machines were also on Scott's agenda, and he created several, including one he named Bandito the Bongo Artist. Bandito could automatically create and perform naturalistic drum improvisations with "an infinite variety of pitches, rhythms, and colors," Scott claimed with parental enthusiasm. "Comparable to, and frequently more exciting than the most brilliant bongo artist anywhere."

Building on the foundations of, and cannibalizing the guts from Karloff and his other devices, Scott developed the first version of his "instantaneous composition/performance machine" in the late 1950s. He named it the Raymond Scott Electronium (no relation to the German Hohner electronium), and it became the most ambitious and resource-consuming project of his life. Laboring for decades, Scott rendered several very different incarnations in hardware, all of which shared his artificial intelligence technology. Although he didn't encourage his human bandmates to improvise, improvisation ironically became a central goal of Scott's Electroniums. "The entire system is based on the concept of Artistic Collaboration between Man and Machine," Scott wrote in a patent disclosure. "The new structures being directed into the machine are unpredictable in their details, and hence the results are a kind of collaboration between the composer and the machine."

Instead of a traditional piano-style keyboard, the Electronium was "guided" by a complex series of buttons and switches arranged in orderly rows. The system was capable of "instantaneous composition and performance" of polyphonic rhythmic structures, as well as tasking preset programs. With Scott controlling the sonorities, tempos, and timbres, he and his machine composed, performed, and recorded all at once. The parts weren't multitracked; rather, voices, rhythms, and melodies originated simultaneously in real time.

"A composer 'asks' the Electronium to 'suggest' an idea, theme, or motive," Scott wrote in the user manual. "To repeat it, but in a higher key, he pushes the appropriate button. Whatever the composer needs: faster, slower, a new rhythm design, a hold, a pause, a second theme, variation, an extension, elongation, diminution, counterpoint, a change of phrasing, an ornament, ad infinitum. It is capable of a seemingly inexhaustible palette of musical sounds and colors, rhythms, and harmonies. Whatever the composer requests, the Electronium accepts and acts out his directions. The Electronium adds to the composer's thoughts, and a duet relationship is set up."

"It was always this metaphysical, almost magical thing, about literally thinking things to the point where they would happen," says Herb Deutsch, a Hofstra University music professor who worked with Bob Moog to develop the first Moog synthesizer in 1964. Deutsch, who also worked for Scott, remembered one of his colleague's visionary objectives. "He wanted to take the work out of being a musician," Deutsch says. "That used to really get me upset. He said, 'Look, I just want to sit here, and I'd like to turn this machine on, and whenever it does something good, I just want to record it at that point.' It was not that he was a lazy guy—far from it. He worked incredibly hard to take the work out of being a composer."[17]

"What Ray did was recognize that music has repetitions and patterns, and he envisioned a machine that would incorporate those patterns," says circuitry expert Alan Entenman who assisted Scott. "He thought of it as 'an orchestra with a thousand voices.' It had plug-in modules, and each module was a synthesizer—of his design—that was capable of making a wide variety of sounds. He kept telling me: if you listen to music, it's repetition. You could repeat notes in a different tone," Entenman explains. "What made his Electronium successful was his knowledge of composition. Being a composer, he knew how to construct music from these things—and it really worked. This thing could make any kind of music you could imagine."

"I understand the secret, to some extent," Entenman continues. "The harmonics are precise mathematical multiples, and when something vibrates, there are overtones. The way you blend these overtones, and the amount of offset they have with one another, gives it warmth. That's what he would do to get it to sound rich. He'd couple that with the melodious, rhythmic patterns he built into it. He would program how it was repeated, and in what key it would be repeated, so it was like gears within gears."[18]

Refining the Electronium concept remained Scott's primary focus throughout the 1960s, when integrated circuits made smaller and more efficient versions possible. He asked Bob Moog to "sophisticate my equipment. The concept is the same as I've had for many years now. And you're the scientist who will make these things small, more compact, and with fewer parts." Scott replaced his eight-stage "sequential timer" relays with Moog's electronic stepping switches.

Figure 17.5
The final, Motown version of Raymond Scott's automatic composition machine, the Electronium. © The Raymond Scott Archives: RaymondScott.com

Destination: Hitsville, U.S.A.

Despite another bout of heart trouble in 1967, Raymond Scott continued to focus full time on his Electronium technology. By the end of the 1960s, he had invested well over a decade—and more than a million of his own dollars—in refining his brainchild. In 1968, he finally filed a patent to protect the Electroniums' interactive circuitry concepts. But Scott's health was faltering, and his once-substantial royalties were dwindling.

In August of 1970, Motown Records founder Berry Gordy read an article in *Variety* about Scott and the Electronium. Motown virtually controlled the '60s pop charts with stars like Stevie Wonder, Marvin Gaye, and Diana Ross. And with the Jackson 5 as his latest smash supergroup, Gordy was at the height of

The Focus and the Fax

During his decades of pioneering audio endeavors, Raymond Scott was also a dedicated photographer who assembled darkrooms and photo labs alongside his self-built recording studios. Never a "people person," Scott seemed to love his cameras as much as his microphones; they allowed him to capture, manipulate, and interact with the outside world, yet stay within the comfortable context of his technology.

Stereoscopic 3-D photography was Scott's interest during the 1920s and '30s, and one of his earliest patent disclosures, from March of 1946, was for a darkroom innovation. As Scott's only son Stan Warnow remembers, his dad, who was too impatient to manually agitate pans of photo chemicals, somehow found the time to design and build efficient robotic armatures to do the work for him. Scott's "sequential timing circuits" precisely timed and adroitly executed each step of the darkroom ritual.

Figure 17.6
Raymond Scott with his audio-visual invention, the Videola (late 1950s). © The Raymond Scott Archives: RaymondScott.com

The Focus and the Fax
(continued)

Scott was also involved with movies and their soundtracks. Beginning in the late 1930s, his music was featured in a series of Hollywood films (including Hitchcock's *The Trouble with Harry* in 1955). "For writing film scores, Scott has developed an instrument which he calls the 'Videola,'" reported the September 1959 issue of *Popular Mechanics*. "The mechanism operates a movie film in a projection room in another part of the house by remote control. The movie is flashed on a television screen, so that Scott can watch the film as he composes appropriate music. A recording apparatus is hooked up to the Videola so that he can stop, play back, listen, rub out, and rewrite."

In the mid-1960s, Scott began collaborating on a series of experimental short films with an emerging artist named Jim Henson. Henson would later create *Sesame Street* and *The Muppet Show*, but the Henson/Scott collaborations were not intended for children. Instead, the films are serious, even creepy, with a surprisingly modern feel, often featuring intense, cyberesque barrage collages built from hyperspeed edits.

Scott was 61 years old, but eager to risk a new venture when he established yet another electronics company in 1969. It was an optics corporation called Electronic Transmission Systems. In 1970, Scott patented his "Optical System for Facsimile Scanners," which was "referenced" years later in patents for new developments by General Electric, A. B. Dick, and Xerox. Today, of course, this type of digital imaging technology is still being utilized daily in millions of cameras, fax machines, and image scanners.

his influence. But as a new decade was dawning, the Los Angeles–based music mogul wanted to modernize his "Hit Factory." Gordy phoned Scott and asked to see and hear this miraculous invention in action. The following week, a sizable Motown entourage arrived at Scott's Long Island facility in a fleet of limos. "It was genius meeting genius," Motown executive Guy Costa recalled. "Berry certainly respected Ray and his knowledge, and Ray admired Berry."

"Berry felt that the power of the Electronium, the ability to numeralize the music process, was important," Costa explained. "Berry was always a formula man. He'd find a rhythm or a progression and build on that. The Electronium gave you the ability to play a chord, and the ability to store rhythms, and resequence those things. To have all these new effects was a turn-on."[19]

Gordy had a famous ear for talent, and Scott was his new discovery. Following a month of discussing details, he ordered a customized version of Scott's

Where Are They Now?

At least one Raymond Scott Clavivox is still known to be in working condition. Its one of many vintage electronic instruments owned by the Audities Foundation in Calgary, Alberta, Canada, under the directorship of David Kean. (The Clavivox can be rented, and was used by Tom Petty and the Heartbreakers on their 1999 album *Echo*.)

The final, Motown version of the Raymond Scott Electronium was bought from Scott's widow, Mitzi, by composer–musician and Devo cofounder Mark Mothersbaugh, who houses it at his Mutato Muzika studios in Hollywood. At Mutato, Scott's unique device for "Instantaneous Musical Composition and Performance" has been collecting dust since 1996. Partly eviscerated by the inventor for spare parts, it no longer functions. Mothersbaugh has promised to have it restored to working order.

Electronium. The initial down payment was $10,000, but it would eventually cost Motown millions. Costa arranged for shipment of the device from New York to Gordy's home in Los Angeles. Scott planned to spend six weeks tutoring the Motown chief on the device. When Gordy asked Scott to make further modifications, the inventor was happy to comply and continued working in sunny California, with his client becoming involved in the progress.

Six weeks turned into six months. Eventually Gordy offered Scott a position as head of Motown's Electronic Research and Development. Scott accepted, and in 1972, he relocated to the West Coast with his third wife, Mitzi. He also had a heart bypass operation that year, but this was a new beginning. Equipped with his own on-site Motown research studio facility, Scott continued to develop the Electronium (eventually renamed "The Scottronium") and other technologies through the '70s.

"Berry was looking at the Electronium as a source of inspiration and new ideas, and as a methodology—as a sophisticated programmable sequencer," Costa said. Scott programmed the Electronium to invent bass-lines, riffs, grooves, and melodies that could later be replicated by Motown's adept studio musicians. "It was an idea stimulator, a creative thought processor. Maybe [they would] find combinations that hadn't been tried," Costa continued. "It could do anything he wanted it to do."[20]

Hoby Cook was a technician at Motown's MoWest facility who tested Scott's Electronium extensively. "I wanted some reactions, so as an experiment, I'd open the door and turn the volume up—loud." Cook's technique worked. Motown personnel heard the curious sounds and wandered in. "Cal Harris did a lot of recording with it, and Michael Jackson was fascinated," Cook recalled. "He was just this kid sitting there, starring at the flashing lights. He said he wanted The Jackson 5 to use the Electronium somehow."[21]

Following a serious heart attack in 1977, Scott's health forced him to finally retire at age sixty-nine. "Ray was a wonderful guy," Costa said. "I can't tell you how much fun we had together. He was the experimenter—the mad professor." Exactly what Motown had to show commercially for its substantial investment remains a mystery.

Time Runs Out

After continued heart problems in the late 1970s, Raymond Scott was no longer on music technology's cutting edge. He upgraded his devices with microprocessors but lost valuable research time due to illness. "By then, he had destroyed the Electronium by vandalizing it for parts for other things he was working on," Costa said. "And new electronics had come so far, they could do with one little chip what he had tons of wiring doing on the Electronium. It didn't pay to keep working on it."[22]

But Scott didn't give up. Despite his deteriorating health, he continued to work, even while bedridden. In the mid-1980s, he modified a Yamaha DX-7 and used MIDI to connect the keyboard to an Electronium through a PC assembled in 1981. "I got involved in an exciting project," the 75-year-old wrote in his journal in June 1983. "For 3 months I slept an average of about 50 hours per month. Then I folded. Symptoms of folding: extreme fatigue, wobbly walking, accumulation of chest pains, zero energy output capability." A major stroke in 1987 closed down shop completely. Even more tragic, Scott could no longer speak, rendering him unable to answer questions when interest in him revived in the early 1990s. He died in February 1994 at age 85.

His technology, meanwhile, had been developing a life of its own. When developers submit an invention to the patent office, existing patents can be "referenced" as part of a new design. Perhaps an indication that his concepts were ahead of their time, Scott's patents have been referenced by Xerox, General Electric, and other high-tech entities. IBM was awarded a patent in 1977 that referenced Scott's early '50s technology. In 1981, Sony was awarded patents referencing Scott's '53 magnetic tape developments. His "Electronic Audible Signaling Devices" patent (for Electronium circuitry) has been referenced many times, including by the Atari corporation: filed in 1980, this patent represented the technology for producing sound effects for Atari's popular arcade and home video game systems. The referencing of Scott's patents continued throughout the 1980s, '90s, and the list is still growing into the next century.

Visionary Outlook

"I understand his ideas about the collaboration between man and machine, which to me is the most important thing he did, in terms of electronics and music," says Berklee professor Dr. Thomas Rhea. "He anticipated some artificial intelligence concepts and some compositional concepts that people believe somebody else did. The idea of collaborating with a machine, and allowing the machine to make certain decisions, was pretty avant-garde."[23]

"Raymond was the first! He foresaw the use of sequencers and electronic oscillators to make sounds. These were the watershed uses of electronic circuitry," Bob Moog recalled of his old friend. "Scott was definitely in the forefront—no doubt about that. He was in the forefront of developing electronic music technology, and in the forefront of using it commercially, as a musician."[24]

"I don't think it was a matter of man versus machine," Moog theorized. "From time to time, there are people who are influenced by the future. Not by the past, not by the present, but by the future. These people do things that later turn out to be directly for the future. I think Raymond Scott was one of those people."[25]

© 2007 Jeff E. Winner

Acknowledgments

Thank you to: Gert-Jan Blom, Deb Scott, Stan Warnow, and Susan V. Davis. Very special thanks to: Irwin D. Chusid.

Notes

1. David Harrington, private correspondence with the author, 1994.

2. Joel Chadabe, *Manhattan Research, Inc.* (compact disc), Basta Audio/Visuals, 2000.

3. Will Hermes, *Spin* magazine, September 2000, 185.

4. Email correspondence with the author, May 2000.

5. Raymond Scott, personal documents, 1968.

6. Pearl Winters, interview by Jeff Winner and Irwin Chusid, May 20, 2000.

7. Johnny Williams, *The Men Who Made The Music: Raymond Scott* (liner notes to sound recording) by Michele Wood, Time-Life Records, 48.

8. Anita O'Day with George Eells, *High Times, Hard Times* (autobiography) (Putnam Publishing Group/Limelight Editions, 1983), 83–85.

9. John Blowers, telephone interview by Irwin Chusid, December 19, 1993.

10. Joel Chadabe, *Manhattan Research, Inc.* (compact disc).

11. Joseph Kaselow, *New York Herald Tribune,* July 19, 1960.

12. Thom Holmes, *Electronic and Experimental Music: Pioneers in Technology and Composition,* 2nd ed. (Routledge, 2002), 149–150.

13. Bob Moog, interview by Laura Spencer, KCUR Radio, June 2000.

14. Carrie Makover, private correspondence with author, ca. 1998.

15. Bob Moog, public lecture, "Reckless Night on Board the Bottom Line," The Bottom Line, New York City, September 27, 1997.

16. Thomas Rhea, telephone interview by Irwin Chusid, March 27 and 29, 1997.

17. Herb Deutsch, telephone interview by Irwin Chusid, May 19, 1993.

18. Alan Entenman, interview by Gert-Jan Blom and Irwin Chusid, December 28, 1997.

19. Guy Costa, telephone interview by Irwin Chusid, 1996.

20. Guy Costa, telephone interview by Irwin Chusid, 1996.

21. Hoby Cook, telephone interview by the author, February 2001.

22. Guy Costa, telephone interview by Irwin Chusid, 1996.

23. Thomas Rhea, telephone interview by Irwin Chusid, March 27 and 29, 1997.

24. Bob Moog, interview by Laura Spencer, KCUR Radio, June 2000.

25. Bob Moog, telephone interview by Irwin Chusid, May 19, 1993.

From Hip-Hop to Flip-Flop: Black Noise in the Master–Slave Circuit

Ron Eglash

Rather than think of race in terms of a fixed biological identity attached to each individual's genotype, cultural anthropology examines the social use of racial signifiers—whether learned or inborn—in the construction of identity. In the connection of black racial signifiers to technology we should thus look at race not as a reflection, but rather a refraction, Paul Gilroy's bifurcating wavefront linking African, European, and American shores. This essay examines the possibility of racial signifiers in the history of electrical engineering—in particular the "master–slave circuit" of flip-flops and the problem of "colored noise" in transistors—and shows that there are subtle connections to the cultural history of Black Americans and African diaspora.

Contrary to Gross and Levitt's claim that there is an undercurrent of revenge in social studies of science, this is not a revenge story. In fact it's really about my love for electrical engineering, and my interest in trying to understand its cultural dimensions. When I was first introduced to the "master–slave flip-flop circuit" as an engineering student at UCLA, I was taken aback by this starkly social metaphor. But I don't think it's necessarily racist. A good ergonomics engineer like Lillien Gilbreth might point out that certain machines are excellent examples for how we should *not* arrange human relations, and a good feminist like Gayle Rubin might point out that not all S&M relationships should be pathologized as sexist. I'm very much against simplistic, mimetic reductions of science = society; this is not about finding race as a

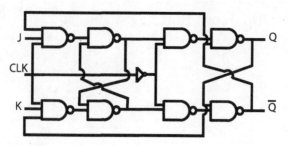

Figure 18.1
Typical diagram for master–slave flip-flop circuit.

reflection, but rather a refraction, of Paul Gilroy's bifurcating wavefront linking African, European, and American shores.

Why is the flip-flop so important? Because every digital circuit, from thermometers to supercomputers, is based on the binary code, on ones and zeros, and the flip-flop is how ones and zeros are generated. The first flip-flop was created by Eccles and Jordan in 1919, and was used to implement binary code in Geiger counters in the 1930s. The binary code actually originated in the work of Leibnitz around 1670, and historian Stephen Skinner shows that it was probably inspired by the binary divination system of geomancy. European geomancers included Thomas Aquinas, Raymond Lull, Robert Fludd, and John Dee. The system was brought to Europe through Islamic sources in twelfth-century Spain, and previous to Islam it was practiced in sub-Saharan Africa. There is, however, an important difference between the original African system and its later European use. The Africans use a random generation to create the first four symbols, and then recursively apply mod 2 to create the other symbols, so that even though it's an aperiodic sequence, it is, after the first four, deterministically generated. The Europeans persistently replaced the deterministic aspects of the system with chance, mounting the sixteen figures on a wheel and spinning it; thus they maintained their society's clean division between determinism and unpredictability.

This deterministic aspect of the African worldview is precisely the point on which anthropologist Evans-Prichard, and others following him, laid claim to a distinction between African knowledge and science. Africans were supposed to have a closed worldview because they could not see that nature operated by statistical chance, that the diversity we see is entirely random, or to put it in terms of spectral density function, that the world is ruled by white noise.

Figure 18.2
The binary divination system of geomancy.

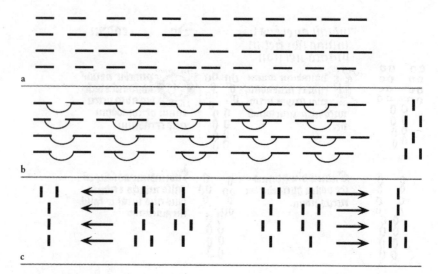

Figure 18.3
Bamana and divination. a. Four random sets of dashes are rapidly drawn in the sand. b.
The dashes are paired off. An odd number of dashes is represented by one stroke; an
even number of dashes is represented by two strokes. c. The process is repeated four
times, resulting in four symbols. Each row of the first two symbols and the last two
symbols are again paired off to generate two new symbols. Recursive application of
this operation (addition modulo 2), along with some other operations, produces a
pseudorandom number sequence that is used by the divination priests to make predictions of their client's future.

According to the mathematics of Evans-Prichard's society, the linkage between determinism and predictability was unbreakable. Deterministic systems
could only give repetition, a periodic noise; and aperiodic, unpredictable noise
could only come from systems which were random, that is, undetermined.

By the late 1970s this mathematical characterization was found to be incorrect. Deterministic chaos, which was inherently unpredictable, could be found
in extremely simple deterministic systems. Its spectral density function is neither the vertical line of periodic noise, nor the horizontal line of white noise,
but rather 1/F noise. The paradigmatic example for binary coding was the
Morse-Thue sequence. Note that the Morse-Thue sequence is extremely similar to African geomancy; both use recursive application of mod 2. That's because both were created through similar motivations: the African divination
priest needs to create symbolic diversity, not periodic repetition. All three

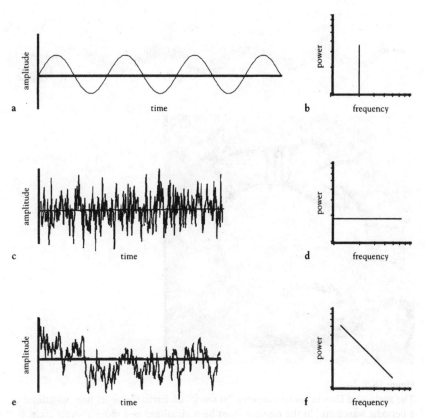

Figure 18.4
Three types of noise. Top: periodic noise—all signal power at one frequency. Middle: white noise—signal power the same at all frequencies. Bottom: 1/F noise—the lower the frequency, the higher the signal power.

categories—periodic determinism, white noise randomness, and deterministic chaos—are components of African geomancy.

Let's take, for example, the Vodhun religion of Benin, known in the New World as Voodoo. The feature of randomness in the world is well known to any Voodoo priest; it is their job to distinguish random events from acts determined by spiritual forces. Of those spiritual forces there are two main categories: the orderliness of Dan, and the deterministic chaos of Legba. Dan is a snake encircling the Earth; he is the cyclic turn of generations, of years, of seasons, of lunar months and solar days. Visual representations of Dan typically

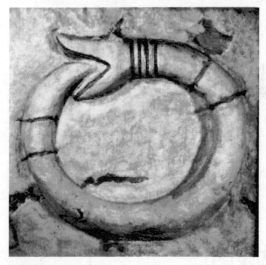

Figure 18.5
The snake god Dan in his two aspects: "at work" on Earth (bottom) he is visualized as
a periodic waveform; in the heavens (top) he is visualized as a more abstract cycle.

show a sinewave, the fundamental periodic signal. Representations of Legba
show bifurcation, the sign of indeterminacy, as in what mathematicians call
"the doubling route to chaos." The same distinction is created through music.
Two years ago I visited the Voodoo convent of Dan in Ouidah, and asked the
head priest to allow me to record his drumming. That of Dan appears to be
more periodic, and that of Legba more chaotic.

In 1712 one particular Voodoo priest in New York followed the geomantic
signs predicting a successful slave insurrection; the prediction was wrong and
they were defeated. The collective forecasts by hundreds of Voodoo priests for
the same in Haiti of 1790 turned out to be correct. In the 1930s, electrical
engineers found that the original flip-flop circuit of Eccles and Jordan was
unstable, and so they adopted the master–slave concept from mechanical

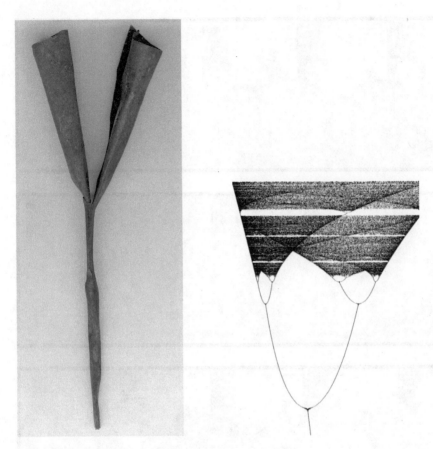

Figure 18.6
The trickster god Legba is often visualized as the crossroads. Each time we arrive at the crossroads, we encounter uncertainty. The graph on the right shows the bifurcation diagram for chaotic behavior in the equation $x_{n+1} = r^* x_n^* (1 - x_n)$.

Figure 18.7
Undulatory dance movements at temple of Dan in Ouidah, Benin.

engineering. During this era, "master–slave" was also used as a metaphor in biological systems: a master molecule inside the cell nucleus was said to command the cytoplasm. African-American biologist Earnest Everett Just opposed this model: "We envision a dynamic self-perpetuating organization of molecular species which owes its specific properties not to the characteristic of any particular molecule, but to the functional interrelationships of these molecular species" (quoted in K. R. Manning's *Black Apollo of Science*). Just proposed that information could be represented by waveforms traveling through the cytoplasm, a concept he portrayed by analogy to music. Music was also cited by Just as the best anthropological illustration of cultural connections between Africa and African Americans.

The flip-flop circuit in vacuum tubes suffered from thermal problems, but in 1948 Bell Labs announced the first semiconductor amplifier, called a transistor. This presented a new problem, however; there was a strange type of noise at the semiconductor contact point. It was neither the periodic signal of deterministic components, nor the white noise of thermal randomness, but exactly halfway in between. It was suspected that this was somehow to the result of a self-organizing activity of electron holes, and became known as 1/F noise because of its spectral density function.

The problem of 1/F noise was solved by William Shockley, who invented the semiconductor junction. Shockley's goal was to eliminate the abnormal presence of this collective activity, because electrical signals could be reliably detected only with the statistically pure white noise background. In the 1950s, during the era of McCarthy's red scares, 1/F signals became know as "pink noise," and after the civil rights era of the early 1960s, it was referred to as "colored noise." In 1967 William Shockley gave a presentation before the National Academy of Sciences, in which he claimed that IQ differences between black and white Americans were due to genetics. In his view empirical evidence for this genetic difference was lost in the statistically impure noise of collective social activity, and he proposed a multimillion-dollar research project in which black and white babies would be provided with economically equal environments, thus leaving only a white noise background for detection of the genetic signal.

Tricia Rose, a professor of history at NYU, published a study of rap music under the title "Black Noise" in 1994 (p. 22): "Worked out on the rusting urban core ... hip-hop transforms stray technological parts intended for cultural and industrial trash heaps into sources of pleasure and power. These transformations have become a basis for digital imagination all over the world." The evidence cited by Rose varies from direct effects of hip-hop—innovations by rap artists which changed practices of recording engineers, for example—to more indirect, intuitive influences, such as breakdancing, as having foreshadowed computer morphing effects. I agree with much of her analysis. In the early 1980s, I was surprised to find that Mathematician Rudy Rucker had used rap signifiers to identify software components in his cellular automata lab, and elsewhere (Eglash 1993, 1995) I've presented my own work showing how comparisons between the fractal dimension of timeseries generated by rap and reggae music can be used to show the difference between analog and digital representation.

In conclusion: the phrase "white noise" was coined by J. B. Johnson in 1928, when he applied the metaphor of the light spectrum—white being the equal presence of all frequencies—to the temporal spectrum of signals produced by thermal noise in electrical circuits. Because red light is at the low frequency end, $1/F$ noise was termed "pink," and since Brownian motion gave the term "brown noise," later the phrase became "colored." It's the perfect internalist story, science providing analogies for itself in a culture-free void. It's a story that leaves me defenseless when I feel disturbed by the off-handed, whimsical way that the phrase "master–slave" is sometimes used.

I am not in favor of banning use of the "master–slave" terminology; I'd rather see engineering professors use it to introduce some cultural and historical discussion. Indeed, as an urban animist, someone who seeks pleasure and enlightenment in electrical artifice, I find many of the overdetermined cultural descriptions from social studies of science to be just as oppressive as the culture-free claims. According to L. S. Keller, obsessive computer programming is—gasp!—masturbation; while Sally Hacker, whose work I otherwise admire, has seen it as the sublimation of male urges for S&M. Even worse are claims of organic superiority, such as D. R. Griffin and Dick Sclove's contention that artificial mediation is inherently dehumanizing. Such writers are covertly imposing their own theology of the natural. During my field work in Africa I never met a divination priest who would hesitate to engage the artificial, to express a love for the synthetic circuits of information and energy that carry our noisy signals through time and space, from one human heart to the next.

References

Dummer, G. (1983). *Electronic Inventions and Discoveries*. Pergamon Press.

Eglash, R. (1993). "Inferring Representation Type from the Fractal Dimension of Biological Communication Waveforms." *Journal of Social and Evolutionary Structures* 16, no. 4.

Eglash, R. (1995). "African Influences in Cybernetics." In *The Cyborg Handbook*, ed. C. H. Gray. Routledge.

Eglash, R. (1999). *African Fractals: Modern Computing and Indigenous Design*. Rutgers University Press.

Gilroy, P. (1993). *The Black Atlantic*. Harvard University Press.

Griffin, D. R. (ed.) (1988). *The Reenchantment of Science*. SUNY Press.

Hacker, S. L. (1989). *Pleasure, Power, and Technology*. Unwin Hyman.

Johnson, J. B. (1928). "Thermal Agitation of Electricity in Conductors." *Physical Review* 32 (July): 97–109.

Keller, L. S. (1991). "Machismo and the Hacker Mentality." In *Women into Computing*. Springer-Verlag.

Manning, K. R. (1983). *Black Apollo of Science*. Oxford University Press.

Milman, S. (1983). "The Role of Theoretical Physics." In *A History of Engineering and Science in the Bell System*. Bell Labs.

Mulira, J. G. (1990). "The Case of Voodoo in New Orleans." In *Africanisms in American Culture*, ed. J. E. Holloway. Indiana University Press.

Rose, T. (1994). *Black Noise*. Wesleyan University Press.

Rucker, R. (1989). *CA Lab*. Autodesk Inc.

Shockley, W. (1967). "The Heredity-Poverty-Crime Problem." *Proceedings of the National Academy of Sciences* 57, no. 6: 1767–1774.

Shockley, W. (1950). "On a Theory of Noise." In *Electrons and Holes in Semiconductors*. Van Nostrand.

Skinner, S. (1980). *Terrestrial Astrology*. Routledge and Kegan Paul.

Voss, R. F., and J. Clarke. (1978). "1/F Noise in Music." *Journal of the Acoustical Society of America* 63, no. 1: 258–263.

Lee Hirsch

In 1992, at age 19, I sold my car, and bought a hi8 camera and a plane ticket to South Africa. Only weeks before, the death of American Fulbright Scholar Amy Biehl had shocked the world. She was an anti-apartheid activist, killed in Gugulethu Township on the outskirts of Cape Town. Stoned to death and a whitey, like me. As I prepared to leave the safety of New York City's wet winter streets, the U.S. State Department called me, urging me not to go; South Africa, they said, was just too unstable. Years later I would find out that my mother had put them up to it.

In the same year, South Africa had just barely escaped a civil war. Tensions were high following the assassination of Chris Hani, a brilliant and much loved young leader of the African National Congress. Some of the first freedom songs I would hear would be in his honor. Against this backdrop, negotiations were underway between the Nationalist Party and the various liberation organizations ... members of the predominately Zulu Inkatha Freedom Party and African National congress were killing each other by the hundreds, in battles that crossed the provinces of South Africa. It was into this climate that I took my first steps on Johannesburg's red soil.

"Zonkisiswe"—Let All the Nations Unite (in the Blood of Chris Hani)

I heard this song over and over again, chanted by 25,000 people crammed into the Orlando Stadium in Soweto for an ANC rally to welcome home hundreds of soldiers from their underground army Umkhonto W'sizwe, better known as MK. They came home as an early outcome of negotiations, and they came home as true heroes. The fortitude, hope, exuberance, and earthshaking harmony I heard that day would hold me transfixed for the next fifteen years.

The man who brought me to this rally was thin and lithe; he had spent his youth in the struggle, and was an expert at not being noticed. If there was a line for food—my instincts drove me to the front while his to the back. If there was a crowd—he would become lost in it. At twenty-five years, my new friend had a powerfully gentle quietness that held me in awe.

Nhlahla (n-tlan-thla) Mabaso would become the first of many amazing friends and guides. His family's was one of two contact numbers I had when I arrived. The first one I called on was an elderly Jewish couple, the grandparents of a girl back home whom I had long had a crush on. I spent only one night with them; they soon realized, over a lavish rump steak dinner at an upscale South African version of Denny's modeled after everything repugnant about America, that I had come to South Africa to learn about freedom songs and meet the very people they feared most. The next morning a supposedly "surprise" visit from a relative would force me to move on.

I called the only remaining number I had, reaching Mam' Zodwa Mabaso on the telephone to whom I explained my situation, why I had come to South Africa, and that I no longer had a place to stay. She didn't ask many questions, and within an hour her son Nhlahla met me, and we went to their farm in a small town on the outskirts of Johannesburg. This would be my home for the next month. It was with the Mabasos that my education began. An incredibly brave family—they were the first black family to move to this small predominantly Afrikaans farming "dorpie" called De Deur, which means The Door. When they arrived they were greeted with death threats. By the time they left they were leaders of that very community.

As a student activist, highly charged by the injustices of apartheid, I expected to see a South Africa that was black and white in every sense. Right and wrong, good and evil—everything followed that logic for me. By the time I left I would understand that there were many shades of gray that coexist in the spectrum. The Mabasos became my link, opening the door into the cultural landscape of the struggle. Nhlahla accepted me as a comrade, and in so doing allowed me access to many events and people who helped me begin my research into what I considered to be the phenomena of South African freedom songs. At night we sat at home listening to recordings the family had kept hidden for years ... Miriam Makeba, Hugh Masekela, Abdullah Ibrahim ... the sounds of liberation etched into scratchy vinyl. Bootleg tapes of "illegal" Radio Freedom broadcasts, the sole recording of the singing done on the night of liberation in Zimbabwe. These songs echoed through the house as this remarkable family shared their stories and culture with me.

As a teenager in exile, Nhlahla had created a tape of various freedom songs which he had overdubbed onto a cassette recording of Paul Simon's *Graceland*—a statement in itself. Shortly into "Diamonds on the Soles of My Shoes," the tape cut into the sounds of AK-47s and a popular lament to a fallen soldier, followed by a powerful call to listeners: "This is Radio Freedom ... the voice of the African National Congress. South Africa's time-tested revolutionary organization, born of the people on the frontline states to spearhead the people's struggle for the seizure of power." He told me about one night when he and some fellow comrades were on an underground mission and were crossing the border back into South Africa. They were searched and the police found this very cassette. The cops made them play it, and Graceland came on as indicated by the label. Had the police made them play it for more than two minutes they would have been caught, the punishment: surely torture ... quite possibly death.

All this for music? I began putting together the pieces.

Song has always been, and continues to be, at the heart of humankind's journey, at times arguably the fuel that keeps us going. From the Negro spirituals of the U.S. to South Africa's impassioned songs for an imprisoned leader who would one day be freed, song has been a life-preserver in the daily struggle to survive.

Within many struggles worldwide, people have used music to give courage, to console, and to strengthen. Nowhere has this been more evident than in South Africa. The voices of South African people have embodied the true spirit of resistance against what seemed to be insurmountable odds.

South Africa's musical history reveals the transition of song in South African culture, from a means of self-expression to a powerful and unified collective voice. Song became a means to mobilize the masses by creating an electrifying climate for change. Through song, South Africans found a nonviolent way to express their anger, fear, and frustration. Song gave the people a voice and a link to their culture in a society that categorically sought to strip it away.

In my feature documentary film *Amandla! A Revolution in Four-part Harmony* we made the case that song was the ultimate catalyst for struggle and ultimately liberation. Music was the glue that bound South Africa's oppressed

populations together, across tribal lines and class differences. Through ingenious channels of communication it carried the messages of the movement
to and from the most isolated communities: songs created at the notorious
Robben Island prison would find their way to school kids in Soweto within
days, sometimes hours.

Activists turned DJs popularized many of these songs through Radio Freedom, a pirate radio station based in Lusaka, Zambia. Its broadcasts found
their way onto South African soil as activists would huddle at great risk listening to the news of the day and the latest liberation songs. At the dawn of liberation in the early 1990s South Africans by and large stood together in a
proud, hopeful, and electrifying collective.

Fast-forward to 2007: as South Africa's economy and democracy thrive, I
am often asked what has become of the liberation songs? A better question
would be; *what's become of the collective?*

These days, many of my friends like Nhlahla actively lament the loss of the
collective spirit, the near disappearance of freedom songs—by the mid-'90s
the writing was already on the wall. While South Africa's racial barriers faded,
her class divisions grew, and community and activist leaders disappeared from
the townships scurrying for their places behind the walls and razor wires of
previously all-white-tree-lined suburbs. Crime and HIV were left behind.
The march of modernity was on and it was centered on the individual.

Across the arts spectrum, expressions of struggle were redundant and losing
appeal; youth wanted to forget the past. In its place rose a new inspirational
voice—bring on the bling! While American and international beats have always been popular on South Africa's airwaves, hip-hop and electronic music
has begun to dominate South African musicians struggling for their place in
rapidly decreasing "local" slots.

Somewhere through this cacophony of sounds and styles competing for
dollars and relevance, the political, cultural, and economic landscape continues to transform. The collective voice can still be heard, albeit more softly:
HIV activists, trade unionists, and those still living in squalor are reinventing
the songs of the past for the struggles of today. They say that song is there, and
can always be used when it's needed; I am not so sure. Can Americans break
out into song as freely as we did during the civil rights and Vietnam war protests? Are there songs being created to mobilize against the Bush administra-
tion? Or, is it possible that just a few generations of plugging in and tuning
out could eradicate that capacity?

The Virtual Breeding of Sound

Manuel DeLanda

Even a casual visit to a complex ecosystem can become an intense musical experience, as the natural sounds that arise from a multiplicity of animals, playing the role of identification, seduction, warning, weave themselves into a rich sonic tapestry. Most of these sounds are genetically hardwired and so have evolved side by side with the genetic materials that form their substratum. But a few of these, like the complex song of the blackbird, have acquired a degree of independence from their genetic foundation. In such cases only the bare structure of a song is inherited, an impoverished backbone which must be supplemented by the actual listening of the adult song with all its flourishing details to become fully developed. What this means is that these songs have become *memes*, patterns of behavior transmitted through *imitation*, and as such, capable of having an evolution of their own. A similar point can be made of some nonnatural sounds, like the phonemes that form the raw material of human languages. Unlike memes, these are patterns of behavior transmitted through *social obligation*, to the extent that learning the identifying sounds of one's speech community is a necessary condition for belonging to that community. (So, rather than "memes," we may call these replicating sounds "norms.") In either case, we have here examples of sonic materials that, having acquired a replicator status of their own, have for the same reason separated themselves from genetic matter and taken flight, following their own evolutionary line.

The realization that evolutionary change may take place in *any population of variable replicators*, and that not only selection pressures like climate, predators, or parasites can steer this process but so can anything that acts as a *sorting device*, is the key to the project of using computers to perform virtual evolution. Perhaps the most famous example here is the *genetic algorithm* created by John Holland, but there are several others (genetic programming, evolutionary strategies, evolutionary programming).[1] Behind the details of each different implementation is the idea that coupling replicators to a sorting device results in an *automatic search process* (the genetic algorithm is classified as a search algorithm in computer science), that is, that as the population goes through many generations a space of possibilities is explored thoroughly (if blindly, given that evolution has no foresight). This search space may be a space of possible bird songs, or of possible linguistic phonemes, or in those cases where artists use genetic algorithms, a space of possible musical compositions. In a sense this simply automates a combinatorial process which, in principle, can be, and has been, carried on by hand by past musicians. As the authors of one genetic algorithm-based music system (Vox Populi) write:

Systems of algorithmic composition evolved side by side with the arising of Western music. One of the first known proposals to formalize composition was made by the Italian monk Guido d'Arezzo, in 1206, who resorted to using a number of simple rules that mapped liturgical texts in Gregorian chant, due to an overwhelming number of orders for his compositions. In the classical era, composers such as Mozart, Haydn, and C. P. E. Bach used an algorithmic decision process called "Würfelspiel" (Dice Game) to compose minuets and other works. The music was constructed by means of random selection of segments from a table of motifs.[2]

The difference between those early attempts and current ones using virtual evolution is in the size and complexity of the search space. Whereas a table of motifs may have only a limited combinatorial productivity, computers allow the creation of much larger search spaces with potentially an infinite number of possible combinations. The first condition for tapping this new reservoir of algorithmic resources is to transform sonic raw materials into replicators. Since we cannot count on a community of imitators to make them into memes, or a social community to obey them as norms, the sounds must replicate themselves through genes. The simplest way of doing this, but by no means the only way or even the most productive one, is to make a conventional digital encoding of the four components of a sound: pitch, timbre, loudness, and duration. Musicians have had such conventional code available for years in the form of the note tables for pitch, velocity tables for loudness, and tables for timbre offered by the MIDI standard. Using this code, the "DNA" of a particular sound can be easily created. In Vox Populi, for example, each replicator is defined as a group of four notes, and its genetic information as a sequence of strings of ones and zeros (one string for each component of each sound).[3] The crucial property of variability (the variation of the replicators is what fuels evolution) may be implemented either as *point mutations* that stochastically change a one into a zero (or vice versa) or, if sexual reproduction is simulated, as *recombinations* of parts of one digital sequence with another. It is not always this simple to decide how to inject variability into the population. In some cases, where the artist needs to reduce the search space so that the evolved compositions stay within a given genre (say, jazz, as in the program GenJam), the design of the mutation and recombination operators becomes more complex.

The next step is to take a *population* of these sonic replicators and unleash them into a virtual environment. It is important to realize that one needs an entire reproductive community of sounds, and not a sonic "Adam and Eve," to get the process going, since the mutations that emerge do so at different places in the collectivity and need time to propagate through it. This is just another way of saying that the efficiency of genetic algorithms as search programs depends on the fact that they explore search space *in parallel*, an entire population moving through that space one generational tic at a time. In the case of Vox Populi, a population of four-note chords is set into motion, each generation yielding a single "winner" which is then added to previous chords to form a sequence that, when sent to the MIDI port, "produces a sound result resembling a chord cadence or a fast counterpoint of note blocks."[4]

Finally, we need to implement the "sorting device," that is, some analogue of natural selection. Short of creating an entire ecosystem of sounds with different functions, some sounds preying on others, some playing host to sonic parasites, and so on, the simplest solution here is to imitate the process of prize-dog or race-horse breeding, where the aesthetic sense of a human being becomes the filter that allows some replicators to survive into, others to disappear from, the next generation. In the case of virtual evolution, the selective action of the breeder may be done in person, the artist checking each generation for aesthetic fitness and directly eliminating those sounds not considered fit, or the judgment of the artist may itself be encoded into yet another program which automatically checks the degree of aesthetic fitness. In either case the process will resemble more that of animal breeding (that is, artificial evolution) than natural evolution, where fitness criteria are not given in advance and tend to change over time, as when a predator and its prey engage in an arms race and change the very rules of the game with every innovation in defensive or offensive adaptations.

Performing the sorting function personally has the advantage that the full complexity and ambiguity of an artist's aesthetic criteria may be brought to bear on the process. Sound sequences that may offer only a faint promise of working may be left in the population for a while, and cliché repetitions that could invade the whole sonic community may be weeded out early. At any rate, the artist's own sense of what works may be allowed to change as he or she experiences the results. The problem with this approach is that it is not only tedious—each sequence of sounds of each generation must be heard and judged—but also time consuming, given that there is no way of speeding evolution up or leaving the system to evolve on its own for long stretches of time. The other possibility, to encode the fitness criteria into a computer program, lifts these limitations, but it has the drawback of forcing the creator into deciding in advance the kind of music that will evolve. In Vox Populi, for example, several fitness criteria are used, two of which are "melodic fitness" and "harmonic fitness," based on the notion of *consonance*, or how pleasing a combination of two simultaneous notes is judged by a listener.[5] Although there are solid technical ways of specifying the degree of consonance of two sounds (by measuring the degree of overlap of the harmonic series components of their fundamental notes), it seems clear that judgments of harmony are highly culturally dependent, so that implementing them as code reduces the search space to that of a particular culture.

There may be solutions to these limitations, such as combining the best features of personal and automatic fitness judgments. Instead of a single fitness-checking program there may be, for example, several such programs (some based on consonance, some on dissonance, and so on), which the artist may let run on their own for a while, or stop and switch to manual mode for a few generations, or even allow the code of the fitness criteria to itself become a replicator, its evolution influenced by the artist's own past choices. These are now questions involving the design of the user interface of the program, questions whose answers determine how an artist may interact with the evolutionary process. For some purposes such as music composition, where the artist may spend long periods of time experimenting with different runs of evolution using them as partial searches of a large musical space, the interface design may be relatively simple. But if, on the other hand, the virtual evolution is supposed to assist the artist in a real-time performance, interface questions become complex and crucial.

A good example of real-time evolution is GenJam, a program for breeding Jazz solos. The program "hears" what a human plays and rapidly evolves a response. Given that there is not much generational time to search the space of possibilities, most of the real evolutionary process occurs away from the stage where the human and the program perform together. The human player must "train" the virtual soloist prior to performance, slowly getting fitness values ascribed to different musical ideas. This is a labor-intensive process, each individual "measure" (a sequence of eight musical events: play a new note, hold an old note, rest) having to be evaluated one at a time. Additionally, knowledge of the dynamics and history of jazz become crucial at the level of the design of the program itself. An example is the tradition of "trading fours" or "trading eights" which provides a structure for the program itself. As the author writes:

One of the most exciting traditions in jazz is the chase chorus, where soloists trade fours or eights. The rhythm section plays the form of the tune as he would for a full-chorus solo, but the soloists take turns improvising, changing off every four measures ... or every eight measures. This typically gets competitive, with each soloist trying to top the previous one. A good tactic is to mine the previous soloist's four for a melodic idea and refine that idea for the next four. This requires good ears, a quick mind, and nimble fingers to pull it off well, but the results are impressive. GenJam accomplishes this one-upmanship by listening to the human performer's last four through a pitch-to-MIDI converter, mapping what is heard as the chromosome structure it uses for a phrase and four measures, possibly mutating those chromosomes, and playing them as its next four.[6]

In this case, knowledge of a certain jazz tradition has influenced the design of the program in that it needs to evolve two populations, one of measures and one of phrases (pointers to *four* individuals in the measure population) in order to be good at the chase chorus game. But more crucially, the responsibility for innovation and creativity falls squarely on the mutation operator, which cannot be a simple stochastic flipper of ones to zeros. In particular, this operator cannot produce random changes but must confine the search space to the area of musically meaningful sequences. In other words, rather than operating at the bit level (flipping a digit in a MIDI sequence) it operates at the *musical event level*, implementing several standard melodic development techniques, such as transposition, retrograde, rotation, inversion, sorting, and retrograde-inversion. The only random aspect about these mutations is which of these alternative techniques is used at any one point.[7] What this shows is that despite the fact that genetic algorithms have become a standard piece of software, artists themselves must become involved in the implementation of the details of the programs they use because only they can bring specific knowledge of their particular field to bear on the design of the different components of the algorithm.

To conclude this brief essay I must add that besides the extra resources which musicians themselves must bring there are certain *philosophical resources*, which are also crucial if the search spaces explored by genetic algorithms are to be rich enough to yield surprising outcomes. These other resources are more general and thus apply to any artistic use of virtual evolution, whether the product is musical, pictorial, architectural, and so on. One of these key philosophical ideas may be explained using biological evolution as an example. As we are vertebrates, the architecture of our bodies makes us part of the phylum "chordata." The term "phylum" refers to a branch in the evolutionary tree (the first bifurcation after animal and plant "kingdoms"), but it also carries the idea of a shared body-plan, a kind of "abstract vertebrate" which, if folded and curled in particular sequences during embryogenesis, yields an elephant; twisted and stretched in another sequence yields a giraffe; and in yet other sequences of operations yields snakes, eagles, sharks, and humans. To put this differently, there are "abstract vertebrate" design elements, such as the tetrapod limb, which may be realized in structures as disparate as the single digit limb of a horse, the wing of a bird, or the hand with opposing thumb of a human. Given that the proportions of each of these limbs, as well as the number and shape of digits, are variable, their common body-plan cannot include any of these details. In other words, whereas the form of the final product (an actual horse, bird, or human) does have specific lengths, areas, and volumes, the body-plan cannot possibly be defined in these terms but must be abstract enough to be compatible with a myriad combination of these properties. Gilles Deleuze uses the term "abstract diagram" (or "virtual multiplicity") to refer to entities like the vertebrate body-plan, but his concept also includes the "body plans" of non-organic entities like clouds or mountains, paintings, or musical compositions.[8]

What kind of theoretical resources do we need to be able to think about these abstract diagrams? In mathematics the kind of spaces in which terms like "length" or "area" are fundamental notions are called "metric spaces," the familiar Euclidean geometry being one example of this class. (Non-Euclidean geometries, using curved instead of flat spaces, are also metric.) On the other hand, there are geometries, such as differential geometry or topology, where these notions are not basic since these geometries possess operations that do not preserve lengths or areas. The operations allowed in topology, for example, such as stretching without tearing and folding without gluing, preserve only a set of very abstract properties. These topological invariants (such as the dimensionality of a space, or its connectivity) are precisely the elements we need in order to think about body-plans (or more generally, abstract diagrams). It is clear that the kind of spatial structure defining a body-plan cannot be metric since embryological operations can produce a large variety of finished bodies, each with a different metric structure. Therefore, body-plans must be topological.

The vertebrate search space is incredibly rich precisely because it is not defined in terms of properties belonging to the final product (fixed lengths or areas) but in a different language. In the musical examples I gave before, on the other hand, the search space is given already in terms of the melodic or harmonic properties of the evolved creatures. It is possible, although I do not know how to theorize this yet, that musicians will have to start thinking in terms of abstract musical structures where the key properties for a sound are not those of fixed duration or a fixed wavelength and the like, but rather are something else corresponding to what we may call "topological music," something we cannot hear (much as we cannot see the topological vertebrate) but which would define a rich search space the final products of which would be audible. In turn, this implies representing within the computer something like the complex embryological processes, which map the genes (the genotype) into bodily traits (the phenotype), given that this complex mapping genotype–phenotype is where the conversion from topological to metric is achieved. Clearly, current uses of genetic algorithms display only the tip of an iceberg, the exploration of which will perhaps take decades. This is a sobering thought, preventing us from being overenthusiastic about our current capabilities of breeding sound, but simultaneously it is a source of excitement at all the unknown domains still waiting to be discovered.

Notes

1. Peter J. Bentley and David W. Corne, "An Introduction to Creative Evolutionary Systems," in *Creative Evolutionary Systems*, ed. Peter J. Bentley and David W. Corne (Academic Press, 2002).

2. Artemis Moroni et al., "Vox Populi: Evolutionary Computation for Music Evolution," in *Creative Evolutionary Systems*, 206.

3. Ibid., 212.

4. Ibid., 208.

5. Ibid., 212.

6. John A. Biles, "GenJam: Evolution of a Jazz Improviser," in *Creative Evolutionary Systems*, 168.

7. Ibid., 175.

8. Gilles Deleuze and Felix Guattari, *A Thousand Plateaus* (University of Minnesota Press, 1987), 141.

Liminal Product: Frances Dyson and Douglas Kahn

Getting out of caves, tunnels, and tombs has preoccupied Western culture for millennia. Western thought itself couldn't function without the vertical axis which has brute matter, primordiality, misery, or evil at the bottom, and the spirit, enlightenment, civility, bounty, or uprightness at the top. But while ascent from darkness into light, from illusion to reality, from moral decrepitude to goodness, from weakness to strength, from the undesirable to the desired, is the central narrative of almost every tale the West has to tell, what is often left out is the equally obsessive desire to return to the darkness, to mess around with its edges, to extract its secrets, to dwell there for awhile, and, of course, to escape and do it all over again. This circularity of entering, exiting, and reentering describes the birth of the subway. The transit underground to the horizontal occasioned the first steam locomotive, built to haul ore from tunnels, which were mines. Engines entered mines in order to transport the fuel they would consume in order to make the trip, instinctively reentering the dark in order to harvest their life blood. The modern subway developed from this solipsism.

Mines, both literally and metaphorically, have provided a space wherein all origins can be retrieved, passages, and ascensions conceptualized, and where sublime tautology and paradox can foment. Along with ore they have provided culture with tragic and fatal narratives for centuries. Unlike the allegorical cave of Plato or the underworld of Orpheus, the mine is not a place of illusion occupied by prisoners unwilling or unable to escape into the light of reason or the truth of sensorial existence. "If the miner sees shapes on the walls of his cavern" writes Lewis Mumford, they are only the monstrous distortions of his pick or his arm: shapes of fear. Unlike Orpheus, the miner's look back into the underworld is enforced with each daily return. What transforms grand illusion into mundane and routine fear has as much to do with the physical transformation of caverns into workplaces and tunnels into the byways of transportation, as with the cultural passage from antiquity to modernity.

As Mumford writes: "The mine is the first completely inorganic environment to be created and lived in by man."[1] Mines are totally enclosed spaces—without the addition of artificial light and air they would be uninhabitable. Conquering the conditions of death, transforming the mine from a tomb to a place of labor is a central theme in the narrative of "progress through technology." The physical environment favors machines, while the life that does intercede necessitates a degree of artificiality, tending away from the biologic toward the inorganic in proportion to the mine's technological sophistication and physical depth. The miner's own presence depletes, with every breath and movement, the conditions of survival. The artificial light opens up the visible space at the same time it eats up the air. The walls that might support the ceiling are destroyed with the advance of labor, as each strike or shovel resounds against the sharp, reflective surfaces. Within these cadenced striations of rock and sedimented dramas of an irrefutable past, the myths of modernity reverberate against the hard walls, closing in on the already claustrophobic passages. It is as though the sounds do not dissipate but take on a physical permanency in the administered air. But while the sounds and activities of humans remain fixed, the juggernaut of progress moves forward into the future in a straight and certain line, leaving the muddling, multidimensional, and obstinately organic tailings of the past in its tracks.

The acceleration of progress transmutes the mine into a tunnel, the locomotive into a subway tram and train. For the millions of people traveling on a daily basis the mysteries of the underground have all been excavated, and what remains is the banality of the daily diaspora. The engine of capitalism has burrowed out the other side carrying with it the commuters, the new ore for its solipsistic regeneration. On-board individuals are alchemically transmuted from individuals, members of communities or circles of friends, family members, into workers. The train which reduces people to inorganic ore has itself taken on a biological character: inseminated at point of departure it sheds its litter upon arrival. During the period of gestation these fetuses, these larvae are known as commuters. The tourist is the only passenger to escape this metamorphosis, moving from station to station, from train to train, from one mode of transport to the next while maintaining his or her identity. What allows this portable identity is the fact of continuous travel, entering the logic of continuous circulation.

If the station had not become banal the ideal commuter could emerge from the mysteries of the underground to survey the glorious revelation of the city and greet the new day. But the station is by definition stationary. It impedes the frenzied desires of progress to accelerate at ever increasing speed, which in modernity found its expression in instantaneous transmission. The key to transport success—to reduce the duration of the passenger moving forward by mechanical means—has made the actual journey irrelevant and the journeying body into something of an interruption in the ideal. There is something of a residue in every passenger—a testament to the fact that bodies, although not stationary, cannot yield to the ideal in transport; they necessarily lag behind in their collective mass, countering the unquestioned violence in this rhetoric of speed with the stubborn stillness of those that wait.

That is why being in transit is experienced most saliently by not moving. Stations are occupied by those who, by definition, have missed the last train. Left behind, like tailings, these stationary passengers stand alone and silent among the hordes. Rarely speaking to one another, the masses gathered in the underground submit to the various tasks of banality: checking the time, listening for announcements, anticipating delays. They wait in a completely inorganic environment without the dialogue which might situate them socially. Instead, they assume a residual status governed by an acoustics and climatics of enclosure. The rock walls, floor, and ceilings of the mine have transmuted into concrete and tiles, which reflect sounds even more sharply. The amplitude of the sounds bear down on the individual as the sounds of trains from different parts of the station arrive from every direction, reflecting repeatedly, over and over again, off every gleaming surface.

The pressure from this acoustical envelopment is reinforced by the constraint of air, at once controlled by ventilation systems, singed by the electrified drives of the trains, and depleted by crowds of waiting passengers. Asphyxiation, as Antonin Artaud has shown, is there at the root of the scream, fueled by a huge compensatory gasp. The nascent scream of controlled air can be heard in the high-pitched sounds of metal wheels grinding on the inside of the rails, the sparking and scraping along the electrical contacts, the acoustically tuned engines which raise in pitch as they accelerate, the overtones of noises interacting with themselves off the tiles, and in the flickering of the gaseous lighting. In the lower range, the platform rumbles and masses of air are shoved aside under the weight of the cars. The passage from hum to measured clang; the doppler of the passing train truncated by its entrance from and exit into the tube. And these are but what we hear or feel, while electrostatic and electromagnetic winds sweep through the innermost reaches of everyone waiting. Trains approach, depart, pass, and the repertoire scrolls by day after day.

Such a volume of sound provokes a qualitatively different experience from simple listening. Lingering in the underground, sound finds a materiality it never enjoys above ground, imprinting on its captive audience the booms and shudders of pneumatic backwash. Sound is a carrier, a medium, something always on the move. Transitory by nature, sound is the perfect passenger, embarking and disembarking quickly, continuously, and without a trace. On the surface of the city, in the bustle of everyday life, this is certainly the case. Heard but not seen, the sounds of the city have only a limited existence. Despite the virtually constant roar of traffic, beep of signals, screech of brakes, wail of sirens, thunder of jackhammers, hum of ambient muzak and shrill tones of mobile phones, its presence is ephemeral, circumstantial, accidental. But in the subways beneath the city, the rapid passage from sound to silence, from ravaging noise to irritating hum is interrupted. In the underground sound hangs around—reverberating off the walls to reencounter itself, repeating and amplifying some of its frequencies, reproducing a limited range of sounds that lack the multiplicity, circumstantial quality, and mutual interruption, of the sounds above.

Asserting and reasserting its exclusiveness in an occluded environment, sound adopts the station as its home, becomes derelict. A failure of transience gives way to the success of "the transient"—the body that is by nature always on the move but stationary for too long. What is the problem with sound underground? Are we witnessing the repressed resonance of urban transport, the collective screams and roars that have nowhere else to go? Or is this the inevitable detritus of noise and bodies that forms at the edges of further and faster?

In the clinical, denatured spaces of the underground the passage of time also takes on a perverse materiality. While there is no night or day, the hours are given measure by the sweaty crush of commuters or scary absence thereof.

The coming together and moving apart of bodies is one of the most mesmer-izing aspects of contemporary transit. Watching the swarms of passengers move it's difficult not to see the underground rail network as did writers in the late nineteenth century, who imagined a mega-body, with the arteries carrying the "lifeblood of a nation" in the same way that telephones "feel out and determine the course of that circulation, which is a condition of national prosperity." But progress has already accelerated through the underground and has come out the other side, the tube lifting its wheels and sprouting wings, taking flight and, reaching its destination, laying eggs like some mega-alien into the pods that reconnect them with the ground, easing that transi-tion from air to surface by providing another well-conditioned tube. In the airport, the sight of passengers deplaning gently morphs with representations of cyber travel in which an infinite number of tiny tubes criss-crossing, link-ing, mapping, and connecting the world create a hyperorganism—a child of evolution doing its thing.

In the contemporary imagination tubes have been replaced by fibers and streams, encircling the globe, a sticky vehicle for the transmission of anything and everything immaterial. "Travel" and "commuting" can now happen at a distance. The visuality of Western culture and its obsession with acceleration has produced a new kind of movement, a new axis of transcendence if you will, which is speed at a distance: visual acceleration. Or, in the vernacular, the *zoom*. The zoom is an onomatopoeia, a four-letter doppler represent-ing the sound of objects passing quickly by a hypothetical listener, that has somehow found its way into the visual vernacular. The zoom is to data trans-fer as the tunnel is to commuter throughput. The quicker the zoom the more transcendent, where all has been burrowed through, where time and space have collapsed, and the passage to another plane has been completed.

The zoomer moves through different simulated zones, displacing the me-chanical movements of the train, the corporeal movements of the passengers and the pneumatic movements of air. With this displacement all the sound, the wind, the sweaty crush, the semidarkness, the dubious atmosphere and the mythological meaning of the underground is lost. With telecommuting, there is no physical necessity attached to the passage of communication, nor is there the need to transform passengers into workers, tourists, consumers. Nothing lingers in the data streams; there is no opportunity for that subtle conversion of the aural into the palpable, or time into measurements of sweat. There is no opportunity for the reversal that has allowed the underground to accommodate the ground under, for transience to manifest in the bodies of transients.

Despite the silence of visual acceleration, it is important to remember that zoom is first and foremost an aural term describing a sound that can only be heard if the listener is stationary. Being stationary has as much to do with standing at the station as with being tied to the work station, as with knowing one's station. Just as sound is the residue, the repressed of rapid transit, so too the body is the repressed that the myth of visual acceleration conceals. Before jumping from one telecommunications platform to the next, it is worthwhile listening to the transfer and sniffing the air. What kinds of sounds inhabit the work station and who or what is left standing once the train has gone?

Note

1. Lewis Mumford, *Technics and Civilization* (New York: Harcourt, 1934), 69.

Carlo McCormick

Hired as a young man by the fledgling Columbia Records label as their first art director, Alex Steinweiss proved to be the rare musical-visual visionary that comes around far too infrequently in the history of popular culture. As the man who single-handedly transformed the drab artless covers of the old 78 RPM (revolutions per minute) record albums into a mass media canvas of infinite creative possibility, Steinweiss's influence has shaped the way every generation has seen, purchased, understood, and appreciated music over the past half century. We first made contact with Mr. Steinweiss in the process of curating an exhibition on the art of the record cover. And on the occasion of our first meeting, while we were installing this show at its original location at Exit Art in New York City (it would later travel to the Experience Music Project museum in Seattle and the Warhol Museum in Pittsburgh), Alex looked at the endless stacks amounting to thousands of albums, pulled us aside and whispered confidentially—"you know, all of this stuff you got here, it all came out of my left elbow."

A man of immense modesty considering his impact on our culture, Steinweiss just wanted to be sure we understood that somehow, this sprawling mass of commerce was indeed his baby. Perhaps all he wanted to make clear in the light that our show was about the 33 RPM LP (long-playing) record, was that it was he who actually came up with that precise way of cutting, folding, and gluing together cardboard that became the industry standard of what we now call a record cover. In fact, having discussed his work with some of the most celebrated artists to ever put their hand to record cover design, we find that they all in their way consider him as the father—the paternal spirit from whose elbow was born one of the most remarkable mediums of American culture in the second half of the twentieth century. Over the past year, I have been very fortunate to know Alex and his wife Blanche and enjoy their fine company. This phone conversation with him at his home in Sarasota, Florida, is but a small portion of the immense blessing I have enjoyed in getting to know him, and of the great joy that has been more widely experienced by the recording industry, musicians, and music lovers the world over.

Carlo McCormick: Let's start back in the dark ages. It's 1939 and you've just gotten a job at Columbia.

Alex Steinweiss: Yeah. 1939. I was 23 years old. And CBS broadcasting company—radio, that is, because in those days there was no television—they decided to buy a defunct record company up in Bridgeport, Connecticut, and named it Columbia Recording Corporation, and they needed an art director. A good friend of mine told me about it, and I arranged an appointment with the advertising manager—a guy by the name of Patrick Dolan (a good Irishman), and he was a brilliant guy. He's no longer with us, but he was a great guy and we got along very well, and that's the way I came to Columbia. Now I guess you want to know what I found when I got there.

CM: Sure. Basically that the covers didn't have any art at all, right?

AS: No. At that time, there was no art on covers at Columbia Records. There was just a gray or a tan paper wrapped around the album. They were 78 RPMs in those days, and bound with some imitation leather and gold stamping on the spine. And then on the front they had just a little box with the nomenclature. It looked like a tombstone. When I looked at it I said, "Jesus, how the hell can they sell beautiful music in this crap?" So I tried to be very diplomatic and I found an opening and said, "Listen, why don't you give me a shot at doing five covers for some of the stuff and we'll see what happens in the market?" I did five covers and the rest is history.

There was one I did for the "Eroica" Symphony, the third symphony of Beethoven, and the sales went up (oh, I don't know) I think it was 800 percent. It was all picked up by the press, and there were articles in *Time* and *Newsweek* and *BusinessWeek*. It was a phenomenon, and naturally, the company was convinced because I was adding to the income.

CM: I guess that's how you get their ear.

AS: That's right. Anyway, I had a wonderful relationship with Pat and with the president of the company, and I worked up in Bridgeport, knocking my brains out until the army put its arm out, you know, at the beginning of the whole thing.

CM: World War II?

AS: Yeah. I got my induction papers, but before that, there were a whole file of guys that came up to Bridgeport to see me because my reputation had gone around already, and they wanted to come up and see what I could do for them. These are guys who were refugees out of Germany. Europe was full of Mr. Hitler. So these guys got out as fast as they could. There was one guy who used to be with the Bauhaus; he was a student first, then he was a teacher. His name was Xanti Schawinsky, and he told me about an operation that the Navy set up in New York City right on Broadway. It was an unbelievable thing; it was almost like a small imitation Bauhaus. The function was to design posters, booklets, models—anything that could be used to teach young men in the Navy what their job was and how to do it, because a lot of them didn't even finish high school when they came in. So, I spent a couple of years there until V-J Day, and all the time I was there I was doing album covers at night, until about twelve, one o'clock in the morning. I had trained the staff up in Bridgeport to take my very tight sketch and to translate it into black-and-white art for the camera. So, I was adding to my income, which was pretty small in the Navy even as a civilian, and at the same time, I was sort of a consultant to the president, and after the war, I was an official consultant to him. That's when—not too long after that the LP record was born in 1947—I invented the jacket, because that was part of my job as a consultant. And as you know, the jacket was the standard kind of packaging used by the industry until the CD.

CM: Now you managed to convince them, I think, within a few months to do those covers, which is pretty remarkable, but when you start out you're doing the advertising catalogs and point-of-purchase ads.

AS: Yes. I was a graphic designer to industry; I was doing packaging, and originally, when I got out of Parson's School of Design that I went to for three years on a scholarship, I got my first job with a guy by the name of Joseph Binder, who opened a studio in his apartment on 58th Street and 6th Avenue. First I went to a guy who was already here many years and who established his reputation as a poster designer, his name was Lucian Bernhard, and I appeared at his studio on 86th Street without an invitation, without a phone call. I rang the bell, and his son, who was his assistant at the time, came to the door and he says, "What do you want?" I said, "I want a job." He says, "Don't you know that you have to call for an appointment." I thought, Holy mackerel, I really stepped into it; they'll never see me now. He says, "Listen, you brought your portfolio, sit down and I'll bring it in to my father, and we'll see what he can do." So I sat there in a pool of sweat for about twenty minutes until the master came out with a big cigar and my portfolio, and he says, "I just called Joseph Binder who's in from Vienna not too long ago. He's starting to work in New York and he told me he needs an assistant. So, I've already called him up; he says to take the bus over and go up and have an interview." Well I thanked him very much, and I went over to see Joe Binder. He hired me as a second assistant, and you can imagine how I felt right out of school.

He was very busy, he was doing a lot of posters, and in those days they had 24-sheet posters; those are billboards. He did them for beers and all kinds of products. He was very successful, but he had a first assistant who was a little more experienced than I was. He was a big airbrush guy; he always did a lot of airbrush on his posters, on his ads, whatever, and I had never held an airbrush in my life. In the interview he asked, "Do you know how to use an airbrush?" and I said, "Sure," you know, a cocky kid from Brooklyn. So I learned on the job. I learned how to use the airbrush and I learned a lot about color. I stayed with him for three years. Then, you know, when you carry out another person's original ideas it gets a little tiresome. I was bursting to create stuff; so I left amicably and tried to start freelancing. Blanche, my wife, was my representative. I made a deal with a very nice guy on 49th Street. He's gone too—Morris Sanders—he was an architect, took an old brownstone and put a very fancy, modern front on. He gave me space in the studio in exchange for doing some visual work for him—renderings and stuff like that. I was there about six months and I was just about getting an account when I get this phone call about the Columbia Records thing, and you know the rest.

CM: It's interesting that you mention all this poster work because I think that one of the things you bring to album cover art (other than inventing the medium) is kind of a maximizing of that space, which seems to me might have been informed a bit by the history of posters before then.

AS: That's absolutely right. It all started when I went to Abraham Lincoln High School in Brooklyn. It was a beautiful school, just opened, and they had a chairman for the art department, a fellow by the name of Leon Friend.

He's also gone. I think that all the people I knew are gone. This guy was a fantastic teacher. He devoted his life to his kids. I didn't know that I had any talent at all at that time. There was a bunch of guys in the art department that were making signs for school, you know, like sign painters; they were learning how to do lettering, and when I looked at that, I almost fainted. I thought, if I could be a sign painter, that's a wonderful way to make a living. So I started to fool around with it. Well, to make a long story short, I took his graphic design courses for the full four years of high school. But the thing is that while he was teaching, at the same time, he was writing the first book ever published in America on the art of graphic design. He was working with a colleague by the name of Dr. Hefter, mostly weekends putting together this book. Now for illustrative material, he was in contact with western European designers because at that time Britain, France, Spain, Holland, and Germany already had a highly developed poster art. They still have it; we don't have it here anymore; we gave up on it as American designers—we're into the computer age. But at that time, poster art in Europe was very, very active, and he would write to the designers over there and get examples of their work in order to put in the book. Before he put them into the book, he held them up to us to show us what was happening in Europe. And this really sunk in and in my work you can absolutely see traces of influence from the great poster designers.

CM: Those were basically the '30s, then?

AS: Those were the '30s. There were a whole bunch of guys who were doing marvelous work there. They were pieces of inspiration for us kids and it was one of the best times in my life. We used to get into school like 6:30, 7 o'clock and we wouldn't get out of school until about 5, 6 o'clock because we were all so interested. You know it was the Depression here, and you had to find a way to make a living, and this was like it came from heaven with this guy training us the way he did.

CM: What were some of the things you could say you learned from those posters that you applied when you first started designing record covers—what were some of the strategies of how to use the space?

AS: What you had to do was get to the point quickly; you couldn't fuss around with all the little details. Whatever was being handled for publicity, or the subject of the poster—whether it was cigarettes or crackers or whatever the product was—you had to keep it very simple and very direct. You had to communicate quickly because a poster is seen in a fraction of a second as a person is walking by or waiting for a train. In Europe, they used to post the posters three at a time, and they still do that. So that principle stuck in my head and when I designed.

I was a specialist in classical music because I had listened to music since I was in knee pants, and it was part of my whole life. So I really didn't have to listen to music to design. And then I found in reading a lot about music that there were, essentially, two types of classical music. One was what you call "program music," like an opera or a ballet—something that has a story behind it—that you get your teeth into. So right away, you have material to work with. The second type of music is more widely known, and that consists of symphonies, concertos, all kinds of chamber music—pure music with no story behind it. That's very difficult for the designer, but it's a great opportunity to go into spaces that were never done before because you don't have to stick to a story; you can let your imagination run and try to get the smell and the feeling of the music in the design.

CM: How would you translate the essence of something abstract in a kind of graphic art medium?

AS: Well, my collection is full of stuff. For example, let's say you're doing Bartok's Third Piano Concerto—what do you do? Well, you take any kind of elements connected with the piano essentially—so you take the piano apart, and on this design I used several white keys and several black keys, sort of floating, and strings in the background. And then on one of the large white keys within it, I did a little drawing in color of a Hungarian peasant. Because Bartók used to travel all over Hungary and Romania collecting old folk tunes, which he used in his compositions. So with abstract music, you can do a lot of reading about the composer's life; you can understand the type of costumes they wore in the days of the composer's life, the architecture, anything that will give the flavor of the music inside. There's a wealth of material you can use for the abstract music. The program music is a little easier. Let's say *La Traviata*, the opera, you know the lady of the camellias. Right away, you've got to have a camellia and you've got to have the suggestion of Paris and champagne and all of that, and then you put in the color. *La Traviata* I remember had a hot pink color. You use color, you use design, and you use distinctive type or lettering.

One of the shortcomings of working in Bridgeport at that time is that there were very few graphic services, like typographers or engravers or people in the graphic arts, reproduction-wise. It was difficult to get type because Bridgeport itself was an industrial city, and the only thing they knew up there was how to make little catalogs for bullets and the Bridgeport brass and Warner's brassieres. That was the town.

CM: But that was also a big time for typography.

AS: Typographers were the basis of the graphic arts industry. Of course, today, it's all on the computer—they're all out of business.

CM: You created your own "Steinweiss Scrawl" font based off your distinctive cursive lettering style.

AS: That's right, I used the Steinweiss Scrawl because it was quick to do and I had a pretty good hand, and I used that for all the secondary material, like the opus number or the name of the instrument. But the names of the composition and the composer were the most important, and I used typography for them. For the secondary material, I just did this very, very quick, colorful, amusing script.

Then Photo Lettering bought that, and they gave me a royalty for many, many years. Finally they had so many designers that they had to send out checks to they offered me a set price and bought the whole thing outright.

CM: Being informed by posters and getting your visual chops that way, and then being hired to do all the kind of general advertising work you did, what was so unique about this canvas—originally for the 78 and then for the LP—what was the challenge or the opportunity of that particular formatted regular surface for you?

AS: Well the LP is still basically a 12 by 12 thing, so it wasn't much different from the 78 RPM album. Of course, I'm in retirement for many years. But strangely enough, about a year ago, a conductor in New York called me and insisted that I do some CDs for him. I hadn't done album covers for years and years, but he insisted and in spite of the hefty fee that I demanded, I just finished my third one for him.

CM: With this general shrinkage in format, you can't quite work the same way of visually grabbing somebody in one second with a CD, can you?

AS: No, you can't, and what the companies mostly do today is put a big head of the artist in there and some type and a bit of color, and that's it. And if you go to a record shop and take a look at these postage stamps—I call them postage stamps—there isn't too much inspiration to get you to pick up a record. But in my day, you had to hit the guy on the head. We used to have the browser boxes for LPs that people would go through, and as they came across an attractive album, they would pick it up. They also

had in the early days of my tenure in the record business little listening booths
in the record stores, and if you wanted to listen to a record, you'd go in a
booth and play it. So a lot of people would be attracted by the art and would
take the album into the booth and listen, and they would buy the album, but
the prime thing was that they took the goddamn thing up. Once you pick it
up, you practically bought it. That's why the sales went up so fast on all the
stuff, including all the pop stuff I did. I did country music, blues, jazz, I did it
all, but of course, I'm a classical music person. I think Mozart will outlive all
the funk and hunk and bunk and junk.

CM: Is it beyond doing something that's an appealing image—is there an
actual trick or a language on how to grab the consumer, kind of the art of
seduction?

AS: The art of seduction? Well, you can call it that, you try to do it by means
of color, design, typography, and—

CM: And imagery, no?

AS: And imagery, exactly. And there's a whole world of imagery. For example, I've done at least four of each of the most important repertoire. Four record covers for the same piece of music, and each had to look different because
I worked for six companies. And you can't do a Mahler First Symphony for
four companies and they all look alike. But if you love the music and you love
what the composer did and you do enough reading, somehow you get to the
point and you're able to do a very attractive thing. I personally think that CD,
the medium, stinks (don't quote me). And I even think that soundwise.

I remember when I used to go to recording sessions, there was a big orchestra, and in the recording booth, there was the music director and the engineer.
The engineer kept his eye on the needle so that it doesn't jump out of the
meter, but the musical person was there with a score and he alerted the engineer as to what was coming up. Between that and the technique of recording
in those days, when the record finally came out it sounded very natural and
undistorted. I find that on some violin concerto CDs it sounds like the guy is
playing a steel fiddle. It doesn't sound like it was made out of wood. It's too
shrill, and that's because there's only an engineer, and he's worried about that
needle, he's not worried about the music.

CM: You worked in the '40s, '50s, and '60s—that's nearly thirty years in this
industry. Can you describe the evolution of the dialogue within the industry?
Obviously when you started they didn't even know what you were doing,
most people there probably had no idea, and you were entirely responsible

for the look of the cover. I'm curious if at any point the marketing people start coming in, or if the recording artist really starts to exercise a stronger control over the look of their record.

AS: I know what you mean. First of all, the person who made the record, in many cases, they were so pleased with what I did that they didn't make any noise. In fact, I have letters of appreciation in my file from all of the greats—Rise Stevens, Lily Pons, Eddie Duchin, Andre Kostelanetz. They were mostly very, very happy and I had free rein. As far as management, I was helping them. The vice president in charge of sales at Columbia Records was Paul Southard, and he loved me because I made his job easier, I was helping him sell the stuff. So in my particular case, management never pushed their nose in too much. Mary Martin married a guy who took over the management of her career. When she was listed to do an album, he always wanted to see me and find out what I had in mind. I would tell him exactly what I thought I was going to do, and he most of the time agreed, he never made a fuss. The other is Andre Kostelanetz. I can remember only two or three times when he asked me to sit down with him at lunch and asked me, "What are you going to do for this, what are you going to do for that?" I know one in particular, he did an album of his typical light music and I think *Orchids in the Moonlight* was the title, and he wanted some orchids on the cover, so I gave him orchids. I did it my way, he was happy, and I was happy, and it worked out great. But most of the time, I used to get wonderful letters from the different artists. Later on, Stokowski, who was pretty close to ninety, moved to England and signed a ten-year contract with Decca (London). At that time I was doing a lot of London stuff, and it came to a point where he insisted that Steinweiss do all his covers. I guess I was satisfying them.

CM: Didn't the labels start trying to figure out, and intrude more in your creative process? I know they did for the music.

AS: I don't know what the other guys did, but in my case, they gave me free rein. I did some of my best covers for classical music for Decca label, and the reason was that Horowitz, the A&R guy there, never told me what to do, never intruded. You see, the bottom line is, is the stuff selling? And apparently, my reputation and what I did was attractive to people, and then, of course, records were only about 50 percent of my output.

CM: Between all the commercial work you did outside the music industry—the liquor ads and the title treatments for films—and all the record covers, you also did this really big body of work during World War II. Of course during wartime you end up with art that is like propaganda. Is graphic art a commercial art in these ways? Are their forms of persuasion not so dissimilar from what the government is going to do to persuade you?

AS: You mean during the period like the war?

CM: During the war, or at any time. Isn't this art, in one form or another, a type of propaganda?

AS: I was working for the Navy. The posters that I did were mostly instructional posters. The only propaganda posters I did were two. The Navy was the first service that opened all the rates to the blacks. Heretofore, they have these nondescript jobs—they cleaned the floors, they cooked the food, they were stewards, but they never got to do what the white guys were doing. Well the Navy wanted to impress the young people in the Navy that were black to go for the rates so they could have higher pay and recognition. So I did posters trying to get that across to the black personnel, and it worked. Don't forget, there were plenty of black heroes too, who gave up their lives. Then I did a poster for the submarine service because you have to go in that by your own volition. You don't get put into the submarine service; you apply for it, you volunteer. You've got to be under the ocean for who knows how long so your personality has to be correct, you got to get along well with the guys, and all the rest of it. Then I did things for the war effort like for war bonds.

CM: You say that music, by going from analog to digital, has suffered. You're working with T-squares and triangles and traditional materials. Those are tools, as is the computer. Obviously the computer offers a lot of possibilities, but in your mind is something lost artistically?

AS: I have a definite opinion about that. I can only judge by what I see that comes out of art studios and advertising agencies. The computer is a marvelous tool; I don't downgrade it because it is a tool, but you can't depend on the tricks that it can do to replace original thinking. So if you come to a computer with an idea of exactly what you want it to do for you, chances are you're going to come out with something good. But many times the computer is a way to get something done quickly and cheaply. I don't know how good it comes out when you go for the cheap and the speed. Let's face it, it's a fast medium—you knock it off, you come out with a disk and bingo, it comes out printed. Creatively, there's something to be desired. It enables the engineer or the architect to make changes without sitting there knocking his brains out drawing it. When you're talking about pure design, I don't think there's a substitute for a pencil. I'd rather have a pencil than a mouse.

CM: Is there also a moment of inspiration which for you is very connected to the artist's hand? Are you designing while you're listening to music?

AS: The music is in my head, in most cases, except for contemporary music, which sometimes you have to get into by listening. But all the Mozart and the Beethoven, and the Mahler—I've been listening to all of my life. There was a time when I was a kid that my father used to take me up to the Metropolitan Museum of Art, and in those days they had a symphony orchestra. It was a cavernous space with a balcony, and the orchestra used to sit in the balcony, and the conductor would do a concert, and you'd go into a gallery and sit on the floor. I'm talking when I was in knee pants. You'd sit there, you'd listen to the music, and you'd be surrounded by this visual art. It was like living in paradise. I think that crept into my being. That really is something that I depended on all my design career—that knowledge and that appreciation for good music.

CM: Well before computers, well before color separation and dot printing, there was a long process by which artwork went from this sketch to the product that the consumer eventually gets. I'm particularly curious about those first sketches you did for record covers. I know there are these other moments where you're going to redefine it or refine it and work out mechanical issues. But that first sketch now, what's foremost in your mind—is it issues of design or is it about capturing your personal impression of the music?

AS: You're asking me a question that I don't know the answer to. You have a love for doing things and you do them, but you never ask yourself now why the hell am I doing it, what am I doing? It just happens on the drawing board. You strive to incorporate all of the elements that I went through before, you know the color, the typography, the design, the idea (the idea is very important), and then of course, the two major types of music are the take-off points—the abstract and the program music. To tell you what happens to me in my head when I'm doing a creative job is very difficult for me to put into words, it just happens, and I thank the good Lord that the brain is still working.

CM: You're as sharp as ever.

AS: Well I just turned eighty-five, and the magic is still up there; I don't ask any questions.

CM: Since you retired in the early '70s, you've really dedicated yourself to making paintings that are very connected to and inspired by music, often the same classics that you were originally packaging. Now it works more tangibly as fine art.

AS: It might sound corny, but actually, I couldn't wait until I started doing paintings that were related to fine music because it was my way—and this sounds poetic and it might sound like a lot of crap—but I was paying back the composers for the music that they gave me. That's why I call it "Homage to Music." It's a continuing program, I've done 48 or 49 so far, and it will continue until I can't pick the brush up anymore, because if you're in love with something as much as I am with music, you must express it somehow. You can't get a fiddle and play the concerto, but you certainly can do a beautiful painting which gives the story for the viewer that might entice somebody to listen to the music. I've had several exhibitions down here, and I remember one in particular. There was a guy there who used to be the first bassoon player for the Philadelphia orchestra, he retired to Sarasota, and he was looking at my paintings and he came over to me and he said, "you know, Mr. Steinweiss, when I look at one of your paintings, I hear the music."

CM: That's a great compliment.

AS: What else do you need?

CM: The medium shifted, but is there another shift when you shift from graphic arts to painting in terms of representing the music, or are there pretty much the same visual issues?

AS: Well, you don't have to contend with typography. You contend only with subject matter and technique. I developed a technique which is very personal. In doing the images I use acrylic in two ways, on canvas, and on heavyweight French watercolor paper. I am essentially a graphic designer, so when you look at a painting, the colors are very, very important, like on my album covers, as you mentioned before. Acrylic has a tremendous range of color in the material itself. It's difficult to use for me because it's not tempera, it's not poster color, it comes out of the tube slippery. There's a lot of guys who use it on a canvas right out of the tube, and they build up an image three-dimensionally. They sometimes don't even use a brush. But I use the paint like I used to use a brush, and the only difficulty is that when you use it that way, you thin the medium down and you can't cover the canvas with one coat—you have to go over the same area several times to get the color bright and full. So that's a little bit of a handicap, but when you're all finished, it's worth the trouble because it's exactly the way I want to do it.

Ken Jordan

1

When can a sound be an image? Often, of course, sounds are words. In songs, the musical elements that surround lyrics are often more important than the lyrics themselves. The words of few lyricists resonate from the page without benefit of performance. We accept that sound and language can be woven into a synthetic experience. But what about sound and image?

One characteristic of digital media is that they allow for, even encourage, the combination of diverse media into integrated experiences. In a digital artwork words can lead to virtual architectural spaces, in which gestures may trigger images, which may in turn evoke sounds. Disparate media elements can be stitched together in a multitude of ways, layered upon one another so that it is difficult to separate them into their constituent forms. Just as a song combines music and poetry to make something that is distinct from either alone, digital media give rise to forms that wed: sound and movement; sound and space; sound and image.

Since *The Jazz Singer*, when the flickering image of Al Jolson first crooned on bended knee, sound has been part of filmmaking. But with or without a soundtrack, film has always been a medium with its own trajectory. We don't tend to think of talkies as being a different medium from silents. In film, the moving image dominates, and the soundtrack is subordinate. Yes, it's important, it contributes, but it is not essential. But a song without a melody or accompaniment is not a song at all: it's a poem. Dance, like film, does not become another type of artwork when without music.

A song is different, because it unites music and poetry into a synthetic expression. Digital media, too, weave sound with other media to create artworks that are specific and irreducible. The formats are still in their early stages, and not yet codified so they can be referred to easily. But building on the legacy of Max Mathews—the first person to produce sound out of bits—artists, engineers, and theorists are exploring this fertile territory. In their work we glimpse new ways to relate to sound, different approaches to shaping sound, and insights for understanding how sound shapes us, the effect it has on consciousness.

Intriguingly, those engaged in this exploration come from across the globe. Their common interest is not specific to any country or cultural tradition. Rather, it tends to coalesce where the technology exists to support it—on university campuses, at art museums, or at institutions dedicated to digital arts, such as ZKM, in Karlsruhe, or the InterCommunication Center in Tokyo. The desire to pursue works in this emerging medium—which does more with sound than legacy technologies enable us to do—may well be universal.

Our internal, personal experience of sound is far more complex and nuanced than our formal means to sculpt sound into profound expressions. A saxophone can capture a certain emotional moment; a Beethoven symphony or Ellington arrangement can help us encounter the elusive textures of our own feelings. But the possibilities of music-making are limited by the technology of our instruments. Even our experience of the most abstract music is invariably linked to something seen, touched, smelled.

Sound is inherently physical. It is a vibration; it travels through the body, and evokes a bodily response. With digital technologies we can integrate sound at a fundamental level into artworks that employ other media, opening new ways for us to share our private experience of sound with others.

Sound can suggest space, it can suggest color and motion. We often close our eyes when listening to music, and meditate on our private visual landscape. Music is an immersive experience. Sound occurs around us, enters our ears and envelops us. We inhabit sound. (Though this way to relate to sound may change. Recently it became possible to confine sound to a narrow territory within an open space. Tools now exist to shoot a beam of sound across space the same as a beam of light is projected—tightly focused on a distant point. Only by intercepting the beam can you hear the sound. The military is developing this technology to send messages across a battlefield, while retail chains like Kmart will use it to broadcast special sales offers next to the appropriate product display. Some sounds might belong to a restricted space; others might follow you as you walk through the store. Ultimately, every shopper could have a customized soundtrack, without wearing headphones. This will undoubtedly have implications for our notion of sound as a public experience.)

The tools we have inherited for making music tap into some aspects of how we relate to sound, while wholly ignoring others. Though we rarely think of this, musicians have been restricted in their ability to play with sound—to literally construct cathedrals of sound that you could walk through—by the nature of their instruments. To date, a "cathedral of sound" has been, by necessity, a metaphor. One day that will no longer be the case. The human impulse toward mimesis is inspiring artists to employ emerging technology to create hybrid artistic forms that mirror the encounter of consciousness with the world. In the mind, sound is not so neatly sectioned off from space, touch, words, or image. One bleeds into the next, slipping and sliding in a spiral of associations. Digital media has already begun to reflect qualities of consciousness that had been beyond the means of artists to capture. In coming years, this will only accelerate.

2

The basics of digital technology invite artists to rethink traditional distinctions between the arts and to strive for something new. Ever since the emergence of computer-based media, engineers and artists have looked for ways to link diverse media together. This tendency dates back to one of the Ur documents of personal computing, Vannevar Bush's visionary article from 1945, "As We May Think."[1] In it Bush proposed a device that gives the user access to a database of information, in the form of texts, photographs, movies, and audio recordings—although, because digital storage had not yet been developed, he describes this "database" as a desk filled with microfilm, shrunken photographs, tiny movies, and miniature audiotapes. This device, which Bush dubbed the memex, would allow the user to create persistent "trails of association" between discrete media elements, linking them together in a myriad of ways, just as the mind moves from idea to idea in a nonlinear fashion. Part of his intent was to suggest that information can be organized in a way that disregards the formal differences between media types, since consciousness cares little for such distinctions.

In the 1960s, inspired by Bush's vision, engineers and theorists laid the foundation for computer-based media and the wired network that enables the transport of digital media from computer to computer. Much effort went into establishing formats for digital media storage that would adequately capture the essence of an analog original. Technology was developed to transform line drawings or taped recordings into bits and bytes, virtual representations that convincingly mimicked the "real thing." Once saved as files, they could then be indexed in a computer database and made available for instant retrieval.

Visionary engineers, like Max Mathews at Bell Labs, wrote software for computer-generated timbres that strove to achieve the tonality of a musical instrument, or the full flavor of the human voice. Mathews built the first singing computer. Its performance of "Bicycle Built for Two," from 1962, became entrenched in the public imagination as an archetype of computer media when, a few years later, Stanley Kubrick had it sung by the mainframe Hal in his film *2001: A Space Odyssey*. Unlike a digitized recording, this performance was a nascent effort to program bits in a database so that the bits themselves would generate an evocative, humane expression.

It was clear since those early days that computers play no favorites between media types. Rather, from the standpoint of a computer, the basic stuff of the *Moonlight Sonata* and the *Mona Lisa* is essentially the same—they are both strings of ones and zeros, ready to be manipulated by whatever programming sequence a code writer chooses to apply to them.

Ivan Sutherland, the great computer graphics pioneer, was perhaps the first to grasp the full implications of this state of affairs. He was working on how to use computers to create accurate visual representations. Bits in a database, he reasoned, lent themselves to presentation formats as various as the human imagination could conceive. Yes, data might be formatted to look like a simple page of typewritten text, but it was just as feasible to present it as a fully realized three-dimensional environment. While one series of algorithms might structure the output of a set of data as a two-dimensional picture, different algorithms could display that data as a volumetric space. At the tender age of twenty-four, Sutherland proposed building what he called "the ultimate display," an interface to a computer-generated immersive environment that would synthesize all media into a representation of consciousness so convincing that "handcuffs displayed ... would be confining, and a bullet displayed ... would be fatal."[2] Maybe the potential of virtual worlds got the young Sutherland overexcited, but he was not the last to be made breathless by the prospect of virtual reality.

Sutherland understood that a computer could integrate all media seamlessly into a complex experience, given the appropriate display devices and software. In the process, he hit upon one of the defining insights of our day: data are infinitely malleable.

Artists and theorists have since expanded on this insight. The Austrian artist Peter Weibel has observed that, unlike traditional forms such as painting or sculpture, digital media are variable and adaptable. "In the computer, information is not stored in enclosed systems, rather it is instantly retrievable and thus freely variable,"[3] he writes. This quality gives digital media a dynamic aspect not shared by traditional forms. Computer-based media can be called out of a database at a moment's notice, and adapted to the needs of the particular context in which it appears. Referring to the impact digital technology has had on the visual arts, Weibel wrote that "The image is now constituted by a series of events, sounds, and images made up of separate specific local events generated from within a dynamic system."[4] The emergence of the bit has eliminated the strict separation between image, word, sound, and action. Within digital media, when such a distinction does take place, it will be because the artist has made a deliberate choice to do so.

Sound is information, just as are images, words, smells, gestures, or haptic impulses sensed through the skin. The shaping of this information for aesthetic purposes is the common strategy of the arts. But only since the rise of the computer as a media device have we come to regard art as so fundamentally a class of information, albeit information subject to a specific type of formal arrangement.

In our era, an overt understanding of the ways that information can be structured, manipulated, and shared will be central to how we express ourselves through culture. The computer is our primary tool for working with information. But how this tool affects our relationship to information, and the forms through which we engage with it, is only beginning to be examined. Lev Manovich, the Russian new media theorist now teaching at the University of California at San Diego, has done much to establish a systemized approach to this study. In his book *The Language of New Media* he writes, "If in physics the world is made of atoms and in genetics it is made of genes, computer programming encapsulates the world according to its own logic. The world is reduced to two kinds of software objects that are complementary to each other—data structures and algorithms."[5] The consequences of this, he suggests, should be the focus of a new field of "info-aesthetics," which would apply the legacy of analytic resources of the arts to the subject of computerized information.

3

The tools we have at our disposal to make art carry consequences for the art we make.

Charles Rosen has written convincingly about the important role of the written score in the Western classical tradition.[6] Not only was the score used to circulate new compositions, and preserve them for future generations; the audience's ability to read the score, at a time when most of the bourgeoisie learned musical notation, was critical to the reception of new works. Until the end of the nineteenth century, music was in large part a private experience. Most people would first encounter a Beethoven sonata alone at a piano, paging through the score. This private dialogue of discovery, between amateur pianist and composer, suggests that the Western relationship to music was once closer to our contemporary relationship to poetry—engaged with a page, searching, meditative.

Today, conversely, we think of music as belonging mostly to the public sphere. Rosen writes: "Our assumption today, made unconsciously, that almost all music is basically public is a radical distortion of Western tradition. We no longer have a public that largely understands how the visual experience of a musical score is transformed into an experience of sound, and to what extent this transformation is not a simple matter but is capable of individual inflections."[7]

The private quality that Rosen refers to was made possible by the specific means used in the Western tradition to create musical works—the written score, musical instruments, and a system of instruction. The link between the notation on a page and the sound a musician makes when reading it is an interaction that blurs the line between mediums, just as digital media makes possible blurring in other ways.

4

Music had been the most transient of arts. It was ephemeral, of a particular place and moment, then gone. It could not be caught, repeated, transported. Without a plot and text to define it, as in theater, music is particularly challenging to discuss with those who have not heard it. While the score provides an approximate transcription of a musical work, it is rough, open to interpretation. Much of a musical work remains outside the score, not only the sections calling for the performer to improvise (which is common), but more importantly the make-or-break details of tone, texture, pacing—details no written notation can capture.

Before recording and broadcast, music was a medium of immediate presence. Late-nineteenth-century technology turned the medium on its head. Recordings became the primary way that we encounter music. What had been the most ephemeral aspect of music—the detailed intonation of a fleeting performance—became concrete. You hear the exact same tones broadcast over radio, in stores, on television, again and again. Jimi Hendrix's spontaneous deconstruction of "The Star-Spangled Banner," played before a few stragglers at dawn at the end of the Woodstock festival, became the anthem of a generation thanks to the close proximity of a tape deck. Every impulsive swoop and shock of feedback on that recording was as if etched in stone.

Like Hendrix, Louis Armstrong was less a composer than an interpreter of compositions. Had he lived at an earlier time, Armstrong's achievement might be known by rumor only, the way that jazz pioneer Buddy Bolden exists for us largely as legend. Chopin was also famous for interpreting the compositions of others, and although that work may have been as inventive as his own writing, we will never know. However, because of recording technology, not only do we have an extensive catalog of Armstrong recordings; we have come to understand that the brilliance he brought to his interpretations effectively transformed them into original compositions. Generations of jazz players have memorized his solos note by note, treating his improvisations with a reverence previously reserved for the scored works of the canon. Machines fundamentally changed our notion of performance, enabling us to relate to acts of spontaneity as persistent compositions.

It would be hard to overestimate the influence that this aspect of the capturing and replaying of spontaneous expression had on American culture in the last century. Through recordings, it became possible to identify and study the rigor behind apparently off-the-cuff creative decisions. Repeat listening allowed underlying structures to emerge. What had once moved so quickly through the mind that it could not be captured by writing was now readily available, at the drop of a needle. This availability elevated the improvisational act into a central tenet of twentieth-century creativity. Inspired by the jazz process, by mid-century artists across disciplines had developed ways to incorporate improvisation into their art making. Think of Jackson Pollock and Franz Kline in painting; Jack Kerouac and Allen Ginsberg in writing; John Cassavetes and his heirs in filmmaking; the Living Theater and the Open Theater on stage. (The ability mechanically to capture spontaneity coincided with a rising interest in the unconscious, led by Freud, and a belief that the unfiltered, unpolished expression was closer to Truth than a more considered articulation.) Though spontaneity as a goal in itself has since diminished, its legacy continues to be felt.

The development of jazz and the technology of recording are deeply intertwined. Without the mechanical reproduction of sound, such deliberate mining of intimate moment-by-moment creativity—as in the work of Art Tatum, Miles Davis, John Coltrane, and Ornette Coleman, to name only a few— would not have been possible. Though some might be loath to admit it, jazz is as dependent on the innovations of engineers as any art form in history.

Or perhaps it is better to say that jazz matured through its dialogue with technology. The records of old masters provided instruction for emerging artists, who learned their lessons and then kept pushing for more introspective improvisational structures, arriving at the modernist apogee of Coltrane's late recordings and Davis' hard funk mediations (the latter, not so incidentally, were themselves tape collages from a recording studio).

5

One consequence of recording often goes without comment: it brought attention to aspects of performance that before had gone unnoticed, and made them the focus of obsessive scrutiny. Every sonic detail captured on record is here forever. Record collectors, often alone in their rooms, or perhaps with a handful of friends, replay a fleeting moment many times, memorizing every click or buzz while endowing them with significance. What had been transient became concrete, making it available to examination, interpretation.

Whole libraries of criticism are devoted to the minute inflections of particular performances. They become landmarks in time, representing more than an aural experience—they exhibit a lost way of being in the world. The preserving of old sounds invented a contemporary way to fetishize the past.

Nothing makes this point more forcefully than the ultimate record collector's achievement: *The Anthology of American Folk Music*, edited by Harry Smith. The *Anthology* was compiled from Smith's personal stash of 78s recorded between 1926 and 1932, during the first wave of commercial releases by rural folk artists. Most of these sides were long out of print when the box set came out from Folkways in 1952. These remarkable, meticulously arranged disks were a seminal influence on the folk revival of the late '50s, and became a touchstone for generations of people seeking the roots of American folk music. For this one release, Smith received a Chairman's Merit Award Grammy for his contribution to American folk music in 1991.

The *Anthology* conjured in the listener's mind a haunting never-never land of American cultural history; Greil Marcus described it as "the old weird America." This "America" stood in contrast to the whitewashed pop personified by Bing Crosby and Doris Day. The subject matter was dark and reflective; most importantly, the sound was ragged, jarring, unpolished. Though many of the songs in the Smith set were familiar, their delivery was strikingly unlike later recordings, which had been cleansed and made "safe" for the suburbs. It was the performance style of these records that gave them authenticity—their specific modes, rhythms, timbres were unknown by the Eisenhower era.

The *Anthology* was no more objective in its portrait of the nation than a Hollywood product. Nonetheless, it became the cornerstone in a constructed notion of American folk purity. The folk styles of the late 1920s came to be regarded as a timeless folk sound, as if folk music existed in innocent stasis for centuries, until undone by the corrupting influence of records and radio. From the late 1950s onward, folk purists used the mannerisms and inflections heard on 1920s records when they sang and played. Our notion of what it meant to be "folk" was fixed by the sonic specificity of those scratchy performances; they led to a kind of folk fundamentalism. Folk came to represent a Luddite perspective that resisted the perceived dangers of modern technology (like the electric guitar, as Bob Dylan was to learn when he went electric in 1965). Ironically, the codified folk style was itself the product of technology.

Had recordings been made of rural music 50 or 100 years earlier, it would have sounded quite different.

(Of course, trapping the folk idiom in 1926 was likely not Smith's intention. The brilliance of the *Anthology* is how well it represents a coherent world of musical possibilities. It is inherent to the mechanical reproduction of sound that an artist's music is trapped in a moment in time. A lack of documentation about who these folk artists were, how they lived, how they made their music, contributed to the mythification of these shadowy figures. But Smith's interest was less in freezing the past than opening avenues to the future. The *Anthology*'s eclectic sensibility, as many have noted, can be seen as the direct progenitor of rock; its example undeniably turned the tide in popular song, which then had a profound transformational impact on American society. Smith apparently hoped for as much when he put the box set together. "I'm glad to say my dreams came true," he said when accepting his Grammy. "I saw America changed by music.")[8]

What is folk music? Putting aside the genre category at any major record store, the question poses a problem. We had thought of folk as music that arises spontaneously from the masses, without a solitary composer; something that is shared, belonging to everyone. That definition describes nothing better than how electronic music is constructed today through the sharing of music files on the Internet. Once an old English melody would have migrated to the North American continent by boat, where it would reappear in a myriad of variations that differed from region to region. In the same way, today a single sample may reappear in hundreds of different mixes. The elements that are recombined to compose these new songs are shuttled across the wired network (where once they passed from person to person), making a music that reflects the techniques and tensions of our time. As DJ Spooky has suggested, folk music no longer comes from an acoustic guitar, but rather from a hard drive.

6

With the introduction of recording and broadcast, sound was separated from its source and began to exist independently. Today we take this for granted, so much so that it is hard to imagine the impact this separation had on the generation that first witnessed the telephone. An extension of the telegraph—which effectively collapsed time and space, creating a networked planet—

Bell's phone was the first instance of a voice without a body, *sans* divine intervention. In the 1870s, many found this uncanny disembodiment an unwelcome challenge to the spiritual. The voice, it was thought, was too intimate a part of a person to be mechanically cleaved from the self, or the soul.

Attitudes change. Though it took decades for the technology to mature, by the mid-1930s every aspect of music had been touched by the ubiquity of sound detached from its source event. From the electronic constructions of Xenakis and the Beatles, to the hip-hop DJs spontaneously composing dance tunes from extant recordings, the sonic art of the twentieth century has been determined by engineers and their devices that preserve and manipulate sound.

Once sound was separated from source, music traveled across borders and spoke across generations as it never had before. The result: an extraordinary cross-pollination of influences in the century's musical works. For example, the Beatles created rock by combining the traditions of the English music hall with J. S. Bach, Indian raga, Stockhausen, the Goon Show, Chuck Berry, and Elvis Presley (among many others). This would strike us an unlikely mix if we did not already take it for granted.

The recombining of sonic elements has been standard practice for composers and musicians for centuries. The young J. S. Bach spent hours copying Vivaldi scores, for example, and this must have fed his own compositional practices. But with the development of recording technology, many artists, like the Beatles, integrated a particularly wide range of influences (often first encountered through recordings) while composing music from scratch. On their later albums the Beatles took a further step, and began to manipulate sounds from the actual records themselves, cutting and splicing existing audio fragments into wholly new works. These songs set a pop music precedent for the club DJs of the 1970s, who regularly spun new audio experiences from legacy recordings. A generation earlier, John Cage had already begun exploring this territory; his 1939 composition, *Imaginary Landscape No. 1*, was performed using test-tone recordings played on two variable-speed turntables.

The separation of sound from source parallels similar developments in the visual arts, cited by Peter Weibel, which gave the image independence from the physical picture that once contained it. With images and sounds freed from the material circumstances of their origin, they became open to continual recontextualization. Weibel has noted how this dematerialization is leading to the ever more radical combinations of media which digitalization makes possible.

The tendency to recombine fragments of media, to play with the pieces as pieces, has of course been a prominent artistic trope in recent decades. It is seen not only in music, but in a great deal of contemporary artwork, much of which emerged in dialogue with the poststructuralist theory of Lacan, Barthes, Foucault, and others. The theater of Richard Foreman is an obvious example, since he has placed the mixing of disparate elements at the center of his productions, beginning with plays like *Rhoda in Potatoland* from 1975. Foreman's madcap juxtapositions, which go by at a ferocious speed, mirror the barrage we feel from a nonstop flow of media fragments. He arranges these shards of consciousness into elaborate, dynamic constructions that make aesthetic sense out of what in life resists literal sense. The fragments, the little pieces, are the raw material from which he builds a poetic whole.

The avant-garde wing of electronic dance music draws from the same impulse, and uses samples to similar effect. Digital media enable this tendency to go much further. Once saved in a database, a recorded sound can be subject to more manipulations than any two turntables plus mixer is capable of. A sonic element can be reconstituted on the fly according to a particular algorithm, in an interactive collaboration with the person who hears it. A sound can be linked to other sounds, but also to any form of media. A sound can lead to an image, which can in turn provoke a gesture. A sound and a gesture can be compressed into a single, inseparable event—as in life.

The mix-master sensibility is well suited to the possibilities of databases.

7

When audio becomes a digital file, it is stripped of its formal specificity—it becomes raw information, preceding form. As a string of ones and zeros, that data is open to a myriad of creative manipulations. It can be directed in real time to produce certain sounds, as determined by an algorithm. Or the bits of an audio file may be accessed from computer memory to re-create the sound of an originating recording. But the same bits can just as easily be read by a software program to generate an image, for example. The formal presentation of any string of bits is determined by the intentions, and capabilities, of the software that processes them. As Lev Manovich has put it, with the computer "media becomes programmable."[9]

This new reality has already become routine, and we give it little thought. For example, most computer programs for making and manipulating audio have visual components—like waveforms and bar graphs—that help the user to control the precise shaping of particular sounds. The same bits that generate sounds through computer speakers will trigger graphical representations on a computer screen that communicate details about volume, pitch, frequency, beats per minute, and the like. There are many examples of commercial music-making software that produce synched sound and graphics in this way.

Digital artists have also begun to explore the linking of sound and image outputs from a single source of data. In the mid-1990s, the British design team Anti-ROM attracted attention for interactive animations that combined chilly, cerebral abstractions with ambient techno music. Pictures on the screen and MIDI samples would respond together to the clicks of a mouse. This effect was achieved by using the software Macromedia Director, but in recent years artists have expanded on this functionality by writing their own customized programs. The Amsterdam collective NATO has created their own software to generate complex, interactive video images from audio feeds.

It should strike us as remarkable that audio data can have a simultaneous visual representation. But we tend to take it for granted. Why? Because we experience the border between sound and image (or sound and word, or sound and movement) as arbitrary to begin with. In our art, that division has been imposed upon us by our tools. Given the resources, it is conceivable that the line between sound and other media might never have been drawn.

Consider that when Thomas Edison set out to "do for the eye what the phonograph does for the ear,"[10] as he put it, his first attempt was to build a "kineto-phonograph" that treated sound and image as inextricably bound. He intended for the device to add moving images as a supplement to the phonographic experience; moving images alone were not intuitively of value to the nineteenth-century sensibility. Edison described the machine this way: "The initial experiments took the form of microscopic pinpoint photographs, placed on a cylindrical shell, corresponding in size to the ordinary phonographic cylinder. These two cylinders were then placed side by side on a shaft, and the sound record was taken as near as possible synchronously with the photographic image, impressed on the sensitive surface of the shell."[11] Edison's materials, ultimately, were not capable of doing the job, and he settled for moving pictures divorced from sound. But as Douglas Kahn has written,

"The important facet of this enterprise ... was that the world of visual images was to be installed at the size and scale of phonographic inscription."[12]

Kahn also discusses how, prior to Edison's work on the phonograph, he intended to invent a machine that would "fuse speech and writing.... [H]e sought to develop a device that could take the phonautographic signatures of vocal sounds and automatically transcribe them into the appropriate letter. This was, in effect, a phonograph where the playback was printing instead of sound."[13] It apparently took much deliberation before Edison could de-link the intuitive interdependence he perceived between forms of expression, as they are experienced in consciousness.

Digital media expand our ability to recombine formal elements in a way that reflects our intuition. With a computer, a string of bits can be expressed simultaneously as sound, image, word, and movement. The limits of this expression lie only in the software we write, or in the hardware we build, to give it shape.

8

Digital technology can replicate the sound of instruments, just as it can make color pictures that resemble artist's prints, or produce moving images like those shot on film. For all intents and purposes, computer media can convincingly mimic legacy media. But in their essentials, works that rely on a computer are fundamentally different from the forms of expression that preceded them.

For practical and commercial reasons, the software developed for computer media has largely focused on replicating familiar distinctions between disciplines. The media objects these programs produce are meant to fall into familiar categories: images, sounds, shapes, texts, behaviors. It's this easy categorization that leads Lev Manovich to describe computer-based multimedia as having a modular structure. When making a digital media work, Manovich writes, "These [media] objects are assembled into large-scale objects but continue to maintain their separate identities. The objects themselves can be combined into even larger objects—again, without losing their independence." Most off-the-shelf multimedia software, like Macromedia Director, treat discrete media objects as independent pieces (sounds remain sounds, images remain images) while assembling them into complex works. An HTML document is similarly composed of separate, self-contained media elements.

But there is a growing number of computer-based artworks that challenge the traditional division between mediums.

One example is *Mori*, the installation by Ken Goldberg and Randall Packer from 1999. Entering *Mori*, you would pass through a curtain into a dark hallway and walk up an incline, guided only by glowing handrails that increase or decrease in brightness. The hallway turns a corner and leads to a widened space at the end. Under your feet, the floor vibrates, sometimes quite powerfully. The vibrations are created by speakers under the floor, which generate rich, low, quaking sounds—orchestrated rumblings—that rise and fall together with the handrail lights. The effect is of walking into the center of a hushed, meditative space that is part cave, part womb. A computer, out of sight, ties the installation's elements together. Through the Internet, the computer receives streaming seismographic data measured continuously from a site near the Hayward Fault, above the University of California at Berkeley. Using the multimedia software Max, the computer translates this data into two real-time commands—one that controls the lighting, another that sequences the rumbling samples that compose the sound, which then vibrate the floor when played.

The total effect suggests an intimate connection to the physical nature of the universe. The artists offer an interpretive frame through which a profound awareness of the cosmos can be experienced. *Mori* is an example of how new media technologies open avenues for personal expression where they had not been available before. The installation is a real-time communication with the geotectonic activity of the Earth, as expressed through an aesthetic conjoining of light, sound, space, and haptic sensations felt through the skin.

Significantly, while each of these media forms is discernible in itself, the originating data—the impulse at the heart of the work—is of none of these. Both the sound and lighting in *Mori* are interpretations of the real-time seismographic data, as controlled by a set of algorithms. The sound is a live mix, determined by algorithms, of samples of low-frequency sounds. The audio is designed to vibrate through the listener, and to affect her bodily—not unlike dance music on a disco floor, though *Mori* is a far more delicate, nuanced experience.

The technical linchpin of the piece is the multimedia program Max. Named as an homage to Max Mathews, it was introduced in 1990, and has been updated regularly to keep pace with advances in computer processing. Unlike most other media software, Max was not designed to mimic familiar media forms. Rather, it allows for the direct manipulation of media files in real time through the algorithmic processing of data—it effectively allows the artist to control the data and output it in any format he wants. Using Max, a software program that plays music can send information to a program that controls a lighting console, allowing the music program to direct the lights in the room where the music is played. Max is software that recognizes the intrinsic quality of computer-based media—that it is fundamentally nothing but bits—and enables an artist to shape these bits into the media forms most appropriate for achieving his intentions. Max allows for the total abstraction of media objects, because once they have become ones and zeros circulating through Max, it makes no difference what form of media they originally began as; the form the bits take at the end of the process is up to the sole discretion of the artist.

Max points to a future where the purpose of multimedia software will be to blur lines between what were once distinct media.

9

It is actually surprising how little we know about sound. As our tools for playing with sound grow in their capacity for expression, we discover new ways for sound to act on the body, and on consciousness. As artists explore this terrain, their work takes on aspects of the trial-and-error method of science. These artists, like scientists, engage in the act of discovery. They try to identify and exploit qualities of subjective experience—provoked by sound—that had previously gone undetected, or at least were publicly unacknowledged, perhaps because they were considered marginal. New musical tools enable us to pay attention to aural experience in ways we simply were not equipped to address.

The neurologist Antonio Damasio has discussed the process in which a sensory impulse creates a neural pattern in the brain that is converted into what he refers to generically as an "image." As he explains, "the word image does not refer to 'visual' images alone.... [it] also refers to sound images such as those caused by music or the wind, and to the somatosensory images that Einstein used in his mental problem solving—in his insightful account, he called those patterns 'muscular' images."[14] Notice that the distinctions between media forms in the mind are so blurry that, from a neurologist's perspective, a single term—"image"—can refer to them all. Damasio goes on to say that, although we know much about where such mental images come from, the mystery continues "regarding *how* images emerge from neural patterns. How a neural pattern *becomes* an image is a problem that neurobiology has not yet resolved."[15]

In their own way, artists pursue this same question. This exploratory approach has been helped along by the computer, which has led us to recognize how art is essentially a type of information—just as Damasio's images are information. What happens when, rather than treating music as an inviolable art form, we see it instead as a kind of data to be manipulated for aesthetic effect? How might this approach expand our notion of personal expression, enabling us to apply aesthetics to experiences that had been outside the concerns of art—that had been the domain of science?

F. Richard Moore, a computer music scholar and pioneer who worked with Max Mathews at Bell Labs in the 1960s, has written about one matrix of possibilities that arises where science meets sound:

Imagine now a computer-based music machine that senses the musical desires of an individual listener. The listener might simply turn a knob one way when the computer plays something the listener likes, the other way when the computer does something less likable. Or, better yet, the computer could sense the listener's responses directly using, say, body temperature, pulse rate, galvanic skin response, pupil size, blood pressure, etc. Imagine what music would sound like that continually adapts itself to your neurophysiological response to it for as long as you wish. Such music might be more addictive than any known drug, or it might cure any of several known medical disorders.

Where does science end and art begin here, or vice versa? Much of what Moore describes (the monitoring of body temperature, pulse rate, etc.) seems to belong to science. But he applies the legacy of aesthetic practice to this territory. What do we like or dislike in music? No conclusive answers are possible. What we like at any moment depends on the context; nothing could be more subjective, or in greater flux. But inhabiting this subjectivity is the specialty of artists. Scientists will likely find that, when it comes to unlocking the mysteries of consciousness, the strategies of artists will play an increasingly important role.

10

No information exists in isolation. Rather, the pieces of information we come in contact with, and comprehend, are fragments from a continual flow. We grasp passing particles from this flow, and understand them in a contingent manner. Meaning keeps shifting; our understanding evolves as we access subsequent information, which transposes what we had encountered earlier and casts it in a changing light.

Digital media make the contingent nature of information explicit, because the technology reduces all formal means of personal expression into raw data ready for manipulation. It not only blurs the lines between distinct media; it invites the further shaping of this data by the person, or group of people, who are accessing it in real time.

Novels, movies, symphonies are not interactive, because they are not capable of incorporating a direct response from the audience in their formal presentation, in real time (efforts to add interactivity to traditional forms are invariably awkward, and regarded as novelties). But because digital media are at their essence bits coursing through software, they can incorporate live response (as determined by the software), and be made to fit the needs of the moment.

Artists and theorists such as Roy Ascott, Marcus Novak, Char Davies, and Pierre Levy have written about the implications of the radical interactivity inherent in digital media. But for the purpose of this essay, it is enough to note that by exploring interactivity art moves in the direction of science, and toward a deeper concern with the mechanisms of consciousness. In consciousness, we make sense of information based on the context in which we receive and perceive it. What the reader brings to the page is as important as what the page offers the reader. Before the computer, the page could not revise itself in collaboration with the reader, but with digital technology, what had been a recitation from author to reader becomes, potentially, a dialogue. This is to say that our engagement with art can become increasingly like our engagement with the intimate details of life.

The explicit concern of art now becomes: how do we create "images" in the mind (as Damasio discusses), and what effect does the creation of such images have on us? Sound, space, voice, color, composition—do they become indistinguishable as we are better able to represent consciousness? Digital media provide an expanded set of tools, which will lead to new forms of expression and different ways of thinking about art. These tools bring us closer to the underlying mechanisms of consciousness, so we can make art that comes closer to capturing, and representing, our intuitive ways of being.

11

It is hard to predict the consequences of using new media technologies. Edison's invention of cinema never anticipated the close-up or the montage, for example, which themselves had a profound influence on the social organization of the last century. Only two decades after the popular acceptance of film were both of these key cinematic techniques discovered. I say discovered, rather than invented, because the potential for each was latent in the technology of moving pictures from its earliest days. But it took a shift in awareness for this potential to be recognized and acted on.

Even as the shift takes place, however, we may not notice it. For years, jazz and folk music were seen by many as bulwarks of the individual spirit against the perceived dehumanizing effects of modern machinery. Rarely was this music's debt to technology acknowledged by these same people. To even consider the possibility of it seemed counterintuitive, though it would have been apparent to anyone who chose to see it. The question is, what brings one to choose to see it?

We are now entering an era in which the tools at our disposal to affect consciousness are increasingly agile. Digital media is opening new avenues to intimate personal expression—through the recombining of media elements, and the blurring of distinctions between traditional mediums in a way that reflects our intuitive engagement with the world. The line where art blurs into science is at the forefront of the discovery of new aesthetic experiences. New tools for personal expression provide us with fresh ways of understanding ourselves. By using these tools, our sense of self will inevitably be transformed. Technology prompts new modes of subjectivity into being.

What we think of as sound, as music, is going to change, as it changed so drastically in the modern era. Because of their extraordinary difference from what came before, digital media demand our attention. Otherwise, we will not see what it is we are becoming. Our analytical skills for identifying the effects of technology on culture have grown considerably since the days of silent film. If we see the changes, we may well be able to better direct them. After all, we are writing the computer code that is guiding the changes.

As Plato remarked, citing Damon of Athens, "When the mode of the music changes, the walls of the city shake." If you choose to see it, you will notice that the walls around you are vibrating.

Notes

1. Vannevar Bush, "As We May Think," in *Atlantic Monthly* 176, no. 1 (July 1945), 101–108.

2. Ivan Sutherland, "The Ultimate Display," in *Proceedings of the IFIP Congress*, 1965, 505–508.

3. Peter Weibel, "The Unreasonable Effectiveness of the Methodological Convergence of Art and Science," in *Art@Science*, ed. C. Sommerer and L. Mignonneau (Springer, 1998).

4. Ibid.

5. Lev Manovich, *The Language of New Media* (MIT Press, 2001), 223.

6. Charles Rosen, "The Future of Music," in *New York Review of Books*, December 20, 2001, 60–65.

7. Ibid.

8. See http://www.harrysmitharchives.com/1_bio/index.html (May 27, 2003).

9. Manovich, *Language of New Media*, 27.

10. W. K. L. Dickson and Antonia Dickson, *History of the Kinetograph, Kinetoscope, and Kineto-Phonograph* (1985, reprint; Arno Press, 1970), 4. Cited in Douglas Kahn, *Noise Water Meat: A History of Sound in the Arts* (MIT Press, 1999), 93.

11. Ibid., 8–9.

12. Douglas Kahn, *Noise Water Meat*, 94.

13. Ibid., 91.

14. Antonio Damasio, *The Feeling of What Happens: Body and Emotion in the Making of Consciousness* (Harcourt Brace, 1999), 318.

15. Ibid., 322.

Scott deLahunta

One can trace connections between computers and dance back to the 1960s when early computer artists, often mathematicians and computer scientists by training, were experimenting with algorithmically generated graphic images and patterns and forms of computer creativity. Working with Bell Labs in Murray Hill, New Jersey, A. Michael Noll began to explore the possibility of combining digital computers and the visual arts by studying three-dimensional computer graphics and computational aesthetics. In a crude approximation of the Turing test in which human and machine intelligence are compared, Noll invented the algorithms that would instruct a computer to generate an image that would mimic in its patterns and structure Piet Mondrian's *Composition with Lines* (1917).[1]

In 1965, Noll created a work of computer animation he titled *Computer-Generated Ballet*, reported to be the first such use of a "digital computer to create an animation of stick figures on a stage."[2] But perhaps his most significant contribution to the convergence of computers and dance was in January 1967 when he published an article in *Dance Magazine* entitled "Choreography and Computers," in which he described a software program he was creating that would indicate stage positions of stick figures and could potentially be of use to choreographers. In the same issue, Ann Hutchinson-Guest (an authority on dance notation) penned "A Reply" to Noll's speculations, in which she writes that the computer will "never replace" the facility a choreographer has for composing movement with the dancer. However, she does concede that the computer might assist in the overall outlining and editing of a score for a dance.[3]

Around the same period, John Lansdown, an architect by training, was pursuing a different vision of integrating dance and the computer. Based in London, Lansdown was particularly interested in the possibilities for "artificial creativity," to use the computer to contribute to a creative process as an autonomous composer, rather than to support or augment an existing one. In his introduction to "Artificial Creativity," a paper given in 1995, Lansdown describes the computer's ability to make "decisions according to rules." He traces the history of the use of related "regulatory" systems in music composition, architecture, and painting and distinguishes between two types: those that are randomized and those that are rule-based. Contemporary choreographers have used similar systems.[4] Merce Cunningham's and John Cage's well-known experiments with random methods were explored further by experimental choreographers in the early 1960s. In the 1970s Trisha Brown devised "dance making machines"—rule-based systems that generated particular performances such as *Accumulation* and *Locus*.[5] William Forsythe's use of algorithmic structures in the 1990s with the Ballet Frankfurt is well documented.[6]

Back in 1968, Lansdown had begun to experiment for the first time with "computer-generated" dances. He first attempted to use the computer to create all the instructions a dancer would require, but soon determined that "a more satisfactory method" was to provide a looser framework within which there was some room for interpretation by the dancers.[7] He developed the concept of generating "peaks" of movements rather than the movements themselves and allowed the dancers to fill in the material between. Using these methods, Lansdown contributed to many performances between 1968 and 1993 with various dance companies, including London-based Another Dance Group, the Royal Ballet School, and The One Extra Company of Sydney, Australia.

In the 1960s and 1970s access to computers was extremely limited and programming a slow tedious process. A. Michael Noll states optimistically in his 1967 *Dance Magazine* article: "The computer and graphic output equipment might be centrally located and time-shared with many users. Anyone could apply this technology to produce this form of 'dance notation typewriter.'"[8] Perhaps Noll thought the conditions he describes would generate more convergence between computers and dance. It did, but not surprisingly it was choreographers working at academic institutions with access to computer science departments who were best able to explore the possibilities, and the mainstream of contemporary dance practice tended to be unaware of, or uninterested in, the outcomes of this work. Computing aids (either generative or supporting) for choreographic compositions have not proliferated to a large degree as perhaps Noll and Lansdown would have predicted. The piece of technical equipment that has become ubiquitous in the rehearsal studio is clearly the video camera and television monitor, but there has been little incorporation of computer technologies into this setup.[9]

In the 1980s, we saw the emergence of "interactive performance systems" such as Canadian artist David Rokeby's *Very Nervous System* (VNS).[10] The VNS uses a video camera as an "eye," the cable to the computer as an "optic nerve," and the computer as the "brain" to create an interactive "seeing" space in which the movements of one's body triggers sound and/or music.[11] There are several other similar systems available today for performance artists wishing to explore interactive systems, including the BigEye software at the Studio for Electro-Instrumental Music (STEIM) in Amsterdam and EyeCon by the Palindrome Inter-media Performance Group based in Nürnberg.[12]

The classes of input devices for interactive systems can be extended beyond those that are video based to include haptic (touch), for example, pressure and flex sensors, and nonhaptic (distance), for example, ultrasound. However, a "seeing" space—video-based technology like VNS—requiring only a camera and software and being relatively easy to set up, is an attractive option for choreographers and dancers who wish to experiment with an interactive system in performance.[13] In all these systems, performer movement or action triggers some sort of event (sonic, visual, robotic, and the like) in the space around or in some proximity to the performer. The connection between the "input," the performer action that oscillates the data stream, and the output event is determined by "mapping" the input to the output in the computer software.[14]

The concept of mapping is a topic of creative interest and a focus of artistic practice in the field of electronic music in particular. In a paper entitled "Towards a Model for Interactive Mapping in Expert Musical Interaction," Marcelo Wanderley and Ross Kirk review the ways "performer instrumental action can be linked to sound synthesis parameters."[15] They describe two main "mapping" directions: (a) the use of generative mechanisms (e.g., neural networks) to perform mapping, and (b) the use of explicit mapping strategies.

Once completed, however, the instructions that make up the mapping itself are relegated to the invisibility of computation. It is the manifestation of mapping, the performer-triggered event, which enters the field of perception of the viewer–listener, not the mapping itself. This poses a challenge to those artists integrating "interactive performance systems" on the stage (in the conventional sense of a space for performance separated from an audience). Some "hide" the interactive systems, placing the emphasis on what is visible; others prefer to expose their workings.

Many accounts of interactive systems shift the focus of discussion to those occasions in which the viewer becomes a player or participant, rather than questioning circumstances and issues surrounding the more traditional performer–audience separation. An alternative to this could be to reorient a set of questions toward the notion of the performer again, but in the condition of training, practice, or rehearsal rather than in performance.

In the interactive computer music improvisation duo *Interface*, Dan Trueman and Curtis Bahn, build their own technologically augmented stringed instruments that are "extended, surrounded, and obscured ... with a variety of technologies."[16] These "composed instruments," combine idiosyncratic sensor designs with equally idiosyncratic speaker configurations that encourage the development of new playing techniques. Finding a way to practice these techniques outside of the live performance context has produced some innovative strategies. Trueman has developed a method for fine-tuning his playing through the recording of a reduced amount of gesture-derived data that can be played back as a trace of the live performance. He analyzes this "recorded sketch" for the types of adjustments that might be made to the interactive system. In his own words:

So, what I do is take these "recordings" of me playing the instrument and spend hours developing and refining mappings of the sensor data to audio (and video, to a lesser extent) signal processing and synthesis algorithms. This technique could be used in exactly the same manner with dancers, and could offer a better way for dancers/choreographers and composers/electronic musicians to collaborate, compose, and choreograph "offline." It can be so tedious to "mode switch" all the time between playing a mapping and actually composing the mapping. This way, you can sit down, look at the recording of the "performing body," and develop the instrument, away from the instrument.[17]

A similar fascination with the recording or tracking of movement can be traced to the "precursor to film" technologies of the late nineteenth century, for example in the work of French physiologist and instrument inventor Étienne Jules-Marey. But the computer-based technology we commonly refer to today as motion capture has a briefer historical trajectory that is closely associated with the development of advanced computer graphics. In the early 1980s, the MIT Architecture Machine Group and the New York Institute of Technology Computer Graphics Lab experimented with an optical tracking system for human body.[18] Toward the end of that decade, motion capture had evolved into a robust means for recording human (or animal) motion in a simulation of three-dimensional space and using this motion either for analysis (sports science/ergonomics) or to animate a variety of forms (film entertainment industry). With an obvious attraction to those working with movement as their material, several dance artists became involved in using these systems during the 1990s.[19]

Motion capture is a form of sampling, but computer animation is equally concerned with the synthesis of motion using a variety of computational approaches. For example, it has become increasingly possible to instruct animations to perform tasks, to develop behaviors, and to maneuver autonomously in differentiated environments. Computer scientists have developed a variety of classification systems for these approaches. Nadia and Daniel Thalmann (directors of MIRALab in Geneva) have developed a classification in three parts: (1) *locally controlled* motions driven by data via either motion capture or key frame animation; (2) *dynamic simulation* where motions are controlled using equations relating to forces, torques, and constraints; and (3) *behavioral animation* in which motions emerge within an environment in which all objects act in relation to other objects.[20] As these tools increasingly rely on dynamic and behavioral computation to generate motion, the role of the animator shifts toward defining the conditions within which these motions or gestures take place, the environments and the tasks involved.

Susan Amkraut and Michael Girard are software developers and multimedia artists who have had a significant impact on these developments in the field of computer animation through their exploration of human and animal figure animation when they were working with Ohio State University's Computer Graphics Research Group in the 1980s. They contributed to the development of the spline and inverse kinematics approaches and provided key input toward the development of dynamic simulation and behavioral animation. They are now developing software tools for commercial animators, most recently producing a software extension called Crowd, which integrates local control (motion capture data) with dynamic simulation and behavioral animation.[21] Crowd supports the organization of the behavior of large numbers of animated figures by drawing on some of the principles of bird flocking systems. Amkraut is credited with some of the early work in the mid- to late 1980s on flocking systems. Flocking systems use three simple rules: (1) separation: steer to avoid crowding local flockmates; (2) alignment: steer toward the average heading of local flockmates; and (3) cohesion: steer to move toward the average position of local flockmates.[22]

Imagine you have motion captured someone jogging. Make twenty-five copies of this figure. Place these twenty-five figures in the space and give them the following instructions: keep running toward the center of the space and avoid collisions by turning right or left. From just these two simple rules complicated patterns of self-organizing movement emerge on the screen. With Crowd you can also define the terrain or the environment the figures are moving in. Although the rules are entirely deterministic, the emergent behavior appears to be undetermined, something one could not have predicted beforehand. In addition, this would be nearly an impossible task if we had to animate each of these figures individually.

Currently, the amount of time and effort it takes to learn to work with the software and render these complex animations effectively distances this as a creative activity from the choreographer who works with dancers in physical space. However, with eventual advances in computer hardware and software, nearly instantaneous processing should be possible as the gap between adjusting the parameters and rules and seeing the result becomes negligible. Combine this with software interfaces that are easier to use, and we may see the reconvergence of computers and dance in the practice of choreography echoing the creative possibilities A. Michael Noll and John Lansdown set out to explore in the 1960s.

Acknowledgments

Thank you to Susan Rethorst for editing assistance and to Dr. Söke Dinkla and Dr. Martina Leeker for permission to use an extract from the following essay:

S. deLahunta, "Periodic Convergences: Dance and Computers," in *Tanz und Neue Medien* (book and CD-ROM/DVD), ed. Dr. Söke Dinkla and Dr. Martina Leeker, pp. 66–84. Berlin: Alexander Verlag, 2002.

Notes

1. A. Michael Noll, "Human and Machine—A Subjective Comparison of Piet Mondrian's *Composition with Lines* 1917, and a Computer-generated Image," *Psychological Record* 16 (January 1966), 1–10.

2. This quote of A. Michael Noll's is available under the "computer art" heading at http://www.citi.columbia.edu/amnoll/ (accessed April 5, 2002).

3. A. Michael Noll and Ann Hutchinson, "Choreography and Computers" and "A Reply," *Dance Magazine* (January 1967), 43–46, 81–82.

4. John Lansdown, "Artificial Creativity." A version of this paper was given at the Digital Creativity Conference, Brighton, April 1995: http://www.cea.mdx.ac.uk/CEA/External/Staff96/John/artCreat.html (accessed April 5, 2002).

5. Trisha Brown's dance making instructions can be found published in different locations, e.g.: *Locus* in *Contemporary Dance: An Anthology*, ed. Anne Livet (Abbeville Press, 1978), 54–55, and *Accumulation* in *The Drama Review: The Postmodern Dance Issue* 19, no. 1, (March 1975), 29.

6. E.g., in the interview of William Forsythe by Paul Kaiser in "Dance Geometry: William Forsythe in Dialogue with Paul Kaiser," *On Line: Performance Research* 4, no. 2 (summer 1999), 66–69, and in the interview of Dana Caspersen by Senta Driver in "It Starts from Any Point: Bill and the Frankfurt Ballet," *Choreography and Dance* 5, part 3 (2000), 24–39.

7. John Lansdown, "Computer-Generated Choreography Revisited," in *Proceedings of 4D Dynamics Conference*, ed. A. Robertson (De Montfort University, Leicester, 1995), 89–99. See http://www.dmu.ac.uk/ln/4dd/guest-jl.html (accessed April 5, 2002).

8. Noll, "Choreography and Computers," 44.

9. This issue was recently addressed at the *Software for Dancers* London-based research project taking place from September 24 to October 6, 2001, aimed to develop concepts for software rehearsal tools for dance makers. See http://huizen.dds.nl/~sdela/sfd (accessed April 5, 2002).

10. For an online historical account of the development of the "interactive performance system" see Söke Dinkla's seminal paper, "The History of the Interface in Interactive Art," presented at ISEA 1994, available at http://www.isea.qc.ca/symposium/archives/isea94/pr208.html (accessed April 5, 2002).

11. Interview of David Rokeby by Douglas Cooper, "Very Nervous System," *Wired* 3.03 (March 1995): http://www.wired.com/wired/archive/3.03/rokeby.html (accessed April 5, 2002).

12. More information is available from the following sites: Palindrome Intermedia performance group, http://www.palindrome.de/; STEIM: http://www.steim.nl/ (accessed April 5, 2002).

13. Two examples of dance and electronic composers/digital artists developing wearable sensor systems for use in interactive spaces are Troika Ranch based in New York City and DIEM based in Aarhus, Denmark: http://www.troikaranch.org and http://www.daimi.aau.dk/~diem/digitaldance.html (accessed April 5, 2002).

14. There are several options for software for mapping input to output, but Mark Coniglio's Isadora offers one of the best for the nonprogrammer to experiment with: http://www.troikaranch.org/troikatronix/isadora.html (accessed April 5, 2002).

15. The Wanderley/Ross PDF is available at http://www.ircam.fr/equipes/analyse-synthese/wanderle/Gestes/Externe/Hunt_Towards.pdf (accessed April 5, 2002).

16. More information about Interface can be found at http://www.arts.rpi.edu/crb/interface/interface.htm (accessed April 5, 2002).

17. From email correspondence between the author and Dan Trueman on March 10, 2002.

18. David J. Sturman, "A Brief History of Motion Capture for Computer Character Animation," SIGGRAPH 94: http://www.css.tayloru.edu/instrmat/graphics/hypgraph/animation/motion_capture/history1.htm (accessed April 5, 2002).

19. For a description of motion capture technologies and some work involving dance artists, see Scott deLahunta, "Coreografie in bit e byte: motion capture, animazione e software per la danza," in *La Scena Digitale: Nuovi media per la danza*, ed. Armando Menicacci and Emanuele Quinz (Venice: Marsilio Editori s.p.a., 2001), 83–100. An English version is available at http://www.daimi.au.dk/~sdela/bolzano/ (accessed April 5, 2002).

20. N. Magnenat Thalmann and D. Thalmann, "Computer Animation," in *Handbook of Computer Science* (CRC Press, 1996), 1300–1318.

21. The *Crowd* extension comes with Character Studio, one of the 3D Studio Max animation software applications that is specifically designed to work with motion capture data.

22. Simple rules leading to complex results—emergent and unpredictable—is a conception underlying the computer-aided study of chaos and other complex systems. "Artificial Life" refers to the field of modeling and study of such systems using the computer.

Vijay Iyer

As a musician, I believe that musical improvisation can provide some powerful insights about consciousness. I'd like to propose an understanding of certain improvisational music as quintessentially *experiential*, in that it leads us to
re-experience our own practice of perception.

I am a pianist, composer, improvisor, and electronic musician engaged with
a range of experimental and vernacular musical codes (Iyer 2003, 2005; Iyer
and Ladd 2003, 2007; Fieldwork 2002, 2005). In the late 1990s, I wrote a dissertation on the role of the body in music perception, cognition, and performance (Iyer 1998). The central thesis was simply that music is an embodied,
situated activity. This means that music depends crucially on the structure of
our bodies, and also on the environment and culture in which our musical
awareness emerges. Rhythm, especially, is a complex, whole-body experience,
and its role in music makes use of the embodied, situated status of the participant. Such claims have a variety of implications; they lead us to appreciate
traces of the embodiment in instrumental and vocal music, to notice how
musical cultures and individuals variously deal with the role of physicality in
music-making, and to understand music perception as an active, culturally
contingent process.

The claim that music perception and cognition are embodied activities also
means that they are actively constructed by the listener, rather than passively
transferred from performer to listener. This active nature of music perception
highlights the role of culture and context. For example, the discernment of

qualities such as pulse and meter from a piece of music is not perceptually inevitable; rather, it depends on the person's culturally contingent listening strategies (Iyer 1998, 83–104). In addition, I have argued that certain kinds of rhythmic expression are directly related to the role of the body in making music, and to certain cultural aesthetics that privilege this role. In particular, certain subtle microrhythmic variations in rhythmic performance display strikingly systematic structure, bearing sonic traces of the culturally situated music-making body (Iyer 2002).

As I developed these academic arguments, I found that embodiment had become a central concern of my creative work as well. As an artist I began to pay attention to audible traces of the human body in improvisational music—the sound of pianist Thelonious Monk's hands, for example, or drummer Roy Haynes' dancer-like bearing. I started creating music that foregrounded this relationship between music and the body: allowing my hands to enact a tactile–melodic logic at the piano that would form the basis of my compositions, creating rhythmic structures that alternately engage and undermine our inherent dance impulse, and attuning to the persistent rhythms within my own body as a guiding principle in improvisation and composition.

Generally, when considering issues in music cognition, scientists too often gravitate to the well-trodden examples from pre-1900 European classical tonal music, and ignore nearly every other form of music, including all non-Western music, any contemporary or popular work, or any works that might be categorized as "experimental." We are led very quickly to ask: how can you make assertions about cognitive universals of human music-making without studying the music of more than one culture? For this reason, in the course of my intertwined creative and scholarly work, I have drawn heavily from the music of the African diaspora, South Asia, and other non-Western cultures.

In the case of the sciences' general avoidance of experimental music, the tacit assumption is that the experimental arts are not concerned with the fundamentals of perception. But often it is precisely through artistic experimentation that we reach new awareness of our perceptual and cognitive processes. The works of Seurat, Monet, and even Picasso, experimental in their time, are well-cited examples in the visual arts; Noë's (2000) work on Serra and Smith provides a rare example of late-twentieth-century artists considered from the point of view of cognition. But how often does one look to African-American experimental composer-improvisers such as Thelonious Monk, Cecil Taylor, or John Coltrane in terms of the implications of their discoveries for music perception? (Lewis [1996, 1998, 2001–2002] convincingly describes what is called "jazz" as a history of experimental practice, in light of which the artists mentioned here could certainly be characterized as experimentalists.) For that matter, when do scientists consider hallowed twentieth-century composers such as Debussy, Varèse, or Ligeti for perceptual insights?

In what follows, I focus on moments from my musical experiences with two pioneering improvisers, pianist Cecil Taylor and multi-instrumentalist Roscoe Mitchell, and also suggest some ways of thinking about aspects of electronic music, all within the framework of embodiment. But first, I must introduce a handful of basic concepts with which to build our argument.

Time and Temporal Situatedness

A fundamental consequence of physical embodiment and environmental situatedness is the fact that *things take time*. Temporality must ground our conception of physically embodied cognition. Smithers (1996) draws a useful distinction between processes that occur "in time" and those that exist "over time." The distinction is similar to that between process-oriented activity, such as speech or walking, and product-oriented activity, such as writing a novel or composing a symphony.

In-time processes are embedded in time; not only does the time taken matter, but in fact it contributes to the overall structure of the process. The speed of a typical walking gait relates to physical attributes like leg mass and size, and shoulder–hip torsional moment; this is why we cannot walk one-tenth or ten times as fast as we do. Similarly, the rate at which we speak exploits the natural timescales of lingual and mandibular motion as well as respiration. Accordingly, we learn (and indeed we are hardwired) to process speech at precisely such a rate. Recorded speech played at slower or faster speeds rapidly becomes unintelligible, even if the pitch is held constant. The perceived flow of conversation, while quite flexible, is sensitive to the slowdown caused by an extra few seconds taken to think of a word or recall a name.

Over-time processes, by contrast, are merely contained in time; the fact that they take time is of no fundamental consequence to the result. Most of what we call computation occurs over time. The fact that all machines are considered computationally equivalent regardless of speed suggests that time was not a concern in the theory of computation, and that the temporality of a computational process was theoretically immaterial. Though computational theory is more nuanced today, "real-time" computer applications make use of the speed of modern microprocessors, performing computations so fast that one doesn't notice how much time is taken. However, this is not what the mind does when immersed in a dynamic, real-time environment; rather, it exploits both the constraints and the allowances of the natural timescales of the body and the brain as a total physical system. In other words, Smithers (1996) claims, *cognition chiefly involves in-time processes.* Furthermore, this claim is not limited simply to cognitive processes that require interpersonal interaction; it pertains to all thought, perception, and action.

The Temporality of Musical Performance

In intersubjective activities, such as speech or music making, one remains aware of a sense of mutual embodiment. This sense brings about the presupposition of "shared time" between the listener and the performer. This sense is a crucial aspect of the temporality of performance. The experience of listening to music is qualitatively different from that of reading a book. The experience of music requires a "co-performance" that must occur within a shared temporal domain (Schutz 1964). While the essentially solitary act of reading a book also takes time, the specific amount of time is of little consequence. (Literary notions of co-performance, such as Roland Barthes' idea of "writerly texts" [1975], do not fundamentally incorporate the temporality of experience.) The notion of musical co-performance is made literal in musical contexts primarily meant for dance; participatory act of marking musical time with rhythmic bodily activity—dancing, rocking, tapping your foot—physicalizes the sense of shared time, and could be viewed as embodied listening.

The performance situation itself might be understood as a context-framing device. In his study of music of a certain community in South Africa, ethnomusicologist J. Blacking wrote, "Venda music is distinguished from nonmusic by the creation of a special world of time. The chief function of music is to involve people in shared experiences within the framework of their cultural experience" (Blacking 1973, 48). There is no doubt that this is true to some degree in all musical performance, and we can take this concept further in the case of improvised music. The process of musical improvisation in a jazz context can be seen as one specific way of framing the shared time between performer and audience. The experience of listening to music that is understood to be improvised differs significantly from listening knowingly to composed music. The main source of drama in improvised music is the sheer fact of the shared sense of time: the sense that the improviser is working, creating, generating musical material, in the same time in which we are co-performing as listeners. As listeners to any music, we experience a kind of *empathy* for the performer, an awareness of physicality and an understanding of the effort required to create music. Empathy is of course a key aspect of how we listen to others in any context. In improvised music empathy extends to an awareness of the performers' coincident physical and mental exertion, of their "in-the-moment" (i.e., in-time) *process* of creative activity and interactivity. Thus improvisation heightens the role of embodiment in musical performance.

Time framed by improvisation is a special kind of time that is flexible in extent, and in fact carries the inherent possibility of endlessness, similar to that pointed out by Shore (1996) in the case of baseball games. Instances like Paul Gonsalves' twenty-seven choruses (over six minutes) of blues on Ellington's "Diminuendo and Crescendo in Blue" and Coltrane's sixteen-minute take on "Chasin' the Trane"—significantly, both live recordings—attest to the power that the improviser wields as framer of time, deciding both the extent and the content of the shared epoch.

Temporal Situatedness and Musical Form

Accordingly, improvisational music requires a different concept of musical form from that of composed music; improvisational musical form can be described in terms of temporal situatedness. It is enlightening to consider the concept of form in the classical improvised music of India:

Syntactical forms are virtually unknown in the music of India. Instead we hear long, cyclical, chain structures and a general progression of organic growth that reveals the guidance of quite different formal models and metaphor. The tactics of form go hand-in-hand with the prevailing models of structure: hierarchical and syntactical forms are naturally implemented by such tactics as contrast, parallelism, preparation, rise, transition, and the like; serial forms [as in Indian music], however, tend to be modular, decorative, incremental, progressive, and open-ended. The Indian version of musical structure tends to emphasize variation of the module: by permutation of its elements, by inflation and deflation of patterns, by pattern superimpositions, and by progressive organic development. (Rowell 1988)

Improvisational African and African-American music can share many of these traits, particularly in the long-term organization of material. The major role of improvisation in many oral musical traditions, combined with the important function of groove, make possible alternative notions of musical form that do not conform to the recursive hierarchies of tonal-music grammars. A teleological concept of form, in which the meaning of music is taken to be its large-scale structure, may be replaced with an alternative, modular approach, in which the meaning of music is located in the free play of smaller constituent units. Such notions of musical structure appear in many African and African-American musics, from Ewe dance-drumming to Detroit techno. Instead of long-range hierarchical form, the focus is on fine-grained rhythmic detail, the dialogic interplay of various musical elements, and superpositional rhythmic hierarchy. Thus, large-scale musical form emerges from an improvisational treatment of these short-range musical ingredients—that is, from the in-time manipulation of simple, modular components.

A prime example is the late, great vocalist–bandleader James Brown's well-known practice of "takin[g] it to the bridge" (Brown 1991). A typical composition might consist of two different musical spaces or grooves, the transitions between which are cued musically by the vocalist. Hence each section may be arbitrarily long, since all that delineates it is an improvised cue to the next section. Before a given performance of a song like "Sex Machine," Brown and his band may not know exactly what will happen when; rather, they know what the raw materials are and how to manipulate them during performed time. They are skilled at reacting to environmental cues, individually and collectively, in real time.

As another example, jazz drummer E. W. Wainwright (private communication, 1997) described to me a practice of creating large-scale temporal form out of a relatively open-ended musical environment, as it was done by John Coltrane's legendary quartet in the early 1960s (see the title track to Coltrane 1993 [1970]). In such pieces, the group would improvise in 4/4 time, using a certain pitch organization as a loose framework, such as a mode or a pedal point. Eventually, formal small-section boundaries would emerge by the systematic doubling of the musical period. As was told to Wainwright by Elvin Jones (the quartet's drummer and Wainwright's teacher), the group would initially accent the beginning of every four bars, using intensity as well as rhythmic, melodic, and harmonic parameters. As the piece unfolded, they would expand the period to eight bars, then sixteen, and so on. The larger the period became, the greater heights the intensity and dissonant tension could reach, and the more effective the unified release at the beginning of the next period. As Jones told Wainwright, this practice emerged organically over the course of hundreds of improvised performances, never having been discussed verbally by any band members. These two examples suggest that aspects of musical form can stem from the collective experience of shared, lived time, and from the ways in which musical variation is executed "in time."

Perception of Musical Motion

Musical motion is often discussed as a structural abstraction in pitch space, involving the play of forms against one another. A typical view is evident in the following quote from noted composer-theorist Roger Sessions. "The gestures which music embodies are, after all, invisible gestures; one may almost define them as consisting of movement in the abstract, movement which exists in time but not in space, movement, in fact, which gives time its meaning and its significance for us" (Sessions 1950, 20, quoted in Shove and Repp 1995, 58).

A more grounded approach is taken by Friberg and colleagues (Friberg and Sundberg 1999; Friberg, Sundberg, and Frydén 2000), who investigate the psychological associations of music with certain rhythmic gaits and other locomotive phenomena. But a review of the concept of musical motion by Shove and Repp (1995) highlights the important and overlooked fact that musical motion is, first and foremost, audible human motion. To amplify this view, Shove and Repp make use of Handel's (1990, 181) three levels of event awareness: the raw psychophysical perception of tones, the perception of abstract qualities of the tones apart from their source, and lastly the apprehension of environmental objects that give rise to the sound event. At this third level, "the listener does not merely hear the *sound* of a galloping horse or bowing violinist; rather, the listener hears a horse *galloping* and a violinist bowing" (Shove and Repp 1995, 59). In this event-based framework, the source of perceived musical movement is the human performer, as is abundantly clear to the listener attending to music in performance (ibid., 60). We connect the perception of musical motion to human motion; from this perspective, music consists of the sound of concerted human action.

Experientialist Music

With the preceding ideas in mind, I wish to pick up the argument laid out by Nöe (2000), who discusses the possibility of self-reflexive moments that disrupt the *transparency* of experience, by which he means the invisibility of the process of perception itself. As Nöe outlines, when we attempt to perceive the process of perception, we instead perceive the object of perception; the "experience" of perceptual experience, being mediated through the senses, cannot itself be perceived by the senses. Nöe points out that perceptual experience is best understood as a "temporally extended process of exploration of the environment on the part of an embodied animal" (2000: 128)—that is, as *perceptually guided action*. Therefore, "to investigate experience we need to turn our gaze not inward, but rather to the activity itself in which this temporally extended process consists, to the things we do as we explore the world" (ibid.).

Nöe suggests that certain artists' work foregrounds the actual experience of perception (as opposed to the object of perception). He describes the massive sculptural works of Richard Serra as *environmental* in nature, overwhelming in *scale*, *complex* enough to lack a perspicuous vantage point, and *particular* in their uniqueness (i.e., site-specific and not reproducible). Nöe asserts that these traits demand a process of experiential exploration, as opposed to a passive, transparent, instantaneous perception. In this way, they provide an occasion for the self-reflexive experience of perceiving one's own process of perception.

Encapsulating the embodied process of being in the world, Nöe (2000) describes experience as a "temporally extended pattern of exploratory activity." This could be a definition of improvisation: real-time interaction with the structure of one's environment. As with improvisation, it is not a passive interaction, for the perceiver–improviser is engaged in sensorimotor activity, skillfully probing the world at will. This process of embodied action situates the perceiver within the environment; so the perceiver must interact with her embodied self as well. Noë's choice of the word "pattern" suggests that the activity is either learned, or grounded in some repeatable behavior.

In this way, we may understand *musical* improvisation as the real-time interaction with the structure of one's acoustic, musical-formal, cultural, embodied, and situated environment. Musical interaction is not a passive interaction either, because it also *generates* structure—it has its own sonic trace, which becomes part of the same interactive environment, and is perceived as contributing to this environment. This view of musical improvisation has implications for the study of consciousness, as the following examples may illuminate. Nöe's notions of scale, complexity, uniqueness, and environment are addressed (though indirectly) in these examples. What I wish to stress is the way in which these improvisational performances foreground their in-time status, drawing attention to the experiential aspect of real-time music making.

Cecil Taylor

The above concepts came to life in my experience as a performer with Cecil Taylor in 1995. A fearsomely virtuosic pianist–improviser–composer, Taylor has irreversibly influenced contemporary music with his rich and nuanced musical vision. Taylor's exacting pianistic approach is characterized by a fluid, relaxed, yet powerful technique that could best be described as athletic. His performances are rather reminiscent of high-level martial arts: a physical be-havior that is intuitive, improvisational, and interactive, yet at the same time muscular, deeply structured, and surgically precise (Taylor 1975, 2002b).

The occasion was the performance of his "creative orchestra" music, which forty west-coast musicians studied and interpreted under his guidance. (A smaller but similar ensemble can be heard on Taylor 2002a.) Taylor's approach spoke volumes about improvised music as a collective activity. Composition in an improvising context can take on a variety of forms—perhaps some thematic material as a point of departure, or perhaps some music-generative methods or processual cues. Early on, when we were repeat-edly questioning him about the role of the written material, he said, "This [written material] is the formal content of the piece; what I want is for all the players to bring their individual languages to the interpretation and execu-tion of the piece." Taylor desired that we create a collective embodiment of his material by filtering it through our individual "languages," framing the music as discourse, individual sound as personal narrative.

In our week of daily rehearsals with Mr. Taylor, the earlier sessions led us to believe that he was a stickler for detail. I recall that we spent the first three-hour rehearsal on one postage-stamp-sized corner of one of his scores; he would continually repeat and rework the material bit by bit, singing or con-ducting a certain phrase for us, or asking us to permute the written pitches in a certain way. But toward the end of the week, his requirements grew less stringent, his guidance less direct; he would simply set us in motion and leave the room for a while. I realized that somehow he had taught us his language—his sense of phrasing and repetition, his attention to detail, the way he rigorously reworks and dissects a turn of phrase. Once this had happened, we were free to bring our own ideas to this context—to embody his language. When he returned to the rehearsal room, he would find that we had made something out of his cryptic scores. Evidently, Taylor's aesthetic privileges the sound of personalities interacting over conventional concepts of form. Because of the heightened role that group interactivity played, it felt at times as though we had formed not just an orchestra but a small musical civilization.

Indeed, our group experienced in microcosm the conflict, strife, and tension that a society experiences in macrocosm. Much of this was enacted on a musical level in the performance on October 26, 1995. For example, when some musicians reached the stage, they abandoned their allegiance to the unwritten, brittle orchestral aesthetic that had been developed over the course of rehearsals, choosing instead to yield to the temptation to play nonstop with furious intensity. This behavior raised the issue of (physical) power: clearly, a tenor saxophonist can play with enough force to drown out a section of six violinists, and a drummer can bury a pianist's efforts with ease. It was found that the louder instrumentalists possessed the privilege to control the intensity level directly, while the softer instrumentalists were forced to defer to such control. (Fellow musician Matthew Goodheart [1996] has observed the added role played by the self-serving musical choices made by certain individuals who wanted to get noticed by the legendary pianist for possible career advancement.)

Also, in the absence of a more dictatorial leader figure or a hard and fast text to which to adhere, we found ourselves in frequent disagreement as to what was "supposed" to be happening or what to do next. Different factions formed to conduct their own unified small-group activities, allowing for the emergence of pockets of apparent order in the sonic chaos. The resultant performances (which included Taylor himself) featured truly sublime flashes of fortuitous beauty and moments of brilliantly focused small-group improvisation, amid often-inscrutable orchestral noise.

What about this musical instance could be characterized as "experiential"? Nöe's notions of *environment, scale, complexity,* and *uniqueness* were each specifically addressed in this performance. In keeping with Taylor's directions, as the audience entered, musicians also entered the stage from the wings and the hall's aisles, bringing their chairs and music stands onstage while chanting and moving in geometric patterns. The musicians were engaging in a performative ritual of "constructing" the performing environment; this act drew attention to this environment's constructedness, and incorporated the environment into the performance itself. Effectively for the audience, it was unclear at what point in space or time the performance had begun; it was somehow fused with the concert-hall *environment* itself, and with the spectator's entrance into the space. Such performative rituals preface many of Taylor's solo and group concerts; he never takes the setting or occasion for granted, nor does he allow the audience to do so.

The audience members witnessed musical structure emerging in real time as extreme polyphony. From a distance, the overall sound may have seemed vast, dense and unfathomable, fulfilling Nöe's requirement of overwhelming *scale*. But with closer attention, they saw small subgroups of musicians visibly discussing strategies, arriving at collective decisions, and acting on them; they observed individual musicians in the aggregate occasionally electing to foreground themselves by performing soloistically, and they saw and heard the real-time response of other members of the ensemble to such acts. The audience was left to contend with these intra-group dynamics and come to their own conclusions about the proceedings. An individual audience member could zero in on small regions of activity, but no single listener ever possessing one privileged listening perspective. This is the musical correlate to experiential *complexity*, in that there is no perspicuous vantage from which to perceive the entire event, and no particular ordered set of perceptions for the listener to follow passively in order to apprehend the ideal "work." Lastly, the performance was specific to that time and place; as is the case with improvisation in general, it is nonrepeatable in any except the broadest sense of the word, and so it displays the required trait of *uniqueness*.

Throughout this performance, our experience of ensemble-as-social-group highlighted the sense of music as the sound of human action, and the sense of improvisation as an embodied, situated activity. The performance consisted of our enacted, sonorous experience of negotiating the improvisational process. We were an orchestra with our apparatus exposed.

Roscoe Mitchell

In recent years I have had the privilege of working in multi-instrumentalist–composer–improviser Roscoe Mitchell's ensemble. A pioneer in experimental music, Mitchell is a founding member of the celebrated Art Ensemble of Chicago (1991 [1972], 1998 [1975]; see also Lewis 1998) and the hugely influential collective of African American artists known as the Association for the Advancement of Creative Musicians (Lewis 2001–2002). He is noted for his novel approaches to form, texture, timbre, and space, among other things.

Mitchell's work with various wind instruments occasionally finds him exploring the most liminal behaviors of these instruments (e.g., "S II Examples" on Mitchell 1978). He might construct an entire solo improvisation by passing air through the alto saxophone in various fingering configurations so as not to generate an actual tone; the sporadic pitches that arise from this process provide a dramatic emergent form that keeps the listener transfixed. He might circular-breathe through the horn for several minutes, allowing the resultant variation in air pressure to impose a periodic timbral surge on his sound. Or he might find a note on the soprano saxophone that squeaks or cracks, and then work through an understanding of that squeaking right before your ears, constructing a masterful solo piece from this odd, "impure" sound emanating from the horn. On these occasions we witness an intrepid sonic explorer in poignant performative dialogue with his instrument, creating music out of the experiential process of making sound. These performances and the act of listening to them are inherently nonrepeatable, predicated as they are on the process of mutual discovery.

Mitchell's ensemble music covers a wide range of instrumentations, styles, and degrees of complexity, and they vary from fully notated to entirely improvised to anywhere in between. In some of Mitchell's ensemble pieces (e.g., Mitchell 1986), he has the musicians improvise independent, focused streams of musical activity, without self-consciously interacting with the other individual musicians. This would seem at first to go against the standard view of jazz as a highly interactive, dialogic medium. But in fact Mitchell is privileging that very dialogue, insisting on a transparent counterpoint among the various melodic streams. He knows that this dynamic cannot be forced, so his directive to the musicians is to listen closely without "following" or imitating one another. Musical counterpoint can occur in unexpected ways, and in this case it unfolds spontaneously from the juxtaposed sonorous actions of the participants. Having performed such pieces with Mitchell, I can attest to the rich variety and specificity of dynamics, textures, and emergent forms that arise from such deceptively simple principles.

At one point in the course of a weeklong studio recording project (Mitchell 2002), he guided his nine-piece group improvisationally through the sculpting of an introduction to one of his notated pieces, titled "this" and based on a poem by e. e. cummings. A certain utterance he made in the process shed light on his creative perspective. Exploring the available options, he asked percussionist Vincent Davis to tap on a wood block, and then to hit a gong. Then he asked guitarist Spencer Barefield about the sympathetic strings on his acoustic guitar, and had him strum them by way of demonstration. Next, he asked percussionist Gerald Cleaver to try a few tremolo dyads on the marimba, first with hard mallets, then with soft ones. He asked to hear these sounds again, one by one, in various sequences. Then, casually, Mitchell announced, "All right, may I please hear that much music again?"

This request hit me hard, because it hadn't dawned on me that what was happening during this process even was music; I had unconsciously dismissed it all as precompositional timbral exploration. But Mitchell *knew* we had crossed the line into music: a series of human sound events, intentional sonic gestures in organized succession. Of course it was music; how could I have thought otherwise?

In that instant, I learned something profound and difficult to explain. It struck me how the rawest sonic materials and the most primal human acts can be heard as compelling, even beautiful music. I saw that music need not be understood simply as the execution of preordained gestures, and that it can be viewed as a process of inquiry, a path of action, a deliberate sonorous exploration–construction of the world. It struck me, therefore, that perhaps humans are always making music—that counterpoint and form necessarily emerge from the sound of experiential human action in time.

It was also made clear in this exchange that music can be viewed as a consequence of active listening; it is, at some level, *through* informed listening that music is constructed. Placing the skillful listener in such an active role explodes the category of experiences that we call listening to music, because it allows the listener the improvisatory freedom to frame any moment or any experience as a musical one. *The improvisor is always listening; the listener is always improvising.*

Challenging in this way the boundary between music and non-music, Mitchell's perspective suggests a listener-centered, bottom-up inversion of Nöe's characterization. In this view, it is within the improvising listener's power to reconstruct music from sounds in her *environment*, and to reclassify perceptual experiences of arbitrary *scale*, *complexity*, and *uniqueness*, actively reframing the tumult of everyday action as music. The listener is empowered to *constitute* music, self-consciously and actively, from guided sensory input. This view underscores an *essential identity between perceptual experience and improvisation*.

The standpoint indicated by Mitchell's request resonates with Taylor's own all-encompassing view of music as a way of life, as he articulated in an interview:

It seems to me what music *is*, is everything that you do. . . . [H]opefully everything that I try to do in this situation has the same kind of *control over the senses* that the making of, you know, the *particular* art of music is. So to read, or dance, you know, to converse, is all a part of the making of music. So that, you know, when one walks down the street, and one looks, if there is a fuchsia-colored awning sticking out on the thirtieth floor, one says, *oh wow*. So that to *me* what it is, is everything one does. (Mann 1981, transcribed by author)

It is important to situate this perspective on musical improvisation, in many ways common to Mitchell and Taylor, in the context of African-American expressive culture. Without question, African-American music has exerted an immense impact on world culture. This fact is especially remarkable given that African-American history has at its foundation a proximity to terror, and a sustained atmosphere of violence imposed from without (Gilroy 1993, 73). In this light, African-American expressive culture can indeed be viewed as a set of tactics for survival in such a context. Here improvisation takes on a crucial symbolic weight. In this context, the phrase "improvised music" suggests not simply that the notes and rhythms are extemporized because of a cultural aesthetic that privileges improvisation (which is certainly true—see Small 1998 [1987]), but moreover that music is created from a position of disenfranchisement, where sheer survival cannot be taken for granted, where one is perpetually improvising through life by making use of whatever is at hand—especially one's own sensory experience. Hence, it has been suggested that we theorize improvisation as a *condition*, shaped by social, cultural, and economic forces. This is not unlike Harvey's formulation of the condition of postmodernity (Harvey 1991). (For more extensive discussions of these issues, a partial list of sources would include Baker 1984, Baraka 1963, Benston 2000, Gilroy 1993, Moten 2003, Monson 2003, Small 1998 [1987].)

On Electronic Music

Music making and music listening are interrelated, embodied activities. Until very recently in the history of humankind, with few exceptions (such as birdsong or windchimes), the music that humans perceive and respond to has always been human music. Before the last century of technological developments, music was almost always generated by human bodies. This is why the class of events that we recognize as music occur in the timescales of human activity—seconds, minutes, hours—and not in microseconds or decades. Music and humanity have arisen in tandem, the former out of the bodily activity of the latter, and so music necessarily bears rhythmic traces of our embodiment: pulse, phrase, gesture, ornament. We bob our heads or tap our feet to pulsations in the tactus range, and we breathe or sway along with the phrasing of a singer, and we listen to rapid rhythmic filigree as if it were speech (Iyer 2002).

More than a century after the invention of recording technology, we have become accustomed to recorded, disembodied, and electronically generated music. But still, music tends to bear these same traces of embodiment. Pulse-heavy electronic dance music often makes sonic references to the stomping of feet and to sexually suggestive slapping of skin. It is indeed rather telling that today, the most widespread uses of electronic music are in contexts meant for dance; the least humanly embodied music is ironically that which is *most* dependent on our physical engagement with it. It has emerged in recent decades as a cheaper alternative to human music-making. One can re-create the pulsating texture of dance music without the physical exertion previously required to do so. The idea of a drum loop encapsulates this possibility; one can loop a danceable drum pattern indefinitely through digital means, thereby creating a whole new notion of temporality in music that lies outside of human action, but still elicits it.

Often, popular electronic music plays in the grey area between bodily presence and electronic impossibility. Much of the electronica of the most recent decade (e.g., Squarepusher 1997) displays this playful ambiguity. A sampled beat—i.e., a brief recording of a human drummer—is sliced into small temporal units. These units are played back in rearranged orders, sped up or slowed down, multiply triggered, and otherwise manipulated electronically. Because the original sampled recording bears the microrhythmic traces of embodiment, the result sounds something like a human drummer improvising with often amusing flourishes and ample metric ambiguity. Momentarily regular, almost human-sounding pseudo-drumming devolves into inhumanly rapid sequences of rhythmic attacks, fast enough to resemble digital noise. Such electronic manipulation of familiar musical sounds serves to problematize the listener's image of a human drummer. These manipulations are typically carried out "out of time" in the studio, in a fashion similar to composition, but object of these manipulations is a human performance that took place "in time." Hence this approach is able to alternately engage and confound our sense of embodied empathy, constructing and deconstructing our mental image of the person behind the sounds.

Hip-hop DJs also enact the play of embodiment, in treating turntables as a kind of improvisational percussion meta-instrument (e.g., X-ecutioners 1997, 2004). Using strategically chosen segments of a vinyl record, the DJ moves the record back and forth with one hand, while creating amplitude envelopes with a fader on a mixer in the other hand. The sound generated is of two general types: one is a percussive scratch derived from rapid motion of the record, and the other is a recognizable, meaningful fragment of recorded music or sound. The latter stroke type often hides the sophisticated, impeccably timed physical gestures involved in their creation, as these gestures are unrelated to the sonic material. The scratch sound, however, bears a direct sonic resemblance to the physical motion involved. There is an interesting continuum between these two general types, and that continuum is navigated improvisationally. A fragment of recorded sound can be manipulated percussively in real time, in a manner that temporarily overrides its referential content, causing it to refer instead to the physical materiality of the vinyl-record medium, and more importantly to the "in-time" embodiment, dexterity and skill of its manipulator.

These twin art forms each create a sustained interruption of the transparency of perception. The listener experiences the disruption–breakage of the physical act of performance, as recorded fragments of human musical acts undergo ironic, physically impossible manipulations (the root *manus* meaning *hand* revealing the counter-embodiment of the manipulator). This is the subtext of the term "broken beat," itself an ironic re-tensing of "breakbeat": the perceptual experience of this music consists of the *recognition of the act of breaking music with the hands*—the metamusical sound of broken music, of hands breaking the body's beats, of one body taking action upon the sonorous actions of another.

Concluding Remarks

The understanding of music as sonorous human action occurring "in time" is fundamental to our experience of music. It arises as a consequence of embodiment, and it is an aspect of music-making that is largely taken for granted. The experimental musical improvisations that I have described draw attention to this facet of music, helping us realize the inherent musicality of human activity, and the sense of drama we derive from music as sonorous embodied action embedded in time. The examples of Taylor and Mitchell illustrate some ways in which musical improvisation can foreground its own process, playing the role of experience itself, reminding the listener of one's own act of experiencing it.

Taylor's and Mitchell's approaches share with, say, the X-ecutioners' turntable music a grounding in the improvisational music that emerged from African-American experimental practice in the late twentieth century—and they are perspectives too often neglected by the research community. These are the sorts of perspectives that we need when trying to understand the musical mind, or the science of art, or the relationship of the arts to cognition. We need to maintain as full as possible an understanding of the arts, and to do so we must remain engaged with as many forms of artistic inquiry as we are able. As Ione (2000) notes with respect to Cézanne, many artists knowingly spend long periods of time on the frontiers of their own perception and cognition. What they find there often stretches our conventional notions of beauty, aesthetics, and even the fundamentals of expression; precisely because of this, their work has much to teach us about consciousness.

This article originally appeared in slightly different form in *Journal of Consciousness Studies* (2004).

References

Art Ensemble of Chicago (1991 [1972]). *Live at Mandel Hall* (compact discs). Chicago: Delmark Records.

Art Ensemble of Chicago (1998 [1975]). *Fanfare for the Warriors* (compact disc). New York: Koch Jazz.

Baker, H. (1983). *Blues, Ideology, and African American Literature: A Vernacular Theory.* Chicago: University of Chicago Press.

Baraka, Amiri (Leroi Jones) (1963). *Blues People.* New York: HarperCollins.

Barthes, R. (1975). *S/Z.* Trans. Richard Miller. London: Cape Publishers.

Benston, K. (2000). *Performing blackness: Enactments of African-American modernism.* New York: Routledge.

Blacking, J. (1973). *How Musical Is Man?* Seattle: University of Washington Press.

Brown, J. (1991). *Star Time* (compact discs). Compilation of original releases from 1956–1984. New York: PolyGram Records.

Coltrane, J. (1993). *Transition* (compact disc). Reissue of original 1970 release, recorded 1965. New York: GRP Records.

Coltrane, J. (1998). *The Complete 1961 Village Vanguard Recordings* (compact discs). Reissue of original recordings. New York: GRP Records.

Fieldwork (2002). *Your Life Flashes* (compact disc). New York: Pi Recordings.

Fieldwork (2005). *Simulated Progress* (compact disc). New York: Pi Recordings.

Friberg, A., and J. Sundberg (1999). "Does Music Performance Allude to Locomotion? A Model of Final Ritardandi Derived from Measurements of Stopping Runners. *Journal of the Acoustical Society of America* 105, no. 3: 1469–1484.

Friberg, A., J. Sundberg, and L. Frydén (2000). "Music from Motion: Sound Level Envelopes of Tones Expressing Human Locomotion." *Journal of New Music Research* 29, no. 3: 199–210.

Gilroy, P. (1993). *The Black Atlantic: Modernity and Double Consciousness.* Cambridge, Mass.: Harvard University Press.

Goodheart, M. (1996). "Freedom and Individuality in the Music of Cecil Taylor." Master's thesis, Mills College, Oakland, California.

Handel, S. (1990). *Listening.* Cambridge, Mass.: MIT Press.

Harvey, David (1991). *The Condition of Postmodernity.* Oxford: Blackwell Publishing.

Ione, Amy (2000). "An Inquiry into Paul Cézanne: The Role of the Artist in Studies of Perception and Consciousness." *Journal of Consciousness Studies* 7, nos. 8–9: 57–74.

Iyer, Vijay (1998). "Microstructures of Feel, Macrostructures of Sound: Embodied Cognition in West African and African-American Musics." Ph.D. dissertation, University of California, Berkeley. Available at http://cnmat.cnmat.berkeley.edu/People/~vijay/.

Iyer, Vijay (2002). "Embodied Mind, Situated Cognition, and Expressive Microtiming in African-American Music." *Music Perception* 19, no. 3: 387–414.

Iyer, Vijay (2003). *Blood Sutra* (compact disc). Norwalk, Conn.: Artists House Foundation.

Iyer, Vijay (2004). "Exploding the Narrative in Jazz Improvisation." In *New Essays in Jazz Studies*, ed. R. O'Meally, B. Edwards, and F. Griffin. New York: Columbia University Press.

Iyer, Vijay (2005). *Reimagining* (compact disc). New York: Savoy Jazz.

Iyer, Vijay, and Mike Ladd (2003). *In What Language?* (compact disc). New York: Pi Recordings.

Iyer, Vijay, and Mike Ladd (2003). *Still Life with Commentator* (compact disc). New York: Savoy Jazz.

Lewis, G. (1996). "Improvised Music since 1950: Afrological and Eurological Forms." *Black Music Research Journal* 16, no. 1: 91–119.

Lewis, G. (1998). "Singing Omar's Song: A (Re)construction of Great Black Music." *Lenox Avenue* 4: 69–92.

Lewis, G. (2001–2002). "Experimental Music in Black and White: The AACM in New York, 1970–1985." *Current Musicology* 71–73: 100–157.

Mann, R. (1981). *Imagine the Sound* (documentary feature film). Janus Films.

Mitchell, R. (1978). *L-R-G, The Maze, S II Examples* (compact disc). Whitehall, Mich.: Nessa Records.

Mitchell, R. (1986). *The Flow of Things* (compact disc). Milan: Black Saint Records.

Mitchell, R. (2002). *Song for My Sister* (compact disc). New York: Pi Recordings.

Mitchell, R. (2004). *Solo x3* (compact disc). New York: Mutable Music.

Noë, A. (2000). "Experience and Experiment in Art." *Journal of Consciousness Studies* 7, nos. 8–9: 123–135.

Rowell, L. (1988). "The Idea of Music in India and the Ancient West." *Acta Philosophica Fennica* 43: 323–342.

Schutz, A. (1964). "Making Music Together." In *Collected Papers II: Studies in Social Theory*, 159–178. The Hague: Martinus Nijhoff.

Shore, B. (1996). *Culture in Mind: Cognition, Culture, and the Problem of Meaning*. New York: Oxford University Press.

Shove, P., and B. Repp (1995). "Musical Motion and Performance: Theoretical and Empirical Perspectives." In *The Practice of Performance*, ed. J. Rink, 55–83. Cambridge: Cambridge University Press.

Smithers, T. (1996). "On What Embodiment Might Have to Do with Cognition." In *Embodied Cognition and Action: Papers from the 1996 AAAI Fall Symposium*, ed. M. Mataric, 113–111. Technical Report FS-96-02. Menlo Park, Calif.: AAAI Press.

Squarepusher (1997). *Big Loada* (compact disc). Sheffield, U.K.: Warp Records.

Taylor, Cecil (1975). *Silent Tongues* (LP record). Germany: Black Lion Records.

Taylor, Cecil (2002a). *The Light of the Corona* (compact disc). Berlin: FMP Records.

Taylor, Cecil (2002b). *The Willisau Concert* (compact disc). Zürich: Intakt Records.

X-ecutioners (1997). *X-pressions* (compact disc). San Francisco: Asphodel Records.

X-ecutioners (2004). *Revolutions* (compact disc). New York: Sony Music.

Alondra Nelson

Nadine Robinson is a London-born, Bronx-based visual and sound artist. She incorporates various mediums in her work and is the creator of "boom paintings"—objects that interfuse the modernist painting tradition with the aural architectonics of black urban culture. Robinson applies "sampling" to art historical concerns, in the process bringing into relief what she perceives to be the imperfections of modernist art practice, and highlighting what she deems the greater promise of aesthetics, which are informed by the cut and mix strategies of hip-hop and technoculture. Her work has been exhibited internationally including at the Studio Museum in Harlem (SMH), The Project (NYC), the Bronx Museum of the Arts, and P.S. 1. Most recently, Robinson's work was shown at "Tempo," the inaugural show of MoMA QNS (Museum of Modern Art, Queens, New York).

Alondra Nelson: How did you first come to make art that combines music technology and painting?

Nadine Robinson: I live in the Bronx but had a studio on the corner of Canal and Hudson streets in Manhattan. I regularly saw sound equipment at the shops downtown. I also saw many of my relatives, and friends from back in the day in the Bronx, down on Canal Street buying speakers to soup-up their sound systems. After a while, I began to shop at these music equipment stores for new kinds of materials.

I made my first "boom painting" in 1997 while at Skowhegan, an artists' residency in Maine. It was ten inches square. I still have this prototype.

"Boom painting" comes from "boom box," which is slang for a portable radio. In naming a minimalist painting, boom, I aimed to bring modernism to a vernacular level that I thought new or nontraditional art audiences could understand or at least want to understand. The first boom painting was small and portable; but now they're quite large and resemble Jamaican sound systems with their oversized speaker constructions. In Jamaica, sound systems are called "Houses of Joy," and so, the large scale of my more recently made boom paintings makes them implicitly architectural.

Boom is a word that means a sound, like the boom of an explosion let's say. These boom paintings make noise, or have the capacity to emit sounds. And therefore, the color field paintings that I create are also "hearing" field paintings. They extend beyond the scale and range of Barnett Newmann's "zip" paintings, and ultimately challenge the manifested intentions of modernism in the 1950s and after.

AN: Do you consider your work, which refers to Newmann's "zips," to be a critique of modernism, an extension of modernist forms and aesthetics, or both?

NR: Let me clarify some of my creative intentions. One of the funny things about an artist's intentions is that there's always an ambivalence, a creative schizophrenia, or an overdevelopment. (I find it better to refer to psychological pathology and its terminologies when discussing "ART" and me.)

There was a group of painters in the '60s and '70s who responded to the decade of Newmann and the like. For example, Philip Taffe's *We Are Not Afraid* provoked Newmann's *Who's Afraid of Red Yellow and Blue II*, 1967. Similarly, my work is about my place in art history as a woman of color. It's a response to not seeing someone who looks like me provoke modernism and its dangerous exclusivity. It's about presenting paintings that demystify modernism and render it utterly accessible. At the same time, the references I use can be an odd collage of histories, mediums, and inspirations, and are specifically related to my own experience of them. For instance, Ad Reinhardt's and Robert Ryman's paintings were ultimately not as autonomous as the artists intended. Yet, the histories that inform some of my boom paintings are obscure and in that respect mirror the obscurity (or intellectual difficulty) of modernism's metaphysical leanings.

The basic difference between, say, *Big Baby Blue* (*BBB*), 2001, and "zip" painting is that modernism and its philosophers proposed that the objective of art was to achieve absoluteness, exclusiveness, and transcendence, and to hold itself separate from the everyday world in an attempt to reach the infinite sublimity of Kantian aesthetics. Boom paintings have speakers and sound that is abstracted–subtracted from the everyday world. I try to reach that sublime. I can only feel what that means; it's the experience of having my breath taken away. (It happens at certain times in nature, but also through "artificially" created experiences that simulate natural sublimity.) My work must first take my own breath away, then the audience's. Boom paintings are both sublime—through the experience of them as sound, visuals, and historical (and art-historical) references—and very of this world. The sampled sound bites and turntables are materials that I hope will be inclusive of an audience that was not included in early modernism. So, to answer your question, boom paintings are both a critique of modernism and an extension of it. It's ambivalent, as all things are.

AN: The "speaker" tends to have several valences in your work, including its function as a technological artifact, as a declaration of agency, and as a synonym for speech, but most importantly the latter. How does your work address voice and voicelessness?

NR: One piece that I never realized was a response to the Million Man March. I thought, what if I made a million small boom paintings, all with the potential for sound, but with no sound? This is how I understand voicelessness in urban America—as potentiality. Large groups of African Americans are vocal in absentia. Blacks in New York City are vocal on the subways when they sing to their Walkmans, or in large gatherings à la the Million Man March. American media dismisses these voices. Blacks are vocal on BET and at jams. A DJ is louder than most black politicians. I always thought that a person in a souped-up car, bass bangin' down the neighborhood, had more to say about the black community than Al Sharpton or Jesse Jackson.

When these speaker paintings do "speak," sometimes it's through a sampled edition that's cryptic when presented without a context (e.g., laugh tracks, "glossalalia," etc.). These works are not as accessible as *BBB*, which was as close to art for art's sake as I could get. I hope to do more like this. But a lot of my boom paintings are still part of a kind of elitist overintellectualism at least as they are an attempt at creating experience and objects that combine several disciplines: history, media studies, religion, etc.

AN: Your painting vocabulary repeats several colors: white, red, black, and baby blue. What is the significance of these colors?

NR: My painting vocabulary continues to grow. Those colors are ones that I've used recently. The blue in *BBB* is the same shade as that of Sugar Hill Records, the first hip-hop record label, and should be a definite marker of inclusion for urban communities and of exclusion for many in the art audience who I have to explain it to more than to, say, Bronx school children. They get it right away. Just like they get David Hammons' work.

Black is the color, the people, and a reference to Reinhardt's reductiveness. His quote, "I'm just making the last paintings anyone can make," reflected the obnoxiousness of modernism. I want to challenge this with a series of black paintings. The red, white, and blue refer to flags and their symbolic meanings. The part of a flag that is its base is called the "field," and here I use wordplay. How can a field of a flag become a color field painting? Ultimately, any color or surface used is conceptually bounded by its symbolic idea and not by the primacy of color theory.

AN: Your art practice is deeply influenced by hip-hop and DJ culture. As DJs have become celebrities, people at clubs started *watching* DJs with a kind of awe, as much as, or more than, responding to the aural environment by dancing, nodding their heads, or throwing their hands in the air, etc. Your piece, *Big Baby Blue*, which was most recently shown in the "Freestyle" show at the SMH, is notably absent of the DJ *and* the crowd. Do you think that it inspires reverence for sound objects rather than interactivity?

NR: The opening night party for the "Freestyle" show was a jam! Afterwards, a reviewer commented that Sanford Bigger's and my work were curiously hollow on opening night. There was this irony: the turntables in my piece weren't being used at a party.

Well, I thought that *BBB* would mostly be a silent piece, expressing the *potential* of sound, and if one needs to hear it as well as see it, then they can turn it on. In making this work, I was also thinking of Robert Morris and the idea of painting as objecthood: the sense that by its size and reference to sound, the piece controlled its audience.

One has to come before the altar of *Big Baby Blue*, and the DJ is the priest. But it doesn't stop there. Anyone in the audience can be a DJ. They can "spin" the painting. There is a practical side of boom paintings. They are actual sound systems; form does follow function. "Zips" are only "zips."

AN: Is there something about the culture of museums and galleries that works against the impulses of DJ culture? Or against your desire for a viewer–listener to experience the work or interact with it? What would happen if a museum visitor tried to spin some records at the "altar of *BBB?*"

NR: DJ culture is inclusive—a party always is, especially a hip-hop party—and not exclusive. I would prefer that all visitors could "spin" the painting. I encourage spinning at the altar of *BBB*. I hope that the museum uses the piece to draw audiences that normally do not attend. The audience should experience works of art intimately. *BBB's* DJ table undoes modernism's separation of the self and the artistic experience, dispensing with the frustration of coming to a monochromatic painting with little else but a title. *BBB's raison d'être* is not to dispense of the possibility of transcendence through art, but to show that transcendence and the immanence of reality do not have clear demarcations. *BBB* is at once at DJ sound system and a nod to modernism.

AN: In *Tower Hollers*, 2001, you provide a medium for the voices of the mostly black and Latino service employees at the World Trade Center (WTC) who were often forgotten in the capitalist mythology of the "twin towers." This work was conceived in 1999–2000 while you were an artist-in-residence at Worlds Views, the residency program sponsored by the Lower Manhattan Cultural Council (LMCC) that provided studio space at One World Trade Center. On September 11, 2001, a fellow artist, Michael Richards, who was working in his studio on the 92nd floor of the WTC was killed, and the LMCC lost their offices and this residency program. How has the meaning of this piece changed after the events of September 11?

NR: *Tower Hollers* was shown in its entirety in the "Tempo" exhibition at MoMA QNS in the summer of 2002. It consisted of 455 twelve-inch by twelve-inch boom paintings. It was my largest piece to date and was installed horizontally and not vertically as originally intended. It is the voices of three of the number of workers at the WTC at the time of my residency.

It was heartbreaking to see the towers fall. I was in the city on 14th Street duplicating slides of my work. When they fell, I immediately proceeded 111 blocks north to the SMH to turn off *Americana*, 2000, a sound installation that mixed speeches and laugh tracks and was on exhibit there. I knew that my friends and family would use and need these totems to help heal. *Americana* has to do with the ideals of America versus the poor treatment that black Americans receive. Not very "post-black," but Thelma Golden [deputy director, exhibitions and public programs, SMH] still mentioned it in *Time* magazine after September 11.[1] The context of *Americana* changed dramatically after that day.

Tower Hollers has also changed. *Tower Hollers* is about industrialization, globalization, and greed. Good versus evil. I have VHS interviews with some WTC workers, mostly security guards or maintenance workers. I asked them

questions about their work, if they liked it, their wages, their favorite song. I
was to complete these interviews this fall. It now has a memorial quality to it.
The soundtrack of the piece wails, "Go down, ole Hannah. Won't come till
judgment day." Those are the words of a work song that were adapted from
a spiritual. Those words are now prophetic and eerie. Michael Richard's death
was tragic. His work was eerily prescient: the image of his tar baby sculpture
with planes attacking its body makes one shudder!

Note

1. Thelma Golden, "Introduction: Post-Black," *Freestyle*, 14. New York: Studio Museum in Harlem, 2001.

Camera Lucida: Three-dimensional Sonochemical Observatory

Evelina Domnitch and Dmitry Gelfand

If we now envisage the more technical side of a possible future, it is very likely that the artist, tired of the cult for oils in painting, will find himself completely abandoning this five-hundred-year-old process, which restricts his freedom of expression by its academic ties.

Other techniques have already appeared recently and we can foresee that just as the invention of new musical instruments changes the whole sensibility of an era, the phenomenon of light can, due to current scientific progress, among other things, become the new tool for the new artist.

—Marcel Duchamp (1999, 196)

Is it possible to create a sonic rainbow?

Is it possible to translate the wave behaviors of sound into those of light?

Is it possible to render sound visible and allow a musician to work with the shape of sonic vibrations?

Since Ernst Chladni's experiments with vibrating plates (late eighteenth century), much territory has been covered in the field of acoustic observation. However, there have been very few attempts at a three-dimensional and non-virtual visualization of the movement of sound events through space. Outside the anechoic confines of an acoustic laboratory where research is conducted in order to achieve as precise results as possible, there lies an entropic, omnidirectional network of merging and diverging sonic fronts.

In order to visualize the customarily invisible dynamics of sound waves without introducing a simulation mechanism such as a recording–playback medium or a computer interface, one must tap into the delicate juncture between the sensorially separated bandwidths of light and sound. The *Camera Lucida* (light chamber) installation allows one to directly convert sound waves into light by employing a phenomenon called *sonoluminescence.*

The Enigma of Sonoluminescence

Like radioactivity, sonoluminescence was discovered on the accidentally exposed surface of a photographic plate. In 1934, German scientists H. Frenzel and H. Schultes registered traces of light on a photographic plate submerged in an ultrasonically irradiated liquid. It took fifty years for scientists to develop the necessary tools to study this light, which emanates from collapsing gas bubbles during a process called cavitation (fig. 27.1).

All acoustic vibrations generate oscillating vacuums, which make up the anti-nodes or "troughs" of a sound wave. If the wavelength is short enough and the amplitude is high enough, these pockets of emptiness can incite the formation and implosive collapse of microbubbles in a liquid. The bubbles

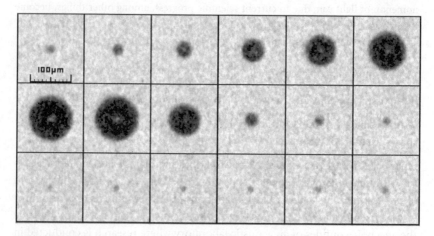

Figure 27.1
Photographic series of a trapped sonoluminescing bubble driven at 21.4 kHz. The bubble dynamics are represented at an interframe time of approximately 2.5 microseconds. (Photo © Reinhard Geisler)

"appear by tearing the liquid with brute force (ultrasound for example). Because they are essentially empty, they are termed cavitation bubbles, i.e., just cavities" (Lauterborn et al. 1999, 296). With the sudden appearance of a cavitation bubble, a tremendous difference in pressure arises between its nearly vacuous interior and the surrounding fluid. Consequently, the bubble rapidly implodes under the liquid's pressure (at over four times the speed of sound), and its gaseous innards shrink into a core so dense that temperatures are reached as high as are found on the Sun (10,000 degrees Celsius). At this stage, which spans far less than a billionth of a second, light is emitted from the center of the bubble. This emission recurs in phase with tens to hundreds of thousands of sound cycles per second as it traces the sounds' detailed patterning and vortices. Although an entirely new science of *sonochemistry* has recently emerged in order to decipher this elusive manifestation, the sequence of events, starting with a bubble's collapse and leading to photonic emissions, remains predominantly unknown.

A widely supported model of sonoluminescence is the hot spot theory, which postulates that the energy fueling the initial expansion and formation of a near-vacuum within a cavitation bubble is focused into a sweltering plasma core upon the bubble's implosion. "The compression of cavities when they implode in irradiated liquids is so rapid that little heat can escape from the cavity during collapse. The surrounding liquid, however, is still cold and will quickly quench the heated cavity. Thus, one generates a short-lived, localized hot spot in an otherwise cold liquid" (Suslick 1994, 142). The hot spot theory also concludes that it is the high pressure arising during a bubble's swift implosion (several thousand atmospheres) that causes explosive shockwave synthesis in solid matter. Other theories have sought to explain sonoluminescence through quantum vacuum fluctuations, optical lasing, and even sonofusion (acoustically induced nuclear fusion).

In terms of duration, pressure, and energy per molecule, ultrasonic irradiation behaves in a manner vastly different from traditional energy sources such as heat, light, or ionizing radiation. Because of the rapidity of tremendous oscillations in heat and pressure caused by a cavitation bubble's collapse, ultrasound offers a highly efficient means by which to synthesize matter at the nanoscale, such as metals, alloys, carbides, oxides, and colloids. A sonochemical preparation of biomaterials, best exemplified by protein microspheres, is also being researched.

Using high-intensity ultrasound and simple protein solutions, a remarkably easy method to make both air-filled microbubbles and nonaqueous liquid-filled microcapsules has been developed. These microspheres are stable for months, and being slightly smaller than erythrocytes, they can be intravenously injected to pass unimpeded through the circulatory system (Suslick et al. 1999, 17).

While numerous practical applications of sonochemistry are flourishing, scientists are still unable to determinine precisely the increase in temperature within a cavitation bubble, and the speed at which it occurs. As with all other behaviors transpiring in nanospace at nanospeeds, one is precisely limited by one's instruments of measurement. Yonder lies the philosopher's and the artist's dominion, where the imperceptible and inconceivable serve to disentangle one's imagination from the burden of finitude.

Preliminary Experiments

The *Camera Lucida* project began as a speculative reverie on observing sound waves with the naked eye. It seemed appealing to us to use a large volume of trapped gas, which would emit light when irradiated by sound converted into voltage. However, as soon as we came upon the phenomenon of sonoluminescence, it became quite clear that we had struck virgin soil. Though imbued with excitement and great potential, this path was riddled with obstacles: most of the physicists, chemists, and acoustic engineers we consulted predicted that our project was destined to fail or that the effects would be barely perceptible to the naked eye.

Nonetheless, after two years of hypothetical wanderings through the thick woods of nonlinear acoustics, optics, and fluid dynamics, we finally donned our sonochemical cloaks in Japan via an invitation from the Institute of Advanced Media Arts and Sciences (IAMAS). On the outskirts of the old samurai town of Nagoya, at the freshly erected "Palace" of Advanced Science and Technology (AIST) crowned by a fountain filled with titanium dioxide spheres, we attended the Eleventh Annual Meeting of the Japan Society of Sonochemistry. It was there that we befriended Werner Lauterborn, director of the Drittes Physikalisches Institut of the University of Göttingen, Germany. Because most of the presentations were in Japanese, we decided along with Dr. Lauterborn to skip some of them in favor of a six-hour dithyramb about the "two or at most three laws that govern the cosmos" (in Lauterborn's words).

By the end of our discourse, having distilled the quintessence of our sonochemical observatory project, Dr. Lauterborn advised us to contact Thierry Lepoint who had allegedly attained the brightest sonoluminescence visible to the naked eye.

Sonoluminescence is usually barely visible even after one's eyes have become acclimated to total darkness. Dr. Lepoint's experiments with xenon-infused

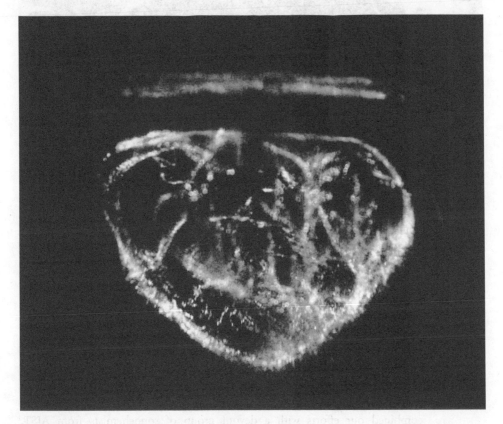

Figure 27.2
Montgolfier figure: Parachute-like sonoluminescent formation within xenon-infused sulfuric acid irradiated by a submerged titanium horn transducer. (Photo © Reinhard Geisler)

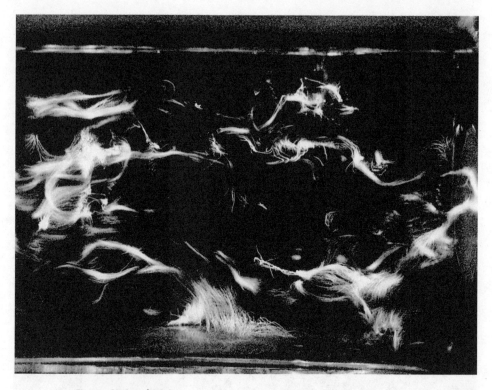

Figures 27.3 and 27.4
Xenon-infused sulphuric acid irradiated by multiple transducers affixed to the outside walls of the resonating chamber. (Photo © Evelina Domnitch and Dmitry Gelfand)

sulfuric acid irradiated by a titanium horn transducer were said to procure sonoluminescence that could be witnessed in broad daylight. Furthermore, by minimizing the distance between the transducer, which projects the ultrasound downward through the acid, and the bottom surface of the chamber (serving as a sonic reflector), one could observe *Montgolfier figures*: parachute-like formations named after the two French inventors of the hot-air balloon (fig. 27.2). As soon as Lepoint sent us all of the specifications, we combined our efforts with a devout group of sonochemists from AIST, doctors Iida, Tuziuti, Yasui, and Kozuka, and began conducting a series of experiments unprecedented in Japan.

Although our initial experiment was successful in terms of brightness, we were not able to create any Montgolfier figures even after numerous recalibrations. The transducer detonated a fiery xenon jet, which was magnificent in and of itself, but in no way alluded to the manifold sound environment within the resonator. On another occasion, we engineered a six-channel transducer system with a humanly audible sound composition modulating the ultrasonics (much like the manner in which mobile telephones permit the human voice to be nonlinearly hoisted onto a high-frequency signal that carries it into outer space). In spite of our efforts, we obtained the same result as before, except that now there were plural jets. After many frustrating hours of delicately tuning the frequency and amplitude modulation, all of a sudden, the unidirectional jets began to swirl and rip apart into trembling, gelatinous vortices. Having inadvertently ignored the ultrasonic amplifier's bleeding voltage

Figure 27.5
60 × 40 × 30 cm resonating chamber with eight ultrasonic transducers affixed to its
exterior. (Photo © Evelina Domnitch and Dmitry Gelfand)

meters, indicative of threshold amplitude levels, we had created a high-
pressure thermo-acoustic wind. The entire chamber was permeated by im-
mensely varied sonoluminescent formations, the quantity of which no longer
corresponded to the number of transducers (figs. 27.3 and 27.4). At last we
were ready to begin the construction of *Camera Lucida*.

Materialization and Operation

With the invaluable help of Honda Electronics, our assorted prototypes
and preconceptions were forged into a singular apparatus (fig. 27.5). Within
a transparent chamber filled with a gas-infused liquid, eight ultrasonic
transducers (four on the sides and four on the bottom) generate an ever-
modulating sonoluminescent environment. After adapting to the absolute
darkness surrounding the chamber, one begins to perceive the highly detailed
configurations of glowing sound waves.

The observatory's sound source is an interactive composition, which modulates the eight ultrasonic transducers individually, within a frequency range of 20–140 kHz. By playing the composition, the viewer–performer is able to activate a vast range of multilayered as well as isolated sonoluminescent behaviors. A hydrophone (a microphone submerged in liquid that is sensitive to high frequencies) simultaneously translates into the human hearing spectrum both the sounds emitted by the transducers and the resultant bubble implosions. As such, the interactive sound composition serves not only as a means of activating the observatory, but also as a large-scale model of the observatory's uncanny acoustic and fluid dynamics.

The Sonoluminescent Universe

While probing nature's inherent capacity to transform sound into light, one necessarily encounters a great many cosmogonical implications. It is revealed in the Vedas that sound is the Creator, Nada Brahma, the vibrational energy which pervades all things (Brahma-Samhita 1990, text 27). After Brahma meditated for a thousand god-years in the directionless, dark, primeval ether, the sound of Krishna's flute entered his eight ears (the earliest promulgation of the musical octave was in India, predating Pythagoras' allegedly Egyptian and/or Chinese resources). When Brahma repeated the sound with his voice (*aum* or *om*), the quiescent particles making up the ether began to heterogenize, and were thereupon cast out from the darkness.

To some such laws the ancient Philosophers seem to have alluded when they called God Harmony and signified his

Actuating matter harmonically by the God Pan's playing upon a Pipe and attributing music to the spheres made the distances and motions of the heavenly bodies harmonical. (Newton, transcribed in Mcguire and Rattansi 1966, 108)

The structure of the cosmos was triggered by a fundamental frequency, followed by overtones upon overtones, cascading omni-directionally into increasingly diversified oscillations, from the 92 periodic elements to the resonant frequencies of one's bodily organs. Everything is made of ceaselessly regenerative wave systems—any level of stasis is just a sensorial illusion generated by gaps in scale between inner and outer space-time. Not for an instant is any particle left unturned in the wake of cosmic renovation. Since energy–mass cannot be destroyed, it must undergo constant, pattern-yielding metakinesis. Consequently, certain harmonic patterns, for example the Fibonacci sequence, can propagate across the entirety of energy spectra from the sonic to the electromagnetic to the gravitational register.

One of the earliest dated sources of the Chinese musical system, Lüi (Lü Bu-Wei, 3rd century BCE), conveys a system based on twelve sounds generated by twelve etalon pitch pipes, whose length is calculated in the relation of progressing powers of two and three (Ravdonikas 2002, 32). Each of the twelve sounds corresponds to a vibratory artifact, stemming from a particular period in cosmic history. The first pitch, Huang Zhong, characterizes the embryonic stage, when the entire mass of beings starts wriggling like earthworms. The second pitch, Tai Cu, corresponds to the striking of a bell, which forced the light, buried among the primal entities, to emerge from stagnation.

According to contemporary astrophysical mythology, the early universe was so dense and torrid that photons remained glued to subatomic particles, together constituting acoustically modulating plasma. At a pivotal moment, the temperature dropped below 3,000 degrees Kelvin, allowing the photons to decouple from electrons, protons, and neutrons, which in their turn assembled into the first atoms (hydrogen), marking the birth of matter. Meanwhile, the emancipated light journeyed across the universe as it expanded and cooled, comprising the cosmic microwave background that one may currently perceive by means of radiotelescopy or by the small percentage of noise it generates on one's television set.

When it was discovered in the 1960s, this cosmic noise floor was found to be remarkably uniform across the sky. It was not until 1992 that the Cosmic Background Explorer (COBE) satellite discovered thermo-acoustic ripples, constituting an entire hundred-thousandth of the otherwise homogeneous flow of faint microwaves. Thermal maps of the cosmic background radiation provide one with a cursory glance of the universe before it flowered into a mosaic of reticulate inhomogeneities. The temperature wrinkles accounted for by the new cosmography denote tiny density fluctuations during the particle evolution of the *prima materia*. These wrinkles were gradually magnified by gravitational attraction into familiar morphologies such as stars, galaxies, and galactic clusters: "gravity and sonic motion have worked together to raise the radiation temperature in the troughs and lower the temperature at the peaks [of the fundamental sound wave and its overtones]" (de Bernardis et al. 2000).

Recent experiments, notably the Boomerang and Maxima experiments, have shown that the electromagnetic intensity spectrum reveals a sharp peak, precisely indicative of the resonant acoustic phenomena long awaited by cosmologists. "The early universe is full of sound waves compressing and rarefying matter and light, much like sound waves compress and rarefy air inside a flute or trumpet," said Boomerang team leader Paolo de Bernardis. "For the first time the new data show clearly the harmonics of these waves" ("Astronomers ...," *BBC News*, April 27, 2001).

Ocular Tuning

There are very ancient traditions scrutinizing the connection between light, sound, and color. From Indian and Chinese to Egyptian resources, Pythagoras collected substantial data during his eastwardly travels, uncovering the correlation between the musical octave and the spectrum of hues making up the humanly visible portion of electromagnetic radiation, broadly referred to as light. It was not until Sir Isaac Newton, however, that the speculations of the Pythagorean School evolved into a pronounced theory. Newton proposed that the light spectrum is "proportional to the Seven Musical Tones [the diatonic scale] or Intervals of the eight Sounds" (Newton 1952 [1730], 154). Historical evidence later arose alluding to the fact that it was his assistant, endowed with better eyesight, who identified the striations of the sunlight spectrum refracted by a prism, but it was certainly Newton who had instructed him to make seven divisions. As a result of this decision, most people today believe unthinkingly that the rainbow is composed of seven colors, called red, orange, yellow, green, blue, indigo, and violet.

Soon thereafter, Newton distilled a far more subtle musical dimension of the spectrum. Pressing together two pieces of glass, one curved like a lens and one flat, to form a gap that enlarges with distance from the contact point made colored rings ("Newton's rings") appear owing to the resultant light-wave interference. When he calculated the spaces between rings—spaces on the order of a ten-thousandth of an inch—he found that they were proportioned as the cube roots of the squares of the Pythagorean string lengths that would have given the corresponding intervals. It was through this discovery that he later calculated the wavelengths of light.

Newton's color research strongly inspired many artists and musicians—among the most exemplary of which was one of his contemporaries, Louis-Bertrand Castel, who spent forty years of his life building a color-projecting harpsichord: "by moving the fingers as on an ordinary harpsichord, the movement of the keys makes the colors appear with their combinations and their chords" (Godwin 1996, 12). Several hundred years later, the advent of electrically harnessed light opened far more elaborate possibilities for color projection, such as Wallace Rimington's "color organ" which accompanied the 1915 New York premiere of Scriabin's *Prometheus* symphony. Having notated precise color indications in the score, the composer held that each tonal mode corresponded to a particular shade of color, and each modulation to a nuance of that shade. Scriabin requested that everyone in the audience wear white clothing so that the projected colors would reflect off their bodies and thus saturate the entire hall. Henceforth, in the 1920s and '30s, the eighteenth century's color intonators were majestically reborn in the hands of various artist–animators such as Oskar Ficshinger and Charles Dockum, whose MobilColor and Lumia had been created during the course of a rivalry between the Museum of Modern Art and the Guggenheim Museum to acquire the superlative light organ. In the 1950s and '60s, the Kinetic Art movement gave rise to even more elaborate acousto-optic instruments; however, much like the vast collective of their predecessors, their interpolation of sound into light was more often than not the result of arbitrary suppositions.

The Art of Science

After a certain high level of technical skill is achieved, science and art tend to coalesce in aesthetics, plasticity, and form. The greatest scientists are always artists as well.
—Albert Einstein (Henderson 1955)

In physics, a nonlinear system, no matter how irregular and unpredictable, is nonetheless governed by deterministic laws. The augmentation of the chaotic propensity of a system makes it ostensibly more difficult to study its laws. However, it is often impossible to discern, let alone quantify, the constituent forces of a system without strategically increasing its instability. Simply to make sonoluminescence visible on a sufficiently large scale, a finely tunable multichannel instrument had to be constructed, and this could only be accomplished by introducing numerous layers of instability to the sonochemical process. In contrast to the customary single-channel, single-transducer systems, an eight-piece ensemble of high-intensity transducers sonicating a massive volume of liquid, tends to get out of tune easily. The more finely tunable the system, the higher its inclination toward nonlinearity. "Despite all of its success, there is still much that goes on in nature that seems more complex and sophisticated than anything technology has ever been able to produce" (Wolfram 2002, 11). Technology and art need not strive to imitate nature, but instead should participate in its multifarious unfolding. Conceived as both a work of art or nature and a scientific research tool, the *Camera Lucida* project seeks to blur the discrepancy between such definitions of intent.[1]

Note

1. For more about the authors, see www.portablepalace.com.

References

"Astronomers Hear 'Music of Creation'" (2001). *BBC News* (April 27).

Brahma-Samhita, Sri, trans. (1990). *Bhaktisiddhanta Sarasvati Gosvami Thakura.* Los Angeles: Bhaktivedanta Book Trust.

de Bernardis, P., et al. (2000). "A Flat Universe from High-Resolution Maps of the Cosmic Microwave Background Radiation." *Nature* 404 (April 27): 955–959.

Duchamp, M. (1999). *Marcel Duchamp: Respirateur.* Ed. K. Von Berswordt-Walrabe. Ostfildern: Cantz Publishers.

Godwin, J. (1996). *Music and the Occult: French Musical Philosophies, 1750–1950.* Eastman Studies in Music. Rochester, New York: University of Rochester Press.

Henderson, A. (1955). "Henderson Recalls Shaw." *Durham Morning Herald.* August 21.

Hu, W., and M. White (2004). "The Cosmic Symphony." *Scientific American* 282 (February): 52.

Lauterborn, W., et al. (1999). *Advances in Chemical Physics,* volume 110. Ed. I. Prigogine and S. A. Rice. Chichester: Wiley.

Mcguire, J. E., and P. M. Rattansi (1966). "Newton and the 'Pipes of Pan.'" *Notes and Records of the Royal Society* 21: 108.

Newton, I. (1952 [1730]). *Opticks: Or a Treatise of the Reflections, Refractions, Inflections & Colours of Light.* Based on the 4th Newton's ed. New York: Dover.

Ravdonikas, F. V. (2002). *Musical Syntax.* St. Petersburg: SPB Publishers.

Suslick, K. S. (1994). "The Chemistry of Ultrasound." *The Yearbook of Science and the Future 1994.* Chicago: Encyclopedia Britannica.

Suslick, K. S., et al. (1999). "Acoustic Cavitation and Its Chemical Consequences." *Philosophical Translations of the Royal Society of London A* 357, no. 1751 (February): 17.

Wolfram, S. (2002). *A New Kind of Science.* Champaign, Ill.: Wolfram Media.

Naeem Mohaiemen

(Amin) Pray Allah keep my soul and heart clean
(Amin) Pray the same thing again for all my team
—Mos Def, "Love" (*Black on Both Sides*, 1999)

Immigrants should understand from Black people what Islam means in America, because African-Americans have been doing it for 400 years.
—Sohail Daulatzai

Journalist Harry Allen once called Islam "hip-hop's unofficial religion." This theme is echoed by Adisa Banjoko, unofficial ambassador of Muslim hip-hop, who says, "Muslim influence was at the ground floor of hip hop. Hip hop came from the streets, from the toughest neighborhoods, and that's always where the Muslims were."[1] Hip-hop's Muslim connection came initially via the 5 Percenter sect, and later expanded to embrace Nation of Islam (NOI), Sufi, and Sunni Islam. Since the 1980s, there have also been shifts where 5 Percenters have moved to NOI or Sunni beliefs. The same artists' back catalog may reflect both his 5 Percenter beliefs and his later NOI faith. Islamic iconography, philosophy, and phrases are in fact so widespread in hip-hop, they show up regularly even in the works of non-Muslim rappers.

In spite of this pioneering and continuing role, Islam as a cultural force in hip-hop is severely underdocumented. In the most recent oversight, Jeff Chang's exhaustive hip-hop history *Can't Stop, Won't Stop* (Picador, 2005) pays only fleeting attention to the Muslim connection. Elsewhere in mainstream media, the Muslim connection is never spoken aloud, even in the middle of otherwise thorough analysis and journalism. Ted Swedenburg calls this "almost willful avoidance." In this, there are parallels to the larger invisibility of black Muslims, who have been shut out of many conversations around the role of Islam in America.

This deliberate invisibility mirrors America's continuing unease with Islam. Black Muslims and hip-hop are frozen out of the larger debate over Islam because they would problematize the entire conversation. If we acknowledge that the largest segment of American Muslims is in fact black, it makes it more difficult to stereotype Muslims as "immigrants" or "outsiders." Furthermore, if we look at Muslim anger and see within it a portion that is African-American, we are forced to confront an indictment of American society. This is a viewpoint that the music press has assiduously avoided. Finally, the image of Islam as an obscurantist force conflicts with its positive influence within hip-hop. Hip-hop scholars have not been able to absorb or observe the Muslim role in creating unique rhyme flows and politically conscious hip-hop. Safer, perhaps, to avoid the topic.

Born Muslim, Born Black?[2]

A dominant discourse links American Islam to Arabs and South Asians, considered new arrivals to America's shore. But statistics tell a contradictory story. According to research presented by the American Muslim Council (AMC), in 1992, between 5 to 8 million Americans followed some variation of the Islamic faith.[3] AMC calculated the largest bloc of Muslims to be African Americans at 42 percent. If African immigrants are included, the number goes up to 46 percent. South Asians are the next highest at 24 percent. Only 12 percent of American Muslims are of Arab descent (the majority of Arab Americans are Christian). Looking at subsections within the black population, we find the proportions even higher: 30 percent of African Americans in the prison system are Muslim, many of whom convert after incarceration—following the trajectory of Malcolm X and Imam Jamil Al-Amin (formerly H. Rap Brown).

There are many reasons why Islam has been popular among African Americans from the very beginning. Scholars point to the roots of Islam within the original slave populations. Sylviane Diouf calculated that "up to 40 percent" of the Atlantic slave trade was Muslim.[4] Although much of the original belief systems was wiped out in the period leading up to the Civil War, residues have transmitted themselves through the black experience and the popular imagination. An example of this emerges in Michael Muhammad Knight's punk Muslim novel *The Taqwacores* (Autonomedia, 2005), when one character says, "There's an old jail in the Carolinas where they used to bring slaves right off the ships ... It's still there, it's like a tourist spot now. But anyway, there's ayats from the Quran on the wall, like two hundred years old, still right there." All of this helped to create a perception within the black community that Islam was not an alien religion. Rather it was seen as something that was "lost–found." James Baldwin diagnosed this accurately in *The Fire Next Time*:

God had come a long way from the desert—but then so had Allah, though in a very different direction. God, going north, and rising on the wings of power, had become white, and Allah, out of power, had become—for all practical purposes anyway—black.[5]

When Muslim preachers first started making inroads into the black community, they were helped by a prevailing sentiment of Afro-Asian solidarity and internationalism. Some of the earliest Muslim preachers to arrive in America in the 1900s were missionaries sent by the Ahmadiya Muslim sect, itself facing persecution in British India. The pioneering missionaries were Mufti Muhammad Sadiq, who came from the region that became Pakistan, and Mutiur Rahman Bengalee, who came from the region that later became Bangladesh. Barred from preaching in white areas and churches, they focused their energies on the black ghettos. Hardened by their own experiences of American racism (Sadiq was initially detained for months by immigration officers fearful he would "preach polygamy"), their message shifted to one of multiracial solidarity. As Sohail Daulatzai has charted in his forthcoming *Darker Than Blue*,[6] the Muslim missionaries found their work easier because of major forces in black radicalism that were pushing for Afro-Asian and pan-Islamic solidarity.

One of the early calls for alliances between pan-Africanism and globalized Islam came from West-Indian born Edward Blyden, in his *Christianity, Islam, and the Negro Race* (Whittingham, 1887). This was echoed by Sudanese-Egyptian scholar Duse Muhammad Ali, who launched *The African Times and Orient Review* and called for solidarity among global populations of color. Duse later mentored Marcus Garvey, whose mission as founder of the Universal Negro Improvement Association "to reclaim the fallen of the race" was adopted by many black Islamic movements. Besides influencing

Garvey, Duse also went on to found Detroit's Universal Islamic Society. This inspired the formation of two separate religious movements, both precursors to the Nation of Islam (NOI)—Noble Drew Ali's Moorish Science Temple and Fard Muhammad's Temple of Islam.

Up until the 1950s, the Ahmadiya message of multiracial solidarity was growing. According to Richard Brent Turner, until the arrival of Nation of Islam, "the Ahmadiya was arguably the most influential community in African-American Islam."[7] But with the rise of Fard Muhammad's NOI, buoyed by the charisma of Elijah Muhammad and Malcolm X, a message of black nationalism eclipsed that of Ahmadiya Islam. Sohail Daulatzai also points to the Afro-Asian solidarity politics surrounding the Bandung era as a key factor behind NOI's success. In a time when Malcolm challenged American imperialism, the black church was fundamentally committed to assimilating within the American nation: "As the struggles around racism and the politics of race began to escalate during this period, Islam came to be seen as an alternative form of radical Black consciousness that was quite distinct from the integrationist goals of African-American Christianity."[8]

The next stages in the rise of American Islam are well documented—the meteoric rise of Malcolm X, Bandung-influenced messages of global revolution, Malcolm's split with NOI, his post-Hajj rejection of racial separatism and embracing of Sunni Islam, Elijah's son Warith Muhammad's renouncing of race theology, NOI's conversion to Sunni Islam, and finally Minister Farrakhan's project to rebuild a splinter group in NOI's old image. In more recent times, after a sizable portion of the NOI converts shifted to Sunni Islam (or "al-Islam" as it is often called), there has been a convergence with the growing immigrant population from South Asia and the Arab world. In the 1980s and '90s, multiracial mosque gatherings became more common, as black Muslims prayed and communed with immigrant Muslims. What was missing, and continues to be missing today, is a multi-ethnic political leadership for American Muslims.

The manner in which Islam spread and regenerated in black America prefigures the style in which Islam influenced hip-hop—myriad strands and theories entered the conversation separately and converged, battled, and complemented each other. As Muslim sects overlapped, new offshoots were born. Shape-shifting is a key aspect of the theological spread, as is the case with Muslim influence on hip-hop. Adisa Banjoko explains it by saying, "Look, when people ask how many people are in NOI, they hear: those who tell don't know, and those who know don't tell. But this obscures the fact that NOI always has high turnover. It's often the passing-through point for people on their way to Sunni Islam. And the same is true of the rappers. You want to know if they are 5 Percenters, NOI or Sunni—well, many of them have very fluid positions."[9]

It is these fluid positions that characterize the Muslim influence on hip-hop.

How Islam Birthed Hip-Hop

Although the usual answer to "who invented rap" is the trio of DJ Kool Herc, Afrika Bambaataa, and Grandmaster Flash, the roots extend further back to black Muslim artists experimenting with rhyme structure and spoken word delivery in the 1960s. One of the earliest influences was the group the Last Poets, whose founding members included Abiodun Oyewole, Umar Bin Hassan, Jalal Nurridin, and Suliman El Hadi. The Poets were black radicals, detonating their lyrics on an America already on fire:

When the revolution comes
some of us will catch it on TV
with chicken hanging from our mouths
you'll know it's revolution
because there won't be no commercials
when the revolution comes

In their most famous spoken-word piece "Niggers are scared of revolution," they pioneered the staccato speeded-up delivery that came to characterize rap rhythms. Simultaneously, this work began the reappropriation of the "N" word, a process now done to death by modern hip-hop:

Niggers are scared of revolution but niggers shouldn't be scared of revolution because revolution is nothing but change, and all niggers do is change. Niggers come in from work and change into pimping clothes to hit the street and make some quick change. Niggers change their hair from black to red to blond and hope like hell their looks will change.

The Last Poets were the original activist–artists, combining their music and poetry with direct action—including alliances with the SNCC (Student Non-violent Coordinating Committee), the SDS (Students for a Democratic Society), and the Black Panthers. Their records were released during a period of violent confrontation, including the murder of two black students and the wounding of twelve others by police at Jackson State University, a daisy-chain of ghetto rebellions in 1970, and the FBI's national campaign to arrest Angela Davis. With their lyrics feeding into the fervor of the times, the Poets were heavily monitored by the FBI and police, and were arrested for trying to rob the Ku Klux Klan. Decades later, these same trends were repeated as the NYPD began surveillance of hip-hop groups, especially those with outspoken politics.

Talking about the explosive effect of the Poets' early work, Darius James called it "a bomb on black Amerikkka's turntables. Muthafuckas ran f'cover. Nobody was ready. Had 'em scared o' revolution. Scared o' the whyte man's god complex. Scared o' subways. Scared o' each other. Scared o' themselves. And scared o' that totem of onanistic worship—the eagle-clawed Amerikkkan greenback! The rhetoric made you mad. The drums made you pop your fingers."[10] Amiri Baraka in turn identified them as rap's root source: "The Last Poets are the prototype Rappers." Baraka himself had converted to NOI, and influenced by that ideology and fever-pitch race tensions, wrote the blueprint gangsta lyric:

All the stores will open if you say the magic
words. The magic words are: Up against
the wall motherfucker this is a stick up.
(Amiri Baraka, "Black People")

Similarly influential, though in a different vein, was the newly converted Muhammad Ali. By dropping his "slave name" of Cassius Clay for Muhammad Ali ("I don't have to be what you want me to be; I'm free to be what I want"), and replacing his cry of "I am the Greatest" to "Allah is the Greatest," Ali became the most visible Muslim in America and a hero of the Afro-Asian and Islamic world. He was in the mold of the defiant black men—Nat Turner, Denmark Vesey, Gabriel Prosser, Jack Johnson, and Paul Robeson. The difference was that his Muslim faith was a key aspect of his righteous rage and political defiance. Ali's refusal to fight in Vietnam, coupled with the incendiary comment "No Viet cong never called me a nigger," enshrined his rebellion in the black psyche. Ali's rebellious spirit was also in his poetry, which led George Plimpton to conclude that "his ability to compose rhymes on the run could very well qualify him as the first rapper."[11] Recognizing Ali's singular contribution to both Islam and the black male image, Ali's artistic descendants later sang,

The man's got a God complex
But take the text and change the picture
Watch Muhammad play the messenger like Holy Muslim scriptures
Take orders from only God
Only war when it's Jihad

(Tribe Called Quest, Fugees, et al., "Rumble in the Jungle," *When We Were Kings*)

As the 1960s gave way to the 1970s, the heady energy created by the Last Poets, Baraka, and others slowly dissipated. The connection between music and Islam then reemerged through the influence of the 5 Percenter Muslim sect. Although the 5 Percenters were never a significant portion of American Islam, their influence has been felt through their singular impact on music. The 5 Percent Nation (or the Nation of Gods and Earths) is a Nation of Islam breakaway sect founded in 1964 by Clarence 13X. In his refashioned version of Islam, Clarence taught that the black man was "Allah." The focus of the 5 Percenters' belief system includes numerology, cryptic scientific theory, and a more extreme race theory. In this theology, 85 percent of the masses are ignorant, 10 percent are "bloodsuckers of the poor," and only 5 percent know the truth. This numeric structure has been used in many rap songs, including those of Wu-Tang Clan, who use whole aspects of 5 Percenter theology:

And then you got the 5 percent
Who are the poor righteous teachers
who do not believe in the teachings of the ten percent
Who is all wise and know who the true and living god is
And teach that the true and living god IS
supreme being black man from Asia
Otherwise known as civilized people
Also Muslims, and Muslims sons

(Wu-Tang Clan, "Wu-Revolution," *Forever*, 1999)

The practices of 5 Percenters included a big focus on rhetorical skills. Clarence 13X was also called "Pudding" because of his smooth oratory. Yusuf Nureddine has highlighted the "eloquent and spell-binding usage of African American inner-city slang. Using the potency and vitality of the black dialect they open up new avenues of logic and thinking, or original ways of perceiving the world."[12] When music was added to this fast wordplay and verbal skills, an explosive cocktail came out the other end. One of the first projects that connected the two was Afrika Bambaata's Zulu Nation, a collective of DJs, graffiti artists, and breakdancers, which was founded in 1974 in New York.

Zulu Nation focused on urban survival through cultural empowerment—making up the core of this new vision were the 7 Infinity Lessons, which combined the dietary restrictions held up by Elijah Mohammed with the racial interpretations of Dr. Malachi York (Imam Isa) of biblical theology and the 5 Percenter "question and answer" and "keyword glossary" format.[13]

Zulu Nation's links to Islam were followed by pioneering rapper and devoted 5 Percenter Rakim. In Rakim's raps, we see the focus on breaking words down into components, a key 5 Percenter practice:

Living on shaky grounds too close to the edge
Let's see if I know the ledge.
(Eric B & Rakim, "Juice (Know the Ledge)," *Don't Sweat the Technique*, 1992)

Elsewhere he broke with the Black Man as Allah concept and praised a deity directly, riding a fluid relation with Islam:

I'm the intelligent wise on the mic I will rise
Right in front of your eyes cuz I am a surprise
So I'ma let my knowledge be born to a perfection
All praise due to Allah and that's a blessing
(Eric B & Rakim, "Move the Crowd," *Paid in Full*, 1987)

As socially conscious rap began to come out in the 1980s, NOI's politics also spread into songs. In 1983, Keith Leblanc released "No Sell-Out," dubbing a Malcolm X speech into the mix. This was the beginning of political rap's obsession with Malcolm, sampling him hundreds of times throughout the 1980s and '90s. Setting the gold standard for politically conscious rap was the group Public Enemy. In this, band member Professor Griff's strong NOI beliefs played a key role. When Public Enemy appeared in battle fatigues, a cocktail of Fruit of Islam and Black Panther, White America was terrified by the specter of revived race riots. The media promptly dubbed PE the "most dangerous band alive," which they scornfully attacked in lyrics:

The follower of Farrakhan
Don't tell me that you understand
Until you hear the man
The book of the new school rap game
Writers treat me like Coltrane,[14] insane
(Public Enemy, "Don't Believe the Hype," *It Takes a Nation of Millions to Hold Us Back*, 1988)

Public Enemy's path was followed by KRS-One, who preached politics and black self-empowerment through Boogie Down Productions. Unlike later 5 Percenters like Wu-Tang, KRS-One stayed clear of numeric theory in favor of more conscious politics:

But last but not least racial prejudice
Is the black man speakin' out of ignorance
Whitey this and Ching-Chow that
Is not how the intelligent man acts
You can't blame the whole white race
For slavery, cos this ain't the case

(Boogie Down Productions, "The Racist," *Edutainment*, 1990)

Kevin Powell has described the 1987–1992 era as the "golden age of hip hop."[15] In this period of restless activity, Sunni Muslims also began to enter the scene. Most notable was Tribe Called Quest (with Sunni followers Q-Tip and Ali Shaheed Muhammad) preaching Afrocentric awareness, collective love, and peace. On the other side of peace was the raw defiance of Paris. His work reflected a mixture of Sunni Islam and Panther ideology, as in his famous song:

Revolution ain't never been simple
Following the path from Allah for know just
Build your brain and we'll soon make progress
Paid your dues, don't snooze or lose
That came with the masterplan that got you
So know who's opposed to the dominant dark skin
Food for thought as a law for the brother man

(Paris, "The Devil Made Me Do It," *The Devil Made Me Do It*, 1990)

While the Afrocentric messages of Tribe were celebrated, the aggressive music of Paris scared tastemakers. *The Devil Made Me Do It* carried the iconic photo of a Black boy in a chokehold by riot police. Record stores refused to carry the album, citing its cover art. Paris' 1992 album, *Sleeping with the Enemy*, carried a photo of him holding a machine gun, hiding behind a tree on the White House lawn. Shareholder pressure over the song "Bush Killa" forced Time Warner subsidiary Tommy Boy ultimately to drop the record. After a five-year hiatus, his follow-up album *Sonic Jihad* (with the infamous image of a plane flying into the White House) was released on his own label. Reflecting ruefully on the commercial price of radical politics, Paris' website notes, "his uncompromising stance on political issues and biting social commentary have both aided and hindered his quest to bring solid music and messages to the masses" (http://www.guerrillafunk.com/paris/bio/).

While Paris is a casualty in the battle over lyrics, many other Muslim artists have risen to become giants of the scene. These include 5 Percenter–influenced Busta Rhymes, Wu-Tang Clan, Big Daddy Kane, Brand Nubian, Nas, Gang Starr, Mobb Deep, Poor Righteous Teachers, Queen Latifah and Ladybug Mecca (Digable Planets); Sunni artists Jurassic 5, Mos Def, Roots (who also have 5 Percenters as members), Kool Moe Dee, and Everlast; NOI-influenced MC Ren, Da Lench Mob, Ice Cube, Kam, and K-Solo; and other artists with more fluid affiliations, such as Eve, Common, Brother Ali, Intelligent Hoodlum, Afrika Islam, Daddy O (Stetsasonic), and Jeru the Damaja. Coming up fast are the next generation of Muslim rappers, who are tipped toward the Sunni scale and include some South Asian and Arab rappers.

The dominance of Muslims in hip-hop came about because of the linkages between 5 Percenters, NOI followers, and music. Islam's success in this area was also aided by the black church's antagonistic relationship with hip-hop. Describing the clergy's ham-handed approach to the music, Banjoko told me, "Reverend Calvin Butts used to ride over CDs with a steamroller. Whereas the Nation, and Minister Farrakhan especially, was having dinner with Ice Cube, Ice T, Sister Souljah, and Chuck D. He was engaging these effective black minds that were connected to young minds. But the Christians really hurt themselves by trying to demonize hip hop. Because they were attacking the most impoverished, and most socially, politically and economically denied people. So the youth heart hardened against the churches."[16]

The Nation of Islam under Minister Farrakhan took a very different approach, embracing the power of music. Farrakhan was a totem for many first- and second-generation rappers. Public missteps have removed him from national screens, but his presence is still strong in the hip-hop nation. During a major "beef" between 50 Cent and Jah Rule, it was Farrakhan who sat with them on live radio to bring a truce. Talking about this approach, Manning Marable said, "The Nation of Islam has understood for decades that black culture is directly related to black politics. To transform an oppressed community's political behavior, one must first begin with the reconstruction of both cultural and civic imagination.... The reluctance of the black bourgeoisie to come to terms with the music its own children listen to compromises its ability to advance a meaningful political agenda reflecting what the masses of our people see and feel in their daily lives."[17]

Sounding a note of the true believer, Banjoko added, "What would Jesus Do? Would Jesus try to ban Ice Cube? I don't think so. I know Prophet Muhammed would embrace Ice Cube and help him be a better man. That's the prophetic tradition!"[18]

Deep in the Flow

The initial link between Islam and hip-hop came via 5 Percent. This came through its focus on wordplay, numerology, and race theory. This trajectory was paralleled by the Nation of Islam, which embraced rap as a preaching tool at a time when the black Christian churches rejected it. Conscious rappers also gravitated toward NOI because its confrontational politics fit with their fierce rhymes. Beyond these initial connections, there were other reasons why Islamic thought influenced rappers. H. Samy Alim has researched the structural and symbolic similarities between hip-hop rhymes and Qur'anic text.[19] Through interviews with Muslim rappers, he has uncovered a key parallel. The Qur'an was revealed to the Prophet Mohammed through an oral tradition, using melodic prose. In this, there are parallels to hip-hop's birth as a means of empowering inner-city griots to transmit stories of urban blight and chaos via rhyme and flow. In conversation with Alim, Mos Def carries the parallel into direct analysis of the Qur'an: "The reason people are able to be *hafiz* is because the entire Qur'an rhymes. *Bismillah Al-Rahman Al-Rahim. Al-hamdulillahi Rabb Al-Alameen* ... I mean it's any *surah* that I could name. *Qul huwa Allahu ahad, Allahu samad. Lam yalid wa lam yulad wa lam yakun lahu kufwan ahad* ... Like there's a rhyme scheme in all of it. And then you start to have a deeper relationship with it on recitation ... Hip hop has the ability to do that—on a poetic level."[20]

Taking the analogy further, Common anoints hip-hop as the new vehicle for reaching people with Allah's message. Although orthodox preachers would dismiss this as *shirk* (blasphemy), Minister Farrakhan's embrace of hip-hop is clearly inspired by sentiments such as

The perseverance of a rebel I drop heavier levels
It's unseen or heard, a king with words
Can't knock the hustle, but I've seen street dreams deferred
Dark spots in my mind where the scene occurred
Some say I'm too deep, I'm in too deep to sleep
Through me, Muhammed will forever speak

(Common, "The 6th Sense," *Like Water for Chocolate*, 2000)

Speaking of the use of metaphor in hip-hop, Bay area rapper JT the Bigga Figga draws an analogy between the creation of black street argot and the creative use of language in the Qur'an to reach believers. Describing the inventive wordplay of fellow rapper E-40, JT says, "It's almost like with Allah how he'll describe his prophets as moonlight. He'll describe his word that he speaks in a metaphoric phrasing. Where he'll say the clouds and when they swell up heavy and the water goes back to the earth, distilling back to earth. The water's heavier than gravity so it distills back to the earth on dry land, producing vegetation and herbs comin up out the ground, you feel me? ... And that's kinda like what E-40 do when he take something and take a word and apply it."[21]

Although many rappers focus on street life, Muslims have also used their knowledge of Qur'anic scriptures to write less worldly musings:

From a lifeless ball of clay, empty as a hollow reed
Until Allah breathed life into my physical frame
From a state of nothingness instead of existing I became
By God, the true and living given insight
Certain colors manifesting physical light
But still earthbound, held down by the physical elements
Spiritual development gives me a higher intelligence
Beyond these concrete streets and the green pastures

(Akbar, "Those Who Say," *Big Bang Boogie,* 2001)

Animated by the convert's sense of righteousness, Everlast also raps against interreligious strife:

This is for the ones who war over whose God is the right one
Can it be the Asian one, the black one or the white one?
The answer to the question really isn't controversial
There is only one God and his love is universal
If you sin and crave redemption, all you need to do is ask him
Then you will be fully prepared for a life that's everlasting
So take heed to the words I say, grab a good book and get hip to
The teachings of the holy Q'uran or the Bible's holy scripture

(Everlast, "What Is This?," *Forever Everlasting,* 1990)

Of course, not all strands of Islam accept parallels between hip-hop and Qur'anic recitations. To more orthodox sects, the Qur'an, the Surah, and the Azaan are all meant to be chanted (*tilawa*) which can be argued to be different from singing (*ghanniya*). Not surprisingly, these rigid structures break down across generational lines, with younger people embracing hip-hop as a boost to their understanding of Islam. Eman Tai, member of the Calligraphy of Thought spoken-word collective, connects hip-hop to Islam's history: "It's part of our history and culture in Islam. The traditional books of law and philosophy in Islam were written in poetry, and students memorize them with drums, basically singing out the poetry. And if you 'beat' that up, it sounds just like rapping."[22]

Beyond a focus on scripture and philosophy, Muslim beliefs guide rappers in very specific ways toward community renewal and progressive politics. NOI focuses on self-sufficiency of the community and this has come to influence the lyrics of rap's Muslim generation. When NOI first moves into a blighted area, they get people to dress well, stop drinking, and clean up crack houses. Then come related programs, such as the push to buy black and boycott racist merchants. All of these programs influenced rap lyrics that sought to uplift the race. But here the contradictions of the music also come bubbling to the surface. When Wu-Tang began their *Forever* double album, the lyrics embraced their Muslim listeners:

These things just took over me
Just took over my whole body
So I can't even see no more
I'm calling my black woman a bitch
I'm calling my peoples all kinds of thing that they not
I'm lost brother, can you help me
Can you help me brother, please

(Wu-Tang Clan, "Wu-Revolution," *Forever*, 1999)

But within the space of one song, the listeners face the contradiction of a "smoking, drinking, fornicating" life:

Bitch ass niggaz counterfeit the funk
I smoke the bead and the skunk, tree top of the trunk
Moonshine drunken monk, Ya HEAD, get shrunk
The touch of skunk, I be fuckin bitches by the chunk

(Wu-Tang Clan, "Reunited," *Forever*, 1999)

The typical explanation given for this apparent contradiction is that the Wu-Tang Clan is a constellation of artists, and some members (like the late Ol' Dirty Bastard who sang the second set of lyrics) were either not Muslim, or "struggling to find the path." Typically when talking about "misguided"

Muslim rappers, the critics focus on 5 Percenter belief as a source for some of these mistakes. This creates new intrasect tensions between Muslim rappers, which we will explore next.

As Muslim as They Want to Be

From the very beginning, the 5 Percenter sect was particularly skilled at creating iconography that appealed to inner-city youth. The school established in Harlem in 1967 was the "Allah School in Mecca," and the five points of the constellation were "Mecca" (Harlem), "Medina" (Brooklyn), "the Desert" (Queens), "Pelan" (Bronx), and "New Jerusalem" (New Jersey). Tracts of 5 Percent concepts were initially circulated as Xeroxed pamphlet "lessons" that passed from hand to hand. But as early hip-hop artists started incorporating 5 Percenter theology into freestyle rhymes, pamphlets were superseded by the more powerful oral tradition. The new urban griots, represented by rappers, beatboxers, and DJs, became preachers, spreading the theology at the speed of music. Key portions of their theories spread through rap lyrics, including black man as Allah ("Praises are due to Allah, that's me"—Poor Righteous Teachers), the Chosen 5 Percent ("Why? That's most asked by 85"—Ladybug Mecca/Digable Planets), supreme mathematics and the supreme alphabet ("Now I'm rolling with the seven[23] and the crescent"—Digable Planets), racial separatism ("No blue eyes and blonde hair is over here"—Poor Righteous Teachers), and the breaking of words into components ("U-n-i-verse—you and I verse"—Roots). In addition, 5 Percenters were the innovators behind early hip-hop slang, including "'sup, G?" (originally "G" meant God, not gangsta), "Word is bond," "Break it down," "Peace," "droppin' science," and "represent."

Five Percent is in many ways a "gateway" theology, which many African Americans passed through to come in contact with other sects of Islam. In this process, the pioneering 5 Percent rappers helped bring large masses to Islam. Yet, because of the unorthodox nature of 5 Percenter beliefs, Sunni Muslims still refuse to grant them credit or recognition. In turn, 5 Percenters call Sunni Muslims "Soon to be Muslim," and refer to the orthodox Muslim teaching "that the almighty true and living god is a spook in the sky" (Wu-Tang Clan). Some of these tensions were expressed by Banjoko, himself a Sunni, in early interviews given in 2001:

No other Islamic sect in the world accepts drinking alcohol. Yet Brand Nubian are known to smoke weed by the pound and drink like fish. Poor Righteous Teachers seem to be the only group from the 5 Percent that shuns drugs, alcohol and foul lifestyles. All the talk about spaceships doesn't help either. The 5 Percent Nation really hurt al-Islam because of their inability to hold on to any theological concept consistently—not to mention their violence and misogyny, which hurts all true believers.[24]

All religions have their strictures against schisms and breakaway factions, and Islam is no different in this matter. The split between Sunni and Shiite has created schisms that affect world politics. Smaller sects such as the Ismailis, Druze, Sufis, Ahle-Hadis, and Ahmadiyas have been branded as heretics. The Prophet Mohammed is said[25] to have warned that there would be 72 sects of Islam after his death and that only one would be the true Islam. Although Islam has no centralized clergy, the battle to create a centralized theological leadership has been waged for centuries. In the current era, some of the main contenders for Islam's leadership are the Saudi Wahhabis, Iranian theocrats, Turkish modernizers, Western philosophers such as Tariq Ramadan, and Asian leaders such as Mahathir Mohammed. Leadership struggles have manifested themselves in voting blocs, as in the recent struggle over the OIC (Organization of Islamic Countries). The volatile Saudi-Iranian rivalry has even descended to violent clashes during Hajj. Most important, as Muslim blocs struggle to assert dominance, minority sects within Islam have become a political target. By waging a battle of fatwas and violence against smaller Muslim sects, the more radical Islamist groups have sought to establish their leadership in the *ummah*.

One of the most prominent targets of these anti-heresy campaigns have been the Ahmadiyas. It was precisely because of the hostile environment in their native Pakistan (then British India) that the Ahmadiyas focused heavily on preaching to the outside world. In this journey, the early Ahmadiya preachers arrived in America and became the first major source for the reinsertion of Islam into black communities. While Ahmadiyas preached to African Americans, back home they were increasingly targets of persecution. A key aspect of the anti-Ahmadiya campaigns was the allegation that they called their leader Mirza Ghulam Ahmed a prophet (in this, there are parallels to the claims of prophethood made by the antecedents of Nation of Islam). Fueled by Saudi funds, the anti-Ahmadiya movement succeeded in banning the Ahmadiyas in Pakistan and banning their books in Bangladesh.[26]

As with Islam globally, so in America. Although there are many pressing problems for American Muslims, a lot of energy has recently been focused on the 5 Percenters in hip-hop. In a 2001 essay, Banjoko accused 5 Percenters of bringing ignorant elements to Islam: "Unless we rid Hip Hop of the *jahiliyyah* elements, we can only expect more of your sharp minded but misguided youth to perish over territorialism, materialism and pursuit of the sensual path."[27] In an interview, 5 Percenter Ibn Dajjal responded to Banjoko: "No amount of fatwas or censorship will ever silence the sounds of the NOI and 5 Percent nations. The group will continue to rise in fame with customers coming from all walks of life: black, white and Bedouin."[28]

Sohail Daulatzai points to another reason for hostility toward 5 Percenters, which is the elitism and sense of ownership some immigrant Muslims feel toward Islam. "They feel that African Americans should be understanding Islam from the immigrant. And that superiority complex does exist because there's a lack of understanding of race. I think the opposite should happen. Immigrants should understand from black people what Islam means in America, because African Americans have been doing it for 400 years." Connecting this elitism with the debate over 5 Percenter influence on hip-hop, Daulatzai says, "It's not just that they are being dismissed based on doctrinal difference. African Americans have a different understanding of Islam. They hybridize it, they mix it with a lot of ideas based on the black experience. Immigrant Muslims don't always see all those differences, whether in the mosque or in hip-hop."[29]

As this debate unfolds within hip-hop, Daulatzai's more nuanced understanding of race, class, and music is reflected among other American Muslims as well. There are now hip-hop fans willing to engage in *ijtihad* (debate) about 5 Percenters. Even Banjoko seems to have softened his stance toward 5 Percenters in recent years. He told me recently, "I still disagree with their beliefs. These guys piecemeal their theology to the nth degree. You'll have these pseudo Wu-Tang affiliates who talk absolute berserk madness. But in spite of theological flaws, they have still been a positive force and I can't deny that. One benefit of the 5 Percenters is that through them, inner-city kids are at least becoming familiar with Islamic terms."[30]

Generation M

One of the most overused text tropes is the phrase "after 9/11." Yet at the risk of oversimplifying, we can at least say that the new realities have brought a

change to Muslim hip-hop. For Muslim youth, there were two new forces in
their lives. First, there is the crackdown on Muslim civil liberties, expressed
through the Patriot Act, INS deportations, "special registrations," "extraordinary renditions," no-fly lists, and torture memos. Second, there are the
continuing U.S. wars of occupation in Afghanistan and Iraq. All this has inspired the rise of new Muslim-identified hip-hop bands. Many of these
are now Sunni affiliated and some are led by children of Muslim immigrants.
Hip-hop remains the singular voice of black America, but that core is now
made larger by Arab, Asian, African, French, and British Muslims. The
center for these new networks is the Internet, especially through websites
such as MuslimHipHop.com and Muslimac.com (Muslim Artists Central).
Among the many they host, the up-and-coming names include Capital D,
Sons of Hagar, After Hijrah 11:59, Arab Legion, Divine Styler, Halal Styles,
Iron Crescent, Jamil Mustafa, Kenny Muhammad, Mujahideen Team, Native
Deen, the Hammer Bros., the Iron Triangle, and Young Messengerrzz.

Taking on a more assertive Muslim identity, many of these new artists identify as "Generation M." Unlike the 5 Percenters' fluid definitions, they adhere
to a more traditional Islamic view and multiracial identity. In their lyrics,
many of the concerns are about being Muslim in the West and the current
civil liberties environment. Sons of Hagar, one of the rising stars, asserts a stri-
dent Arab identity:

My own country is trying to get rid of me
Got no shoulder to lean on and I ain't crying neither
It's the Arab hunting season
And I ain't leavin'

(Sons of Hagar, "INSurrection," *A Change*, 2004)

Just as Islamophobia is now a global trend, the critiques of that force come
from all corners of the world. Sons of Hagar are joined by Paris, who raps:

See me blame it on a foreigner and non-white men
Celebrate my gestapo with a positive spin
Then manipulate the media—it's U.S. first
Get the stupid-ass public to agree with my words

(Paris, "Evil," *Sonic Jihad*, 2003)

Paris is echoed by the Asian Dub Foundations' British-Bangladeshi vocalist,
who links blowback to U.S.–Taliban alliances:

Babylon is really burning this time
coming home to roost on a Soviet landmine
Climbing out the subway burning eyes spinning head
Walking through the station breaking into a cold sweat
Is the ticking time bomb in my head or your bag
Have you been snorting white lines with President Gas
Crawling from the wreckage of my tumblin' tower block
Someone else had to finish the job
It was the enemy of the enemy
The enemy of the enemy
He's a friend
Til he's the enemy again

(Asian Dub Foundation, "Enemy of the Enemy," *Enemy of the Enemy*, 2003)

In the 1990s, Public Enemy surveyed a landscape of police brutality, a crack epidemic, and hostile Reaganomics, and unleashed their rage on the mic. Public Enemy's grand project to channel "Black CNN" into a united political movement foundered on Professor Griff's anti-Semitism. Ten years later, "Driving While Black" has been switched for "Flying While Brown" and the fight back is also in rhymes. The media played a crucial role in PE's downfall, paving the way for the apolitical bling stylings of gangsta rap and an eternal cycle of Hot 97–generated "beefs." With Generation M, some will be equally ready to seize on any missteps and derail the political mission. Guarding against the media glare, while building a deep-rooted Muslim hip-hop movement, where the black experience is core, is the next project for activist–academics like Daulatzai and Banjoko.

Last/Lost Words

In the ongoing debates over Islam, the same South Asian and Arab faces are always brought out. It is always Fareed Zakaria, Fouad Ajami, Imam Feisal, et al. African American Muslims remain the invisible minority in the public eye. Part of this can be attributed to the continuing phobia against Nation of Islam.[31] But the sidelining of black Muslims is also part of the larger project to render Muslims as permanent "outsiders." African Americans complicate the narrative because they are not immigrants. Nor do they have an origin country where they can be deported in times of crisis.

Embedded within the African-American experience is a direct critique of the American nation-state. When we talk about the black experience, we confront the uses of racism and power. In analyzing this, we can start to make sense of the current world crisis by discovering the parallels and overlaps between the black and Muslim experiences. The collapse of the black working class can be traced at least partially to the failure to resolve racism and poverty. Similarly, a global pandemic of radical Islam is a blowback from a foreign policy that embraced dictators and destroyed indigenous political movements. In our recent past, theories of "black rage," "bell curves," and images of hypersexual black males have been deployed to explain all crises and absolve the power structure. Similarly, visions of fanatic hordes and neo-Orientalist fantasies of rescuing veiled women propel anti-immigrant policies and continuous oil wars.

When a black Muslim musician critiques foreign policy or xenophobia, it is still an "angry Muslim voice," but not one that can be easily stereotyped. Hip-hop and the visibility of Muslim artists offers a way to turn racist paradigms on their head. When rappers rhyme over the *azaan* or Qur'anic *ayaats*, mainstream society's perceptions of an "alien" religion are flipped. Enhanced visibility through music can create a dynamic that moves America from hyper-Islamophobia to a dialogue among equals.[32]

Appendix: Who's Who in Muslim Hip-Hop

A very incomplete, always evolving, list of artists who profess Muslim faith (5 Percenter, Nation of Islam, Sunni, Shi'a, Sufi, etc.) or have been influenced by Muslim beliefs:

Afrika Bambaataa
Afrika Islam
After Hijrah
Akbar
Ali Shaheed Muhammad, formerly of A Tribe Called Quest
An Nasr
Arab Legion
Azeem
Big Daddy Kane
Brand Nubian
The Brothahood
Brother Ali

Busta Rhymes
Capital D
Common
Daddy O (Stetsasonic)
DAM
Divine Styler
11:59
Encore
Erykah Badu
Eve
Everlast
Frontline
Generation M
Guru (Gang Starr)
Halal Styles
The Hammer Bros.
Ice Cube
Intelligent Hoodlum
Iron Crescent
The Iron Triangle
Jeru the Damaja
Jurassic 5
Kam
Kenny Muhammad
Kool Moe Dee
KRS-One
K-Solo
Ladybug Mecca (Digable Planets)
Lakim Shabazz
The Last Poets
Lupe Fiasco
MC Ren
Mecca 2 Medina
Mobb Deep
Mos Def
Mujahideen Team

Napoleon (Tupac's Outlawz)
Nas
Native Deen
Old School
Paris
Poor Righteous Teachers
Prince Akeem
Professor Griff (Public Enemy)
Q-Tip (Fareed Kamal), formerly of A Tribe Called Quest
Queen Latifah
Rakim
Roots
Shorty (Da Lench Mob)
Sister Souljah
Sons of Hagar
Tyson
World Famous Supreme Team
Wu-Tang Clan
Young Messengerrzz

Notes

1. Author interview, March 23, 2005.

2. A play on Suheir Hammad's *Born Palestinian, Born Black* (Writers and Readers Publishing, 1996).

3. These statistics were calculated before a new wave of immigration from Muslim countries probably boosted these numbers. To take one example, according to a 2005 census report, the fastest-growing New York migrant group between 1990–2000 were Bangladeshis. Therefore, it is safe to say these numbers have gone up. At the same time, post-9/11 immigration crackdown and worsening of Muslim civil liberties would dampen these numbers.

4. Sylviane A. Diouf, *Servants of Allah: African Muslims Enslaved in the Americas* (New York University Press, 1998).

5. James Baldwin, *The Fire Next Time* (Dell Publishing, 1977), 46.

6. Sohail Daulatzai, *Darker Than Blue: A Cultural History of Black Radicalism and Afro-Asian Solidarity*, forthcoming.

7. Richard Brent Turner, *Islam in the African-American Experience* (Indiana University Press, 1997).

8. Sohail Daulatzai, "War At 33 1/3: Culture and Politics Across the Afro-Asian Atlantic," in *The Vinyl Ain't Final: Hip-Hop and the Globalization of Black Popular Culture*, ed. Dipannita Basu and Sid Lemelle (Pluto Press, 2006).

9. Author Interview, March 21, 2005.

10. Darius James, *That's Blaxploitation!* (St. Martin's Griffin, 1995).

11. *Time* Magazine, "Time 100: The Most Important People of the Century," http://www.time.com/time/time100/index_2000_time100.html/.

12. Yusuf Nureddine, quoted in Hisham Aidi, "Hip Hop of the Gods," Africana.com, April 27, 2001.

13. Known as the "Lost-Found Muslim Lessons," which are arranged in question-and-answer format (and may have been modeled on the catechism of the Masons). See http://www.thenationofislam.org/lostfoundlesson.html/.

14. Here PE may also be linked to John Coltrane's Muslim connection, via Ahmadiya Muslims such as Yusuf Lateef.

15. Kevin Powell, quoted in Manning Marable, "The Politics of Hip Hop," *Along the Color Line*, March 2002.

16. Author interview, March 22, 2005.

17. Manning Marable, "The Politics of Hip Hop," *Along the Color Line*, March 2002.

18. Author interview, March 22, 2005.

19. H. Samy Alim, "Exploring the Transglobal Hip Hop Umma," in *Muslim Networks: From Hajj to Hip Hop*, ed. Miriam Cooke and Bruce B. Lawrence (University of North Carolina Press, 2005).

20. H. Samy Alim, "Three X Black: Mos Def, Mr. Nigga (Nigga, Nigga) and Big Black Afrika X-amine Hip Hop's Cultural Consciousness," *Black Arts Quarterly* 6, no. 2.

21. H. Samy Alim, "Exploring the Transglobal Hip Hop Umma," in *Muslim Networks*.

22. Marian Liu, "Hip-Hop's Islamic Influence," *SJ Mercury News* (see http://www.daveyd.com/commentaryhiphopislam.html).

23. A focus on numerology can also be found in Islam—such as the belief that some elements in the Qur'an are divisible by seven, in a manner impossible to produce without divine intervention.

24. Hisham Aidi, "Hip Hop of the Gods," Africana.com, April 27, 2001.

25. The prophets' sayings are collected in Hadith, with notations about provenance and reliability.

26. Naeem Mohaiemen, *Muslims or Heretics* (documentary), 2005. See www .shobak.org/.

27. Adisa Banjoko, "Hip-Hop and the New Age of Ignorance," *FNV Newsletter* (June 2001).

28. Hisham Aidi, "Jihadis in the Hood: Race, Urban Islam, and the War on Terror," *Middle East Report* 224, fall 2002.

29. Author interview, March 23, 2005.

30. Author interview, March 23, 2005.

31. On a Long Island TV show called *The God Squad*, I was asked by a worried host, "Now when you say black Muslims, I just want to make sure you're not talking about Nation of Islam."

32. Naeem Mohaiemen works as a visual artist in Dhaka and New York City, spanning video, archive, and text. His obsessions include national security panic, failed revolutionary movements, and the jump from utopia to dystopia. For more on his work, see http://shobak.org/.

Three Pieces

Chuck D

Hip-Hop vs. Rap

Don't make me stop this car
Rap is a vocal application
Tell the locals
Rap is not a music, it's a vocal
Application
Crosses all musics and generations
And many nations
Ad libs now owned by corporations
Hip-hop narrowed down to hit pop
The big paycheck
Makes the heads bop
Nonstop
Sometimes it's silly rhymes and catch phrases
Seen this game go thru phases
And crazes
Only the lawyers get raises
Still wit it
I can dig it you can dig it we can dig it
Two turntables

One mic and a mixer
Overdubbed when Doc J was a Sixer
Before stickers
And tippers
Gored vinyl between CDs and tapes
And winos
But like Planet of the Apes
They blew it up

Rap knocked hip-hop out cold
And turned it into disco
Rap can ride any sound
Has no bounds
Hip–hop's a subculture
From a people with culture
Swooped on by vultures
At the same time defining
The creativity behind
The last 30 years on the timeline
The Bronx is the startline
Ladies and gentlemen it's startime
Hip-hop is a state of mind

Blown up
Some say hip-hop is pregnant
Cause rap dun fucked it up
Two different definitions
I love hip-hop to the bone marrow
Sometimes I turn rap down
When it's too narrow
Rhymes like arrows
To the head and heart
Hittin' hip-hop from the start
Hip-hop cannot be bought
But rap can be sold
Thus rap can get cold
Hip-hop's forever hot
Cause we are hip-hop

A Twisted Sense of God (pt. 1)

I was talking to my assistant a couple of months back, and while we were talking about the obvious differences in men and women, I had to give up and say that men couldn't handle the period cycles that women go through. She countered and told me that men do have periods ...

They're called WARS.

There's little words that can describe what happened here in the United States on Tuesday, September 11, 2001. I was in New York when it was goin' down. My heart goes out to those in the aircrafts, the buildings, the rescuers killed on the ground. As a person who has traveled across forty countries in the world, I can attest to the fact that the common peoples on the Earth have long suffered, and swallowed the bullet of the greed of governmental rule and arrogance. Power is a funny thing, when poured on the few individuals that are selected to govern people, no matter where they're at on the Earth ... it makes manipulation a close cousin.

Mad questions abound. Whoever the so-called hijackers or planners answered to, my question is how come their superiors didn't put THEIR lives on the line? I don't buy religious martyrdom if the leader heads themselves can't get in the same box. It's problematic when one is trained and taught to die for religious elevation while the heads of that structure are rich as hell and don't share the wealth with their followers. On the other side, the United States is talking war but who is actually gonna fight those battles, and with whom?

War is not a football game, y'all.

BUSH and the rest of these 50-PLUS-WHITEMEN (C. POWELL included) will not be on the air or field. I repeat they will not be on the air or field. They're making definite decisions and I have a problem with the arrogance of most governments period. I have a problem with the arrogance of MAN period. There is little if any humility on both parts.

The skeptical pendulum is swinging both ways as far as culprits are concerned. I have a problem with dragging innocent people into political high-level bullshit. There will be innocent people catching it bad across both waters, infested with a lethal combination of fact, attacks, myth, dogma and orders.

I have a problem with Amerikkka walking out and damn near shitting on the WORLD RACISM CONFERENCE in SOUTH AFRICA. I have issues with the United States talking cocky, considering while admitting themselves about the carrying out of assassinations. I have a problem with heartless cats training to fly planes in order to kill thousands of innocent people in the air or on the ground. I have a problem with some nations and its protectors how they refuse to acknowledge their major contribution to this cycle of terror and greed. I have a problem that Americans consider it a "over there" issue, as if it was on another planet. I have a problem with Amerikkka with three Ks, and its relentless hyping and macho barroom talks of a "beat-u'down" past. I don't have a problem on what America can be. In NEW YORK, a place known for people not giving a damn about the next person, all of a sudden people are communicating with one another regardless of background unless the person has a Middle Eastern "visual characteristic" and that's where Amerikkka, that's with three Ks, and not America spelled properly, rears its ugliness. Understand the difference y'all ... Twisted.

Why everybody wanna kill God? It's wack when people oblivious to the facts are dragged into war and death. It's wack when cats throw religion into the mix. It's wack that celebrations are taking place in the streets of some nations and just as terrible as some Texans shooting and burning a mosque in Abiline. Just as horrible is the fact that Amerikkkans jumped in celebratory joy when two atomic bombs were dropped on JAPAN in 1945, and updated hate in 2001 about people calling people of backgrounds "dogs," it's documented. I can go on and on and on about the inner and outer, and still continued "terrorism"-endorsed Amerikkkan, that's with three K's style, as eloquently pointed out and covered by my man Art McGee's Black Radical Congress piece. Terror Attacks. Ignoring calls for reparations, only endorses a past of slavery, KKK, COINTELPRO, Japanese World War II concentration camps etc. etc. that's been hosted here in the same land of the free everybody's talking about. When it all boils down to it, power has never been with the people. The people of the Earth are still PAWNS IN THE GAME, while the board-masters, the rulers of countries, corporations, giant and religious leaderships operate under the guise of "IN GOD WE TRUST" or even "ALLA U AKBAR" where an action assumes the position of an act of God. It's not what you say you are, it's what you prove you are. So avoid this latest rhetoric and arrogance that's woven with this "twisted sense of god," while the everyday person is shook by a new existence in this odec, this century, this millennium.

On the real, in all sense of humility may God bless us all beyond the flags.

Why y'all wanna kill God?

A twisted sense of God.

Rap, Race, Reality, and Technology

This is something for the time capsule ... No it ain't tryin' to make the Billboard charts, Emptyv, Rap City, Hot 97, the Vibe or the Source ... This is intentionally tryin' to tell you that this is a counterattack against the mass dumbing down of black culture ... Rap, race, and reality and technology set you free.

This exception to the fool
I ain't provin' no points
Ain't tryin' to sell you
We are gathered here
Hear me, this is called the lecture series
1001 reasons to fear me
As I trek thru the nation
Givin' vibe sessions, massive conversations
Let the def, dumb, and blind see
Lecture series to set your mind free
Lessons on rap race and reality
Education makes you what you really be
All you choose to really be
Communication
Rides on technology
Hit the fertile minds
Like susskind

Rap, race, reality technology

Some who got
Psychoanalysis
To the point of paralysis
Can't think or move to the groove
At the same time
I got no points to prove

Hear me
To think outside how you
Trained to think
Followin' ink
Slippin' in pink
A dozen years
From the Howards to the Harvards
San Francisco States
To Mississippi valley states
50 states
Thru step shows
Homecomings and spring breaks

Now that raps hit the mainstream
Hip-hop is more than get the cream
Forget the dream
The real is
What it is
Who and where it's been
While most average fan fails to understand
It's more than a man
So here I am
Lecture poses like a new black Moses
In street clothes
No flips in the lips
Race flows traces and trips of slave ships
Can't truss it
No doubt
Pow, if you don't know me by now
I raise brains alongside eyebrows
Fed your heads
So stick around
Fed your head
So stay around

Brian Eno

About Bells

The casting of bells is an ancient art that requires the convergence of several technological skills including the making of moulds, and an understanding of the heating and fusing of metals and alloys. The Egyptians made "closed bells"—also known as crotals—using plaster moulds from about 2000 BCE. Over the next 1,000 years, small open bells were cast in northern Iran, and by 850 BCE, Assyrian bronze founders were experimenting with the acoustic properties of different ratios of tin and copper in their bells.

By the fifth century BCE, meanwhile, the Chinese had settled on an alloy of four parts copper to one part tin for bell-making. This ratio is still in common use in modern bell foundries.

The first recorded Christian bellfounders were the smiths Tasag, Cuana, and Mackecht, whom St. Patrick took to Ireland in the fifth century CE, although the bells they made were forged rather than cast—probably more like cowbells. The development of cast churchbells was fostered by the Italian Benedictines beginning in about 530 CE. As their order spread, they established bell foundries in monasteries all over Western Europe, and became the main suppliers of bells.

From about the eleventh century, treatises on metallurgy and bell-founding encouraged improvements in technique and design, and the craft passed from clerical into lay hands, although the secrets involved were very carefully guarded.

The advent of the artillery cannon in the fourteenth century provided an unexpected boost to bell manufacture: the cannon used almost exactly the same alloy as bells and was made by similar methods. In order to have the security of a local arsenal, cities offered foundry sites and special privileges to bell founders who would settle within their walls. The same supply of metal would be made into cannon in wartime and would go back to bells after hostilities were over.

In Europe in the seventeenth century the perfection of clocks increased the usefulness of clock-tower chimes and led to an interest in their musical possibilities. This favored founders who could cast and tune bells in musical scales, and the most prominent early makers of well-tuned bells were the migrant Hemony brothers from Lorraine. Their work was mostly commissioned in Germany, Holland, and Flanders, where they cast many bells including over fifty carillons with ranges of 26 to 37 bells.

During the seventeenth and eighteenth centuries bell-founding was influenced by the wealthy Russian monasteries, who increased the number of small bells in their bell sets and added larger ones. Since these bells were stationary rather than swung they exerted no lateral thrust on the buildings that housed them.

The biggest bells are physically much larger than any other instruments—the great Tsar Kolokol bell which sits broken in the Kremlin weighs 200,000 kilograms and is nearly seven meters in diameter; the "Emelle" bell, cast in Korea in the seventh century, is 72,000 kilograms. Objects such as these remained the largest castings made until modern ship propellers. What has to be borne in mind is that these bells—like all bells—were made in one casting, which means that 200,000 kilograms of metal had to be brought to temperature and poured in one continuous operation. As a technological feat (and allowing for inflation) this is perhaps comparable to the level of coordination required to launch an Apollo into space.

The twentieth century saw many technical improvements in bell-founding, including better mould-making materials, better temperature control, and, importantly, better ways of tuning and measuring the pitch of the overtones of the bells. Recent innovations in Holland have involved the use of computers to design bells, modifying the proposed shape until it produces the required overtone series.

All instruments produce their own characteristic partial or overtone series, but what distinguishes bells is that their overtones are not necessarily in concordant relationships—that is to say, they are not necessarily simple multiples of the lowest frequency. A clarinet, for example, produces strong overtones at even multiples of the frequency of the fundamental tone, whereas bells rarely produce such pure overtones, with many bells having overtones with no numerical relationship to each other.

In England the lowest note of a church bell—the note which lasts the longest—is called the "hum note." The next overtone—which is approximately, but rarely exactly, an octave above it, is the "fundamental." The next two overtones are called the "tierce" and the "quint," and they are approximately a third and a fifth above the fundamental. The tierce is usually a minor third (although recent Dutch experiments with computer-aided design have shown bell-makers how to reliably produce "major" bells). About one octave above the fundamental is the "nominal"—a short-lived overtone which helps to define the perceived pitch of the bell.

When the fundamental and the nominal are not a true octave apart, a partial called the "strike note" may be audible at the instant of striking. This overtone is a difference tone, the result of the interaction of other tones. It is still hotly debated whether its presence adds or subtracts from the overall beauty of the bell.

Above the nominal there are further partials in more or less dissonant relationships to each other and the lower overtones, but their decay is very rapid so they do not affect the perceived pitch of the bell. They do, however, affect the perception of brightness and richness that the bell gives at its attack, and the individual character of a bell has very much to do with the perception of its higher partials. The larger the bell, the lower in frequency the whole overtone series is, and the more perceptible it becomes.

The experiments on this CD sometimes try to simulate existing bells, and (perhaps more profitably) imagine different sorts of bells, bells which may indeed be physically unmakeable. Some of the hypothetical bells have idealized overtone series—where each overtone is the same pure multiple of the one below it. Other hypobells explore reversals or suspensions of some physical laws: what would happen if the highest partials lasted longest? What if the lowest notes were the first to speak, and the higher partials appeared later?

What would a large bell made entirely of glass sound like? What if the first chaotic milliseconds of a bell's ring could be extended over minutes? What if a bell became a drone?

When we started thinking about the Clock of the Long Now, we naturally wondered what kind of sound it could make to announce the passage of time. Bells have stood the test of time in their relationship to clocks, and the technology of making them is highly evolved and still evolving. I began reading about bells, discovering the physics of their sounds, and became interested in thinking about what other sorts of bells might exist. My speculations quickly took me out of the bounds of current physical and material possibilities, but I considered some license allowable since the project was conceived in a timescale of thousands of years, and I might therefore imagine bells with quite different physical properties from those we now know. And as I started trying to make bell sounds with my synthesizers, I got diverted by some of the more attractive failures.

About "January 07003"

Campanology—change-ringing—is one of England's more eccentric contributions to the musical landscape. By the 1600s, many churches had numbers of tuned bells in their belfries, and these seem to have been rung in simple sequence, over and over. About that time a new development arose. Ringers became interested in trying to ring all the possible permutations of their bells, and it is this pursuit that has become known as change-ringing. Stated briefly, change-ringing is the art (or, to many practitioners, the science) of ringing a given number of bells such that all possible sequences are used without any being repeated. The mathematics of this idea are fairly simple: n bells will yield $n!$ sequences or changes. The "!" is not an expression of surprise but the sign for a factorial: a direction to multiply the number by all those lower than it. So three bells will yield $3 \times 2 \times 1 = 6$ changes, whereas four bells will yield $4 \times 3 \times 2 \times 1 = 24$ changes. The ! process does become rather surprising as you continue it for higher values of n: $5! = 120$, and $6! = 710$—and you watch the number of changes increasing dramatically with the number of bells.

What interests change-ringers is finding ways to arrange all the permutations of a given set of bells into a logical, playable, and memorable sequence (since no change may be repeated, no scores may be used, no bell may occupy the same position for more than two consecutive changes, and a whole

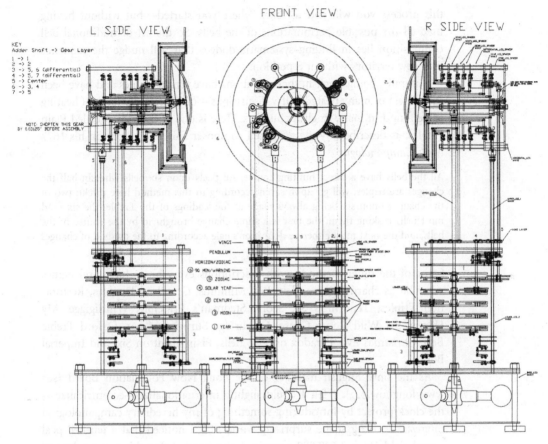

Figure 30.1
Drawings from the first prototype of the Clock of the Long Now, completed 01999.

method must be rung from memory). This becomes an issue with larger numbers of bells, and with a peal of 8 bells and therefore 40,240 changes—not uncommon in English churches—it can be a very complex exercise with many different solutions.

The drawing shown in figure 30.1 shows the first part of an early solution for six bells, as recorded by Richard Duckworth in his 1671 book *Tintinnalogia*. We now call this method Plain Bob Minor: the alternation of three pairs of bells reversing position and then two inner pairs reversing. If you continue this process you will end up back where you started—but without having used all the possible permutations of the bells. So the art of traditional bell composition lies in finding systematic dodges that will nudge the sequence into new territory without repetition.

Naturally, being English, these solutions have arcane names and have been the subject of many heated belfry discussions—often the only form of heating to be found in many English churches. Here is one of the oldest, called Plain Triples, as described by the great bell composer Fabian Stedman in his 1677 book *Campanologia*:

All the bells have a direct hunting course. All peals upon six bells wherein half the changes are triples, will go upon seven according to this method here prickt: two of the changes upon six being always made at the leadings of the Treble, the six hind most bells making them: the first is a triple change brought in by the course of the bells, and the next must either be double or single according to the method of changes upon six.

Some of the other methods, with descriptions every bit as lucid and names every bit as charming, are Plain Bob Minimus, Grandsire Doubles, Restoration Triples, Tendring's Six Score, Stedman's Principle, Whirligigge, My Honey, the Wild Goose Chase, Cambridge Surprise Minor, Oxford Treble Bob, Christmas Eve, Paradox on Five Bells, Plain Hunt on Six, and Imperial Bob.

As the only English member of the Long Now Foundation Board (see www.longnow.org), I felt I could slightly internationalize—eccentricalize—the clock project by introducing something of my hereditary campanological interests. Looking at the surprising world of !, I noticed that a ten-bell peal would yield $10! = 3,628,800$ changes. I also noticed that this is very close to the number of days in 10,000 years—the proposed minimum lifespan of the Clock.

This attractive near-coincidence made me imagine a method which would produce such a series of changes but which would also be generated in such a way as to act as a calendar. What that means is that a listener, hearing the bells on a day in the future, should be able, if the algorithm that generates the series is known, to calculate exactly the number of days since the series started playing. Seen from the other end, it would enable me as a composer to know what change would be playing on a given day in the future. That was the part that interested me: I wanted to hear the bells of the month of January 07003—approximately halfway through the life of the Clock.

Figure 30.2
The Clock of the Long Now.

I had no idea how to generate this series, but I had a good idea who would. I wrote to Danny Hillis asking whether he could come up with an algorithm for the job. Yes, he wrote back, and in fact he could come up with an algorithm for generating all the possible algorithms for that job. Not having the storage space for a lot of extra algorithms in my studio, I decided to settle for just the one.

Danny's explanation of his algorithm and a mechanism by which it could work begins as follows:

Each day the ringer mechanism rings a change, which is a ring sequence consisting of one permutation of the bells. The mechanism is designed to work through all of the permutations of ten bells before repeating.

To understand the algorithms used for generating the permutations, try writing down the permutation of a smaller number of bells, say three, on a piece of paper. First write down the name of the first bell, 1, in the center of the paper. Now notice that the second bell can ring either before the first or after it—in other words it can occur in one of two places, with respect to the first bell. Write down both of these possibilities on the next line, one on either side. Now, notice that when we have two bells in place, there are three places to put the third bell. You can write down each of these on the line below. That generates all six permutations of three bells.

To generate the permutations of four bells you would need to place the fourth bell in each of the four possible positions for each of these six three-bell permutations, and so on. The proposed mechanism uses an algorithm very similar to this to generate the permutations. The mechanism is modular, with one ring module for each of the ten bells. Each module has a wheel that counts the position of the bell in the sequence, relative to the lower numbered bells. For example, the third bell has a wheel with three positions, selecting whether the third bell appears before, between, or after bells one and two. The fourth bell has a four-position wheel, and so on. These wheels are used to count through all of the possibilities, advancing to a new combination each day.

The mechanism actually needs not only to generate the index positions of the bells, but must translate those indices into a sequence. For this it uses another counting wheel in each module that keeps track of how many bells have rung so far in the current change.

A campanologist will notice that Danny's algorithm produces a result which breaks some rules of traditional bell ringing—that no bell shall occupy the same "place" on more than two consecutive changes, and that place shifts are such that they are physically possible for ringers to play (so a bell isn't expected to be rung at the end of one sequence and then the beginning of the next, for example). I considered that these rules were breakable because the changes were being generated by a machine, and would be played far enough apart in time (one change a day) for their positional similarities to be irrelevant.

Tracks 2, 8, and 15 all use the sequence for the month beginning Saturday, January 1, 07003. Track 8, which shows the changes for the whole of that month, employs the bells made from a very heavy ceramic-metal compound in the year 05102 (shortly after the original bronze set had finally deteriorated beyond repair due to the hyperacidity of the late fourth millennium). The last track, in some parallel universe, plays the first two weeks of that same January on the original bronze set. Track 2 plays the first few days but in such a way that each bell is struck as many times as its number—so bell 10 is always struck ten times. This breaks every known rule of bell-ringing but makes a pretty noise.

Other tracks explore noncampanological approaches, such as the German "hit every bell as often as and as hard as possible" approach (track 6), and the Russian "shock and awe" style (track 14). Track 9 got its title because Inge, who looks after the studio, said, almost with tears in her eyes, that it reminded her of her homeland's bells. The bells on the first track are constructed in such a way that their harmonic series is intensely idealized, with each harmonic being precisely 1.66 times the pitch of the one below it.

"Tsar Kolokol III (and Friends)" is an attempt at a sonic reconstruction of the biggest bell ever made—which was never heard because it cracked during a fire shortly after being cast. In this piece I imagine the big bell with a few similarly large companions.

Technical and historical information adapted from the following sources:

Benade, Arthur H. (1976). *Fundamentals of Musical Acoustics.* Oxford University Press.

Change Ringing: The History of an English Art (1987). Ed. J. Sanderson. Cambridge: The Central Council of Church Bell Ringers.

The New Grove Dictionary of Musical Instruments (1984). Ed. Stanley Sadie. Oxford University Press.

Daniel Bernard Roumain (DBR)

What One Must Do

you have to challenge yourself.
you have to stretch your imagination.
you have to play as though you will not be able to play tomorrow.

you have to play when it hurts because no one else will.
you have to play until it hurts because no one else can or will dare to.
you have to play until the pain is gone.

you have to think about your mother.
you have to think about your mother murdered.
you have to think about your mother's murderer and play to him.
all the rage.
all the anger.

you have to think of your first child.
you have to think of her name.
you have to play to her and be as gentle as the mother you might be.
all the tenderness.
all the patience.
all the pride.

you have to beat your instrument.
you have to play your cello like a bass drum.

you have to play your violin like an electric guitar.
you have to play your drum like a flute.
you have to play your flute like a drum kit.

you have to have so much pressure on the bow it all becomes pure noise.

you have to listen with your whole body.

you are way too comfortable with what you think you know.

you have to keep learning.
you have to want to.
you have to go to new places and then you can take me there.

you have to have balls and know when not to.
you have to see with your father's eyes; no one is blind.

you have to find the beauty in one note and then share it with me.

you have to want to be new.
you have to listen to things you don't want to listen to.

you have to make NIN a part of your DNA.

you have to play tired and make it beautiful.
you have to be poor and shallow and play rich and deep.

you have to try 1,000 times harder and that is only a start and you
have to know that.
you have to count and make it count.
you have to not take it for granted and i think you do.
you have to not become a broken record doing the same things every day.

every day do the same thing and see how it feels; tomorrow do one thing
different and see how that feels. pick one and repeat.

ask yourself, "why would i want to listen to you?"
i ask myself, "what am i playing that hasn't been played before, better?"

are you original?
where does originality exist?
is there anyone in the world like you?
no?
prove it!

you can.
play it!

you have to decide.
you have to make the choice to be a great musician in the hopes that
you might make good music.
you have to be able to make great conversation first.

there is nothing i can teach you that you don't already know.
don't you know this?

*

Music Changed My Life

Music changed my life and saved my life. Statistically speaking, as a young
Black man in America, I should have at least one child; I should have used
or should be using illegal drugs; I should have been arrested, been to jail
and/or prison at least once; I could be HIV+; I could be unemployed; I
could be dead. When I tell you music changed my life and saved my life,
that is not an exaggeration.

*

In Service to Music

You have to decide whether or not you are going to have music serve
you or if you are going to live your life in service to music.

*

It Is, Is It?

History, tradition, and classical music—are these words related?
Who decides what it is or when it is—is it you or them?

*

Composers Are

Composers are historians, documentarians, ethnomusicologists, and
pathological liars.

*

B to MJ to M to PRN

Brahms is to Michael Jackson as Mahler is to Prince. The formers are most concerned with melody with little attention paid to timbre. The latters provide substantial melodic construction supported by overwhelming timbral patterns and design.

*

SSS

When everything else is over, music and silence should be about selflessness, selfishness, and pleasure.

*

Listen and Move

If you want to understand music, take a dance class. If you want to learn how to dance, don't ask a musician. Listen and move to your favorite music instead.

*

Listen to Your Lover's Voice

If you want to understand timbre, or the color of sound, that is, what distinguishes the sound of a piano from the sound of a violin, listen to your lover's voice. Have you ever recorded the voice of someone you want to love and listened back to it? Have you ever called someone's voicemail just to hear the sound of their voice if only for a few, passing moments? Have you ever kept a message from them on your cell phone for days, weeks even, because you love the sound of their voice that much? That is timbre, or for me, the best definition.

*

SHMRF and, and

The five essential parameters of music are sound, harmony, melody, rhythm, and form. There may be one or two more yet to be discovered.

*

G-Harmony

Great harmony is just like great sex. Supportive, elusive, mysterious, complex, contrapuntal, synergetic, clear, and sometimes, exhausting. Harmony is the notion of one idea pitted against another.

*

Melody

Melody is the notion of a singular idea, a singular thought, a clear and definite line. Make no mistake about it—melodies are all around us all the time. I am inspired by the sounds in my head and the sounds under my feet.

*

Form

Form is the definition of space over time.

*

Rhythm

Rhythm is a more specific and substantive aspect of form.

*

What's Going On?

Most young people, between 7 and 39 years of age, are already listening to very sophisticated music. Hip-hop, rock, dub, techno, grunge, heavy, death, and speed metal, reggaeton, house, jazz, classical, and electronica, these really have a lot "going on" in terms of the five essential parameters of music in sound, harmony, melody, rhythm, and form. If you were to do a musical analysis of that music, and I have, you'll find that, on a rhythmic level especially, most commercially available music is exceedingly complex. It's contrapuntal music. It's an easy sell, once you start demonstrating that. Eminem and Bach are using the same musical scales. Joni Mitchell is a great American composer and melodist. Snoop Dog is a twenty-first-century

chamber musician. Most young people come equipped with all the listening
and analytical skills they need to appreciate the most complex classical
music. No one's turned them on to it. It seems no one will.

*

David Parsons and the KKK

I would like to think that a devoted, loving husband, father, and Ku Klux
Klansman, full of hate for all things Negro, and David Parsons, the African-
American CEO of AOL Time Warner, might both have a hidden passion for
50 Cent or Willie Nelson.
Imagine . . .

*

Lennon

John Winston Lennon was born on October 9, 1940, in Liverpool, England.
John Winston Ono Lennon was murdered (assassinated?) on December 8,
1980, on 72nd Street in New York City. Today, he would have been 65 years
old.
Imagine . . .

*

iPod

The iPod is the greatest musical instrument and musical invention of the
twenty-first century. Like any instrument when you buy it, it's blank, empty,
and waiting to be filled. You input your tastes, your music, your ideas.
You input your arrangements of those ideas exemplified by your playlists.
You make it your own. By shuffling your ideas, or allowing them to be
randomized, you are participating in a compositional idea, a compositional
technique, an aleatoric procedure. The unexpected nature of what might
come next, of what might be heard next, helps to liberate the mind and the
ear and expand the very personal nature of one's perception of music, and I
think, one's taste. And like any great musical device, the iPod can grow and
expand and respond along with the player. Several companies offers ways in

which two iPods can be used as two turntables. Podcasts are becoming more
and more common and blue collar (the NYPD features one now on its
homepage). Today, I noticed there were 181,000,000 "hits" when the word
"iPod" was googled.

Imagine . . .

*

Cobain

"Jam! for Piano" was the first work I composed in which I was purposefully
trying to combine hip-hop music with something, anything else, in this case,
my take on classical music, cluster chords, and Cobain—Kurt Cobain and
that grunge sound inspired "Jam! for Piano" as much as anything else that
was in the air at the time.

*

The Truth, So Help Me . . .

I used to be very interested, as a composer, in documenting the African-
American experience. Now, I'm interested in the human experience. I'm
interested in reaching a broader audience, but I'm not as interested in
celebrity as community. I believe classical music's beginnings were founded
in the idea of delivering the words of God to the common man and woman,
in the hopes of creating a more informed, tolerant, and moral society. I
believe hip-hop music's beginnings were founded in the idea of delivering
the words of brothers and sisters to brothers and sisters, in the hopes of
creating a more informed, tolerant, and moral society. I still believe in
classical music and I will always love hip-hop music. And I believe that
composers represent these original, noble, and in some ways holy and sacred
ideas; as musicians and artists, we are the keepers of the flame.

It is up to us.

Hans Ulrich Obrist and Philippe Parreno

Translated by David Kidman

Philippe Parreno: When did you come to realize that, as a composer, you had to invent your own means of production? Jaron Lanier, the inventor of virtual reality, which has become such a metaphor for everything, is also a musician. In the beginning, his intention was to invent a musical instrument. In a way, you were the first to initiate such methods. So, when did you realize that?
Pierre Boulez: I started to think about this kind of thing in 1948, because Pierre Schaeffer had asked me to take part in some recordings, he wanted some chords that he would be able to manipulate. He had set up a little studio in the rue de l'Université. To see how these methods were likely to develop, I joined his *musique concrète* group in 1951–52. I realized pretty quickly that it was really just do-it-yourself stuff, so-called poetry—but in the end, with poetry, I find that you camouflage things rather than discover them, at least with that kind of poetry. Afterwards, around 1958, I got in touch, through Stockhausen, with the electronic music studio in Cologne, where I had seen that they worked much more seriously. And, more interestingly, simply because it was far better musically. After that there was the Südwestfunk, when I moved to Baden Baden, which had set up a little studio to produce "Poésie pour pouvoir," which was a mixture of orchestra, voice, and technology, the technology of the time, of course. I found it unsatisfactory, though, because it was still handmade; I had thought right from the beginning that the technology should be more responsible than that. In the early 1960s, then, when I

traveled regularly to Munich to conduct the *Musica Viva* concerts, I had been
put into contact with the Siemens studio. They had a studio which was being
tried out at the time. And there, really, I realized that those aspects of technology were much more gratifying, because they evolved in phase with the state
of musical philosophy. All the previous experiences had seemed to me to be
unsatisfactory because written musical theory was much more advanced than
technology theory. So there, in the Siemens studio, which didn't last for very
long, unfortunately, I already had a notion of the potential of the work. There
had been a project to establish a music laboratory in the [Foundation] ...
[Boulez cannot remember the name of the foundation], and I was asked to
oversee a department of contemporary music. That is when I began to think
about the means necessary for such a place. In the end, it came to nothing.
That was somewhere around '68. And later, president Pompidou asked me if
I could participate in the Pompidou Centre, which he was in the process of
founding. I said yes. I presented a project which was an advanced version
of what I had done for that foundation (still no name on that ...). At that
time, I concentrated on putting all the tools of musical theory into phase
with the tools of technology theory. The development of information technology was what interested me most. I got in touch with the different studios that
existed then; with the Benlams in New York, Max Mathieu in particular. That
is when I saw that information technology was in its infancy.

Hans Ulrich Obrist: You also met Billy Kluver in New York ...

PB: Yes, absolutely, I met Billy Kluver in New York. At that time, I wanted
to give the computer its rightful place—while knowing quite well that the
conditions were still far from adequate. But I had to reserve a place for it, in
order to foresee its developments. As it happened, during the years it took to
found the IRCAM, at the beginning of the '70s, computers developed enor-
mously. I was in contact with MIT and the Center at Stanford. They helped
a great deal in establishing the IRCAM. I am still really grateful to them, because without their help the IRCAM wouldn't have been up and running so
quickly.

HUO: So it starts at the time of the big studios like Baden Baden, with those
huge computers. Then comes miniaturization which entails decisive developments. Did that change the way in which you work?

PB: Yes, it changed because at the beginning it was an enormous machine
and we worked on it using time shares. If there was, for example, somebody
who had a program which took a long time to calculate, the others simply had

to wait. And for so long that you couldn't really talk about spontaneity. I went to Stanford myself, in 1975 (that is a pretty long time ago, twenty-eight years already) to learn how to program, etc. At the time, it was still a pain, especially if you didn't have the right education: when you forgot a comma, or a semicolon in the program, nothing worked anymore and you didn't know the reason why. Later there was an error detector, which made it easier to redirect when you had gone astray. And then in terms of the interface there was progress, too—it was in black and white at first, then in color—which gave you a much more intuitive relationship with the machine. At the beginning, though, that relationship was difficult, because it was based on elementary didacticism.

PP: You had to write the codes for your programs ...

PB: Yes, that's right.

PP: So it might be that this enabled you to develop new ideas, since you had to create your own programs. I belong to the software generation.

PB: Yes, of course. But it is also much easier today, using an existing program, you can think along the same lines on which the program has been conceived. At that time, we were really light-years away from that. We worked like madmen, between five and eight hours in the morning to get a second or two of sound, and even that wasn't very rigorous. Today, if you try something, you can have the result almost instantly. Given that the techniques of today are infinitely more sophisticated, the relationship is also infinitely more intuitive, more direct. That doesn't mean that you invent anything new. It means that you can use these things; inventing is still very difficult.

HUO: Does that change the way music is written? I mean: you see a lot of young composers today who work on computers and don't write the musical score. You might get the impression that electronics are going to lead to the disappearance of the musical score. Do you think that the score should be saved?

PB: Yes, it must exist, because it enables musicians to combine things. And for our collective memory. You know that technique is in a transitory period, however perfect it is, even nowadays. As time goes by the transitory periods are getting shorter. You know, even work made twenty years ago has to be re-recorded onto new support. Hardware is completely renewed every five to ten years, so we have to adapt the old to the new, copying into another language, onto another piece of hardware. We have less problems with nineteenth-century pianos than with twenty-five-year-old technology—and it is impossible to work with such time gaps, so the score is absolutely necessary. That doesn't necessarily mean that it is a score with the notes and scales. It can be a different type of score, numbered and digital, any imaginable form is possible. But it must be written so that whatever future developments take place, any technical incompatibility can be rethought, taking into account the new hardware. In other words, you can rethink the way in which the score is written, but its data is still needed.

PP: In a sense, would you say it's the score of the score?

PB: Exactly.

HUO: Regarding the score of the score, you often talk about the "provisional state" of your work, to say that it is always work in progress. This is a paradox, since on the one hand you work on the score, which fixes your work in a certain way, and on the other had you keep it open, as if in a spiral, your research ...

PB: Yes, the score fixes things, but at the same time it is a provisional state—as far as I am concerned, at least. I have often compared it to the Guggenheim Museum, in New York. I really like going to that museum, whereas a lot of curators, both freelancers and those from other museums, don't like the Guggenheim because the structure forces you to follow a one-way path, and you cannot determine your own trajectory according to the exhibition in question. What is interesting, though, is that because you cannot alter the trajectory, you have the future of the exhibition and its past at the same time as its present. You see a certain number of things; you back up, you see what you have just seen once again; and then you look up and you see what you are going to see, later on, by going around the spiral. A system of comparison is established, a way of placing time in the visiting process, which seems very interesting to me. Otherwise, you are obliged to walk, to look behind you, to come back into a room that you have already left, etc. You have to do the moving. At the Guggenheim, though, it's only your point of view that moves. I find that particularly interesting. To come back to scores, it is true that some of them are finished and fixed. When you get to the end of the spiral, you are not going to come down to specially make the trip in the other direction. But when you have got the impression and the intuition that the work can be developed, it remains in your head, so when you pick up the work later on, you can identify and resolve problems. Especially when you are in my position, since I usually perform at the same time: if I hear the piece of work and I am not satisfied, I draw conclusions from that and rework the piece.

Not necessarily the next day—I mean that there is a problem to resolve and I will try to resolve it, whether in the short or the long term.

HUO: Philippe mentioned Jaron Lanier earlier, who invented virtual reality in the early 1980s, and in other interviews, I noticed that you often refer to the *l'explosante fixe* as a virtual score. What is a virtual score?

PB: The virtual score doesn't quite exist yet. I was talking about it to colleagues at the IRCAM only yesterday. The virtual score is one which is able to change itself according to certain parameters. In other words, you have a series of numbers and they can mean something else, something different: tone or length or dynamics, etc. You have a score which is solely virtual: taking it from there, you can imagine installations, installations where the path taken by someone would trigger modifications, for example, using a motion detector. For the same score, instead of being within an expanded ambit, you would be in a reduced one. Instead of being in that scale of things, you could use different scales, of a different sort. Instead of using very dense polyphony, for example, you could reduce it and have a very spare version. Discursively, the changes will be signposted, but the data could be changed. Such data is completely virtual, since it does not exist—it is purely digital. The numbers contained within the data may correspond to a form of reality. What is really interesting, on the other hand, is interactivity. If the virtual score is triggered by a performer, who plays it on the clarinet, for example, or on the piano, his performance is analyzed in terms of dynamics. Certain dynamics are going to influence the virtual score. Beyond a certain level of dynamics, the virtual score will be changed—let's say it could change scale. Or, equally, the density of the writing. If a performer has a very densely written piece, very fast, then that density in the succession of events will give, for example, a very spare density in the virtual score, thus creating a contrast. If the instrument possesses a rarified density, then the virtual score will be a headlong affair, and so on. It is an alternative form of interactivity. In an installation, it is a fixed interactivity. You move in front of a laser beam, and trigger a modification, or perhaps even a new score, while there, it is the acts of the instrumentalist, an activity which can only take place in the present, which trigger something different in the future score. That is the project, I haven't yet produced it, but I want to.

HUO: So it is an unproduced project. The following is the only question that I ask everybody: do you have any other unproduced projects which are dear to you?

PB: Yes, but that is the one which is the most important, because it puts into play a conception of time and events, of the interaction of time and events and the correspondence of the digital with that which exists.

PP: And then it also mixes the aspects of composition and performance that interest you . . .

PB: That's right. The act of playing can influence the data which has already been built up.

PP: They are time games . . .

PB: Yes, the constraints involved in synchronization pushed me in that direction. I had worked with English electronic composers on commissions for the BBC several times. The score was written in its entirety and the tape had been recorded, so the main preoccupation was the *exact* synchronization of the two. An exact synchronization of both score and tape over ten minutes removes any possible freedom of action for the performer, because your only concern is the synchronization. If you are late, you have to speed up, if you're ahead, you have to slow down, to such an extent that even the most flexible aspects of the musicians' interpretation are subjugated to the timescale of the tape and its written equivalent, leaving no room for intuition. So much so, in fact, that having had this experience, I swore to myself that I would never again put myself under that kind of constraint. It is quite simply the antithesis of musical interpretation in general.

HUO: In your book you deal with the writing of gesture, and you often refer to organization. From that point of view, what is your view on the emergence of the notion of self-organization—which is very much to the fore in different disciplines these days—to what extent does that notion, as well as that of the loss of control, interest you?

PB: Loss of control of what? You are always in control to some extent. And a score always encourages gestures which are not always the same each time, fortunately, but is contained within certain limits. What is a rhythmic signature, for example? You're going to hear a meter which is imposed and cannot be deformed to the point of non-recognition. It is always recognizable even with variations. It was the same in the past: if you had a tone, you heard a false note immediately, since it deviated from the norm that you had established. Nowadays, it is just about the same: there are norms, they might be more flexible or more open in some ways, but they are still norms. When you write music, you can always transpose it or manipulate it, but its properties as an object are already determined. The existence of the object, once it has been established, is stronger than the person who manipulates it, since you can only manipulate it in terms of its dimensions and properties as an object.

HUO: Perhaps, in relation to that idea, you could talk to us about *Marteau sans maître*, about the relationship between knowledge and practice, between understanding and not understanding . . .

PB: Yes, one always thinks that the reading of a text gives you complete freedom, you take it and it is yours. That isn't all, though; a text can only really exist if we look at the internal as well as the external relationships and are not straitjacketed into a digital definition. First, there is a hierarchy of events—for our (Western) music, but also for all the different types of music that I have studied. The frequencies of notes fundamentally exist, there is no doubt about it. You cannot cheat with that. You can entirely transpose music: for example, if a piece has been written throughout in C major, you can play it in D, or in E, the relationships are the same. But the internal hierarchy is more powerful than the transposition that you add. If, for example, you change the intervals, you change the meaning totally. Note frequency is something that requires the greatest discipline. After that, everything is relative, with more or less relativity, in spite of everything. As long as the rhythm depends on a meter, a pulsation, you can control it. And you cannot escape from that pulsation because it dominates you. It might be more flexible: there is a relationship with the digital, but the pulsation, whether regular or irregular, Mozart or Stravinsky, it remains a pulsation. But if you have no pulsation at all, if the spaces are purely graphic, in that case, the eye is a very poor judge, only judging digitally. Your intuition tells you that it is a little longer or a little shorter, but you have no point of reference. The rhythm can be very precise or quite vague; it is not at all like the frequency of notes. The dynamics, though, are uncontrollable. What is a *fortissimo*? Is it a hundred decibels, or ninety, or ninety-five? A *fortissimo* of trumpets is nothing like a *fortissimo* of mandolins, and is not perceived in the same way either. Everything to do with dynamics is beyond control, without even mentioning the acoustics of the concert hall. There are so many parameters that you absolutely cannot be rigorous about that. Besides, this phenomenon is reflected in the developments in musical notation. First and foremost it is fixed on the frequency of note. The relationships are described using nodes. It is not very accurate yet, but the frequencies of notes are described. The first efforts are concentrated on the writing of musical notes. After that, the notes are placed into meter, but much later. In Baroque literature, for example, they didn't write any tempo or dynamics, because they knew that the dynamics were subsidiary. They used dynamics in a sense, but it wasn't very important, sometimes not important at all. The first time that dynamics became important was with Mozart, and above all with Beethoven, who was the first composer to indicate the *sforzato*, the contrasts, and the like. After that, though, it developed very quickly, although timbre came relatively late. In Baroque music, there are a thousand examples in Bach: he changes the instruments, he adapts a piece of music to another context, he changes constantly. While as time goes by, we move toward a precision of timbre. In Schoenberg's third piece, Opus 16, *Farben*, you cannot change it. It is really written using the specific character of each instrument's color. Therefore in the history of musical notation there has been a development of precision or lack of it. It isn't possible to quantify timbre either. It is not continuous. Of course there are timbres which are more or less full-bodied; but even though we might try to establish scales, they are not satisfactory. Apart from the timbre that you play, there is also the ease of articulation, and so on. A lot of factors come into play which make a simple description of the development of timbre difficult to simplify.

HUO: Continuing on the theme of organization and self-organization, on the role of conductor, you say that you are wary of the notion of the "genius" conductor; you also talk about physiology, about the gesture that guides the musicians, without them understanding it . . .

PB: It is both mysterious and not at all. If your gestures are suitable, they work. But it only works, no more, remaining on common ground. It is much more difficult to put personality into the gesture, to know how to ask questions of the musicians, and to induce them to give something else. Because you can be very rigorous and accurate, but the interpretation can still be dead. On the other hand, if you can affect the existence of the musician, without worrying about rigor, then the interpretation can take on a different meaning: it can be exuberant, but completely out of control. You need passion, but at the same time there must be some distance from that passion. There is a form of schizophrenia, split between the desire for expressivity and the control that you want to maintain over things. As far as the public goes, it is even more curious. It is something that one honestly cannot explain—or at least can explain only by using external criteria. But suppose that you were playing a piece for the first time, a new work. The public can feel more or less how well the piece has been rehearsed, if the musicians are on top of their parts. And you ask yourself, why? Probably because of the tone; the more sure the musicians are of themselves, the more they pay attention to the tone. If they are not certain, they either become aggressive or shy. I mean that you will not obtain a fullness of the ensemble's tone. There is that of course, and then there is the visual aspect: if the musicians master their instruments, they are hooked, their body language is different. It is an indicator, but nothing more. It is not enough. You might ask yourself why the public reaction to one piece was so positive even though they knew nothing of it beforehand. It remains a mystery.

PP: Perhaps that is the problem that music poses. It makes me think of something that Clément Rosset said to us recently: that music is a reality in itself . . .

PB: Yes, but you can make comparisons with the help of the existing repertory, with your memories, what you already know, and so on. In the case of a new work, you don't have any point of comparison at the beginning. You have what I call "contracts of confidence." The conductor has chosen a group of musicians and a piece of work: so he believes in the value of both. For that reason, he will trust the musician. But that trust has no real foundation; it is only a calculation and that is really curious. In spite of everything, the contract of confidence means that there are more positive reactions even before you start work. Maintaining that positive reaction when you play the actual piece, though . . .

PP: It is as if the listener, at the time that he hears the new work, situates himself according to a sonic reference. He tunes in.

PB: More or less, yes. People who go to a lot of contemporary music concerts, just like those who see a lot of contemporary art, acquire, not a sixth sense, that would be an exaggeration, but a sort of sharpened judgment. They can be wrong, too. But they are aware that you need to make value judgments, and they have the necessary baggage to make that judgment.

PP: Speaking of the public, you can define modernity as a politics of detachment, in other words as a time when the consequences of acts had only a limited importance—I am thinking of the theories of Ulrich Beck—and the idea that today we are in the midst of the politics of attachment, of the management of the effects of our actions. Has music also been affected by that change?

PB: Well, music has been subjected to that change more than it actually wanted to be. Very contemporary music is destined to have a very restricted audience, obviously. But we don't *want* a very restricted audience, we are forced to accept the situation. Because the principle of invention, of creativity, is not to be obsessed with a larger audience. The main thing is to do something as you believe that it must be done. If it only takes later on, I mean that it doesn't find its audience immediately, too bad. If it does find it straight away, so much the better. It is more "pleasant," but that is it. That doesn't represent any kind of criteria for the work. For me the most important thing is to do what you *must* do, what you think you must do. I am not in favor of saying "I did that. Whether it exists now or in thirty years' or in fifty years' time is all the same to me." I think that a composer, an author, a playwright especially, must try to communicate what he does immediately. That is why I have always hated those arguments and discussions about things that we have neither seen nor heard. How many people can read a score? Very, very few, in the end. When people discuss one's work, I often find that the discussion is based on ideas that have nothing to do with the work itself, as it exists. The discussion is about what others say, or "somebody once heard that," etc. That means that the discussion takes place on a very ... virtual basis. Since my younger days, I have always tried to establish lines of communication. "This is what I have to offer. You can judge it, that is in your power. But you cannot get around my presentation of my work, or if you do, it is because you take it in bad faith."

In my opinion, you must take into account the criteria of good or bad faith. That is why, as soon as I was able to, I organized concerts, initially for my generation (when I was young), then for younger generations, so that it would be possible to debate on the basis of things as they exist and not only their potential existence.

PP: Do you think that a project like the IRCAM would not be feasible today?

PB: It would be more difficult. First because of economic conditions—the necessary generosity no longer exists. And second, because at the time that the IRCAM was founded, there was a French president who was in favor of its creation.

HUO: But there were also others who were involved, ministers ...

PB: Yes, there was Jack Lang, who did become involved, but it was after the establishment of the IRCAM. His contribution was to help the expansion of the IRCAM and that expansion was largely due to Lang. But we owe the project's existence to Pompidou. When a politician is highly cultivated and takes an interest in art forms in general, his political complexion is secondary; I look beyond it. But I am not going to take a position as a musician which denies the importance of politics and the way it affects me. If I am given the opportunity to do something, I do it. I wouldn't say that if Hitler had been the one to give me this opportunity, I would have taken it [laughter]. But in a democracy, though it might veer to the right or to the left, there is a balance, and the fact that antagonistic forces are sometimes in power and sometimes in opposition is one of the strengths of democracy. My relationship with the political world is very clear in that respect. I won't take their side, but if they give me a chance to do something I will. I will say, too, that such things can be above them, as well as above me. If we created the IRCAM, it was neither to build political capital nor for my own personal benefit, but to be able to provide, independently, the tools that they need for the artists who request them.

PP: Do you think that the economic problems of music have become a real constraint today?

PB: Yes, yes. Listen, we have been hearing about a new hall with an auditorium for orchestras that need one, and we still don't have it. The project at La Villette (La Cité de la Musique, in the North of Paris) was complete when it was proposed: three concert halls, the conservatory, the museum, and even an opera. The opera was built elsewhere, OK. But there were still three halls to build. However, after the first petrol crisis and the economic problems that ensued, the budget was cut. And the project remains unfinished, even today. As long as there is no political will, I mean really political—no more will come of it. Mitterrand, in the end, wasn't interested, neither was Jospin, so, nothing happened. Right now, Chirac has other problems, Raffarin too, so ... You know, it is very symbolic. There are two very big cultural projects at the moment, since yesterday in particular: the restoration of Versailles, in other words of heritage. Because it is visible on a global scale, it gets the money, and everything is considered on a large scale: seventeen years ahead of time! And second, the road and rail infrastructure, etc. That is a project over the next twenty-five years! With enormous sums of money earmarked. But for music, they don't give a toss! They really couldn't give a toss! At least for now ...

HUO: It is the same for contemporary art ...

PP: Politicians are preoccupied by the restoration of heritage ...

HUO: So you have built up a network of political contacts in relation with the music world in France. There was, among the politicians, another that you knew, Michel Guy ...

PB: Yes. Of the two culture ministers who really were *culture* ministers, because they really were interested—and didn't use it as a jumping off point for their political ambitions elsewhere, there was Jack Lang and Michel Guy. Lang had a very good idea at the end; becoming both the minister of culture and the education minister, thus linking the two, which had been, and once again are, completely separated. It didn't last for very long, since he only held the two positions simultaneously for two years and didn't have enough time to develop projects. Then there was Michel Guy, who didn't belong to the political world, even if he was right-wing. He was Chirac's minister, but Valéry Giscard-D'Estaing was behind his appointment. And Michel Guy was in his element, he knew everybody, he was very familiar with contemporary painting and painters, he knew a great deal about the contemporary art world. He was one of those people who were interested in music without having the disadvantage of only discovering that interest at the last moment—he was interested well before he became a minister. As a result, we could open up a real dialogue with him. It was the same with Lang. He understood what we were saying. Because sometimes, you would find that the minister (from both the right and the left) would listen to you as though you were speaking double-Dutch! You were completely off their radar. Catherine Tasca was also very well informed, but she took the job in a preelection period and was unable to do anything concrete, especially as she had a Prime Minister (Jospin) who didn't help her at all. She was buried; despite all her good ideas and good intentions, she wasn't in a position to decide. If Bercy (the Finance ministry) and the Prime Minister aren't interested, the culture minister is powerless. The great advantage of Michel Guy and then Lang was to have the ear of their president. Lang remained for a very long time, because the various elections protected him, but Michel Guy lasted for two years and as the effects of Giscard's election faded, Michel Guy disappeared. We can see the same thing with Jean-Jacques Aillagon right now: people without any political weight, those who are unelected are sidelined by ministers who have a political base because they are elected.

HUO: Maybe we could watch the film now?

PP: Yes, fine.

HUO: I was wondering, where can I find copies of your scores?

PB: They are published by Universal in Vienna. I have been with Universal since 1952.

PP: And the scores of the scores?

PB: Well, those, I can let you have them from here.

PP: I am quite interested in the idea of the score of the score.

HUO: In fact, how is the collaboration with Gehry going; it is going to be published by Domus. The museum agreed to let us use it. We only need Gehry's reply, but that is only a formality.

PB: In addition to that, right after the festival de Lucerne, we are going to be involved in a public debate. You have got to admit that his Los Angeles project is sensational. I have known him for twenty-five years. We were friends before he became so famous ... besides, even though he has become so well known, it hasn't changed him at all.

Ibrahim Quraishi

Trucks race across the dusty roads and highways through the pathologically heightened Utopia known as the *Ummah*,[1] honking endlessly through the imposed architectural structures of so many informationally perplexed urban squalors inside much of Muslim landscape. Blaring radios, yes or no? Women veiled but voices unveiled. The magnification of mimetic form: the scale is synthetic or syncopated, in a way those inside the squalors are totally incapable of *Hakam*.[2]

The mindset, every source of music comes from the Qur'an. Inside Islam, music is one of the most controversial flash points. The *Adh'an*[3]—a call to prayer—is a mechanical reproduction in search of a moment, the density of blankness within a mindset looking outside the Minaret filled with electrical pulses, loops going over and over for 1,500 years, more in syncopated reverb.

The gap between the external and internal, the rational critique inside the sounds of the *Adh'an*. One language in collaboration and standardization of the 99 names of God. Divine in their self-embodiment, the *Ijmah's*[4] aversion to technology beyond the *Adh'an*, is the very negation of cultural fluidity of a sonic Islam, a mixed loop, a *djing* of sorts. Organically adapted, accepted, or evolved through the complicated web of indigenous cultures and sounds, classical Islam embraced those forms, pulses, fluids, rhythmic patterns that were not afraid of producing emotional senses and frequencies, neurologically linking the body and mind. It is here, in a mere space of 500 years of *Dar al–Islam*,[5] that classical mixes and remixes brought the *Dhikr Madh* (vocal meeting), chanting with *Kiai Kanjeng* (Islamic Gamelan music from Indonesia) to *Sama'* or *Inshad*, those vocalized poems sung in Sufi gatherings in contrast to *Litanies* (the remembrance form), called for example *Khatm-e Khwajegan*, originally from the Naqshbandi Order through Sufi Rhythms for the Daf passing right through Kawali. These are just a few examples of an age where hybridity occurred openly across those lands dominated by the call of the *Adh'an*.

Sound as commodity: it is the extension of the mosque. Sound as a mode of consciousness generates a state of suspension. Sound as a means of social interaction inhabits the exotic transactions of a *Medina*[6] inside the reflective threads of the Aristotelian logic that gave Islam her sense of *logos*. Decision to debate represents the counterpunch to the vocal *fatwas*, the crystallization of human thought. Experts on, for, off, by, with, or against Islam agree that the Qur'an represents the permissibility of music. The Word itself is Divine: The Qur'an.

The Arabic word *Musiqa* or *Musika* by contrast generates a narrow sense of control. *Musiqa* can be said to represent the popular folk, pop, and especially classical instrumental transaction, frivolous in its consistency. The *Adh'an* and Qur'anic recitations stand as the modes of the Islamic conciseness, its divine medium.

The consensual concentric circles within the Five Pillars of Islam break the sonic negation beyond the *Adh'an*, the ongoing toxic drive, that has become often too lyrical, imprisoning culture in the process of the tonal consensus.

The *Adh'an* is a reflective mix (or in most cases an outdated remix), understood or misunderstood by those who most advocate it, promote it, and demand it as the sole vehicle of spinal thought, demanding that a singular form can be the embodiment, the neurological nexus of all movement and form.

Notes

1. *Ummah*: The Muslim community.

2. *Hakam*: Sound judgment.

3. *Adh'an*: Heard five times a day, the major public genre of Islamic music.

4. *Ijmah*: Consensus that gives legitimacy to a legal decision.

5. *Dar al–Islam*: Territory under Islam.

6. *Medina*: The center.

Catherine Corman

Joseph Cornell's box sculptures represent muted worlds, where the only people are images collaged onto the back wall, disappearing into the paint. Movement is hinted at by the suspension of movement: two wooden balls nearly touch. Wooden birds sit frozen, glancing sideways through a glass wall.

Poets are drawn to the quality of silence in Cornell's work. John Ashbery, Octavio Paz, and Charles Simic have all written of it. Ashbery felt Cornell's work recovered from childhood "the dazzling, single knowledge we get from the first things we see in life, things we look at daily and come to know through long, silent experience."[1] He describes a sort of contemplative wisdom born of reflection, rather than the worldliness of a man of action who has traded innocence for experience.

The duration and the quiet of Cornellian understanding allows for a return to wonder. Objects never really became objects, but retained hidden mythic qualities, which Cornell the magician (as Ashbery calls him) restores to the patient viewer. In this brief passage on silent experience, Ashbery pays homage to Cornell's subtlety. Unlike the provocative grand gesture more common in late-twentieth-century art, Cornell's work rewards, and almost commands, the stillness of solitary reflection.

In his poem "Objects and Apparitions" dedicated to Cornell, Octavio Paz writes, "You constructed / boxes where things hurry away from their names." Paz finds Cornell's images excessive to language. They shed whatever words try to attach themselves and exist on a plane speech cannot touch.

Cornell's work has often been called literary, and Paz also writes of the transformative power of Cornell's art, changing ideas into sculptures, leaving words behind. Paz writes, "Joseph Cornell: inside your boxes / my words became visible for a moment."[2] Their visual poetry touches Paz the poet, for whom meaning is primarily constructed through language.

In his book of poetic meditations on the art of Joseph Cornell, Charles Simic (1992) writes, "Empty space and silence. The city like a chessboard on which the few remaining figures are motionless and unnamed. Inside the white buildings, more empty space and silence." Cornell's later sculptures were almost bare. Sometimes a few small pieces of white wood were the only objects. Again, quiet connotes solitude: an interior space hinted at by the "few figures," their stillness, and the silence endlessly surrounding them.

On another page of the same book Simic writes, "The near darkness of old movies is that of dreams.... Images surrounded by shadow and silence. Silence is that vast, cosmic church in which we always stand alone."

Simic describes the expanse of silence, calling it "vast, cosmic." It is as if Cornell uses silence as a key to the universe, taking us beyond one location with its specific, identifying sounds, to an unlimited space of devotion— what Simic calls the "cosmic church."

Cornell created a fragile, oneiric cinema, which, in its silence, offers the impression of solitude Simic feels in Cornell's work. Cornell spliced and reconfigured old films to create poetic narratives, hinting at internal life, receding from action in the world.

Cornell's first collage film, often called his masterpiece, was *Rose Hobart* (1936). Most of the footage comes from the 1931 jungle melodrama, *East of Borneo*. In the original film, a young American woman, played by the actress Rose Hobart, travels to the jungles of Borneo to find her husband, who is now the personal doctor to a Sorbonne-educated jungle prince. The prince tries to seduce Rose, and she tries to rescue her husband.

Cornell has removed the plot of the film almost entirely. He edited the hour-and-twenty-minute film down to twenty minutes. With all the action gone, what remains are interstitial moments: a loaded glance, a glass being lifted, palm trees swaying in the wind. He removed the sound, slowed the film down to silent speed, and played a record of Brazilian music while projecting it.

Brian Frye (2001) describes the combined effect of erased sound, deceleration of image, and the addition of exotic music: "As a result, the characters

move with a peculiar, lugubrious lassitude, as if mired deep in a dream."
P. Adams Sitney (2002) writes, "By stripping it of its dialogue and mood
music, he transformed its banality into an oneiric mystery.... By projecting
Rose Hobart at silent speed, Cornell retarded the gestures and action of *East of
Borneo*, not enough to make them look like slow motion, but to lend them
a nuance of elegance and protraction." Cornell plays the film at silent speed
while restoring to it the poetic qualities of silent film.

He turned a jungle action picture into an underwater ballet, a fragmented
tropical dream. Smoldering passions that once drove the film are now only
hinted at by a glimpse of a volcano behind a curtain, a crocodile descending
into water, a line of dancing girls in sarongs.

Jonas Mekas believes Cornell's films are "so unimposing that it's no wonder
his movies have escaped, have slipped by unnoticed through the grosser sensibilities of the viewer, the sensibilities of men who need strong and loud
bombardment of their senses to perceive anything."[3] But when Cornell first
screened the film, it hardly slipped past the notice of one prominent audience
member. Salvador Dalí knocked over the projector in rage, ending the screening. Legend has it he yelled, "Joseph Cornell, you are a plagiarist of my mind."
Dalí, at the forefront of the avant-garde, had conceptualized such a film, but
had not yet mentioned it to anyone. Cornell, a reclusive young man from
Queens, had made work that threatened an artist he called "a master." Aside
from Dalí and his wife, no one in the room that night understood what had
happened.

Joseph Cornell once wrote a paean to the sublime nature of silent film, in
the form of an appreciation of the actress Hedy Lamarr, who he felt retained
some of the elusive qualities of that extinct medium. Published in *View* magazine, it was titled "Enchanted Wanderer." This essay gives us a clue to what
Cornell did that so startled Dalí, but remained incomprehensible to others.

Cornell begins "Enchanted Wanderer" with this passage:

Among the barren wastes of the talking films there occasionally occur passages to remind one again of the profound and suggestive power of the silent film to evoke an
ideal world of beauty, to release unsuspected floods of music from the gaze of a human
countenance in its prison of silver light.

Silence allows for poetry. The intrusion of sound destroys the possibility of
subtlety and suggestion, the formal communication of an ideal. Speech creates
a "barren waste." The "mute gaze" is profound and overwhelming because
unlike speech, silence can ascend to the sublime.

Cornell continues:

But aside from evanescent fragments unexpectedly encountered, how often is there
created a superb and magnificent imagery such as brought to life the portraits of Fal-
conetti in "Joan of Arc," Lillian Gish in "Broken Blossoms," Sibirskaya in "Menil-
montant," and Carola Nehrer in "Dreigroschenoper."

It is significant that he calls these "portraits." Cornell's assistant and collaborator, Stan Brakhage, describes the film *Rose Hobart* as an expression of
Cornell's adoration for the actress Rose Hobart. He calls the film a communication of her essence as a human being: in other words, a portrait.

Rose's image is constantly on the screen. Cornell's film is so exclusively
about Rose that we rarely see any other person with whom she is speaking.
The camera barely lifts its gaze from her.

Brakhage writes:

[Cornell] took this movie, and . . . cut it down to what he cared about the most. . . . He
began making it a film really about the deepest of all possible problems that women
can have and how desperate their situation is, and the magics that they have and how
fragile those are, and made a piece that's, I think, one of the greatest poems of being a
woman that's ever been made in film, or maybe anywhere. This is like carving out
slowly the deep essence of this movie that he could see because of his love of Rose
Hobart.[4]

In Brakhage's understanding, Cornell took *East of Borneo*, and pared away
everything that was not an expression of the essence of Rose Hobart. Michel-
angelo is thought to have said, "To determine the essential parts of a sculpture, roll it down a hill. The inessential parts will break off." This is what
Joseph Cornell did with *East of Borneo*. What remained was Rose Hobart.

As Cornell's "Enchanted Wanderer" continues, he writes,

And so we are grateful to Hedy Lamarr, the enchanted wanderer, who again speaks the
poetic and evocative language of the silent film, if only in whispers at times, beside
the empty roar of the sound track.

By removing the invasive soundtrack of East of Borneo, Cornell lets Rose
speak through "mute gaze" alone. He erases the "empty roar" that might interfere with understanding her fragile, soundless communication. No longer
speaking in dense, clumsy language, Rose is rescued from the mundane jungle
drama and restored to the realms of poetry.

Sitney (2002) interprets "Enchanted Wanderer" as it relates to *Rose Hobart*:

[T]wo principles of cinema emerge: that facial expression and gesture are its essential
language and, more crucially, that the coming of sound has destroyed the immanent

spiritual music of films.... In this difficult time for cinema—the era of the sound film—the "poetic and evocative language" can appear only in "evanescent fragments" and their "realms of wonder" are necessarily mediated by the memory of silent films.

Cornell understands that Rose is a spiritual heiress to the world of silent film. She is somehow misplaced in a sound film, and, as he did for tragic historical figures such as Lorenzo de Medici and Paolo and Francesca in his sculptures, in this film he rescues her. Silence will reveal her spirit.

Paz has called Cornell's sculpture a "theater of the spirits."[5] *Rose Hobart* is almost literally that. Cornell has created a ballet in which the only dancer is the spirit of Rose Hobart as he perceived it.

Toward the end of "Enchanted Wanderer," Cornell writes, "Like those portraits of Renaissance youths she has slipped effortlessly into the role of a painter herself." This is the secret of Cornell's collage film. He is not painting a portrait of Rose; he is collaborating with her to create her self-portrait. He helps her do this by editing out what is not Rose, by removing the sounds of the outside world, even by removing her own voice—her communication with other people, external reality. All we have left is interior experience, a patiently sketched watercolor of inner life.

The film opens not with a shot of Rose Hobart, nor even with footage from *East of Borneo*, but with a shot of people looking through binoculars at something beyond the frame. This is a reference to Eugene Atget's photograph, *The Eclipse*, once the cover of the journal *Surrealist Revolution*.

In Atget's photograph a crowd stands on a bridge looking at an eclipse occurring outside the frame. They have no idea that they are the subjects of a photograph. From their collective action, we gather they think the subject is elsewhere: in the sky. But the subject becomes the crowd, the direction of their gaze, the way they watch the eclipse. They unwittingly give us a glimpse of themselves in natural positions, not posing for the camera, but engaging with their environment.

Walter Benjamin (1979) identified Atget as a proto-Surrealist because his photographs implied "a salutary estrangement between man and his surroundings." In this photograph, the object of the crowd's gaze is extraordinarily distant, completely unreachable. They are focused intently on something they can never touch.

Atget and the crowd are analogous to Joseph Cornell and Rose Hobart. Cornell selects those moments of the film when Rose reveals herself, when hidden emotion and vulnerability emerge, as if she were caught unaware like the crowd on the bridge. And Cornell's subject, however devoted to her he may be, will always remain beyond his grasp. He is not interested ultimately in the image of Rose Hobart, or even the living woman, but her spirit, the mystery of her existence.

Writing about "Enchanted Wanderer," Sitney (2002) calls Hedy Lamarr "a metaphor for the mediation of the broken and fragmented sound cinema. Identification with her dramatizes the cinephile's eagerness and distance from what is attracting him or her." In the case of Rose Hobart, Cornell is attracted to what is ultimately distant from him: the interior life of another human being.

In order to approach this, his first step was to remove the sounds of the world. By silencing the actors, the sound effects, and the ambient noise of the locations in the film, Cornell gave it a glaze of interiority. We are further removed from the actual world of the film, and retreat into contemplation of it.

The heroine, whose words were futile, and the prince, whose words were deadly, are both changed to mute figures moving around the screen. Their verbal battles become ballets of yearning without any clear objective. We see Rose in almost every shot, and so identify with her perspective. We have moved from the world of the film to the world of Rose Hobart.

As Frye (2001) writes, "the world appears as a sort of strange theatre, staged for her alone." Cornell works his magic. Her expressions of emotion are collaged together until we are overwhelmed with images of Rose Hobart feeling. This becomes, as Brakhage said, the subject of the film.

The images are overlaid with exotic music building slowly in complexity and tension, then relaxing back to its original strains. When Cornell screened the film, he would alternate between both sides of the same record, creating a sound collage to match the film collage on screen.

The intermittent rupture is momentarily jarring, but the music soon flows back into the environment of the film, as palm trees cast dark shadows and native men carry torches along the river. The exotic is this Hollywood version of a jungle, but it is also Rose Hobart herself, the unreachable continent. Like the music, Rose is beautiful and haunting, intriguing but unstable. If we feel we are approaching her, the scene shifts abruptly, the music flips to the other side of the record.

Just as silence allowed access to interiority, so music was a route to inner life. Cornell's assistant Larry Jordan says, "Music was important to Cornell. He talked as much about that as anything else. He talked about a man he'd known who was a violinist who played Debussy in a certain way … it was something special, the way that this man was inside the real Debussy."[6]

The record *Brazilian Holiday* does not itself transport us to the inner depths of Rose Hobart's being. It does not lead us "inside the real" Rose Hobart. But it paves the way, bringing a dreamlike ambience to the film, preparing us for something foreign and captivating.

Sitney (2002) calls Cornell's films "the area where the conscious and the unconscious meet." As Cornell played the record—slowing it down and flipping it back and forth unexpectedly—it was the soundtrack for the meeting of conscious and unconscious, for the uncertain terrain leading from a person's existence in the exterior world to the dark, mysterious interior.

Jonas Mekas writes that Cornell's films have "something to do with retracing our feelings, our thoughts, our dreams, our states of being on some other, very fine dimension from where they can reflect back to us in the language of the music of the spheres."[7] In *Rose Hobart*, Cornell collages together a portrait of the unknowable woman, whose interior life remains forever elusive.

In his essay "On Dolls," Rilke imagined a child dying, clutching a doll. In his scene, a tiny soul arises in the doll to mirror, or witness, the disappearing soul of the child. So, in *Rose Hobart*, Joseph Cornell mutes the exterior world to more clearly witness the ephemeral spirit of another person. The faltering appearance of her spirit forms a silent mirror, faintly, tentatively, reflecting his own.

Notes

1. Quoted in Mary Ann Caws, *Joseph Cornell's Theater of the Mind* (New York: Thames and Hudson, 1993).

2. Octavio Paz, "Objects and Apparitions," in *A Joseph Cornell Album*, ed. Dore Ashton (New York: Viking Press, 1974).

3. Jonas Mekas, "The Invisible Cathedrals of Joseph Cornell," in *A Joseph Cornell Album*.

4. Stan Brakhage interview on the DVD-ROM, *The Magical Worlds of Joseph Cornell* (Washington, D.C.: The Voyager Foundation, 2003), published as a companion to *Joseph Cornell: Shadowplay … Eterniday* (New York: Thames and Hudson, 2003).

5. Octavia Paz, "Objects and Apparitions."

6. Larry Jordan interview on the DVD-ROM, *The Magical Worlds of Joseph Cornell*.

7. Jonas Mekas, "The Invisible Cathedrals of Joseph Cornell."

References

Ashton, Dore (1974). *A Joseph Cornell Album*. New York: Viking.

Benjamin, Walter (1979). *One-Way Street and Other Writings*. London: Verso.

Caws, Mary Ann (1993). *Joseph Cornell's Theater of the Mind*. New York: Thames and Hudson.

Cornell, Joseph (1941–42). "Enchanted Wanderer: Excerpt from a Journey Album for Hedy Lamarr." *View* 1, no. 9–10.

Frye, Brian (2001). "*Rose Hobart*." Available at http://sensesofcinema.com.

Joseph Cornell: Shadowplay ... Eterniday (2003). New York: Thames and Hudson.

Lehrman, Robert (2003). *The Magical Worlds of Joseph Cornell* (DVD-ROM). Washington, D.C.: Voyager Foundation.

McShine, Kynaston (1996). *Joseph Cornell*. New York: Museum of Modern Art.

Perry, Idris, ed. (1995). *Essays on Dolls*. New York: Viking.

Rilke, Rainer Maria (1959). "On Dolls." In *Rilke: Samtliche Werke*, vol. 5. Ed. Ernst Zinn. Insel-Verlag.

Simic, Charles (1992). *Dime-Store Alchemy*. Hopewell: Ecco Press.

Sitney, P. Adams (2002). *Visionary Film: The American Avant-Garde, 1943–2000*. Oxford: Oxford University Press.

Jaron Lanier

I'm 41 now so I've decided I need to develop my grumpy side. So here's a rant about the sorry state of pop music.

There's a question I've been asking myself for about a decade: Why can't kids make up their own styles of music these days? They seem to be stuck listening to their parents' music for the first time since electrification.

I'm only talking about big-time commercial music in the United States. Of course music is gloriously seething in odd corners of the planet as it should. But it's important to be concerned with the state of pop culture in industrialized countries. These cultures are made of human beings just like other cultures and something has gone awry in the last decade or so.

Of course I am free to try to ignore this problem. I can team up with some compatible friends and we can go find or make our own music in any of a number of accommodating environments—on the Net, in the forest, or in some dank club late at night. But pop culture is important. It drags us all along with it; it is our shared fate. We can't simply remain aloof.

I must be clear about the nature of my grumpiness: I'm not complaining about how crummy the new pop music is. If only! I'm complaining that there is no new pop music to complain about.

Yes, there are new bands, but they almost always sound just like old bands—really old bands. "Mainstream" (white) kids are listening to the youth music of the baby boomers, which at this point is often the music their grandparents listened to. They accept either the originals or pale contemporary copies. Black or "urban" music hasn't been stuck in freeze frame for as long, but it's still stuck.

Pop music can be grand. Louis Armstrong was a pop star, as was Jimi Hendrix. I'm even happy to stand up and risk the wrath of some of my cynical music-world friends and say I enjoy and respect a lot of what's on the radio today. I just went out to get a burrito and Destiny's Child was playing while I waited. I like Destiny's Child, but how different are they from, say, En Vogue? We're talking about a difference in dates of well over a decade. Now, I'm not trying to equate the two groups. I like Destiny's Child better, for the plain-truth lyrics, the fun production, and the great voices. But still: Think about Aretha and then think about what was happening ten years before her. It was a different universe. The very idea of what music was for had shifted. Think about the Beatles and think about what was around ten years before them. We are not seeing motion today, just churn.

Once again, I want to be clear about what I'm lamenting here. I'm not whining about how crummy the latest pop music is. I'm whining about how there isn't any latest pop music.

If I thought the problem was that new pop music was schlocky or low quality or too mean-spirited or something like that, I'd still probably bitch and moan for the pleasure of it, but there would be less reason to take me seriously.

Schlock, for instance, annoys me, but the annoyance only runs so deep. It's only a minor infraction. Only people can make schlock. A bird can't be schlocky when it sings, but a person can. So we can take existential pride in schlock, and even view it as a safe outlet for Nietzschean urges. Ego and schlock go well together—from Nietzsche's beloved Wagner to Worldwide Wrestling.

If only I could complain about the schlocky music the kids are listening to! My discontent is instead with the lack of contents.

What the hell's going on?

Well, here's a roundup of six familiar theories:

(1) The first is that kids who grow up with digital technology instinctively seek to remix established cultural fragments as their method of experience and enjoyment. Pop semiotics is their natural language. After all, the last genuinely new styles (such as hip-hop) were based on remixing.

This is the optimistic view. I want to believe it—I've wanted to believe it for over a decade. So far, though, whatever might be happening along these lines underground doesn't seem to be potent enough to move a new generation to transcend the retro stupor.

One sad problem might be that we've discovered that the language of reuse just doesn't communicate well enough. It's one thing to artfully remix some old R&B artist, but something very different to just rehash old music. Somehow the former seems to degrade into the latter too easily and quickly, so that you miss the smart stuff if you blink.

We might have an "odd bedfellows" situation here, as when Feminists and Fundamentalists joined together to fight porn. There's a natural economic affinity between postmodern academic types and some stinky weasel at a label who wants to be able to remarket some old tape in the vault. Both of them will promote recontextualization.

But that brings us to another theory that might be more important ...

(2) The second theory is that the music industry is powerful enough to determine what happens, and it is devoid of imagination, courage, faith, or vitality. It is populated by frustrated boomer executives who wanted to be rock stars in their youths and failed. They put their own neurotic superstitions ahead even of their greed, but they're too powerful to realize that they're doing it, because competition can't get in the cracks to wake them up. They have shut down the evolution of popular music.

Musicians believe this one. All of us have heard brilliant demos from kids who ought to be the new superstars but were shut out of the labels because some stiff idiot with power "couldn't see how to market them."

Don't even get me started on the labels. I'm sure you know the drill by heart. They put out crap no one wants to buy and then blame Napster.

Speaking of which: Napster could be the key piece of the puzzle here. Maybe it was the solvent the next nascent pop music was waiting for. Maybe it was the new electric guitar and the new Marshall-stack-in-waiting.

I can't help but wonder what would have happened if Napster, or something like it, had been allowed to gain some critical level of momentum. I think we might have seen a genuinely new pop music emerge from it.

Then I would have had to find something else to rant about.

(3) Another possibility is that we don't trust our own authenticity anymore. We're trapped in bourgeois banality. Maybe when you get up to the tippy top, vertigo-inducing, highest altitudes of Maslow's old hierarchy, it's mostly the quest for authenticity from a distant external source that drives people to listen to music.

So Moby samples old blues guys. The old-timey soundtrack album for *O Brother, Where Art Thou?* becomes a rare mega-seller in a period of moribund record sales. (By the way, notice how people still buy CDs in a case like this when they like the music. The record industry's Napster mania is such a crock.)

But back to our theory number three: Maybe some vague, almost mythic interval from the 1960s into part of the 1970s was the last time well-off people in industrialized countries felt authentic.

It feels plausible, but I don't buy it entirely.

If this theory were right, then you would expect to see not just good music, but shocking new styles of music arise from more recent shocking new anxieties and possibilities, just as they did in the 1960s, and in each decade before. The last new styles (like hip-hop) were responses to digital technology, the degeneration of the urban experience, and many other things, but by now hip-hop is, dare I say it, getting more than a little old.

Hey, I want to digress for a moment to talk about hip-hop. Outside of hip-hop, digital music usually comes off as sterile and bland. Listen to a lot of what comes out of the university "computer music" world or new age ambient music and you'll hear what I mean. Digital production usually has an overly regular beat because it comes out of a looper or a sequencer. And because it uses samples, you hear identical microstructure in sounds again and again, making it seem as if the world were not alive while the music was playing. But hip-hop pierced through this problem in a shocking way. It turns out these same deficits can be turned around and used to express anger with incredible intensity. A sample played again and again expresses a feeling of stuckness and frustration, as does the regular beat. Hip-hop was a great example of a new technology inspiring new aesthetic invention that expressed its time in a way that went beyond words. That's what I'm talking about when I'm talking about a new style!

But as I say, more time has passed since hip-hop soared out of the box than passed between, for example, the big band era and Motown.

Where are the new musical styles that respond to AIDS, biotechnology, globalization, or terrorism? The pop musical responses to 9/11 were a resurgence of the song "America the Beautiful" and a particularly lame Paul McCartney single.

And here is where I think we can't entirely separate ourselves, no matter how esoteric or oppositional we might care to frame ourselves, from what we observe in pop music. I live right by the poor WTC and I've seen some musical response in the neighborhood, but astonishingly little. It's as if the cultural response mechanism has atrophied from lack of use.

(BTW, I made dark music after 9/11—you know I live right by the poor WTC—an example is a track that I recorded with the flute player Robert Dick, mostly on instruments that were damaged in the attack. Might be worth compiling tracks from the neighborhood from that period.)

(4) Another potential culprit is the anemic and mean-spirited culture of the "high arts" educational and other institutions. Most young people from industrialized countries interested in music have at least a brush with a music department at a university or, outside of the United States, with a public arts funding agency. The elitism, nepotism, back stabbing, and ass kissing that saturate such institutions are highly traditional and seem to have served past musical epochs reasonably well. What is new in the last fifty years or so is the aversion to joy, the arms race of cynicism.

Maybe this is an institutional reflection of the authenticity problem. If your music teacher doesn't believe in music or in his or her soul, then careerism is all that's left.

Another idea is that back in the early-to-mid-twentieth century academic and institutional arts people wanted to feel more like scientists, who were winning the prestige game, and so they tried to create a more "technical" culture, where emotion mattered less, and where it was hard to understand, appreciate, or do anything. A lot of these posers got into permanent power and we still haven't recovered.

So the theory would be that a critical number of kids get infected with the attitude and are nullified.

(5) Then there are the systemic arguments. Here's the simplest version: Once you have the possibility of making a lot of money from something, you have to become more conservative about taking risks because more is at stake. You also have more to gain by trying to squeeze out competition, at least from the attention of the audience, if not from actual access. That's why television seems to get less varied and lower quality on average as more cable stations are added.

Thus the music industry pushes clichés and kills alternatives because of market pressure, and the only way to fix it is to change the way markets work, or the relationship of music to capitalism. According to this theory, it doesn't have anything to do with the individuals who happen to have power in the music business or government right now; anyone would be drawn into the same bad behavior if they were in the same positions.

These are devilish difficulties. You can have a population of wonderful authentic and starving musicians living RIGHT THERE in the middle of a huge population of potential fans seeking authenticity in music, a frustrated population that dutifully pays monthly cable and online bills without finding what they seek, and yet there doesn't seem to be a way to connect the two groups together.

(6) And yet another possibility: This state of affairs isn't "post" anything. It's the normal coming of age of a culture. We denizens of postmodernity now have a canon just as every culture before us has had. There's nothing new or unusual about that. It took us a few centuries to get here and now we've arrived. We don't need no new culture.

There aren't too many deep conflicts between the theories I've assembled above. They can for the most part all be true at the same time.

I guess I've reached the word count you're looking for, so this is the place to stop. But I simply wouldn't know what to say next anyway. I'm perplexed!

Afterword: The Rhythm of History

Jeff Chang

The life of a people and a culture, master musician Gilberto Gil once said, is produced through an permanent, uninterrupted process of transformation. But at some points in history, change accelerates like a motive wind. In these moments fences fall and creativity is freed; the ridiculed and the ridiculous suddenly resemble prophets and blueprints.

Change is not always good. Americans like to believe Martin Luther King, Jr.'s hopeful dictum that the arc of our universe bends toward justice. Yet how much of our morning-dew optimism comes from our refusal of a bloody imperial past, under which are buried bodies of native knowledges and traditions?

It is not that, as Tony Kushner's right-wing true believer Joe Pitt argues, "The rhythm of history is conservative."[1] If we were really listening, history would sound like a New Orleans second-line, slow in tempo now but perhaps faster later, interlocking, inclusive, rhythms multiplying, ancient and futuristic at the same time. (The remix, after all, is nothing new.) As the march to justice passes down our streets, it is as much a work of recovery and restoration as of forward motion.

The world in which the artist works is that of the barely heard and the hardly seen, the one, as Afrika Baby Bambaataa of the Jungle Brothers put it, "so dirty you didn't want to deal with it, so funky you didn't want to get with it."[2] The creative process is birthed from the places that too much of society doesn't want to see by the people too many don't want to recognize. Then the spectacle is celebrated, not the work. Artists and art making are alienated from their art.

For decades the de facto cultural policy in America has been to confuse the culture industry with the source of creativity, to abandon the production, promotion, distribution and enjoyment of arts and culture to the dictates of the boom–bust marketplace. The result has been the spread of "lifestyle economies" that are merely new forms of monoculturalism and the rise of an environment increasingly antithetical to creativity. A wave of deregulation in the culture industry has consolidated distribution channels and destroyed local scenes, locked away sources of inspiration behind fences of "rights management" and copyright and favored a "blockbuster or die" approach that raises barriers to entry and creates diseconomies of scale. Call it the privatization of the imagination.

In 1963, President John F. Kennedy honored the poet Robert Frost by celebrating his contrarianness. "The great artist is thus a solitary figure," Kennedy said. "In pursuing his perceptions of reality, he must often sail against the currents of his time. This is not a popular role."[3] Amid the cold war, Kennedy argued the artist was indispensable to democratic society precisely because his dissent strengthened it. Where the nonconformist Russian or Chinese artist would be repressed, the American artist would be welcomed in from the cold. The NEA was one fruit of this consensus.

But as the cold war waned, right-wingers began to describe artists as a disease to the state. Artists were not just outsiders; they were unpatriotic, overprivileged, and antisocial. They certainly didn't deserve our tax money. Better to let them find their way in the marketplace. (Some of them did, and this is another complex discussion.) Kennedy's script had been flipped, and the culture wars began. This conservative backlash, combined with rampant corporate consolidation, plunged artists into a dark era.

In its disdain for creativity, the United States has stood almost alone. Many countries recognize the centrality of artists and culture as an economic stimulus and social glue. In 2003, in his first speech as Brazil's minister of culture, Gilberto Gil stated that his aims were to forge "the opening of territory for creativity and new popular languages," ensure "the availability of space for adventure and daring," and secure "the space of memory and invention." His storied tenure left a framework for a new-millennium cultural policy, one that preserved national arts legacies, seeded new-generation movements such as hip-hop arts and activism, tried to balance corporate interests with individual expression, and promoted a radically connecting spirit of diversity.

Against less accommodating conditions, U.S. artists didn't stop trying to find their way. Hardship engendered a defiance, an impatience. "Waiting around for my shell to crack," said Baby Bam just at the moment the NEA was imploding. "After that you can't hold me back." So they tugged the national unconscious forward, plying a fearless, sometimes even unruly kind of polyculturalism. By the final months of the 2008 election season, they had secured Obama as the waking image of hope and change.

Now in this moment of flux, it's fair to ask the question we have not stopped to answer for a generation: Why must we estrange our artists? Artists develop new forms of knowledge and consciousness. They open new perceptive windows. Creativity does not only enable individual, but social transformation. It jump-starts the engine of change, the kind of change that Dr. King might recognize. What are the possibilities available to us if we truly set artists free to propel us—our pulses locking together in a loud joyful noise—toward the justice at the end of that great arc?

May 2009

Notes

1. Tony Kushner, *Angels in America*, part II: *Perestroika* (New York: Theatre Communications Group, 1993), p. 204.

2. "Beyond This World," from Jungle Brothers, *Done by the Forces of Nature* (Warner Bros. Records, 1989).

3. http://www.arts.gov/about/Kennedy.html.

Contributors

David Allenby is Head of Publicity and Marketing at Boosey & Hawkes, a classical music publishing and rights group.

Pierre Boulez is both a composer and a conductor. He has taught musical analysis, composition, and conducting. He was for several years a professor at the Collège de France (Paris). As a researcher, he organized IRCAM, l'Institut de Recherche et de Coordination Acoustique/Musique (the Institute for Acoustical/Musical Research and Coordination). He is also the author of many books and essays.

Jeff Chang is an author, journalist, and activist. His first book, *Can't Stop Won't Stop: A History of the Hip-Hop Generation*, won the American Book Award and the Asian American Literary Award, among other awards. He was also the editor of *Total Chaos: The Art and Aesthetics of Hip-Hop*. He was a founding editor of *ColorLines* magazine and cofounded the influential hip-hop indie label, SoleSides, now Quannum Projects. He was a 2008 USA Ford Fellow in Literature and a winner of the 2008 North Star News Prize. His next book is *Who We Be: The Colorization of America*.

Artists **Beth Coleman** and **Howard Goldkrand** began collaborating in 1995 with the SoundLab Cultural Alchemy project, a nomadic, multimedia installation and event (www.soundlab.org). Coleman and Goldkrand work with sculpture, installation, sound, code, and text. Their collaborative and individual projects have been exhibited internationally in venues such as Whitney Museum of American Art, P.S.1 Museum of Contemporary Art, New Museum of Contemporary Art, Mirror's Edge international exhibition, James Cohan Gallery, the Venice Biennale 2004, ARC/Musée d'Art moderne de la Ville de Paris.

Howard Goldkrand's sculpture and installation work have been exhibited at the James Cohan Gallery, Andrew Kreps Gallery, Mirror's Edge international exhibition with curator Okwui Enwezor, P.S.1 Museum of Contemporary Art, Artist's Space, Studio Museum of Harlem, the Ludwig Museum, Cologne, Massachusetts Institute of Technology List Gallery, Henry Art Gallery Seattle, New Museum of Contemporary Art, EAI, and Exit Art. He was a 1999 artist-in-residence at P.S.1 museum of Contemporary Art and a 2001 artist-in-residence at the Chinati Foundation, Marfa, Texas. Goldkrand is a 2003–2004 Rockefeller New Media Fellow.

Beth Coleman is Assistant Professor of Writing and New Media in the Program in Writing and Humanistic Studies and Comparative Media Studies at the Massachusetts Institute of Technology. Her writing has been published in a variety of catalogs, presses, and journals. Coleman is a 2003–2004 Rockefeller New Media Fellow, a 2004 Ford Foundation fellow, and a 2006 AAUW Emerging Scholar fellow. Her artwork has been exhibited internationally at P.S.1 Museum of Contemporary Art, Whitney Museum of American Art, Parkett, Mirror's Edge exhibition, ARC/Musee d'Art moderne de la Ville de Paris, and MIT's List Gallery, among other venues.

Catherine Corman is the editor of *Joseph Cornell's Dreams* (Exact Change, 2007). She has lectured on Joseph Cornell at the New Museum of Contemporary Art, Anthology Film Archives, and Sarah Lawrence College.

Chuck D, leader and cofounder of rap group Public Enemy, addressed issues of race, rage, and inequality with the release of PE's debut album, *Yo Bum Rush the Show*, in 1987. The group's subsequent seven albums were released over the next thirteen years, all meeting with critical acclaim from publications as disparate as *Time* and the *Source*, with worldwide sales in the millions.

Chuck has since hosted his own segment on the Fox News Channel and published a best-selling autobiography, *Fight the Power*. He is a speaker on the college lecture circuit (lecturing at universities ranging from Harvard to Howard) and a member of music industry nonprofit organizations MusicCares and Rock the Vote (which honored him with the Patrick Lippert Award in 1996 for his contributions to community service), and he started the record label SlamJamz. He has served as national spokesperson for Rock the Vote, the National Urban League, and the National Alliance of African American Athletes, and has appeared in public service announcements for HBO's campaign for national peace and the Partnership for the Drug Free America. He is also a regular guest on numerous television shows including *Nightline*, *Politically Incorrect*, and shows on CNN.

Most recently, Chuck has been a major proponent of music on the Internet. In September 1999, he launched a multiformat "supersite" on the Web, Rapstation.com, a site that hosts a TV and radio station with original programming, a slew of hip-hop's most prominent DJs, celebrity interviews, free mp3 downloads, social commentary, current events, and regular features dedicated to empowering rap artists. The site has partnered with several companies on the Web, including RealNetworks, House of Blues Digital, Launch, Tucows, Rioport, Communities.com, New World Culture, All Earth, and AudioGalaxy. Chuck has also launched a radio station on the Internet, Bringthenoise.com, and has made Public Enemy the first multiplatinum selling act to release their album via the Web before it was available in retail stores. He also arranged for the album to be the first-ever released on a Zip disk. Chuck has appeared on the cover of *Net, Wired, Bomb*, and *Yahoo Internet Life* magazines, and he was the guest editor of the 1999 year-end issue of *Red Herring*. He has also been a guest contributor to *Time* magazine. His advocacy of the Web also been profiled in *Forbes, Time, USA Today*, and the *Industry Standard*, and he was named to *Upside* magazine's "Elite 100" list of Internet leaders. He is currently working on a second book.

Erik Davis is a San Francisco–based writer, culture critic, and independent scholar. He is the author, most recently, of *The Visionary State: A Journey through California's Spiritual Landscape* (Chronicle, 2006), with photographs by Michael Rauner, and he also penned a short critical volume on *Led Zeppelin IV* for Continuum's 33 1/3 series. His book *TechGnosis: Myth, Magic, and Mysticism in the Age of Information* (Harmony, 1998), on visionary media studies, has been translated into five languages. Davis has contributed to scores of magazines and books, was a contributing writer for *Wired* for many years, and has taught at UC Berkeley, UC Davis, and the California Institute of Integral Studies. A collection of his work, *Nomad Codes: Adventures in Pop Esoterica*, will be out in the fall of 2008. Some of his work can be accessed at http://www.techgnosis.com.

Manuel De Landa is a New York–based philosopher and science writer with a cross-disciplinary body of work. He has written extensively on nonlinear dynamics, theories of self-organization, artificial life and intelligence, and chaos theory, as well as architecture and history of science. Born in Mexico City, he moved to New York in 1975 and became an independent filmmaker. In 1980 he turned his attention toward the computer and computer art, before he emerged as one of the leading theorists of the electronic world. Major books include *War in the Age of Intelligent Machines* (Zone Books, 1991); *A Thousand Years of Nonlinear History* (Zone Books, 2000); and *Intensive Science and Virtual Philosophy*.

Scott deLahunta works from his base in Amsterdam as a researcher, writer, consultant, and organizer on a wide range of international projects bringing performing arts into conjunction with other disciplines and practices. He is an Associate Research Fellow at Dartington College of Arts, Research Fellow with the Art Theory and Research and Art Practice and Development Research Group, Amsterdam School for the Arts, and Affiliated Researcher with Crucible (Cambridge University Network for Interdisciplinary Research). He lectures on the Amsterdam Master in Choreography and serves on the editorial boards of *Performance Research, Dance Theatre Journal*, and the *International Journal of Performance and Digital Media*.

Cory Doctorow (craphound.com) is a science-fiction novelist, blogger, and technology activist. He is the coeditor of the popular weblog Boing Boing (boingboing.net), and a contributor to *Wired, Popular Science, Make*, the *New York Times*, and many other newspapers, magazines, and websites. He was formerly Director of European Affairs for the Electronic Frontier Foundation (eff.org), a nonprofit civil liberties group that defends freedom in technology law, policy, standards, and treaties. In 2007, he served as the Fulbright Chair at the Annenberg Center for Public Diplomacy at the University of Southern California. His novels are published by Tor Books and simultaneously released on the Internet under Creative Commons licenses that encourage their reuse and sharing. He has won the Locus and Sunburst Awards, and has been nominated for the Hugo, Nebula, and British Science Fiction Awards. He cofounded the open source peer-to-peer software company OpenCola, sold to OpenText, Inc., in 2003, and currently serves on the boards and advisory boards of the Participatory Culture Foundation, the MetaBrainz Foundation, Technorati, Inc., Stikkit, the Organization for Transformative Works, Areae, the Annenberg Center for the Study of Online Communities, and Onion Networks, Inc.

Frances Dyson is an Associate Professor in Techno-Cultural Studies at University of California at Davis. She is currently a fellow at the Davis Humanities Research Institute and a researcher in residence at the Langlois Foundation for the Arts and Sciences. Her publishing and exhibition have focused on sound, new media, and culture, and her audio artwork has been broadcast on Australia's premier audio arts program, *The Listening Room*, for over a decade. Her current research focuses on relationships between sound, virtuality, and posthumanism, with reference to developments in wireless technologies.

Ron Eglash holds a B.S. in cybernetics, an M.S. in systems engineering, and Ph.D. in the history of consciousness, all from the University of California. A Fulbright postdoctoral fellowship enabled his field research on African ethnomathematics, which was published by Rutgers University Press in 1999 as *African Fractals: Modern Computing and Indigenous Design*. He is now an associate professor of Science and Technology Studies at Rensselaer Polytechnic Institute. The National Science Foundation has sponsored his culture-based software for math and computing education, available for free at http://www.rpi.edu/~eglash/csdt.html.

Brian Eno is a musician, composer, and producer of audio and visual landscapes. Eno's synthesizer work and electronic manipulation of audio textures was first featured during the early 1970s when he was a founding member of Roxy Music. His solo and collaborative musical compositions with John Cale, Robert Fripp, and David Bowie have been in circulation worldwide over the last twenty-five years. Eno has produced records for numerous artists including U2, David Bowie, Jane Siberry, and performance artist Laurie Anderson, and has executive produced the "Help" benefit album. He performed with Pavarotti, Bono, and The Edge at 1995's Modena Festival to benefit the War Child charitable organization.

Eno has been involved in the design and production of audio-video gallery installations including "Music for White Cube" at the White Cube Gallery in London in spring 1997 and "Lightness" in the Marble Palace at the Russian Museum, St. Petersberg, in November 1997. In October 1995, a permanent exhibition of his work opened at Austria's Swarovski Museum. His diary and essays *A Year (with Swollen Appendices)* was published in May 1996.

Dmitry Gelfand and **Evelina Domnitch** create sensory immersion environments that merge physics, chemistry, and computer science with uncanny philosophical practices. Current findings, particularly regarding wave phenomena, are employed by the artists to investigate questions of perception and perpetuality. Having dismissed the use of recording and fixative media, Domnitch and Gelfand's installations exist as ever-transforming phenomena offered for observation. The immediacy of this experience allows the observer to transcend the illusory distinction between scientific discovery and perceptual expansion. In order to engage such ephemeral processes, the artists have collaborated with numerous scientific research facilities, including the Drittes Physikalisches Institut (Goettingen University, Germany), the Institute of Advanced Sciences and Technologies (Japan), The Yin Group (University of California, USA), and the Meurice Institute (Belgium).

Cultural critic and theorist **Dick Hebdige** has published widely on youth subculture, contemporary music, art and design, and consumer and media culture. His books include: *Subculture: The Meaning of Style* (Methuen, 1979); *Cut 'n' Mix: Culture, Identity and Caribbean Music* (Methuen, 1987); and *Hiding in the Light: On Images and Things* (Routledge, Methuen, 1988). His current interests include the integration of autobiography and mixed media in critical writing and pedagogy.

Lee Hirsch's debut feature film, *Amandla! A Revolution in Four Part Harmony*, which chronicles the history of the South African antiapartheid struggle through a celebration of its musical heroes, won the Audience and Freedom of Expression Awards at the Sundance Film Festival, as well as one of the five Emmy awards it was nominated for, among many other honors. Currently, he is directing and producing a one-hour special for the Discovery Channel on the future of urban transportation. Hirsch is also a director of music videos. He was born and raised on Long Island, New York, and attended the Putney School in Vermont, Hampshire College, and the New York Film Academy.

Described in the *The Village Voice* as "the most commanding pianist and composer to emerge in recent years," **Vijay Iyer** was named No. 1 Rising Star Jazz Artist and No. 1 Rising Star Composer by the Downbeat International Critics Poll for both 2006 and 2007. His most recent recordings include *Tragicomic* (2008) under his own name; *Door* (2008) with the collective trio Fieldwork; *Still Life with Commentator* (2007) in collaboration with poet-performer Mike Ladd; and *Raw Materials* (2006) with saxophonist Rudresh Mahanthappa. Iyer tours frequently as a composer-performer, and has received numerous awards and commissions, among them the CalArts Alpert Award in the Arts and the New York Foundation for the Arts Fellowship. Iyer teaches at New York University, and has published articles in *Music Perception, Journal of Consciousness Studies, Critical Studies in Improvisation, Current Musicology, Journal of the Society for American Music,* and *Uptown Conversation: The New Jazz Studies.* http://www.vijay-iyer.com

Ken Jordan is a New York–based writer, theorist, and digital media producer. In 1995 he led the development and was founding editorial director of *SonicNet.com*, the Web's first multimedia music zine and digital music store, which later became part of MTV. He collaborated with the legendary playwright and director Richard Foreman on the book *Unbalancing Acts: Foundations for a Theater* (Pantheon, 1992), is coeditor of the anthology *Multimedia: From Wagner to Virtual Reality* (W. W. Norton, 2001), and is coauthor of the white paper "The Augmented Social Network: Building Identity and Trust into the Next-Generation Internet" (FirstMonday.org, August 2003), about creating an "open source" system for digital identity. He has written for *Wired*, *Index*, and *Paris Review*, and is publisher of RealitySandwich.com and Evolver.net.

Douglas Kahn, Professor at the University of California at Davis in Art History, Music, and Technocultural Studies, is author of *Noise, Water, Meat: A History of Sound in the Arts* (MIT Press), editor of *Wireless Imagination: Sound, Radio and the Avant-garde* (MIT Press), and journal editor of *Senses and Society* (Berg) and *Leonardo Music Journal* (MIT Press). He received a 2006 Guggenheim Fellowship to research the historical discovery of natural radio.

Daphne Keller is Senior Product Counsel for Google Inc. She is the lead counsel on copyright, privacy, content regulation, and related legal issues for a portfolio of Google products including Web Search and Book Search, and was previously lead product counsel for assorted Google products including News, Video, and the Google Toolbar. Daphne specializes in particularly geeky legal issues, including counseling Google's Open Source Group, and has worked on academic partnerships including planning Google and Stanford's 2008 Legal Futures Conference (http://cyberlaw.stanford.edu/node/5685).

In private practice, Daphne was in the litigation group at Munger, Tolles, and Olson in San Francisco. Previously, she taught courses on intellectual property and the Internet as a Senior Fellow at Duke Law School, where she also coordinated student work with public interest groups including EFF, CDT, and EPIC. She has also been a resident researcher at Wolfson College, Oxford and lectured at Cardozo Law School.

Beryl Korot lives and works in New York. An early video-art pioneer and an internationally exhibited artist, her multiple-channel (and multiple-monitor) video installation works explored the relationship between programming tools as diverse as the technology of the loom and multiple-channel video. For most of the 1980s, Korot concentrated on a series of paintings that were based on a language she created that was an analogue to the Latin alphabet. Drawing on her earlier interest in weaving and video as related technologies, she made most of these paintings on hand-woven and traditional linen canvas. More recently, she has collaborated with her husband, the composer Steve Reich, on *Three Tales*, a documentary digital video opera in three acts and a prologue. In the context of Korot's body of work, which began with her early video tapestries, *Three Tales* extends and deepens her interest in both technology as a material in which to make work—video, weaving—and as a relevant exploration of history in which to base her work.

Jaron Lanier is a computer scientist, composer, visual artist, and author. His current appointments include Interdisciplinary Scholar-in-Residence, CET, University of California Berkeley. http://www.jaronlanier.com/

Joseph Lanza writes impressionistic histories, specializing in film and popular music. He is perhaps best known for his book *Elevator Music: A Surreal History of Muzak, Easy Listening, and Other Moodsong* (University of Michigan Press), a foray that *Entertainment Weekly* called "one of the few pop-history books that won't put you to sleep." His other books include *Vanilla Pop: Sweet Sounds from Frankie Avalon to ABBA* (Chicago Review Press), which *Publisher's Weekly* described as "surprisingly flavorful"; and *Fragile Geometry: The Films, Philosophy, and Misadventures of Nicolas Roeg* (PAJ Publications), which the British Film Institute declared as "by common consent, the best book" on the subject. He also produced the two-volume CD release *Music for TV Dinners* and helped compile Time-Life Music's *Instrumental Favorites* series. His latest book is *Phallic Frenzy: Ken Russell and His Films* (Chicago Review Press), hailed by London's *The Independent* as an "enjoyable biography of a frustrating visionary." http://www.myspace.com/moodsong

Jonathan Lethem is the author of *You Don't Love Me Yet* and six other novels. His fifth, *Motherless Brooklyn*, won the National Book Critic's Circle Award and has been translated into over twenty languages. His essays and stories have appeared in the *New Yorker, Harper's, Rolling Stone*, and a variety of other periodicals and anthologies. He lives in Brooklyn and Maine.

Carlo McCormick is senior editor of *Paper* magazine.

Paul D. Miller aka DJ Spooky that Subliminal Kid is a conceptual artist, writer, and musician working in New York City.

Moby is an influential figure of electronic music culture in America, best known for his chart-topping album *Play*. He lives in New York City.

Naeem Mohaiemen does art interventions in Dhaka and New York. His projects include *War of 666 against sixty million* (Finnish Museum of Photography), *Visible Collective* (2006 Whitney Biennial: wrong gallery), *Muslims or Heretics: My Camera Can Lie?* (UK House of Lords), *Penn Station Kills Me* (with Gensler+Gutierrez, Exit Art gallery, New York), *Sartre kommt nach Stammheim* (Pavillion, *Documenta XII* magazine), *Oppose Us and Rome Will Not Forgive You a Second Time* (Himal, Nepal), and *Mind Crimes Trials for (Sweetly) Silent Artists* (Aprior, *Documenta XII* magazine). His essays include "Guerillas in the Mist" (Sarai Turbulence, part of *Documenta XII* journal project), "Beirut: Illusion of a Silver Porsche" (*Men of Global South*, ed. Adam Jones, Zed Books), and "Why Mahmud Can't Be a Pilot" (*Nobody Passes*, ed. Matt Bernstein ed., Seal Press). http://www.shobak.org/

Alondra Nelson teaches African American studies and sociology at Yale University. She is editor of *Technicolor: Race, Technology, and Everyday Life* (with Thuy Linh N. Tu)

and of *Afro-Futurism*, a special issue of the journal *Social Text*. Her book *Body and Soul: The Black Panther Party and the Politics of Health and Race* is forthcoming from the University of California Press.

Keith Townsend Obadike + Mendi Lewis Obadike are artists whose work has been published in *Catch the Fire*, *Black Arts Quarterly*, *Indiana Review*, and the College Art Association's *Art Journal*. Their sound/net art projects have been exhibited in Race and Digital Space at MIT/List Visual Art Center, the Studio Museum in Harlem, Infos 2000 (Slovenia), Sonik (Denmark, Danish Film Institute), Audiophfile 6.0, and Collective Jukebox (France, Frac Paca), and in the upcoming Only Skin Deep: Changing Visions of the American Self, at the International Center of Photography. Their most recent project is *The Sour Thunder*, a net.opera supported by the Yale Cabaret, the Afro-American Cultural Center at Yale, and the Yale Digital Media Center for the Arts.

The Swiss curator **Hans Ulrich Obrist** joined the Serpentine Gallery as Co-director of Exhibitions and Programmes and Director of International Projects in April 2006. Prior to this he was Curator of the Musée d'Art Moderne de la Ville de Paris since 2000, as well as curator of museum in progress, Vienna, from 1993–2000. He has curated over 150 exhibitions internationally since 1991, including *do it*, *Take Me, I'm Yours* (Serpentine Gallery), *Cities on the Move*, *Live/Life*, *Nuit Blanche*, First Berlin Biennale, Manifesta 1, and more recently *Uncertain States of America*, First Moscow Triennale, and Second Guangzhou Biennale (Canton China). In 2007, Hans Ulrich cocurated *Il Tempo del Postino* with Philippe Parreno for the Manchester International Festival. He is the editor of *Hans Ulrich Obrist: Interviews: 1.*

Pauline Oliveros is an American composer. Her career spans five decades and includes composing, improvising, writing and educating. She currently teaches at Rensselaer Polytechmic Institute, and is Darius Milhaud Composer-in-residence at Mills College. She is the founder and president of Deep Listening Institute, Ltd. http://paulineoliveros.us

Philippe Parreno is an artist and filmmaker. He was born in 1964 in Oran, Algeria, and lives and works in Paris, France. http://www.airdeparis.com/parreno.htm

Ibrahim Quraishi is an artist whose works, shown recently at the Japan Foundation Tokyo, BAM Next Wave Festival (New York), Springdance (Utrecht), Holland Festival (Amsterdam), ImPulsTanz (Vienna), and iDANS Istanbul, among others places, challenge our understanding of performativity and its relationship to the broader cultural perspective. Currently dividing his time between New York, Lahore, Amsterdam, and Istanbul as a writer, director, choreographer, and conceptual artist, Quraishi examines the dynamics of "migration," dispossession, and cohabitation within the highly rigid sociopolitical spheres of imagined communities. Coming from a diverse/nomadic cultural and artistic background, Quraishi was formerly a student of Edward W. Said at Columbia University, New York.

Steve Reich was recently called "America's greatest living composer" (*Village Voice*), "the most original musical thinker of our time" (*New Yorker*), and "among the great composers of the century" (*New York Times*). From his early taped speech pieces "It's Gonna Rain" (1965) and "Come Out" (1966) to his and video artist Beryl Korot's digital video opera *Three Tales* (2002), Reich's path has embraced not only aspects of Western Classical music, but the structures, harmonies, and rhythms of non-Western and American vernacular music, particularly jazz.

Robin Rimbaud aka Scanner is a conceptual artist, writer, and musician working in London, whose works traverse the experimental terrain between sound, space, image, and form. Since 1991 he has been intensely active in sonic art, producing concerts, installations, and recordings, the albums *Mass Observation* (1994), *Delivery* (1997), and *The Garden Is Full of Metal* (1998), hailed by critics as innovative and inspirational works of contemporary electronic music. He recently scored the hit musical comedy *Kirikou & Karaba* and will premiere his six-hour show *Of Air and Eye* at the Royal Opera House in London in late 2008. He has collaborated with Bryan Ferry, Radiohead, Laurie Anderson, The Royal Ballet, Steve McQueen, Philips Design, Mike Kelley, and Douglas Gordon. His work has been presented throughout the United States, South America, Asia, Australia, and Europe. http://www.scannerdot.com

Nadine Robinson is a conceptual artist who presents artwork situated at the crossroads of the white modernist canon and the African American contemporary aesthetic. She works in a minimalist vocabulary, combining appropriated music and sounds, DJ equipment, and unconventional materials. Her large-scale installations reflect social, cultural, and historical politics and are informed by an array of influences, from Christianity to Rastafarianism to hip-hop culture. Her work often speaks to the disconnection between Western and non-Western culture, the past and the present, and art and popular culture.

Known for fusing his classical music roots with a myriad of soundscapes, Haitian-American artist **Daniel Bernard Roumain (DBR)** is a composer, performer, violinist, and band leader. From Australia's Sydney Opera House to Boston's ICA Museum, DBR continues his 2008 worldwide tour premiering solo works and pulsing duets off of his debut international solo album *etudes4violin&electronix* (Thirsty Ear Recordings). His pieces range from orchestral scores and energetic chamber works to rock songs and electronica. DBR's *One Loss Plus*, his multimedia premiere at BAM's 2007 Next Wave Festival, kicked off the festival's three-year residency of DBR-commissioned works. The second commission to be premiered at BAM's 2008 Next Wave Festival is *Darwin's Meditation for the People of Lincoln*, a quartet concerto featuring the chamber orchestra SymphoNYC and a setting of a new pocket play by Daniel Beaty exploring an imagined conversation between Darwin and Lincoln. Other upcoming projects include *24 Bits: Hip-Hop Studies and Etudes* and *Event Pieces* performed by DBR on piano and laptop; the score for Carl Hancock Rux's contemporary opera *Makandal*; a fusion of contrasting cultures and instruments with Elan Vytal aka DJ Scientific in DBR's *Sonata for Violin and Turntables;* and ongoing collaborations with the Orchestra of St. Luke's, Bill T. Jones/Arnie Zane Dance Company, Philip Glass, Ryuichi Sakamoto, and DJ Spooky. His ensemble DBR & THE MISSION makes its international debut at Australia's 2008 Adelaide Festival. http://www.dbrmusic.com

Alex Steinweiss is a graphic designer. In 1939, he was the first art director for Columbia Records, where he invented the concept of album covers and cover art. Steinweiss was active in record cover design from its inception in 1939 until 1973, when he semi-retired to devote himself to painting. He lives in Sarasota, Florida where he still paints and designs posters for community and cultural events.

Bruce Sterling is an author, journalist, editor, and critic. Best known for his eight science fiction novels, he also writes short stories, book reviews, design criticism, opinion columns, and introductions for books ranging from Ernst Juenger to Jules Verne. His nonfiction works include *The Hacker Crackdown: Law and Disorder on the Electronic Frontier* (1992) and *Tomorrow Now: Envisioning the Next Fifty Years* (2003). He is a contributing editor of *Wired* magazine and a columnist for *Make* magazine. During 2005, he was the "Visionary in Residence" at Art Center College of Design in Pasadena. In 2008 he was the Guest Curator for the Share Festival of Digital Art and Culture in Torino, Italy. He has appeared in *Time*, *Newsweek*, the *Wall Street Journal*, the *New York Times*, *Fortune*, *Nature*, *I.D.*, *Metropolis*, *Technology Review*, *Der Spiegel*, *La Repubblica*, and many other venues. http://blog.wired.com/sterling

Lucy Walker won a Fulbright Scholarship to attend NYU's graduate film program at Tisch School of the Arts, where she won various awards and received her M.F.A. She is best known for directing *Devil's Playground*, a feature documentary following the struggles of Amish teenagers. Lucy was named one of *Filmmaker* magazine's "Top 25 New Faces in Film," and her other directing credits include music videos, promos, award-winning short films, and children's television. As a musician and DJ, during the 1990s Lucy performed both solo and as a member of Byzar, whose releases on Asphodel included *Beings from the B'yond Wythyn* and *Gaiatronyk vs. the Cheap Robots*. Her most recent film is *Blindsight*, a feature documentary about six blind Tibetan teenagers who climb up the north side of Everest. She is currently directing her third documentary feature for Participant Productions and Lawrence Bender.

Saul Williams is a poet, writer, actor, and musician. His new album, *The Inevitable Rise and Liberation of Niggy Tardust*, produced by Trent Reznor and mixed by Alan Moulder, is available as a free download from his website: http://www.saulwilliams .com.

Jeff E. Winner is an experimental music historian and researcher who has written feature articles for *Electronic Musician* magazine, contributed liner notes to the Ellipsis Arts series, *OHM: The Early Gurus Of Electronic Music*, and edited the Devo biography from Firefly Publishing. Winner also coproduced *Manhattan Research Inc.*, a book and two-CD set detailing Raymond Scott's pioneering electronic music and inventions.

Audio File Credits

For a free download of the audio files for this book, contact digitalproducts-cs@mit.edu.

Sound Unbound: Excerpts and Allegories from the Sub Rosa Catalog

Produced by Paul D. Miller aka DJ Spooky that Subliminal Kid
Project Engineer: Howie Kenty
Recording Studio: Subliminal Kid Studios, Manhattan

1. RadioMentale and Matthew Herbert, "Cool Noises"
2. Martyn Bates/Allen Ginsberg, "Once Loved/A Footnote to 'Howl' (DJ Spooky Remix)"
3. Jean Cocteau, "Le buste (DJ Spooky Remix)"
4. Sun Ra, "Imagination"
5. Mikhail/Gertrude Stein, "Untitled in CoF Minor/A Valentine to Sherwood Anderson (DJ Spooky Remix)"
6. DJ Spooky vs. Rob Swift, "Scratch Battle"
7. Marcel Duchamp/The Master Musicians of Joujouka/RadioMentale, "The Creative Act/Interview with George Heard Hamilton/Boujeloud (Solo Drums)/I Could Never Make That Music Again"
8. Raymond Scott, "The Paperwork Explosion"
9. Alter Echo/Pamela Z, "Perpetual Next/Pop Titles 'You'"*
10. Liam Gillick/ RadioMentale and Aphex Twin, "Sarah (Los Angeles Soundtrack)/I Could Never Make That Music Again"
11. James Joyce/Erik Satie, "Eolian Episode/Gnossiene (DJ Spooky Dub Version)"

12. Steve Reich, "Reed Phase"

13. Shukar/RadioMentale/Raoul Hausmann, "Cika-Laka/Cool Noises/Bbb"

14. Augustos de Campos/Bill Laswell/To Rococo Rot, "Dias Dias Dias (Spoken by Caetano Veloso)/Above the Earth/Contacte"

15. John Cage, "Rozart Mix"

16. Antonin Artaud, "Pour Finir avec le Jugement de Dieu (To Have Done with God's Judgment) (DJ Spooky Remix)"

17. DJ Spooky, "One Laptop Theme"

18. Susan Deyhim, "The Spilled Cup (DJ Spooky Remix)"

19. Raymond Scott, "General Motors: Futurama (Interstitial)"

20. Marcel Duchamp/George Lewis and Aki Takase, "Erratum Musical (Score for Three Voices)/Voyage for Three"

21. Bill Laswell/René Magritte, "Ghost Dub/Le Surréalisme et les Questions"

22. Anthony Braxton and Evan Parker/Pauline Oliveros, "The First Set— Area 4 (Solo)/A Little Noise in the System (Moog System)"

23. Bora Yoon, "// (DJ Spooky Remix)"

24. Pierre Schaeffer, "Cinq études de bruits: Étude violette"

25. Daniel Bernard Roumain and Ryuichi Sakamoto, "The Need to Be"**

26. Phillip Glass, "Music in Fifths"

27 Edgard Varèse, "Poème électronique"

28. Iannis Xenakis, "Concret PH"

29. Ryoji Ikeda, "One Minute"

30. Sonic Youth, "Audience (DJ Spooky Remix)"

31. Alter Echo/Ge-te Do-pe, "Aftermath of Creations Dub (in Three Parts)/ Dong Lim"

32. Terry Riley/Alter Echo, "Dorian Reeds/Aftermath of Creations Dub (in Three Parts)"

33. Luigi Russolo/DJ Spooky, "Corale/FTP > Bundle/Conduit 23"

34. Fanfare Savale/Vladimir Mayakovsky, "Rumba Lu Georgel/I Know the Power of Words"

35. Droma/Trilok Gurtu and Bill Laswell, "Pilgrim's Song (Trala Shepa)/ Kala"

36. Nam Jun Paik, "Hommage à John Cage"

37. Morton Subotnick/DJ Spooky, "Mandolin/Acid Bassline"

38. The Master Musicians of Joujouka/Hans Arp, "Mali Mal Hal M'Halmaz/ Boujeloud (Solo Drums)/Dada-Sprüche"

39. Sub Swara/Kurt Schwitters, "Koli Stance/Anna Blume"

40. Walter Ruttmann/Troupe from Taschingang, "Week End/Ache Lhamo"
41. Raymond Scott, "Bendix 1: The Tomorrow People"
42. Martyn Bates/Trinlem, "I Can't Look for You/The Palaces of Gesar's Family (DJ Spooky Remix)"
43. Otto Luening and Vladimir Ussachevsky, "Incantation for Tape"
44. Carsten Nicolai, "Time ... Dot(3)"
45. William S. Burroughs and Iggy Pop with Techno Animal, "The Western Land"

Translation of Vladimir Mayakovsky's "I Know the Power of Words":

"I know the power of words" ...

I know the power of words, I know how words give alarm
These ain't the words to whom the crowds applause
These words make coffins move ...
Make it walking on its four oak legs

Sometimes it happens that they throw away, never print it, never publish.
But words rush with speed,
Ages jungle and trains crawl up
To lick the horny hands of poetry....

Acknowledgments

*From Pamela Z's *A Delay Is Better* CD released by Starkland (www.starkland .com).
**"The Need to Be" is from DBR's album *etudes4violin&electronix* released on Thirsty Ear Recordings.

Thanks to Sub Rosa Records for the use of many of the tracks on this compilation. Sub Rosa Brussels, Belgium, www.subrosa.net

Index